RESEARCH IN LABOR ECONOMICS

Supplement 2 · 1983

NEW APPROACHES
TO LABOR UNIONS

RESEACH IN LABOR ECONOMICS

A Research Annual

NEW APPROACHES
TO LABOR UNIONS

Editor: JOSEPH D. REID, JR.
Center for Study of Public Choice
Virginia Polytechnic Institute
and State University

SUPPLEMENT 2 · 1983

 JAI PRESS INC.

Greenwich, Connecticut   *London, England*

CONTENTS

PART III.   EMPIRICAL ANALYSIS OF LABOR UNIONS

PART IV.   ARE NEW APPROACHES TO
LABOR UNIONS NEEDED?

LIST OF CONTRIBUTORS

John T. Addison	Department of Economics University of South Carolina
Armen Alchian	Department of Economics University of California at Los Angeles
John Burton	Department of Economics University of Birmingham England
Gregory M. Duncan	Department of Economics and Statistics Washington State University
Ronald G. Ehrenberg	Departments of Economics and Labor Economics Cornell University
Roger L. Faith	Department of Economics Arizona State University
Henry S. Farber	Department of Economics Massachusetts Institute of Technology
Richard B. Freeman	Department of Economics Harvard University
Michael M. Kurth	Department of Economics Emory and Henry College
Edward P. Lazear	Graduate School of Business University of Chicago
Bernard Lentz	Department of Economics Ursinus College

David Lewin   Graduate School of Business
                                Columbia University

H. Gregg Lewis   Department of Economics
                                Duke University

James L. Medoff   Department of Economics
                                Harvard University

Wesley Mellow   Office of Research and Evaluation
                                U.S. Bureau of Labor and
                                Statistics

Jacob Mincer   Department of Economics
                                Columbia University

Eli Noam   Graduate School of Business
                                Columbia University

Mel Reder   Graduate School of Business
                                University of Chicago

Joseph D. Reid, Jr.   Center for Study of Public Choice
                                Virginia Polytechnic Institute and
                                State University

Gordon Tullock   Center for Study of Public Choice
                                Virginia Polytechnic Institute and
                                State University

EDITOR'S INTRODUCTION

In October of 1981, a conference on *New Approaches to Labor Unions* was held at the Center for Study of Public Choice at Virginia Polytechnic Institute and State University. Over 40 economists interested in analyzing labor unions participated in the conference, organized by Joseph D. Reid, Jr. This special volume of *Research in Labor Economics,* for which Joseph Reid is serving as guest editor, contains revised versions of 10 papers presented at the conference as well as the written discussion of some conference participants.

As Reid's introductory remarks indicate, economists' approaches toward analyzing unions as institutions and union behavior have evolved significantly in recent years. It is our hope that this volume will provide the reader with a sense of the direction in which professional research on the subject of unions is moving and also convey the intellectual excitement that the conference participants felt.

Ronald G. Ehrenberg
Series Editor

PREFACE

In October 1981, 10 papers, all indicating general unease with economists' current understanding of labor unions, were presented at a Conference on New Approaches to Labor Unions held at the Center for Study of Public Choice at Virginia Polytechnic Institute and State University. Over 40 leading contributors to the analysis of labor unions participated. This volume reports the (revised) proceedings of the conference, in hope of encouraging further elaboration and testing of the new approaches to labor unions illustrated here.

Most participants in this volume agree that the standard model of a labor union is inadequate. That model, of a static labor monopoly that exploits inelasticity in its demand and in other inputs' supplies in order to raise wages, at once predicts too little and too much. It predicts too little, for a labor union without monopoly power can raise the wages of members, as the opening and closing contributions to this volume argue. It predicts too much, for a labor union does not raise members' wages proportionately or identically, nor does it attain some outcome and then rest; rather, the aims of a labor union are formed and its outcomes achieved as the results of interplay between an exogenous environment and endogenous strategies (of unions and firms) that evolve over time. In addition, several contributors argue that a union must be distinguished from its members, if union acts and accomplishments are to be understood. Just who a union does represent is one question to be investigated. Whether it adopts recruitment, constitution, and negotiation strategies in order to transform its constituency is another question worthwhile to investigate. The old implicit assumption that each union represents all of its members faithfully no longer can be maintained without substantiation.

Individually, the mildest of modifications to received theory are proposed. To admit that unions can raise productivity, as well as wages, and to admit that unions are strategic institutions optimizing a dynamic maximand to suit a changing constituency do not seem a sufficient foundation for an analytical revolution. But immediate results are many. For one, if wages are an instrument of strategy, as well as a goal, then the success of a labor union is not measured unambiguously by its impact on wages today. Nor is the impact of a union upon wages evidence that a union succeeded at monopolization of labor. Thus, those many past estimations of union power from union wage premiums are thrown into question. In the same vein, workers' preferences for a union are not predictable from the positive or negative impact of unionization upon the average or median wage.

Applications of these modifications of received theory have large results in analysis of unions in the public sector as well. Although union membership has grown explosively there and has stagnated in the private sector during the last 20 years, public-sector unionism commonly has been treated as but a twin of private-sector unionism. But contributors' insistence that a union be analyzed in its particular environment directs a new look at public unions' growth. The reason is that public employers did *not* recently guarantee the right to organize to the public employees most prominent in organizing and striking since 1960: state and local employees. The applicable legal change (the executive order of President Kennedy that permitted government employees to join independent unions) affected only unmilitant federal employees. More so than private employees, therefore, unionized public employees must suit rather than defy their employers, politicians. Directly applied, this means that the growth of government unions must benefit some politicians, at least in the first instance. Further applied, it suggests that a union that on balance does not retard measured productivity is not surprising in the public sector.

In one sense, in their call for a dynamic analysis of what unions do, the contributors are rediscovering the wisdom of the institutionalists. Analysts such as John Commons and Arthur Ross emphasized the dynamic and strategic aspects of analysis of labor unions. But they and other institutionalists stopped there—stopped at the uniqueness of each union's record, so to speak. The contributors to this volume are emphasizing the dynamic and strategic facets of labor unionism not to stop analysis, but to improve analysis and to better prediction. Each contributor is saying that the analysis of labor unions is an important part of economics, so important that development of union theory and union facts require the very best economic practice. The contributors show that the very best practice is challenging, indeed. But in the end, they prepare a new entree for economists' menu of *institutions* of society ripe for new and deeper analysis: Government, family, and firm preceded. Labor unions now are ready for understanding.

Joseph D. Reid, Jr.
Guest Editor

PART I

THEORIES OF LABOR UNIONS IN

THE PRIVATE SECTOR

THE LABOR UNION AS ITS MEMBERS' AGENT

Roger L. Faith and Joseph D. Reid, Jr.

ABSTRACT

To analyze what unions do and how they do it, a union is modeled as the agent of some principal. Most generally, a union is its members' (workers') agent, although a union can also be the agent of an employer (as when the union helps to cartelize an industry) or of third parties (for example, racketeers or a federated national union). Like all agents, the union seeks to enhance its own welfare, subject to constraints imposed by its principal and by laws. The varied accomplishments and policies of different unions thus are modeled as results of different principals and differences degrees of malfeasance by the union agent. The wide range of testable implications of the union qua agent model testifies to the potential robustness of our approach and significantly extends the theory of unions.

New Approaches to Labor Unions.
Research in Labor Economics, Supplement 2, pages 3–25.
Copyright © 1983 by JAI Press Inc.
All rights of reproduction in any form reserved.
ISBN: 0-89232-265-9

3

I. INTRODUCTION

When George Johnson (1975) surveyed economists' analyses of trade unions, he concluded that "the study of the behavior and effects of trade unions is not currently one of the major growth industries of the economics profession." Economists' two questions about labor unions—What do they do? and How do they do it?—were already answered: unions raise members' wages "approximately 10 to 15 percent" (Lewis, 1963, p. 5), and unions do so by monopolizing labor. Few asked other questions about the impact of unions. Disagreement, if any, was over whether employers' monopolies of jobs justified unions' monopolies of laborers. But disagreement was muted, perhaps because the cost of unions seemed so slight and the aims of unions seemed so worthy. Thus, in 1975 all questions were answered and the study of labor unions was moribund.

Since then, there has been a remarkable revitalization of the study of labor unions. Returning to the old questions, new data are being mined with new econometric tools to remeasure unions' relative wage effects. These efforts perhaps indicate some reduction in unions' impact on members' relative wages.[1] More importantly, these efforts have forced economists to recognize that in order to better understand and estimate the accomplishments of unions, a richer and more insightful model of a labor union is required (Lewis, 1980; Dertouzos and Pencavel, 1981). It is our aim here to provide the model of a labor union needed.

II. THE NEED FOR A LABOR UNION MODEL

Others have recognized that a model of a labor union would be helpful for understanding of union behavior and impacts. But few appreciated that a model is prerequisite for any but the most general understanding. Dunlop (1944, p. 4), for instance, proposed that a union maximizes the total of members' wages (the wage bill) by setting the wage (seemingly so that analysis of a union's behavior would resemble economists' analysis of other economic actors' behavior: maximization subject to constraints). Fellner (1949) and Cartter (1959) generalized this maximand by making members and wages separate arguments of a union's goal function, although the union's control variable remained member's wage. Freeman and Medoff (1979) implicitly generalized the wage control; they argued that a union somehow may increase members' productivity.

These approaches to analysis of unions share several attributes. First, they are static: flow variables (such as the wage bill) are maximized, implicitly for all time, without concern for longer-run implications for employment or membership. Second, all imply that a union is its members' (or at least its surviving members') fair and perfect agent: that is, the union represents each member as well as any other, and each without malfeasance.[2] Third, none considers explicitly why an agent is wanted, nor why the union in question fulfills so perfectly the wanted agent role.

There is another strand in the modeling of labor unions, however. Simons (1944) and Ross (1948) emphasized that a union's objective function is determined by a political process. Immediate implications are that not all members will be served equally well and that a union's goal might change as its electorate changes (for empirical confirmation, see Farber, 1978). Berkowitz (1954) extended this approach. His union sells (unspecified) services to members, with the goal of maximizing profits (dues income less costs of gaining and keeping members), subject to the constraint of selection by a majority of employers.

It is this strand that we build upon. Our model union strives to achieve some objective, not necessarily identical to those of all or of a majority of its members. This union is a perhaps imperfect agent of some principal: ideally, worker-members, but perhaps employers or even the union itself. This conceptualization of a labor union forces us to address explicitly why an agent is wanted by workers, how a labor union fills workers' and other principals' wants, how well a union will serve its members, and how a union's services will evolve over time. We proceed from the ideal union that raises workers productivity by faithfully representing workers' legitimate interests, and end with a more realistic union that uses all means available to achieve its own private goal. To begin, we consider the roles of an employees' agent in firms.

III. EMPLOYEES' AGENTS IN FIRMS

The conventional view of firm and employee is that of a two-party exchange: the employee agrees to provide labor in return for some remuneration. In our view, a labor union is a *third* party additional to firm-employer and employees, even when the union perfectly represents the legitimate interests of one or both of the conventional parties in the firm. So the first question we must answer is: What legitimate (that is, nonmonopolizing) interests can a labor union represent? In other words, what is there for a nonmonopolizing labor union to do within a firm? To see, let us discuss possible roles of an agent of employees' within a firm.

First off, consider payment to employees. Remuneration seldom is paid concurrent with the delivery of effort. Typically, a worker gives effort for some period before he is paid. Nor is remuneration fully in cash. Some is paid in psychic coin or is deferred to reduce taxes. Economies of providing pay collectively (such as working conditions) or indivisibly (such as group insurance) mean that employees' choices need to be aggregated by the firm and to be evaluated by the employees. Furthermore, many

components of pay are not specified fully (such as promotion considerations), but are left to custom or good faith for their determination. Thus,
to raise utility or reduce costs, workers' pay is in part deferred, or is
provided on the job, or is provided collectively or indivisibly, or is defined
implicitly and is provided probabilistically.

Each transformation of pay from cash concurrently received puts expense or risk upon the employee. Pay deferred or received probabilistically may not be received at all: pensions might be bankrupted and promised considerations for promotion might not be given, for instance.
Understandably, workers would welcome oversights by a trusted agent
to assure that probabilistic and inexplicit components of pay are handled
fairly. Here, then, is one legitimate interest that an employees' agent might
serve: ombudsman—like oversight and evaluation of workers' probabilistic and inexplicit components of pay.[3]

The economies of pay provided collectively and indivisibly may so
dominate in many instances that none will want his unique recompense.
Few factory laborers, for instance, insist upon private floor stations isolated within private walls, in order to bask in their most preferred color.
Rather than pay with reduced wages for so much wall and so much im-
pediment of work flow, factory workers take working conditions provided
to all. As to shared conditions, it is unrealistic to expect that employers
are so abundant relative to preferences that each worker can find coworkers with identical preferences, and thence can secure his most preferred collective outcomes completely, without incredibly high costs of
search or dislocation. Thus, employees appreciate that some of their preferences best are aggregated. But they would like them to be aggregated
fairly. Revealed openly to an employer, however, workers' preferences
let the employer choose the least-cost benefit that provides his employees'
required minimum. Understandably, utility-maximizing workers would
rather have a choice of conditions from alternatives of equal cost.

To decide whether to accept this employer's offer or to search for another job, an employee would like some idea of his opportunities. Clearly,
the firm has some incentive to undervalue an employee's opportunities
elsewhere and overvalue its own pay offer. Not too much should be made
of this, for any advantage to the firm of overvaluing its offers relative to
the market will dissipate eventually, and doubtless will leave behind a
residue of ill will and hard feelings quite costly for the firm to eradicate.
On the other hand, there possibly is some profit at some time in such
misrepresentations by the firm, which a cautious employee would like to
guard against. Without fear of exploitation, some expertise is needed to
ascertain workers' value here and there, for pay components and living
costs differ. Thus, employees will welcome help in figuring their oppor-

tunity value, and will believe an independent calculation more readily than their employer's.

Employees' expense and risk of directly negotiating pay to be deferred or received collectively or implicitly increase with the scale of the establishment (the "bargaining unit," in NLRA language). For one thing, employees' aversion to the risk of such contracts will increase as employees collect more yield from capital specific to their employer, and more earnings from specific capital become more likely as scale rises, for the firm more can profit from essentially fixed-cost outlays for accomplishments suited uniquely for the firm. Furthermore, the close contact and trust that alleviates the employees' risks in a small firm decline as the firm grows. The decline in trust accelerates as routinization of the work increases, when routinization further decreases contact with supervisors (its typical purpose). The employer no longer fully trustworthy, it is not surprising that employees at larger plants might seek an agent solely in their employ skilled at collecting pay data, skilled at aggregating preferences, skilled at discerning possibilities, and skilled at preventing unilateral renegotiations of work terms.

To get help with negotiation and monitoring of employment contracts, movie and sports stars seeks individual agents. Ordinary workers have fewer unique inputs to supply, fewer unique opportunities of employment, and less income to spend on unique demands than do stars, of course. Hence, ordinary workers have less demand for a unique agent or a unique employment outcome. Furthermore, many of the wage bargain clauses that like-skilled workers want from their agents will be very similar: bargains with the same employer, temporal transformation of identical wage profiles, analyses of similar current and future job prospects, and so forth. Such services performed for one can be provided to another nigh costlessly, which means that an agent's service to ordinary workers possesses economies of scale and joint-production characteristics. Unlike stars in sports and movies, therefore, ordinary workers will *share* an agent.

The argument that employees will want a shared agent can be summarized succinctly in symbols. To start, consider that every worker has a multitude of possible wage sequences over time. Formally, represent the set of all of worker j's earning possibilities as

$$_jW^* = \{_jW_1, _jW_2, \ldots \}, \tag{1}$$

where

$$_jW_k = (_jw_{k1}, _jw_{k2}, \ldots, _jw_{kT}) \tag{2}$$

and $_jw_{kt}$ is the value of marginal product of the jth worker in the tth year at the kth employment this year.[4] For concreteness, let $_jw_{kt}$ also be what his best employer offers to pay him at time t, when he works this year for the kth employer. Of course, any worker's wage at any task will depend upon the quality of cooperating inputs, his effort, the organization of the market, and all the other parameters and variables in production and demand functions. But, to move the argument forward, we ignore all aspects unaffected by presence of an employees' agent.

A worker wants utility rather than cash, of course, so he will choose among employers so as to maximize the utility of alternative wage profiles. Thus, the jth employee chooses employer k in order to

$$\max_{k} \; U(_jW_k). \tag{3}$$

Now, if $U(_jW_k)$ is a utility production function, then an agent might be wanted because it reduced the cost of transforming wages into utility (by capturing economies of scale in providing surrounding future wages, for instance). Or an agent might be wanted because it improved $_jW_k$ (be keeping employees better informed of opportunities elsewhere or by enabling employees to devote full attention to their jobs, perhaps). In short, because it promises to better wages or to reduce his cost of getting utility from wages, an agent might be wanted by an employee.

To embody choice of agent in our formal calculus, let $_jW_{ki}$ be the wage vector and $U(_jW_{ki})$ be utility of employee j associated with the kth employer and the ith employees' agent. Thus, the jth employee chooses employer k and agent i in order to

$$\max_{k,i} \; U(_jW_{ki}), \tag{4}$$

where i ranges across agent-representatives possible with employer k. Perhaps there are many potential employee agents at employment k. In this case, i would range over a large domain, which would include self-representation under various pay and work management schemes, such as incentive pay and Taylorism, might include sure and constant wages, and might index a large number of independent competing agents wishing to represent employees at the kth employment.[5] Often in the past, i would have been chosen by the employer, so that to choose employment k was simultaneously to accept representative i. Since passage of the National Labor Relations Act in 1935, the domain of i generally has included one or more independent labor unions, such as the United Steelworkers, and has excluded a separate shared agent paid for by employers, or a company union. But before we take up the constrained evolution of employee agents, we wish to finish our discussion of unconstrained agent choice.

To identify the forum for provision of an agent's employment services to ordinary workers, we have used various synonyms for the place of employment: the factory, the plant, and the bargaining unit. By all, we mean that employment locus over which scale economies in representation are realized. To achieve this intent, it seems that the employment locus should be delimited by discontinuities in the characteristics of work or workers that would prompt discontinuities in the costs or benefits of an agent's help. Skilled craftsmen frequently change employers. A plumber, for instance, works at the Jones house in the morning and the Smith house in the afternoon—but always on pipes. It makes sense to us that skilled craftsmen will share needs for an agent to represent them beyond their current employment: to keep tabs on demand and supply over a wide area and to keep them up to date on new developments in their trade. Common laborers, in contrast, will want an agent (if at all) to represent them at their current job only, where their skills (if any) are specific; their lack of general skills reduces their similarity of concern about other opportunities. For the same reasons, it makes sense that craftsmen will perceive higher personal benefits from an agent than will common laborers. Furthermore, with craftsmen's homogeneity of interests off as well as on the job and their scattered employers, it makes sense that craftsmen's agent would provide off-the-job consumptions to subscribers (such as burial assistance and unemployment benefits), as well as negotiate for pay packages. These, in turn, would prorate the costs of agent representation across a larger base. We therefore predict that craftsmen would hire an agent before common laborers would, and that their agent would offer services craftwide, rather than firm- or plantwide, other things equal.[6]

Unlike craftsmen, unskilled workers' similarities decrease abruptly at the plant door, and their employer is more constant (if perhaps their employment is not). Within their plant, homogeneous employees will find it easier and more rewarding to bargain collectively, if for no other reason than that the preferences of each more closely are the preferences of all, and the language of each is understood by all. It seems no surprise, for instance, that the unskilled Brewery Workers, all with the wants and understandings derived from the same strong ethnic heritage, formed one of the first unions of noncraftsmen (Weber, 1967).

To be sure, many pay outcomes are quasi public—work conditions and pace on an assembly line, for instance—in response to economies of scale. This might seem to make a shared agent vulnerable to free riders who enjoy the collective benefits without contributing to the remuneration of the agent (Olson, 1965, chap. 3). Our preceding analysis, however, suggests that the cost of free riders is not so burdensome, because of great economies of scale in production of agents' services for ordinary workers. In addition, the prosecution of grievances is to some extent provided by an agent on an individual basis, and plausibly these are of sufficient value to a worker to offset his proclivity to free ride.[7]

Thus, there are several reasons (unrelated to monopolization of labor, we emphasize) that prompt employees to share an agent who bargains in their behalf. But employees are not the only ones to welcome such a bargaining agent to the scene. Although we above have identified an "employers' incentive to cheat," we do not mean to suggest that the incentive prompts the act. Yet employees' guarding against that incentive prompts turnover, unwillingness to shoulder long-term employment costs and to acquire employer-specific skills, and indiscriminate attention to gossip and rumor, for employees have much to lose from a cheating employer, even if the probability of loss is low. This suggests that employers seeking to avoid being discriminated against in the labor market would be about as willing as employees to hire an independent agent to evaluate the firm's performance for employees. Further, the employer could anticipate savings from negotiation of terms of employment and resolution of grievances with someone better aware of broad market conditions and better able to understand cost accounts than is the average employee, especially when this someone can relate what he has learned to the workers without question of credibility. Such an agent would speed and make less disruptive contract negotiation, and thereby would raise employees' productivity.

If workers' enhanced productivity accrues to their employer, likely the employer will pay for the agent. If the employer pays, then we predict that the employees will get paid what they could get elsewhere, and that the employer will keep the benefits from the rise in productivity. But the employees could pay for the agent, even if all of his benefits are specific to the employer. If the employees pay, then their wages will capture the value of their increased productivity. Obviously, employer and employee could share expenses as well. There seems no strong reason to expect one or the other to pay, for the employer-specific agent is analogous to firm-specific capital (Becker, 1964). If workers' enhanced productivity is not captured with certainty by any one employer or if the agent merely improves workers' bargaining skills (as when the agent keeps workers abreast of opportunities elsewhere), we expect with more assuredness that workers will pay for their agent and that the value of workers' raised productivity will be passed on fully in members' wages.

IV. THE HISTORICAL RECORD

Over the nineteenth century, behemoths grew in American industry. As the strife-ridden records of Carnegie's Homestead Works testify (Brody, 1969), these firms were too large to secure satisfactory labor relations from the normal contacts between manager and worker on the job. With the new technologies and the new organizational forms, contacts between worker and manager were not sufficiently innocent for the trust and the candid flow of information necessary for labor harmony (Edwards, 1979). In consequence, new means of achieving labor peace grew. One means was Taylorism, which for our purpose is best characterized as detailed design and monitoring of laborers' tasks. What we mean to convey is that Taylorism became scientific determination of labor's tasks, rather than a means toward management of labor. By and large, Taylorism did not achieve harmony in relations between workers and managers. As an alternative or a supplement to Taylorism, large employers established corporate welfare programs for employees: typically recreation and education programs, health care, and pensions for employees. Within large firms, scientific management and corporate welfare came to be administered by an intermediary between boss and worker. This intermediary often was called the personnel department, and was charged with maintaining control of and winning cooperation from workers. Especially when wearing its welfare hat, it did so with actions, *in the opinion of management,* beneficial to workers. Hence, it seems reasonable to designate such a personnel department as the agent of management, even though it served management and labor.

There grew another means of achieving labor peace. In addition to scientific management and corporate programs, large firms introduced company unions into the workplace, in order to improve labor relations. From firm to firm, company unions—or, by their other name, systems of industrial democracy—varied considerably in design and accomplishments (Department of Labor, 1937; Lauck, 1926; Nelson, 1975, pp. 156–62). But it is not stretching to describe company unions as a means for an agent of workers *selected by workers* to represent workers to management. To be sure, the company union-agent was constrained by management: in the issues that it could raise, in its access to workers, and in its remedies for disagreements. Within these (characteristically evolving) constraints, company unions looked after the collective interests of worker-members, as those interests were perceived by workers. In contrast, personnel departments looked after workers' interests, as perceived by management. Thus, just as it seems it is appropriate to view a personnel department as an agent of management, so it is appropriate to view a company union as its members' agent.

That a company union typically embraces all at a plant, that the workers covered disproportionately were unskilled, and that the expense of the company union generally was paid for by the employer conform to our expectations. Many of an agent's benefits to craftsmen with portable skills likely will not benefit any one firm with certainty. So we expect that mobile craftsmen will pay their agents and will reap the benefits directly. Thus, inclusion of craftsman in company unions was incidental. But many large employers of unskilled laborers provided company unions through the 1920s—indeed, until company unions were outlawed by the Wagner Act in 1935. These company unions acted to enhance productivity by electing employee-leaders who communicated managements' responses and justifications to employees and brought employees' questions and responses to management.

Employer sponsorship or even encouragement of unions was rare, however. So we next take up why, if unions potentially promise to lower labor costs, especially at factories employing many unskilled, that strike rather than harmony accompanied unionization.

V. A UNION AS ITS MEMBERS' AGENT

It is more common for economists to view a union as raising members' wage through restriction rather than facilitation of production. The union as monopolist of labor fully occupied Marshall's analysis and has prompted the bulk of advance in theory since (Marshall, 1964; Hicks, 1932; Johnson and Mieszkowski, 1974). This preoccupation is for good reason. To the extent that a union is its members' "perfect" agent, it should raise members' utility however it can. We have discussed above how a union can raise members' productivity and thereby members' wages. We have argued that such possibilities for raising productivity will be largest for craftsmen and for unskilled laborers at integrated jobs (so that collective provision of working conditions is economical) using much fixed capital (so that small improvements in the work process yield magnified returns) in large establishments (so that collective provision of benefits is economical).

But a union of craftsmen is an engine for restricting use of growth of the craft, as well as for reaping economies in provision of valued services. A union of unskilled is an engine for transferring quasi-rents from management and capital to labor. Such rents will be larger at those same establishments where a union can raise productivity more, that is, where there are many workers (and therefore rapid replacement is difficult) performing integrated tasks (so that shutdown is costly) and using fixed capital (so that net cash flow exceeds profits). Hence, it is not suprising that many employers who recognized the productivity-raising advantages of a company union still hesitated to permit one. They feared that a union, if its members agent, would seek higher wages as readily from monopoly as from productivity.[8] Granted the power to strike and de facto the right to use violence, and armed with employment terms necessarily bargainable collectively, it would be malfeasance if a union today did not press both productivity and monopoly for wage gains.

To sum up our progress to here: There are reasons to believe that a labor union acting as its members' agent could increase labor productivity and reduce labor costs by making more efficient the production process and the means of payment. There are reasons that job-mobile craftsmen would form such a union before less skilled industrial workers and that a union of craftsmen would be independent of employers and would embrace craftsmen employed by many employers. Less skilled industrial workers, by the same reasoning, would perceive less gain in productivity from a union, but more of their gain would flow from industrial-democracy–type accomplishments within the plant. Accordingly, we predict that industrial workers would form unions after and less readily than craftsmen, that unions of industrial workers would be plant- or firm-specific, that such unions would be formed in the largest firms, and that employers would bear much or all of the cost of an industrial union. Finally, we note that such an industrial union would possess some power to coerce rents from other inputs. There is evidence that fear of such monopolistic coercion kept some employers from aiding in establishment of company unions prior to the 1930s. By the National Labor Relations Act (Wagner Act) of 1935, an employer was prevented from giving to any particular union certain help (such as payment of employees dues) or hurt (such as refusing to bargain in good faith) (Gregory and Katz, 1979, chap. 9). This act and associated laws and practices effectively outlawed a company union and gave to an independent union greater monopoly power over the supply of labor. Independent industrial unions responded predictably by increasing in size (from perhaps 700,000 members in 1930 to 4 million members in 1939)[9] and militancy [work stoppages over wages and hours expanded threefold in the period (U.S. Bureau of the Census, 1975, Series D 978, 983)]. Almost surely the proportion of union wages got from monopoly extraction increased and the proportion from productivity gain declined after 1935.

At this time, this commonsensical statement is the most that can be said. For sure, a plethora of regressions run recently report a positive impact of labor unions on productivity (Allen, 1979; Brown and Medoff, 1978; Clark, 1980). But there are reasons to question these results. If the union unilaterally raises members' wages, an employer will substitute alternative inputs for labor. The employer will use more management or more tools or more higher-skilled workers. All such responses are moves along an isoquant that minimize the burden of a wage raised by a union exercising monopoly power. If labor's productivity now is measured, almost certainly it will be higher than before. Of course, the correct measure of changed productivity here wanted is the shift in the isoquant map induced by labor's unionization, not the movement along an isoquant induced by labor's raised wage. If the qualities and the quantities of inputs are measured accurately, and if the production relation is specified and estimated correctly, then such cost-reducing moves along an isoquant will be distinguished from shifts in isoquants. But these are big ifs. The requirements for proper measurement are notoriously difficult to meet, and econometric studies generally confound the impacts of changes in inputs and changes in productivities. The typical result is misattribution of too much impact to productivity and too little to substitutions of other inputs for laborers of the original quality.[10] Because factor substitution gets cheaper as time passes, misattribution from mismeasurement or misspecification will show up as continuing growth in productivity.

Measured productivity is raised and true productivity is reduced by a monopoly union because laborers cannot legally be bound to a lifetime contract. If laborers could be bound and through their union-agent could monopolize the sale of labor to the bargaining unit, then an all-or-nothing offer would transfer in a lump sum all rents to the employees, but would not affect factor ratios at margins. The monopoly union then would charge the employer a fixed fee to regain access to a competitive labor market. In the first instance, only the distribution of income would be affected by a monopoly union.

Because workers cannot be bound by a lifetime agreement, a firm will not pay a worker's union a once-and-for-all amount equal to the present value of labor to the firm, for the employer has no assurance that soon after payment a similar lifetime demand will not be repeated. Accordingly, an employer facing a monopoly union will pay only that portion of the amount appropriate for the enforceability of contracts (the duration and certainty of a "no-strike" clause). Further, he will insist upon paying enough of the lump in the form of higher wages or in deferred compensation to assure the availability of laborers throughout the contract period (with attendant effects on factor ratios). Finally, an employer will strive to reduce the cost of subsequent wage demands by making capital more variable and other laborers more accessible, if he can. Thus, the inability to transfer property rights from firm to union will prompt inefficient labor use and continued struggle between union and employer that will reduce productivity. In contrast, if a union represented a permanent labor monopoly and could be expected to honor permanent contracts, then the union would help the employer to deter shirking and productivity-reducing behavior that would reduce the value of the monopoly (Faith and Tollison, 1981; Martin 1980). Varied degrees of enforceability of contracts and the permanency of labor monopolies thus also prompt varied impacts of unionization upon measured productivity.

Labor's marginal value is its marginal product multiplied by output price. So another way that a monopoly union can get a higher wage is by raising the price of output. One way for a union to raise output price is to increase output demand. Another way is to restrict output and move the market back up a given output demand function. In the usual analysis, where the industry in question otherwise would be competitive—for instance, where economies of scale are slight and inputs are dispersed among owners—a many-member cartel of producers would be required to allocate and enforce the output restriction on each member firm and to set the higher prices. Typically, after formation of a cartel, cheating would become rampant and the cartel eventually would fall apart. If not, it would end up with an unwieldy and inflexible managing bureaucracy, which would produce reams of evidence of illegalities. Here, then, is a real opening for a union: a union can share output data (proportional to the number of members at work), enforce agreements (backed up by punishment with strikes, for instance), and reduce output (through employment and work-practices restrictions) (Faith and Lentz, 1980; Maloney et al., 1979; Thompson, 1980).

The classic historical incident of a union joining with manufacturers to maintain a cartel occurred in the 1880s, when a union of window glass workers used strikes and restrictive work practices to police a cartel of window glass producers (Ulman, 1955, pp. 526–31). More recently, Weiss (1966) found that union members' wages were higher in industries of lower concentration. Since lower concentration suggests a greater need for cartel enforcement for optimum monopolization of the product market, union members in less concentrated industries perhaps are paid more because their ability to police a cartel is more needed.

VI. WHAT ELSE UNIONS DO

Thus far, unions have been presented as monopolists of labor (their traditional role) and as spokesmen of employees (their revisionist role). As members' agent, of course, unions should perform both rules. But with a need to be selected by members, the union should win votes by enhancing its value to members in every way. In particular, perfect-agent unions would not confine their efforts to raising rents from the firm and its customers or to enhancing labor's productivity by actions on the job. As its members' agent, the union would seek rents from society at large through politics, in addition. The union would use its political power to raise protective tariffs and minimum wages to standardize workplace conditions and length of workweek, and to achieve other outcomes beneficial to members.

In fact, unions have done so: recent successful uses of political power include the negotiated import restrictions on the importation of Japanese cars (achieved by the United Automobile Workers) and the standardization of working conditions enforced by the Occupational Safety and Health Administration (OSHA), heavily supported by the AFL–CIO.

Such legislated accomplishments depend more upon a union's political power than upon its successes at monopolizing or raising the productivity of workers. In the first instance, there is no reason that a union's job power (proportional to the scarcity of substitutes for union workers) or productivity power (related to technology and demography, it seems) would be correlated closely with a union's political power (proportional to the number of pro-union voters), so there is no reason that the union best organized for direct impact at the job site would be best organized for strength at the polls.

In politics, power accrues to a pressure group in proportion to the pressure group's ability to get its members to vote and to vote the issue. Pressure groups vary in ability to do these, of course. But there are reasons to believe that almost any pressure group has some, if only because the group presents members with a desirable outcome and gives promise that enough will vote the recommended way that the desirable outcome might be achieved. Further reasons for a group to have political strength disproportionate to its number might be advanced, such as the members' personal satisfaction from recognized participation in a group project and members' disproportionate exposure to one-sided "persuasion" (Reid, 1977). It seems that an unaffiliated voter will not be so informed or so sure to vote his preference (if any) as a group member will, for the expected marginal impact of one vote is nil.[11]

Distinction between the job power and the political power of a union prompts speculation that local unions' associations in nationals and federations are means to gain political power without unnecessarily lessening job power (cf. Dalton, 1982). Increasing returns to scale and to more appropriate geographical distribution of political pressure groups makes a national union or a federation of nationals a much stronger political force than the unaffiliated total (Pincus, 1975).

The alternative argument is that national unions and federations of several nationals raised or cheapened job power. Admittedly, this is so to some extent. The power to blacklist a strikebreaker doubtless raises unions' job power. Likewise, any ability to coordinate better the production of new practitioners of a craft with growth in demand achieved by national crafts unions surely keeps the wages of craftsmen above what would prevail.[12] As discussed above, it also is admitted that some collective benefits might be provided for less if pooled over large numbers of like persons, such as practitioners of the same craft. If the benefit were probabilistic, such as insurance, however, the "large number" for most beneficial pooling would be reached long before the number in a national was. Furthermore, covariance and cost likely would be lessened by including diverse rather than like participants in the pool. Even if not, since the cheapest pool for life insurance would not be the cheapest pool for health insurance, etc., it seems that diverse but advantageous pools of beneficiaries would be organized by diverse providers, not one union, if cheapness of provision controlled the result.

For craftsmen, perhaps, a national union may provide information about job opportunities efficiently. For less skilled industrial workers, a national union or a federation makes little sense as a means to raise productivity or to cheapen provision of benefits. It makes more political sense.

VII. MALFEASANCE

Increasing returns to scale in political pressure groups make the national union a stronger political force than the same number of members fragmented into several locals. However, the existence of the national union also contributes to the erosion of the members' position as principal. For one thing, federation and political involvement obfuscate the facts of union representation. When a local leader argues to do x because it will produce y on the plant floor and z in the paycheck, the worth of the argument is soon and clearly measured. When he argues to do x or to vote y because the national requests it for administrative or strategic reasons, the relation between request and accomplishment is hidden. Even when union leaders' political positions so radically diverge from members' that differences are obvious—as in the case of AFL–CIO lobbying for increased welfare payments (Kau et al., 1980; see also Heldman and Knight, 1980)—these divergences arguably can be attributed to intelligent logrolling, rather than to leaders' malfeasant self-indulgence. Unionists' efforts on the political margin thus carry the risk of reducing their union-agent's faithfulness of service.

The affiliation of a local union with a national and a federation of nationals threatens more than a dimunition of information necessary for control of the local by its members. With the instruments of exclusive jurisdiction and union security agreements, these affiliations make more possible the monopolization of union services.[13] To the degree that monopolization occurs, the extent of malfeasance to be expected increases. To be sure, malfeasance is not the benefit to members generally attributed to exclusive jurisdiction and compulsory unionism. Exclusive jurisdiction strengthens unionism by rationalizing unions' efforts to organize new members—this is the official justification (Reynolds, 1974). It is argued that exclusive jurisdiction does this by stopping raids by another union on members already organized and by assigning rights to organize those currently unorganized by one particular best-fitted union. Thus are the thin ranks of union organizers best allocated to aid workers and wasteful competitions avoided. Likewise, union security agreements officially are justified as necessary to prevent free riders from enjoying benefits collectively negotiated and collectively received without payment (Olson 1965, chap. 3).

But in plain English, "exclusive jurisdiction" means "one seller," and "union security" means "forced purchase." If the benefits of unionization are so individualized in the handling of grievances that free riding is checked, as argued in Reynolds (1980), then there is no argument for exclusive jurisdiction and union security that leads to a benefit for members. Exclusive jurisdiction and union security together give a particular union the power to compel members to honor strikes. Of course, the ability to strike effectively will benefit a labor monopoly. If that monopoly benefitted the members of the local directly, however, compulsion to strike would be unnecessary. Employees' direct and immediate interest would prompt their strike support. Possibly, a strike would directly benefit others disproportionately, as when a strike by those least substitutable is settled by pay raises to all. But side payments proportional to value of marginal product as easily can be arranged for strikers as for vice-presidents, so that even these public benefits (to unionists only, to be sure) do not seem to require coercion of employees' behavior. Indeed, competition of unions for members, which now is blocked, would ensure that crucial unionists indeed received their monopoly worth. In practice, exclusive jurisdiction and union security permit heavy fines for wildcat strikes, requirement of national union approval of locally bargained contracts, and selective parceling out of strike rewards. These are the means used to cartelize, without full payment of profits to union members.

VIII.   IMPLICATIONS OF AGENCY

Modeling labor unions as agents in service of some principal, we have shown that a union's actions to benefit its principal will vary with the preferences and the opportunities of the principal. In particular, we have shown that the true impact of a union on labor productivity will depend upon the ease of raising efficiency relative to the ease of raising rents. Albeit briefly, we have argued that exclusive jurisdiction and compulsory unionism will help to capture monopoly rents. Finally, we have emphasized that to a greater or lesser degree a union will strive to serve its own ends, rather than those of its formal collective principal.

These observations lead to several implications. First, it is unlikely that any agent is the perfect agent of its principal. This truth applies to analysis of unions, as well as to analysis of other agency–principal relationships. The patterns of union affiliations so productive of political power lessen members' oversight and control of their agents. As discussed, exclusive jurisdiction, union security agreements, and the outlawing of company unions restrict competition among union-agents for members and thereby reduce members' control of their agent's performance. The equations modeling members' demand for union representation can embody the possible deterioration in members' (principal's) monitoring ability. Now we write the jth employee's choice criterion as

$$\max_{k,i} \ EU(_jW_{ki}),\tag{5}$$

where EU represents expected utility; k indexes the employer, as before; j indexes temporal sequences of unions experienced in some probability. If the kth employer currently is unorganized by a union, i will index a large number of potential sequences of representatives (including no representative), with varying probabilities. If the kth employer already is organized, i still may range across alternative agents, but the sum probability of alternatives to the current agent will be low (for it is held down by exclusive jurisdiction and no-raiding agreements). Introduction of the union index and associated probabilities explicitly with the employer index k into an employee's job decision calculus emphasizes the risks and imperfections in the relationship between employee-principal and his agent. As argued above, a union-agent with more involvement in politics and with a safer constituency more likely will display less adherence to his principal's wishes. At the same time, an agent with political margins to exploit and cooperant unionists to utilize doubtless can improve his principals' wage (or, more accurately, W vector) relative to any competitive alternative. Leaders' malfeasance and members' profits from unionism, that is, grow apace. But if average profits to members grow with expansions of leaders' stage of action from productivity enhancement to redistribution, so does variability of profits. Thus, the substitution of expected utility for utility in the maximand emphasizes the need to incorporate members' risk preferences.

Second, it is clear that econometric studies of union wage effects need to allow for indirect and collectively provided remuneration. For instance, preliminary study of blue-collar workers' wage profiles show that union members gain "better" (less strenuous, cleaner, and so forth) jobs as tenure rises with more certainty than do nonmembers. Duncan and Stafford (1980) estimate that compensation for undesirable working conditions explains two-fifths of the wage premium of union workers. Thus unionists' relative wage advantage is not as much compressed with age as commonly thought.

Third, typically it is presumed that a union's principal is its membership democratically aggregated. Henry Simons (1944) long ago questioned that assumption for monopoly unions. The logical principal, he suggested, would be half of the original union members, and would halve again at each opportunity. But there is a complication. As we discussed, because workers are unable to execute lifetime contracts, even monopoly unions must maintain a continuing existence. This requires the continuous addition of members. To add members, the union must offer entrants a competitive wage (or more accurately, a competitive expected present value of lifetime earnings), but it need not offer entrants more. Thus, a union's principal might include a subset of all members. For example, because the original members always will be senior to new hires, the stronger seniority provisions and deferred fringes of union contracts well may effect an accrual of rents to the founders. If unions do benefit subsets of members, then we would expect membership challenges to union contracts after upsurges in employment that redistribute votes away from current beneficiaries. Such a challenge well may have occurred recently in United Mine Workers (UMW) coalfields (Farber, 1978).

Deferring highest earnings keeps workers pro-union. Deferring earnings keeps young employees, who due to layoffs by seniority are not yet or are seldom employed at union wages, supportive of union monopolies. Underfunding or renegotiating pensions keeps retired unionists' support strong thereafter. Deferring high earnings, so to speak, keeps a carrot in front of a potential or one-time unionist who otherwise might cross a picket line or vote for freer enterprise. Seniority pay and promotion provisions, accordingly, likely are the means used by a union to effect a long-lived monopoly. Once in place, seniority provisions keep many more than the immediate beneficiaries interested in the maintenance of the monopoly, for even those who in present value will earn at the union employment only their opportunity earnings over their lifetime—that is, all those hired after the formation of the perfect monopoly union—will support the union fervently when earnings are deferred, so that the promised yield of their immediate payment (of dues, layoffs, and long times in low pay grades) will be realized (cf. Lazear, 1979). Thus, it seems smart thinking for a group of employees at some job to implement their monopoly of labor in the form of sharp and rigid links of pay and employment to seniority. To exploit more fully the incentives to seniority, it is natural that these original workers expand from job action to political action. Seniority, in sum, is not the substitution of average preferences for marginal preferences championed by Freeman and Medoff (1979), but is the means of enlisting many in a benefit program for a few.[14]

IX. CONCLUSION

Our agent–principal conceptualization of unionism attributes the diversity of union accomplishments in part to the diversity of principals, in part to differences in the cost providing the same benefit here and there, and in part to flaws in the relationship between agent and principal. In particular, we make the conjecture that not all union members qualify as principals. Above, we mentioned young workers employed under a high seniority–pay gradient contract. Also only grudgingly represented are those complementary to the true principals. The cooperation of complementary workers can raise the cost of strikebreaking greatly, although their subsequent agitation to share the gains can sustain union-weakening strife and prompt changes in the principal. Finally, we expect continuous attempts by each union-agent to build its independence, that is, to become its own principal.

ACKNOWLEDGMENTS

We wish to thank participants in the Workshop on Labor–Management Relations and the Public Choice Seminar at Virginia Polytechnic Institute and State University, in the Labor Workshop at the University of Chicago, the Management Workshop at the University of Rochester, the Transactions Cost Workshop at the University of Pennsylvania, Bernard F. Lentz, Francis A. O'Connell, Jr., Jonathan Pincus, Robert McCormick and Adrian Throop, who discussed an earlier version presented at the meeting of the American Economic Association in Denver, and Conference participants, for helpful comments. We thank the National Right to Work Legal Defense Foundation, Inc., for research support.

NOTES

1. Most often, from explicit estimation of the simultaneous impact of higher wages on the extent of unionization (Lee, 1978); but also from explicit consideration of employees' quality (Weiss, 1966) and psychic compensation (Duncan and Stafford, 1980). Addison and Siebert (1979), Lewis (1980), and Parsley (1980) survey recent econometric studies of unions' wage effects.

2. For an introductory survey and analysis of the agency literature, see Faith and Tollison (1981).

3. Several studies conclude that union members view grievance processing as more important than contract negotiation, and that a union is most likely to win election after a "violation" of implicit contract terms (Miller et al., 1965; Sayles and Strauss, 1953; Seidman et al., 1958).

4. "This year," to allow for opportunities to change employers in subsequent years. For instance, the kth employer might not pay well this year, but might open up advantageous opportunities later on.

5. As discussed in the text, unique representation of an individual would be too costly for ordinary workers, so that $U(_jW_{k1}) < \max_{i>1} (_jW_{k1})$ for every k, where i = 1 corresponds to representation by an individual agent.

6. We still are considering only *legitimate* (that is, nonmonopolizing) efforts by an agent in behalf of employees represented.

7. See Bennett and Johnson (1979) and M. Reynolds (1980) for persuasive arguments for this conclusion.

8. This interpretation is supported by research materials in Boxes 141, 243, 255–57 from Accession 1411, National Association of Manufacturers, Eleutherian Mills Historical Li-

brary, Wilmington, Delaware. I am indebted to the Library staff for guiding me to these materials.

9. Seven hundred thousand members is the rough average of alternative measures of total union membership less American Federation of Labor membership in 1930. Four million is reported membership in the Congress of Industrial Organization for 1939 (Department of Commerce, 1975, Series D 931, 940–41, 943–44).

10. See Kalachek and Raines (1980). For elaborations, see Addison (1981), Brown and Medoff (1978), Lewis (1980), or Reid (1979, pp. 158–66). For an imaginative response—unsatisfactory in the end, however—see Mandelstamm (1965).

11. This is an implication of a recent seminar argument by James Buchanan.

12. That craft unions did affiliate in national unions in order to stop "overproduction" of craftsmen is the principal theme of Ulman (1955).

13. Union security agreements secure the following: exclusive representation, which designates one labor union to represent all employees in a bargaining unit; maintenance of membership, which requires membership during the life of the contract; union shop, which requires employees of a bargaining unit to be a member of the union; agency shop, which requires employees of a bargaining unit to pay dues to the representing union; and dues checkoff, which permits employees to have union dues deducted from pay and paid directly to a representing union by the employer (Reid, 1981).

14. Our argument that union seniority provisions are a payoff to the original members and a way to extend union power has an interesting implication for right-to-work states. If unions in right-to-work states do monopolize jobs, then seniority provisions would be even stronger (that is, the gradient of pay against tenure would be even steeper) than in non–right-to-work states. The reason is that without compulsory union dues, the only means to insure dues collection and continual union support is through exploitation of grievance procedures (so that nonmembers' grievances are pressed poorly). Conversely, if unions do not monopolize jobs in right-to-work states, their weakness should show up in a flatter seniority–pay gradient. This is so, as argued above, because pay by seniority asks subsequent hires to pay now for the promise of collecting later. But an infirmed monopoly cannot credibly promise a later rent. Therefore, any rent (reward) must be paid immediately to one and all, for all are continually of equal value in its procurement. We argued above that exclusive jurisdiction and compulsory unionism are necessary to make a strike effective, and that a strike is the means to effect a significant labor monopoly. By our logic, therefore, unions in right-to-work states should be weak, and that means that their seniority–pay gradients should be flatter. In fact, it seems so. Our very preliminary finding is that the seniority–pay gradient is much flatter in right-to-work states, which we interpret as evidence that unions there do not monopolize jobs. Right-to-work laws do matter (Faith et al., 1982).

REFERENCES

Addison, John T. (1981), "Are Unions Good for Productivity?" Mimeo, University of South Carolina.
Addison, John T., and W. Stanley Siebert (1979), *The Market for Labor: An Analytical Treatment*. Santa Monica, Calif.: Goodyear Publishing Company, Inc.
Allen, Steven G. (1979), "Unionized Construction Workers Are More Productive." (Mimeo).
Becker, G. S. (1964), *Human Capital: A Theoretical and Empirical Analysis*, NBER. New York: Columbia University Press.
Bennett, James T., and Manuel H. Johnson (1979), "Free Riders in the Labor Union: Artifice or Affliction?" *British Journal of Industrial Relations* 17 (July):158–172.

Berkowitz, Monroe (1954), "The Economics of Trade Union Organization and Administration." *Industrial Labor Relations Review* (July).

Brody, David (1960), *Steelworkers in America, the Nonunion Era*. New York: Harper & Row.

Brown, Charles, and James Medoff (1978), "Trade Unions in the Production Process." *Journal of Political Economy* 136 (June):355–378.

Cartter, Alan (1959), *Theory of Wages and Employment*. Homewood, Ill.: Richard D. Irwin Publishing Company.

Clark, Kim B. (1980), "The Impact of Unionization on Productivity: A Case Study." *Industrial and Labor Relations Review* 33 (July):451–469.

Dalton, Allen D. (1982), "Determinants of National Union Dominance." Ph.D. Dissertation. Virginia Polytechnic Institute and State University.

Dertouzos, J., and J. H. Pencavel (1981), "Wage and Employment Determination Under Trade Unionism: The International Typographers Union." *Journal of Political Economy* 89(6):1162–1181.

Dunlop, John T. (1944), *Wage Determination Under Trade Unions*. New York: Macmillan Company.

Duncan, Greg J., and Stafford, Frank P. (1980), "Do Union Members Receive Compensating Wage Differentials?" *American Economic Review* 70 (June):355–371.

Edwards, Richard (1979), *Contested Terrain, The Transformation of the Workplace in the Twentieth Century*. New York: Basic Books, Inc.

Faith, Roger, and Bernard Lentz (1981), "The Intertemporal Impact of Strikes on Profits." Working Paper No. E 79-8-2, Department of Economics, Virginia Polytechnic Institute and State University, May.

Faith, Roger, Bernard Lentz, and Joseph Reid (1982), "Union Wage Policies." Working Paper, Center for Study of Public Choice, Virginia Polytechnic Institute and State University.

Faith, Roger and Robert Tollison (1981), "Contractual Exchange and The Timing of Payment." *Journal of Economic Behavior and Organization* 1 (December):325–342.

Farber, Henry S. "Bargaining Theory, Wage Outcomes and the Occurrences of Strikes: An Econometric Analysis." *American Economic Review* 68 (June):262–271.

——— (1978b), "Individual Preferences and Union Wage Determination: The Case of the United Mine Workers." *Journal of Political Economy* 86 (October):923–942.

Fellner, William (1949), *Competition Among the Few*. New York: Alfred A. Knopf.

Freeman, Richard B., and James L. Medoff (1979), "The Two Faces of Unionism." *The Public Interest* LVII (Fall):69–93.

Gregory, Charles O., and Harold A. Katz (1979), *Labor and the Law*, third edition. New York: W. W. Norton & Company.

Heldman, D., and D. Knight (1980), *Unions and Lobbying: The Representation Function*. Arlington, Va.: The Foundation for the Advancement of the Public Trust, Inc.

Hicks, John R. (1932), *Theory of Wages*. London: Macmillan.

Johnson, George E. (1975), "Economic Analysis of Trade Unionism." *American Economic Review* 61 (May):23–28.

Johnson, H. G., and Peter Mieszkowski (1970), "The Effects of Unionization on the Distribution of Income: A General Equilibrium Approach." *Quarterly Journal of Economics* 84 (November).

Kalachek, E., and F. Raines (1980), "Trade Unions and Hiring Standards." *Journal of Labor Research* 1 (Spring).

Kau, James B., Donald Kennan, and Paul H. Rubin (1980), "A General Equilibrium Model of Congressional Voting." Mimeo, University of Georgia. Presented to the American Economic Association, September.

Lauck, W. Jett (1926), *Political and Industrial Democracy 1776–1926*. New York: Funk & Wagnells Company.

Lazear, Edward P. (1979), "Why is There Mandatory Retirement?" *Journal of Political Economy* 87 (December):1261–1284.

Lee, L.-F. (1978), "Unionism and Wage Rates: A Simultaneous Equations Model with Qualitative and Limited Dependent Variables." *International Economic Review* 19(2):415–433.

Lewis, H. Gregg (1963), *Unionism and Relative Wage Rates*. Chicago: University of Chicago Press.

—— (1980), "Interpreting Unionism Coefficients in Wage Equations." Mimeo, Duke University, August.

Maloney, Michael, Robert McCormick, and Robert Tollison (1979), "Achieving Cartel Profits Through Unionization." *Southern Economics Journal* 46 (October):628–634.

Mandelstamm, Allan B. (1965), "The Effects of Unions on Efficiency in the Residential Construction Industry: A Case Study." *Industrial and Labor Relations Review* 18 (June): 503–521.

Marshall, Alfred (1964), *Principles of Economics*. London: Macmillan.

Martin, Donald L., (1980), *An Ownership Theory of the Trade Union*. Berkeley: University of California Press.

Miller, Robert W., Frederick A. Zeller, and Glenn W. Miller (1965), *The Practice of Local Union Leadership*. Columbus: Ohio State University Press.

Nelson, Daniel (1975), *Managers and Workers*. Madison: The University of Wisconsin Press.

Olson, Mancur (1965), *The Logic of Collective Action*. Cambridge, Mass.: Harvard University Press.

Parsley, C. J. (1980), "Labor Unions and Wages: A Survey." *Journal of Economic Literature* 18(1):1–31.

Pincus, Jonathan J. (1975), "Pressure Groups and the Pattern of Tariffs." *Journal of Political Economy* 83 (August):757–778.

Reid, Joseph, D. (1976), "Sharecropping and Agricultural Uncertainty." *Economic Development and Cultural Change* 25 (April).

—— (1977), "Understanding Political Events in the New Economic History." *The Journal of Economic History* 37 (June).

—— (1981), "The Importance of Union Security Agreements in Explanation of the Extent and Nature of Union Representation." Working Paper, Center for Study of Public Choice, Virginia Polytechnic Institute and State University, October.

Reynolds, Lloyd J. (1974), *Labor Economics and Labor Relations*. Sixth Edition, Englewood Cliffs, N.J.: Prentice-Hall, p. 342 and *passim*.

Reynolds, Morgan O. (1980), "The Public Goods Argument for Compulsory Dues." *The Journal of Labor Research* I (2):295–313.

Ross, Arthur (1956), *Trade Union Wage Policy*. Berkeley: University of California at Berkeley Press.

Sayles, Leonard, and George Strauss (1953), *The Local Union*. New York: Harper.

Seidman, Joel, et al. (1958), *The Worker Views His Union*. Chicago: University of Chicago Press.

Simons, Henry (1944), "Some Reflections on Syndicalism." *Journal of Political Economy* 52 (March):1–25.

Thompson, Earl (1980), "On Labor's Right to Strike." *Economic Inquiry* 18(4):640–653.

Ulman, Lloyd (1966), *The Rise of the National Trade Union*. Cambridge, Mass.: Harvard University Press.

U.S. Bureau of the Census (1975), *Historical Statistics of the United States, Colonial Times to 1970, Bicentennial Edition, Part 2*. Washington, D.C., Series D 978, 983.

U.S. Department of Labor (1937), "Characteristics of Company Unions 1935." BLS Bulletin, No. 634, June.

Weber, Arnold (1967), "Stability and Challenge in the Structure of Collective Bargaining." In Lloyd Ulman (ed.), *Challenge to Collective Bargaining.* Englewood Cliffs, N.J.: Prentice-Hall.

Weiss, L. W. (1966), "Concentration and Labor Earnings." *American Economic Review* 56 (March):96–117.

UNIONISM, WAGES, AND CONTRACT ENFORCEMENT

M. W. Reder

There is wide, if not universal, agreement that unionism is somehow related to wages. However, in the extensive literature on the subject, there is no consensus either as to the direction of causation or as to the relative importance of various possible channels of interaction.[1] Given the complexity of the subject, this is not surprising.

In the first section of this paper, I present a model in which unionism and the wage rate (a proxy for worker compensation per hour) are jointly determined with the legal status of unionism being the key exogenous variable.[2] I do not portray unionism as a variable that is associated with differential wage rates between otherwise identical workers, but as a cause of changes in the wage level of a homogeneous group of workers each able to choose whether he will work under union conditions. That is, I consider two possible states of nature—unionism permitted and unionism not permitted—and compare the equilibrium wage rate in the two

New Approaches to Labor Unions.
Research in Labor Economics, Supplement 2, pages 27–52.

states. If there are both union and nonunion firms, their wage rates must be equal (in either state) but may vary from one state to the other.

The model presented in Section I is of little direct empirical interest and serves primarily as an introductory exercise to the more complicated two-period model of Section II which does have potential empirical application to explaining the intertemporal behavior of union–nonunion differentials as well as the long-run equilibrium differential.

I. UNIONISM AND WAGE RATES IN THE LONG RUN

Assume an economy that produces a single commodity by a process homogeneous of degree 1, that is sold at a price of $1. Employers are pecuniary maximizers, each hiring exactly one worker and supplying all other imputs. In the *absence of unions*, all employers pay the same hourly wage rate w, use the same technology, and have the same unit cost c. (Technology given, $c = \alpha w$, where α is the reciprocal of man-hour productivity.)

Let each employer's technology be idiosyncratically sensitive to unionism so that in the presence of a union, employer i's production function is $\bar{\phi}(i) = N\phi(i)$, where N, the nonunion level of output per man-hour is assumed the same for all firms; $0 < \phi(i); \phi(i) < \phi(i + 1); i = 1, 2, \ldots,$ m. Now $N - w = z$ for every nonunion employer and $\phi(a) - \bar{w} \geq z$ for all unionized employers, where a is any unionized employer, $\bar{w}$ is the wage rate given that unionism is legal, and z is profit.[3]

Assume that, absent unionism, all employees are (i) equally productive regardless of their employer and (ii) have zero reservation wage rates. Further, assume that (iii) absent unionism, each employee derives the same utility from a given wage regardless of the identity of his employer, but that (iv) each employee also has an idiosyncratic "taste (or distaste) for unionism."

Let this taste be defined by the condition that $U(\mu^s w) = U(w)$, where $\mu > 1$, $\bar{w}_s = \mu^s w$, and $U(\cdot)$ is utility of $(\cdot)$; i.e., the utility of μ^s times the nonunion wage is equal to the utility of the union wage. Now $\bar{w}_s$ is the union wage that makes s indifferent as to whether or not he is unionized when the nonunion wage is w. Let employee k's (k = 1, 2, \ldots, m) taste for unionism be such that he would be indifferent between unionization and nonunionization if the same wage rate prevailed in both states;[4] i.e., $U(\mu^k \bar{w}) = U(w) \mid \bar{w} = w$, implying either k = 0 or $\mu = 1$, where $U(\cdot)$ is the *common* utility function of all employees. As it is inconvenient to let $\mu = 1$, assume k = 0;[5] also assume $U' > 0$ and $\mu > 1$.

Call k the "union-neutral" employee and designate any employee $v < k$ as a union preferrer and any employee $j > k$ as a union avoider. Let employee 1 be designated as $-(k - 1) = 1 - k$ and employee j as $j - k$;

thus for $v < k$, $\mu^v < 1$; and for $j > k$, $\mu^j > 1$. Assume the taste for unionism to be such that μ^v and μ^j are independent of both wealth and the wage rate. Employers are assumed indifferent to union status except as it affects profit.

The assumptions of this model are such that, absent unionism, total output would be independent of how employers and employees were matched. That is, if there were a law that effectively prohibited unionism, workers (employers) would be indifferent as to the particular employer (worker) with whom they were affiliated and total output would be the same for all pairings. Of course, union-preferring workers would obtain less utility in the presence of such a law than in its absence.

Now suppose this law were changed to permit unionism provided both parties agreed, i.e., employer and employee are allowed to negotiate union status and the wage rate simultaneously. Under the changed law, there are three possibilities: (i) some pairs unionize, but not all; (ii) all pairs remain nonunion; and (iii) all pairs unionize. In case ii, the legal change has no effect on the wage rate; in case iii, the effect might be either to raise or to lower the wage rate (see below); and we shall analyze case i in detail.

The important point to note is that all employees receive the same (equilibrium) wage regardless of union status, although that wage may differ from the wage they would have obtained if unionism were forbidden. The reason for this is that, by assumption, (a) all union employees must receive the same wage; and (b) all nonunion employees must receive the same wage. Optimization requires that the union-neutral employee must receive a wage only "negligibly different" from both the union and the nonunion wage, and therefore (approximately) equal to both.[6]

In analyzing case i, it is convenient to distinguish among two subcases, $\phi(k) = 1$ and $\phi(k) \gtrless 1$.

(a) $\phi(k) = 1$: This is the special case where the employer of the union-neutral employee k is equally productive under union and nonunion conditions. Equation (1) states that in this case the productivity of match k (worker k, employer k) under union conditions is such that (a) it yields an output just sufficient to pay the employee the same wage and the employer the same profit as they could earn under nonunion conditions, and (b) the union-neutral employee is indifferent between union status and nonunion status at the same wage.

$$\bar{\phi}(k) = N = w + z = \bar{w} + z \tag{1}$$

$$= \mu^0 U(w) = U(\bar{w}) .$$

Equation (1) implies that w must be equal to $\bar{w}$ and that their common value is such that the union-neutral employee remains indifferent as to whether he is unionized. It further implies that changing the law (from not permitting unionism to permitting unionism) will not affect the equilibrium wage rate. The intuitive rationale for this is as follows: Since all employees are equally productive when affiliated with any given employer, any employee can place himself in the union-neutral employee's position and thus obtain the same wage in the union as in the nonunion status. Therefore, no employee will accept less than w. But he cannot obtain more than w because all nonunion employers (1, . . . , k − 1) have the same technology as k and therefore cannot earn z if they pay a wage higher than w.

Union employers (k + 1, . . . , m) can hire employee k (who accepts w under union conditions), and therefore will not pay more than w. Employers 1, . . . , k are nonunion, and hence have identical technologies and earn z at wage w. Employers k + 1, . . . , m all have a production function, $\bar{\phi}(j) > N, j > k$, and pay w, thereby generating profits in excess of z; these profits increase in j.

Therefore, in this special case, changing the law to permit unionism (provided both parties agree) has the following effects: (i) all "union-avoiding" workers are left with both the same wage and the same utility as before; (ii) "union-preferring" workers gain utility without loss (or gain) of wages; (iii) employers who are less efficient under unionism are left with undiminished profits and not unionized; (iv) employers whose efficiency is increased by unionization benefit, the benefits increasing with the gain in efficiency associated with unionization.

(b) $\phi(k) \gtrless 1$: For $\phi(k) < 1$, the employer of k cannot earn competitive profits and pay w, given the productivity associated with union status. Hence the kth pair will not unionize. But for $\phi(k) > 1$, the employer of k can pay w while earning more than z, given unionization; therefore, the kth pair will unionize. As I will now show, where $\phi(k) < 1$, there are some pairs, v, . . . , k − 1, who will not unionize, but who would unionize if $\phi(k) = 1$; also, where $\phi(k) > 1$, some pairs, k + 1, . . . , j − 1, will unionize who would not do so if $\phi(k) = 1$.

To see this, consider the panels of Figure 1, whose vertical axes measure dollars and whose horizontal axes are an indicator of the order number of a pair in an array satisfying the rule $\phi(i + 1) > \phi(i)$. Panel 1a describes the elements of this diagram: in this panel $\phi(\cdot)$ gives the value of output for each pair under union conditions and N (=constant) gives the value of output under nonunion conditions. Here z = constant and w = constant are the profit and wage rates, respectively, when unionism is prohibited. [The positive slope of $\phi(\cdot)$ results from the rule $\phi(i) < \phi(i + 1)$ that determines the ordering of employers under union conditions.]

Panel 1b describes the case where $\phi(k) = 1$. Here $\phi(k) = w + z =$

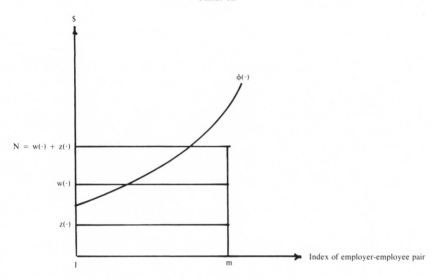

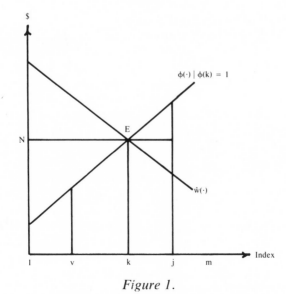

Figure 1.

Panel Ic

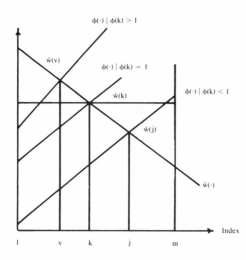

Panel Id

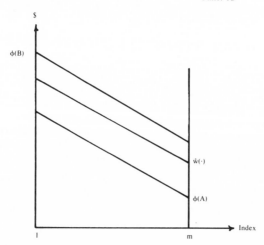
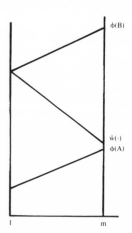

Figure 1 (continued)

32

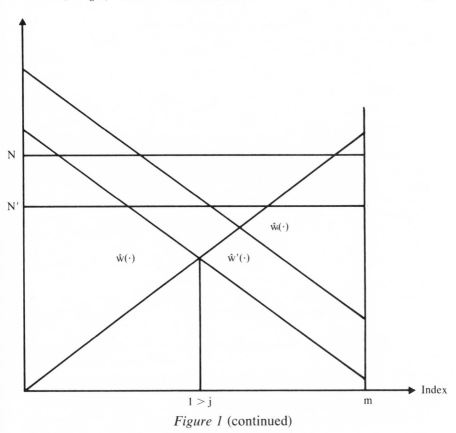

Figure 1 (continued)

$\bar{w}(k) + z$ as k (the union-neutral employee) will compel $\bar{w}$ to equal w. In this special case, legalizing unionism will not affect the wage rate as employee k will not accept union status at a wage lower than w and employer k cannot earn (as much as) z under union status at a wage higher than w. Hence the kth pair will be indifferent as to whether they unionize.

For any employer $v < k$, $\phi(v) < \phi(k)$; therefore, v would be unable to earn z if he paid as much as $w = \bar{w}$. Therefore, v will be nonunion (with productivity $= N$) and will employ a worker v for whom $\mu^v < 1$. Given the nonunion wage rate, it is possible to construct the curve $\hat{w}(\cdot)$ whose ordinates measure the *minimum* wage rate the corresponding worker would accept under union conditions.

In panel 1 b all pairs to the left of k (i.e., from 1 to $k - 1$) are nonunion and all pairs to the right ($k + 1$ to m) are unionized. All workers are paid $\bar{w} = w$; all nonunion employers earn a profit of z and all union employers earn z plus a differential rent of unionism equal to $\phi(\cdot)$ − N. Stable equilibrium requires that $\hat{w}(\cdot)$ cut $\phi(\cdot)$ from above at E. Otherwise the wage premium (in excess of w) necessary to induce employee k + 1 to accept unionism would exceed the gain in productivity from unionizing the (k + 1)st employer compelling him to accept profits less than z, in which case pair k + 1 would not unionize; the converse would apply to the (k − 1)st pair. This would imply that (at least) one pair, k + 1, which was more productive under unionism and whose employee member was union-preferring, would choose nonunionism, while another pair, k − 1, with the opposite characteristics would unionize. Obviously, such a result would be nonoptimal and unstable.

As drawn, panel 1b (and panel 1c) imply uniqueness of equilibrium. However, nothing in the structure of the model requires this result, and it is postulated (ad hoc) only to avoid irrelevant complications. The assumed monotonicity of both $\hat{w}(\cdot)$ and $\bar{\phi}(\cdot)$, together with the equilibrium requirement $\phi(k)N = \bar{w}(k) + z(k)$, assure that employer k and employee k are "matched" in equilibrium. Also, equilibrium requires that if a firm consists of a union-preferring worker and an employer whose productivity is greater under unionism, it must be unionized; and that firms consisting of a worker and an employer with the reverse characteristics must be nonunion. But beyond these requirements, the model does not determine which employer–employee matches will be made nor, for our limited purpose, need it do so.

Panel 1c is a generalization of 1b. The equilibrium at v refers to the case where $\phi(k) > 1$, and that at j refers to the case where $\phi(k) < 1$. Now $\phi(k) < 1$ implies that the productivity of the union-neutral employee is less under unionism than otherwise, so that he would choose to be nonunion. Thus the equilibrium position will lie southeast of $\hat{w}(k)$; i.e., the (unionism legal) equilibrium wage will be lower than $\hat{w}(k)$ and some union preferring workers (k + 1 to j) will be induced to be nonunion. The effect of legalizing unionism is to *lower* the wage rate. The reverse of these statements apply in the case where $\phi(k) > 1$.

In effect, if $\phi(k) < 1$, equilibrium is attained where the lower productivity of the employer under unionism is just offset by the maximum wage sacrifice that the "marginal union worker" will make to become unionized, leaving the employer a profit of (exactly) z. If $\phi(k) > 1$, equilibrium is reached where the greater productivity of the "marginal union employer" is just sufficient to provide the wage premium necessary to induce the "marginal union worker" v to accept unionization and leave a profit of z.

Panels 1b and 1c refer only to nonboundary equilibria, i.e., to equilibria where there is at least one union firm and one nonunion firm. But boundary equilibria are possible: for example, in panel 1d $\phi(A)$ lies below $\hat{w}(\cdot)$

at all abscissae so that worker m requires a higher wage to accept unionism than employer m could pay while earning z. Hence worker m (and, a fortiori, all others) would choose to be nonunion and earn w. In such case, legalizing unionism has no effect upon either the equilibrium wage or the number of union members (which remains zero).

Panel 1d also shows that, where $\phi(B)$ lies above $\hat{w}(\cdot)$ at all abscissae, under unionism worker 1 would accept a wage below that which would reduce employer 1's profit to z. Therefore worker 1 (and all others) would unionize and earn a wage in excess of w; in this case, w would not be determined by the variables operative in Figure. 1.

Qualifying Remarks

The construction of Figure 1 involves several quite arbitrary assumptions that are essential to the results obtained. I comment on these, seriatim:

(1)   Figure 1 describes a matching model in which a firm consists of exactly one worker and one employer; where the economy contains an equal number, m, of workers and employers; where no worker has a (positive) reservation wage and all possible employer–worker matches are equally productive, in the absence of unionism. These assumptions imply full employment of both workers and employers—conceivably at a negative wage rate—and preclude any possibility of variation in the worker/employer ratio. Finally, every employer is assumed to receive a minimum profit of z.

The combined effect of these assumptions is a model with a strong Ricardian favor. Indeed, considering nonunion firms as the analogue of uncultivated units of land, and unionized firms as the analogue of cultivated units, the above model translates into a simple variant of the Ricardian model used to determine the (extensive) margin of cultivation, the return per input unit of labor-capital, and the "differential rent" to the various land plots selected for cultivation.

As our model contains no analogue to the landowner, it is necessary to assign the benefits of differential productivity under unionization (the analogue of differential land rent) arbitrarily; I have assigned them to the employer. However, with equal justification, these differential benefits could be assigned to unionized workers with the consequence that any unionized worker j would receive $\bar{\phi}(j)$ − z and all employers would receive a profit of z.

(2)   In the model presented, unionism may affect the equilibrium wage rate, but cannot create a union–nonunion wage differential such as is usually supposed to result from partial unionization, and which emerges from Lazear's model presented in this volume. My result follows from

the assumption that both workers and employers are free to consider (at zero cost) all possible matches and to select among them without penalty. This implies, inter alia, that among two workers of equal productivity there cannot be a wage differential, regardless of unionism.

For the "ultralong run," where there is opportunity to relocate to avoid or facilitate unionization, this case may have some analytical interest. However, I shall not press the point. For the short run, it is surely more realistic to assume the existence of a union–nonunion wage differential, together with union-imposed job rationing, etc. Even in the long run, union monopoly over a class of employment opportunities, with effects similar to the short run, is possible though not so common as the literature might suggest. In any event, in this section I abstract from the possibility of a union–nonunion wage differential. However see remark 6, below.

(3) As used here, "productivity gain from unionization" is not restricted to the effects of technical change, induced or otherwise. This is because the model described by Figure 1 abstracts from the very important role played by nonhuman agents of production, some or all of whose owners may earn rent. If unionization causes transfer of such rents either to workers or employers, they are reckoned as productivity gains to the recipient firms, just as though they had arisen from a union-induced shift of the production function. Regardless of how unionism accomplishes the shift from N to $\bar{\phi}(\cdot)$, the productivity gain (or loss) to firm j is $\bar{\phi}(j) - N$.

Absent unionism, the rents of which I have been speaking would accrue (i) to owners of "fixed" factors such as land, patent rights, etc. and (ii) to consumers, part of whose surplus may be appropriated by product monopolies generated by unionism. While employers may "happen" to own some of the rent-earning inputs, this is incidental to the argument; qua employer, the nonworker member of a firm earns only competitive profits, z.

In short, so long as the exogenous variable is unionization, the argument summarized by Figure 1 is the same regardless of whether $\bar{\phi}(\cdot)$ reflects rent transfers, technical change, altered supply of worker effort per real dollar of compensation, or some combination of all three. Thus the model is broadly applicable; however, it has serious shortcomings.

(4) The model offers no explanation of how the differential gains of unionism are divided between workers and employers. I am not aware of any such explanation that would not involve, at least implicitly, the exclusion of rival sellers of labor services and/or product. To take account of such exclusion it would be necessary to construct a model very different from the "competitive" theory implied by Figure 1. In particular, such a theory would not permit equalization both of wages across workers and of profits across firms. Whatever $\bar{\phi}(j) - w$ might happen to be, its division between worker j and employer j would depend upon how effectively

their rivals were prevented from competing away any supercompetitive earnings that might obtain. These forces cannot be considered within the framwork of Figure 1.

(5) Embedded in the theory of Figure 1 is the assumption that legalizing unionism does not affect the (competitive) levels of wages (w) and profits (z) that would obtain in the absence of unions. Put differently, the assumption is that w and z are determined by the forces operative in a competitive general equilibrium model, and only negligibly influenced by unionism and/or other impediments to intersectoral factor mobility. However, if unionism has an impact upon the tax structure, thereby shifting the saving function, and/or upon social welfare programs that affect labor supply and the wage rate, this assumption may be inappropriate.

(6) Perhaps the most important limitation of the argument of this section arises from the assumed independence of the nonunion production function and the legal status of unionism. Whether this independence exists depends upon what unions are legally permitted to do to induce employers to accept them. In one sense, employers cannot be compelled to accept unionism, so long as they are free to go out of business rather than unionize. But in a more important sense, employers may be subjected to varying degrees of pressure to accept unionism, depending upon what a union may lawfully do to induce such acceptance.

This pressure may take the form of picketing, boycotting, etc. that reduces productivity under nonunion conditions. This is expressed in panel e of Figure 1, by a downward shift of N to N', consequent upon legalizing unionism. The distance N − N' increases with the degree of duress the law permits a union to impose upon a nonunion employer. The $\hat{w}'$ curve in Figure 1e is the same as the $\hat{w}$ curve in Figure 1c but with each ordinate reduced by N − N', so that $\hat{w}'$ measures the premium that must be paid to make a given worker indifferent as to union status, after adjusting for the diminution of wages resulting from the decrease in productivity under nonunion conditions that is caused by union actions.

Thus the greater is N − N', the greater will be $\hat{w} - \hat{w}'$ at any abscissa, and the further southwest the equilibrium position. That is, the greater the cost increase (w given) the law permits a union to impose on a nonunion employer, the *lower* will be the equilibrium wage rate, and the greater the fraction of (both) employers and employees who will choose to be unionized.[7] Now N − N' = 0 may be considered as a limiting case where the law permits unions to exist but does not permit them to utilize "normal" organizing tactics to reduce the productivity of nonunion firms.

The same reservations apply to Figure 1e as to Figure 1c. If $\phi(\cdot)$ is interdependent with N − N', or if N' should be nonmonotonic, or if w should vary from pair to pair, the remarks of the preceding paragraph may not apply. In general, legalizing unionism permits unions to impose costs upon employers (i.e., losses in man-hour productivity) if they elect to remain nonunion. These costs are likely to vary from one firm to another with circumstances and permit the union to impose variable wage premia to offset interfirm differences in the costs of remaining nonunion.

II. UNIONISM IN SPOT LABOR MARKETS AND WITH LONG-TERM CONTRACTS

In recent years there has developed a substantial literature on the effects of long-term employment contracts, explicit and otherwise, on the behavior of wage rates.[8] However, there has been virtually no consideration of how unionism interacts with long-term contracts to influence wage behavior.

For simplicity, consider a two-period model in which the contracting parties have perfect information concerning realizations in period 1, but are uncertain about those anticipated in period 2. Uncertainty about period 2 realizations reflect concerns about both the state of the world and the interaction of the (period 2) state with the fixed characteristics of one's contracting partner. Assume uncertainty about the period 2 state to concern only the level of product demand and suppose that all calculations are made as of the start of period 1.

First consider the case where unionism is forbidden by law: assume, as in Section I, exactly m workers and m employers with zero reservation wage rates and zero requirements for quasi-rent in *both* periods, and a common production function such that it is always optimal to pair off, one to one, for productive activity. At the outset of period 1, the parties are assumed simultaneously to choose partners and decide whether their contract is to last one period or two. One-period contracts will be called spot contracts and two-period, long-term contracts.

A. Long-Term Contracts

The problem of determining the equilibrium set of matches (pairings), and the terms of spot and long-term contracts (i.e., the spot and long-term wage rates) presents a strong analogy to the matching problem of Section I. However this problem is more complicated and so, to avoid irrelevant complications, I shall make further simplifying assumptions.

(1)   Assume that d < m workers and employers possess a characteristic, "Reliability," such that in period 2 a Reliable party will (if necessary) sacrifice some positive gain, available through the spot market, in order to honor a commitment made under a long-term contract. Now m − d workers and employers do *not* have this characteristic.

As of any moment a given individual (worker or employer) either possesses Reliability of does not (zero–one), and there is universal agreement as to whether he possesses the characteristic.[9] But however acquired, a reputation for Reliability may be destroyed by un-Reliable behavior. Since such a reputation is valuable (see below), all parties believe that Reliable individuals will sacrifice some expected gain in period 2 to preserve their reputation, though they also believe that there is some upper limit to the sacrifice that anyone will make.

For simplicity, assume that (i) it is (universally) believed that un-Reliable workers will bear no sacrifice of current advantage obtainable from contract breach and (ii) this belief implies that zero investment will be made in specific training. Further assume that every Reliable employer will sacrifice the potential gain from breaching an employment contract to a maximum expected present value (calculated as of the start of period 1) of \$b > 0, and that this warrants a specific training investment of \$a > 0 by a paired Reliable worker (a $\leqq$ b). Analogously, every Reliable worker will sacrifice a potential gain of \$B > 0 (obtainable by quitting in breach of contract) which warrants specific investment by a Reliable employer of \$A > 0 (B $\leqq$ A).[10]

When Reliability is the same, all employers are homogeneous (i.e., equally productive when paired with any worker of given Reliability); an analogous assumption applies to workers. Reliability is a source of superior productivity because each pair can learn a *pair-specific* secret of production during period 1 that will multiply period 1 productivity in period 2 by $\gamma > 1$ if the pair stays together. This "secret" will be of no effect (i.e., $\gamma = 1$) if the pair separates.

Thus if a Reliable worker–employer pair teams up at the outset of period 1, they can make their expected joint product in period 2 greater than if either were to team with an un-Reliable partner. Given our assumptions about the public nature of each party's Reliability and the numerical equality of Reliable employers and Reliable workers, it follows that individual maximization will segregate the market into (un-Reliable) pairs who transact on the spot market in both periods and Reliable pairs who enter into long-term contracts. Among un-Reliable pairs, all matches are equally productive; this is also the case among Reliable pairs.

(2) Assume that there is a number of employers N(h), N' > 0 (N > 0 if h > 0; N = 0 if h = 0), who will enter production in period 2 if h > 0, but not otherwise. All of these Transient Employers (Transients) are less efficient than employers 1, . . . , m, but differ among themselves in productivity when paired with any given worker. However, their productivity is independent of the worker with whom they are paired. Define p(2) and w(2) as the realized price and realized (spot) wage rate in period 2; E[p(2)] and E[w(2)] are the expected values of p(2) and w(2), the expectations taken as of the start of period 1, h $\equiv$ h[p(2) − E[p(2)]]; h' > 0, h(0) = h(<0) = 0.

The level of realized product demand is indicated by h; h is a random variable. Assume also that the realized level of derived demand for labor is an increasing function of the demand for product so that sign $[w(2) - E[w(2)]]$ is the same as sign $[p(2) - E[p(2)]]$.

This amounts to positing the traditional Marshallian short-run response of product price, and both price and quantity of variable input, to levels of product demand greater than expected. A higher-than-expected product price offsets the productivity deficiency of Transients, causing them to enter production and thereby shift upward the spot market (derived) demand schedule which, given an inelastic short-run labor supply function, drives up the spot wage rate.

(3)   Assume that all employers earn an expected competitive rate of return per dollar of investment s; that all employers employ $X in period 1, X(1), but that Reliable employers use $Y in period 2, Y(2), Y > X, while un-Reliable employers use $X(2) = X(1)$. Abstracting from discounting, the expected return to an un-Reliable employer as of the beginning of period 1 is $s[X(1) + X(2)]$. Similarly, the expected return to a Reliable employer is $s[X(1) + Y'(2)]$, $Y' > Y$. The difference, $Y' - Y$, reflects the productivity of Reliability which, in the present context, may be treated as an endowed characteristic. While a Reliable employer earns only a competitive return s on his investment in pair-specific technology, such an investment is essential to earning *anything* on his Reliability.

For all workers, both the expected and realized wage in period 1 is $w(1)$. For un-Reliable workers, the expected wage in period 2 is $w(2) = w(1)$, but for Reliable workers the expected wage in period 2 is $w^*(2) > w(2)$; $w^*(2) - w(2)$ reflects the effect of the pair-specific technology on worker productivity and hence on the period 2 expected wage.

The expected joint return (in period 2) to Reliability, for any Reliable pair, is $G = w^*(2) - w(2) + s[Y'(2) - X(2)]$. Nothing that has been (or will be) argued will suffice uniquely to allocate G between a Reliable employer and a Reliable employee. However, G must be positive to motivate the investment in learning the technology and sufficient to yield (at least) the competitive return on the employer's investment in such learning, sY.

Further, it is reasonable to assume that the worker also incurs a training cost (e.g., foregone leisure) to acquire training. Let this cost be $C; for convenience, let the expected rate of return on C be s also, so that (in period 2) the worker must receive an expectation of at least sC implying $w^*(2) - w(2) \geq sC$; thus $G \geq s(Y + C)$.

Where the inequality in the preceding two expressions applies, the excess reflects return to Reliability. But the allocation of G as between employer and worker cannot be explained without relaxation of the assumed internal homogeneity of the membership of each of the following groups: un-Reliable workers, un-Reliable employers, Reliable workers, and Reliable employers. To avoid irrelevant complication, I maintain the (counterfactual) assumption of (internal) homogeneity and posit that the (Reliable) employer receives a period 2 expectation of $\pi = sC + s'$ so that $G = s(Y + C) + s' + s''$, where s' and s'' are chosen to maximize the expected utility of the relevant individuals as of the beginning of period 1. Here s' and s'' may be interpreted as the returns to the characteristics of Reliability in an employer and employee, respectively.

(4) If Reliable workers were certain to honor long-term contracts regardless of the relation of the period 2 spot and contract wages (i.e., regardless of the loss entailed by honoring the contract), employers would have no incentive to condition the period 2 contract wage upon either the (period 2) spot wage or product price. But such extreme fidelity is highly unlikely; (even) Reliable workers will break contracts with some probability, ω, if the gain from doing so is sufficient. Therefore, given the positive association of the period 2 product price, $p(2)$, with the contemporaneous spot wage, $w(2)$, a higher $p(2)$ will be associated with a higher ω. Assume that employers recognize this and, to induce greater fidelity, condition the period 2 contract wage, $\bar{w}(2)$, upon the realized product price, the realized spot wage, or both.

But while such conditioning may serve to reduce the risk of contract breach somewhat, it will not completely eliminate it. Consider: If an employer wishes to breach the contract without overtly refusing to pay the contractual wage, he can increase work duties or worsen employment conditions beyond what was understood (by both parties) when the contract was negotiated. If a worker wishes to breach, he can supply less effort than the contract implied.

Obviously, there are very great practical difficulties in *completely specifying*, for each possible state of the world, the working conditions and performance expected of one another by the parties to a long-term contract. Thus, neither party can be effectively bound to honor long-term contracts by making compensation and/or required performance vary with the state of the world. Stated alternatively, the cost of specifying a long-term employment contract (with its terms state-dependent) in such detail as to eliminate concern about breach would be greater than the expected benefit from elimination of such concern. Therefore, concern about breach remains a feature of long-term employment contracts.

To limit such concern, both employers and workers occasionally seek to obtain performance bonds (or posted forfeits) from one another. While these forfeits may be explicit, typically they are hidden in the details of the intertemporal expected wage structure. For example, the employer may obtain an (implicit) forfeit from the worker (if he should quit before the end of period 2) by making part of the period 1 wage payable at the end of period 2 and conditional upon his working both periods. Such a practice might be reflected in a "length-of-service" wage differential between periods 1 and 2 in excess of the increment in the worker's marginal product. To induce the worker to accept the implied increase in the expected cost of changing employers (i.e., breaching the contract) in the event of an unusually large $p(2) - E[p(2)]$ in period 2, the employer must somehow increase the expected present value (as of the start of period 1) of the entire two-period earning prospect.[11]

Similarly, a worker (or his union) may require an employer to post a schedule of severance pay and/or vest part or all of the worker's accumulated pension benefits, so that the employer would incur a penalty should he breach the contract by an "uncaused" dismissal. If an employer agreed to an implicit penalty (for breaches) that was greater than average, then an employee who stayed the full two periods would receive a lower (two-period) wage than would be paid a (two-period) worker whose employer agreed to pay only the average penalty. This is because competition among employers who offer long-term contracts will equalize the expected (two-period) compensation across all contracts.

To summarize: Among Reliable parties there is some residual danger of contract breach (though less than among the un-Reliable). To limit this danger, the terms of contracts are (sometimes) conditioned on states of the world and, in addition, performance bonds or forfeits may be required by either party, or both. As such bonds may be reflected in length-of-service differentials embedded in the employer's wage structure, their presence may account for otherwise inexplicable wage differentials associated with length of service. However, the cost and/or practical difficulty of protecting against contract breach through bonding is such that few if any parties ever require bonds to the point where they feel no need for retaining some further capability of deterring breach of their (employment) contracts; it is here that the union enters.

B. Unions in a Two-Period Context

Let $\hat{p} = p(2) - E[p(2)]$; $\bar{w}(2) \mid \hat{p} > 0 = \bar{w}^{(+)}$, and $\bar{w}(2) \mid \hat{p} \leq 0 = \bar{w}^{(-)}$; write the Reliable employer's expected profit in period 2 (the expectation taken as of the start of period 1) as

$$\phi\{g_1[E(\hat{p} \mid \hat{p} > 0) - \bar{w}^{(+)}] + g_2[E(\hat{p} \mid \hat{p} \leq 0) - \bar{w}^{(-)}\} \qquad (2)$$

Here $\bar{w}^{(+)}$ and $\bar{w}^{(-)}$ are determined by the long-term contract, conditional upon the sign of $\hat{p}$, and are assumed to be uniquely determined by the two-period contract; g_1 and g_2 are the (exogenous) respective probabilities, estimated as of the start of period 1, that $\hat{p} > 0$ and $\hat{p} \leq 0$ will obtain; $\bar{w}^{(+)}$ is the contract wage in period 2 conditional upon $\hat{p} > 0$; and $\bar{w}^{(-)}$ is the analogous term conditional upon $\hat{p} \leq 0$.

Assume that the long-term employment contract is so constructed that the employer's concern for his reputation as Reliable, together with the effect of any bonding provisions, is sufficient to insure observance in all states where $\hat{p} > 0$. But if $\hat{p} \leq 0$, especially if $|\hat{p}|$ is large, the balance of considerations favoring contract observance may be reversed. In paricular, if $\hat{p}$ is so low that, given $\bar{w}^{(-)}$, there is real danger of bankruptcy, the employer may break the contract no matter what the consequences for his reputation.[12] Given our assumption about the specificity of worker training, such breach would compel the worker to accept any wage not less than $w(2)$.

Under a long-term contract conditional on states of the world, the realized wage will be determined by the contract terms applicable to the realized state only if $\hat{p} > \hat{p}_a > 0$. For $\hat{p} < \hat{p}_a$, $\hat{w}(2) = \psi(\hat{p})$, which invalidates equation (2). [$\hat{w}(2)$ is the wage realized by a Reliable worker in period 2.] Thus equation (2) must be replaced by (2a). In (2a), $g_2[\cdot]$ is replaced by the sum of $g_3[\cdot]$ and $g_4[\cdot]$, where g_3 and g_4 are the probabilities of the corresponding states arising in period 2:

$$\phi\{g_1[\cdot] + g_3[E(\hat{p} \mid 0 < \hat{p} > \hat{p}_a) - \bar{w}^{(-)}] \tag{2a}$$
$$+ g_4[E(\hat{p} \mid \hat{p} \leq \hat{p}_a) - \psi(\hat{p} \mid \hat{p} \leq \hat{p}_a)]\}.$$

The rationale for equation (2a) is as follows: Assuming the parties to be rational and reasonably experienced, they will recognize that if $\hat{p}_a < \hat{p}$, $\bar{w}^{(-)}$ will be determined by $\psi(\hat{p})$, $\psi' > 0$, regardless of contract provisions. Accordingly, workers will "pay little" for employer promises applicable to such states. In the present two-period framework, $\psi(\hat{p}) \geq w(2)$; but in reality a Reliable worker might "invest" in his employer's survival beyond period 2, by temporarily accepting $(\bar{w}(2) \mid \hat{p} < \hat{p}_a) < w(2)$. However, such possibilities lie beyond the purview of this paper. In the present context, $\psi(\hat{p})$ should be interpreted as "the maximum a Reliable worker can get in period 2," given (i) the contract, (ii) $p(2)$, and (iii) $w(2)$.

Equations (2) and (2a) refer to situations where unionism is not permitted. But if a union is allowed, matters will be different. If a union is present, an employer who replaces $\bar{w}^{(-)}$ by $\psi(\hat{p})$ will not only lose reputation but in addition may be faced with a strike.

It is not always, or even typically, the case that a union insists upon receiving the contract wage, no matter what the product price. Usually, a credible threat of bankruptcy will lead a union to abate implicit contract terms to help an employer survive. Consequently, the effect of unionization is to relate the expected wage to the product price, whenever the latter falls below the "bankruptcy threat price," $\hat{p}_a$. Thus, regardless of unionism, $\hat{w}(2)$ will be a diminishing function of $p(2)$, if $\hat{p} < \hat{p}_a$.

However, in the absence of a union, $\hat{w}(2) = \psi(\hat{p} \mid \hat{p} < \hat{p}_a)$, $\psi' > 0$. Present a union, $\hat{w}(2) = \bar{\psi}(\hat{p} \mid \hat{p} < p_a$, $\bar{\psi}' > 0$, but $\bar{\psi} > \psi \mid \hat{p} < \hat{p}_a$. In words, given that bankruptcy is threatened, the wage rate will vary in the same direction as the product price, but (for given $\hat{p} - \hat{p}_a$) its *level* will be higher in the presence of a union than otherwise. Thus, the employer's quasi-rent in period 2, conditional upon $\hat{p} < \hat{p}_a$, will be lower if a union imposes $\bar{\psi}(\cdot)$ than if the nonunion wage function, $\psi(\cdot)$, prevails. The employer is induced to bear the "excess cost" $\bar{\psi}(\cdot) - \psi(\cdot)$ by the union's threat of a strike that would reduce the employer's quasi-rents even further, if he did not comply.

Thus unionism is likely to raise the expected wage in those period 2 states where $\hat{p}_a < \hat{p}$. But why should the effect of unionism differ with the state of the world? The answer must lie in the fundamental asymmetry in the positions of the union, the worker, and the employer during the life of an employment contract.

Employer's Position

If, for any reason, an employer should desire to alter or break a (two-period) contract, a union can to impede use of his business property (by striking) until the employer induces it to stop. As nonunion workers cannot do this, by definition, breaking a nonunion contract costs the employer no more, and probably less, than breaking an otherwise identical union contract.

Worker's Position

Suppose the worker decides to break his employment contract, accepting the associated loss of reputation. This loss will be the same, regardless of whether or not he is unionized. A union might suffer some incidental loss of reputation because its members quit in violation of implicit understandings to the contrary; but only rarely, if ever, would it seek to impose sanctions on its members to inhibit voluntary job changes or individual shirking. Thus unionization inhibits contract breaches by employers, but not those by workers. But employer breaches are more likely to occur when $\hat{p} < \hat{p}_a$ than in other states because it is in these states that employers are most likely to revise downward their valuation of "reputational capital."

The reason for this is that the employer is assumed to have a set of desired or target terminal values for his stocks of assets, as of the end of period 2. These targets are part of the optimization plan adopted as of the beginning of period 1. One of these asset targets is his stock of reputational capital—reputation—as an employer who honors his labor contracts.

The employer invests in building this reputation and does not sacrifice it casually. But if he bcomes bankrupt, his reputation is destroyed in any case. Hence he will sacrifice reputation to whatever extent is necessary to avoid bankruptcy, violating implicit labor contracts to conserve liquidity, so long as he can keep operating. Absent a union, he can keep operating so long as (i) $\bar{w}(2) - w(2) > \epsilon$ and (ii) he pays his creditors. A union may compel him to sacrifice his reputation as a reliable debtor, and partially default on his loan contracts, in order to share his quasi-rents with his employees; i.e., it may compel him to set $\bar{w}(2)$ well above $w(2)$.

Thus, if $\hat{p} < \hat{p}_a$, unionism is likely to inhibit a wage cut (i.e., make period 2 wages higher). But if $\hat{p} > \hat{p}_a$, the converse of this argument does not hold (see below).

Long-Run Union Wage Effects

Consider only Reliable workers and employers: assume their (two-period) wage contracts to be determined by a market-clearing mechanism at the outset of period 1, and assume further that all characteristics of workers and employers assumed in constructing Figure 1 continue to hold. Then, assuming a noncorner equilibrium, the present value of two-period wage contracts will be equal for all workers regardless of union status as in Section I.

The probabilities of $(\hat{p} - \hat{p}_a)$ being positive or negative for a given employer may be thought of as characteristics of his technology and determining the effect of unionization upon his productivity. Thus an employer j for whom the probability of $\hat{p} < \hat{p}_a$ was relatively high would be correspondingly anxious to avoid unionization, and conversely. For j, long-run equilibrium under unionism might require paying a substantially lower wage when $\hat{p} > \hat{p}_a$ than would be paid under nonunion conditions.

But this is only one possibility: equilibrium could be maintained if employer j could collect an initial side payment at the start of period 1 as a bribe to accept unionization. All that equilibrium requires is that any special advantage to unionism in one state of the world be somehow offset by other disadvantages so as to maintain the equality of present values of union and nonunion two-period wage contracts.

There is not much more to add unless we alter the (rigid) assumptions of the Section I model, in particular the assumption that worker attitudes toward unionization are known in advance of hiring. However, relaxation of this and other assumptions would take us far afield.

Accordingly, I shall not push the long-run general equilibrium analysis further, but concentrate upon a few particular points.

Unions as Foul-Weather Friends. As argued above, when $\hat{p} < \hat{p}_a$, wages are higher under unionization. Nothing is asserted about the effect of unionization on wages when $\hat{p} \geq \hat{p}_a$. But, assuming competitive product markets, negligible rents, and a technology insensitive to unionization, the greater expected cost of a union contract in states where $\hat{p} < \hat{p}_a$ must be offset by lower expected cost of union contracts in states where $\hat{p} \geq \hat{p}_a$. In effect, even if a union cannot transfer employer wealth to its members, its contract-enforcing power will induce trades of wage rates "across states of the world" (i.e., from states where $\hat{p} \geq \hat{p}_a$ to those where $\hat{p} < \hat{p}_a$) though without cost to the employer.

This is reminiscent of the empirical finding of Lewis (1963)[13] and others that union–nonunion wage differentials are greater in nonprosperous periods than otherwise. However, it should be noted that these empirical findings refer to general business conditions, while the present argument refers to individual product and factor markets.[14] Thus, if a particular firm or industry exhibits (i) a countercyclical pattern in its product price(s) and (ii) has a labor force that embodies much firm-specific training, its union–nonunion wage differential wage movements should also be countercyclical (rather than procyclical, as Lewis found).

Unions as Instruments of Wealth Transfer. Thus far the argument has assumed that, unionized or not, employers earn a competitive rate of return. The argument has referred only to ex ante long-run equilibrium and said nothing as to the effect of unanticipated unionization, nor of the effect of various states of the world on the propensity of unionize. I shall continue to abstract from failures of anticipation and state-induced unionization, but relax the assumption that all employers earn a competitive rate of return.

If an employer has a patent on a product or process, or in some other way has secured a source of monopoly profit, a union that is able to impede operation of his facilities can compel him to share it. De facto, this is tranferring employer wealth to union members. Similarly, the owner of a land parcel or other nonhuman resource which is appreciably more productive in one use than in any other can be compelled by a union, with an appropriate jurisdiction and strike effectiveness, to share his rents with its members. In addition to transferring wealth from owners of monopolies or rent recipients, customers of product market monopolists may be compelled to bear losses of real income and consumers' surplus imposed by the monopolists in "passing on" part of the cost of meeting union wage demands.

Beyond appropriating monopoly revenues that exist independent of the union, union wage pressure may induce (compel) formation of monopoloid marketing arrangements (oligopoly, cartel, etc.) to permit satisfaction of union wage demands. Union shelter from antitrust prosecution may facilitate the success of such attempts, but the main contribution of unionism is its ability to impede competition from lower-cost nonunion sources of supply. That is, in varying degree, unions protect the product markets of unionized employers by organizing otherwise nonunion competitors, by organizing boycotts of nonunion products, and by discouraging workers from working in nonunion establishments.

All of the above are familiar explanations of (ex ante) union "power" to set higher wage rates than would be obtained under nonunion conditions. That is, they are explanations of why the present value of the two-period employment contract that a union negotiates prior to period 1 may be greater than a two-period nonunion contract. However, none of these factors explains, or even suggest, how the distribution of the union advantage across period 2 states (or between periods 1 and 2) will be determined.[15] While I conjecture that there is a bias toward realizing long-run union advantage in states where $\hat{p} < \hat{p}_a$ or, more broadly, where $\hat{p} < 0$, rather than in states where $\hat{p} > 0$, the rationalization is incompatible with the "one worker–one union" assumption of this paper, and therefore I shall not pursue the matter further at this time.[16]

Unions as Productivity Boosters: Market Signaling.   Finally, let us consider the possibility that unionization changes the productivity of the parties affected. For this purpose, consider Figure 2: thus far our analysis of the wage effects of unionism has been, in effect, comparison of boxes III and IV [i.e., a comparison of the (two-period contract) wages paid to Reliable workers by Reliable employers, under union and nonunion conditions]. But suppose that unionization causes (some) otherwise un-Reliable workers to become Reliable (Figure 2).

Analysis of this case would require a comparison of boxes I and IV in Figure 2. Such a case could arise under the following circumstances: Contrary to previous assumption, suppose that Reliability is not a "fixed effect," but varying with the expected difference in payoff from being Reliable instead of un-Reliable. Suppose, for simplicity, that un-Reliable workers and employers are characterized by "less trust" than Reliable ones, but are otherwise identical. "Less trust" means that the un-Reliable parties *estimate* the expected utility of the return to investment in firm-specific knowledge to be less than that estimated by Reliable parties; i.e., $\lambda_n < \lambda_R$, where $\lambda_{(\cdot)}$ is the estimated return to firm-specific knowledge and the subscripts n and R refer to un-Reliable and Reliable parties, respectively.

When unions are illegal, un-Reliable workers do not consider the expected return to the investment in firm-specific knowledge to be worth the cost because they believe employers are "too prone" to break long-term contracts by refusing to pay more than the spot wage in period 2. But given the union option, (hitherto) un-Reliable workers make a higher estimate (conditional on unionization) of the probability that an employer

	Non-Union	Union
Un-Reliable	I	II
Reliable	III	IV

Figure 2.

will honor a period 2 commitment (even at a temporary loss), thereby increasing λ_n to λ_R. Perceiving this, hitherto un-Reliable employers (correctly) increase their appraisal of the probability that contract workers will resist the possible temptations of the period 2 spot market and also raise their λ_n to λ_R. In effect, unionization increases the estimated productivity of investment in firm-specific knowledge, thereby raising (as of the start of period 1) both ex ante expected wages and expected employer returns from being Reliable.

Thus changing the law to permit unionization (from a law forbidding it) may act as an environmental signal to workers and employers that the return to Reliability has increased, thereby inducing greater investment in Reliability and match specific investment.[17,18] This suggests a constructive role for unionization; i.e., unions serve as guarantors (bonding agents) of employer Reliability, thereby increasing worker trust which, in turn, causes market signaling that increases employer trust.

But while possible, this outcome is far from certain: it is not true, a priori, that unions are lowest-cost bonding agents. If bonding Reliability were important practically, an employer commitment to arbitrate all relevant issues of period 2 employment terms, backed by money in escrow and enforceable as a voluntary contract, would seem a strong competitor to unionization. However, the issue is clearly an empirical one.

The main purpose of comparing boxes I and IV is to point out that unionization may involve two distinct sources of wage change. Boxes III and IV suggest comparing the wages of Reliable workers under union and nonunion conditions; but boxes I and IV contrast the wages of un-Reliable workers under nonunion conditions with those of Reliable workers under union conditions.

To be valid, any analysis of the effect of unionism upon wages must specify whether in the nonunion state the workers are considered to be Reliable or un-Reliable. Movements from I to IV are likely to induce investments in firm-specific human capital that would raise wages regardless of unionization; such movements might be termed "decasualization of the labor force consequent upon unionization." The wage effect of unionization in these cases should be larger than where movements were from III and IV and the workers are Reliable even when not unionized.

If workers become unionized without becoming Reliable, would their wages rise? (This case might arise where migratory workers unionize without otherwise altering their behavior.) This is the case to which a comparison of boxes I and II would apply. The answer is that, absent a shift to Reliability, there is no source from which a wage increase could be paid except by exploitation of a monopoloid market structure or from a government subsidy.

Since our focus is upon unionization, comparison of boxes I and III is irrelevant, which leaves the comparison of boxes II and III. This is difficult because it involves comparing the wages of unionized un-Reliable workers with those of nonunion but Reliable workers. I have no conjecture as to the effect of unionism in this case, and can think of no examples to which it might apply.

ACKNOWLEDGMENT

I am indebted to Edward Lazear for valuable criticism.

NOTES

1. The literature is neither sharply focused nor cohesive. A rather extensive bibliography can be collected from the references of the various articles in *Journal of Labor Research*, Volume 1, Number 1, Spring 1980.

2. In this paper a union is assumed to have only one capability, i.e., to impede production until it obtains acceptable terms. This power to impede production by, say, striking imposes a potential cost on the employer for the avoidance of which he can be made to

pay. This is a source of a positive union wage effect. But exercising this power entails a cost (both pecuniary and nonpecuniary) to the workers, varying from one to another, with the result that some workers feel that unionization is a net benefit while others believe the reverse.

3.   This assumption is convenient, but not "neutral." In effect, it says that unionization can never lower employer profits, so that any associated reduction in productivity and/or increase in wages must be paid by "someone else."

4.   Operationally, a "taste" for unionism that varies across workers is indistinguishable from differences (across workers) in the net benefits of unionization.

5.   N.B. it is assumed that the number of employers is equal to the number of employees, m. This assumption is convenient, but inessential. It is made solely to facilitate the formation of a "matching equilibrium" without being compelled, somehow, to account for unmatched individuals.

6.   The reason for "negligibly different" and "approximately" is the discreteness of the quantity variable.

7.   The discussion of this paragraph implicitly introduces the union as a third party to the bargaining process. To reformulate the model to allow explicit consideration of this fact would not be worth the trouble it would cause.

8.   For example, Hall and Lillien (1979), Hall and Lazear (1981).

9.   It is of course possible to assume that c workers and d employers, $c \neq d$, are Reliable and/or make Reliability a "matter of degree" (e.g., a continuous variable with an associated price), thereby adding realism and complexity to the argument. However, such embellishment would not advance the present argument.

10.   The willingness of Reliable individuals to sacrifice a potential (short-run) gain from breaching a contract reflects a concern for their reputation as "Reliable" which is a terminal asset value as of the end of period 2. In a complete dynamic optimization model, a, b, A, and B would all be conditional on the desired terminal asset values of reputation at the end of period 2. However, such elaboration is unneeded for the present purpose.

11.   Schemes to induce worker performance by deferring payment are discussed by Becker and Stigler (1974).

12.   "Bankruptcy" is used here as a generic term to cover any state of period 2 quasi-rents that imperils the wealth position of the employer sufficiently to cause him to lower the value he attached (as of the beginning of period 1) to maintaining his reputation as Reliable.

13.   Lewis, H. G., (1963), pp. 188–194.

14.   We assume, without discussion, that the state probabilities, $g_1, \ldots, g_4$, are independent of unionization.

15.   The reader is reminded that in reality (i.e., when we relax our simplifying assumption that all consequences of unionism for wages occur in period 2), there may be substitution of expected payoffs across periods in addition to substitution across states in the same period.

16.   The conjectured asymmetry arises from the distinct possibility that a union will have a different marginal rate of substitution between wages (benefits) per member and a change in number of members, when the change in membership is an increase than when it is a decrease. As already stated, development of this point requires a model of the union–member relationship and the distribution of union benefits among members, which cannot be encompassed in the one-worker firm, one firm–one union model used in this paper.

17.   Thus, Freeman (1980) finds that, after controlling for a member of other variables, unionized workers have appreciably lower turnover than nonunion.

18.   A general equilibrium analysis would carry the argument further to trace out the effect of a legal change to permitted unionism on the supply of Reliable and un-Reliable workers and employers and the consequent effect on period 2 spot and contract wages. Manifestly, I have not attempted this.

REFERENCES

Becker, G. S., and G. J. Stigler (1974), "Law Enforcement, Malfeasance and Compensation of Enforcers." *Journal of Legal Studies* 3(1):1–18.

Freeman, R. B. (1980), "The Exit-Voice Tradeoff in the Labor Market: Unionism, Job Tenure, Suits, and Separations." *Quarterly Journal of Economics* XLIV(4):643–673.

Hall, R. E., and E. P. Lazear (1981), "The Excess Sensitivity of Layoffs and Quits to Demand." Palo Alto, Calif.: Hoover Institution.

Hall, R. E., and D. M. Lillien (1977), "Efficient Wage Bargains under Uncertain Supply and Demand." *American Economic Review* 69(5):868–879.

Lewis, H. G. (1963), "Unionism and Relative Wage Rates in the United States." Chicago, Ill.: University of Chicago Press.

A MICROECONOMIC THEORY OF LABOR UNIONS

Edward P. Lazear

The last two decades have witnessed the growth of an increasingly rigorous brand of labor economics. The theories of labor supply, labor quality, information in the labor market, and labor contracts have received a significant amount of attention and the construction of theories with micro-economic foundations has led to a greater understanding of the phenomena. This is less true with respect to the analysis of labor unions and how they function within the labor market. Models of union behavior usually treat the union rather than the individual in it as the basic unit of observation and suggest some behavior for that entity. This paper will adopt a micro-level approach and will argue that one can go surprisingly far toward the analysis of union behavior by employing a simple model where workers and firms are the rational basic unit.

The goal is to predict which industries, occupations and time periods are most likely to be characterized by strong unions and to analyze the

New Approaches to Labor Unions.
Research in Labor Economics, Supplement 2, pages 53–96.
Copyright © 1983 by JAI Press Inc.
All rights of reproduction in any form reserved.
ISBN: 0-89232-265-9

behavior of unions under a variety of circumstances. A central theme is
that it is unproductive to think of the union as having an objective function.
The point is perhaps best understood by considering some points which
arise when the union, rather than its more fundamental elements, is the
basic unit of analysis. First, most models of union behavior allow a labor
market which does not "clear." Some workers who would like to work
are turned away from union jobs. What happens to those workers? How
do they influence the union's strategy? Second, given the highly hierarchical nature of most unions where seniority plays a major role, why don't
the least privileged workers within the union join forces with nonunion
workers to undermine the power of the union? In particular, the young
workers could form their own union, making employers and themselves
apparently better off while destroying any union equilibrium. Why doesn't
this happen more often? Finally, few models (Sherwin Rosen is an exception) allow the firm to play an active role. There is no allowance by
the union for the possibility that the firm will react differently to different
wage demands except as expressed by labor demand.

This paper starts from utility and profit maximization by worker and
firm respectively and builds a model which deals with these issues explicitly. Labor markets clear in the sense that anyone can enter the industry and claim a nonunion job, but there are queues for union jobs. The
length of the queue is the direct result of union and firm behavior and the
union takes this into account when announcing its wage demand. The
product market clears as the firm pushes its anti-union activity to the
point where costs are equalized across union and nonunion firms. The
life-cycle nature of union benefits provides the young workers with an
incentive to remain "true" to the union at the expense of short run gain.
Since the young inherit the seniority rights from retiring workers, all workers are better off by this deferred payment structure. This is among the
most important innovations since it is through this mechanism that a union
equilibrium of a particular kind is achieved. Finally, the firm plays a
central role in determining the outcome of the union's efforts and its
behavior is taken into account by the optimizing workers who potentially
comprise the union.

"Union" is defined here as a collection of workers who act together
to call out wage (and later, quantity) demands to firms. Firms buy labor
from the union at the union wage or, at some cost, fight the union and
buy labor in the competitive "fringe" (which may be much larger than
the union sector). Product markets are competitive, and the equilibrium
that emerges is a well-defined blend of competition and monopoly, not
unlike the dominant-firm-with-competitive-fringe equilibrium found in the
industrial organization literature. This one simple structure yields a num-

ber of implications, some of which conform with earlier work, some of which do not.

The following are major implications of the model:

1. Consistent with Marshall, inelasticity of product demand increases the likelihood that the industry will be unionized.
2. Contrary to Marshall's assumption, inelasticity of demand for labor does not imply an increase in union power manifested by an increase in the union membership or wage differential.
3. The more elastic is the supply of labor to an industry or occupation, the lower is the probability that a union will exist in that industry or occupation.
4. As expected, an increase in the cost of running a union and enforcing wage demands lowers probability that a union exists. Less obvious is that the union wage and wage differential increase as costs rise. A corollary is that anti-union legislation results in a smaller likelihood of a union, and a smaller proportion of union workers within a unionized industry, but larger union wage and wage differential. Also, as a corollary, as the attrition rate rises, the occupation is less likely to be unionized, but will have a higher wage differential if unionized.
5. Under reasonable circumstances, the observed wage differential overstates rather than understates the true effect of a union on wage rates and the overstatement is smallest for industries or occupations where the proportion of union workers is close to zero or one. In addition, there is no straightforward connection between wage differentials, proportion in the union, and union power.
6. "Featherbedding" is both rent maximizing and Pareto Optimal. Further, a union which can select quantity as well as price selects the preunion employment level.
7. Union workers take a greater part of their compensation in the form of fringes than do nonunion workers.
8. In a steady state union workers are older than nonunion workers and older workers receive more of the benefits of the union. Yet, young workers have no incentive to break the coalition.
9. Age-earnings profiles are flatter in unionized firms.
10. Union-nonunion wage differentials move countercyclically.

The strategy is to define the relevant labor supply function and then to maximize the lifetime utility of a representative individual. In a one-period context this amounts to maximization of expected utility. In the multiperiod context, the ex ante equilibrium is achieved and maintained by the way in which union membership is distributed over the lifecycle; young workers are willing to remain passive nonunion members as a precondition for admission to the union at a later date. This discipline insures that lifetime utility is maximized.

First, a one-period setting is considered because results are easier to obtain in that context. Those results are explored in the second section. The final section examines what happens when a multiperiod world is considered. There, it is shown that the equilibrium that was achieved and enforceable in the one-period setting is achieved and enforced in the multiperiod world as well, by appropriate manipulation of the age structure of union membership.

I. A ONE-PERIOD MODEL

Consider an industry comprised of S competitive firms each of which has a demand for labor given by $L = d(W)$ where W is the wage rate and L is the number of workers in the firm. There are $R(W)$ workers in the occupation or industry. Assume (relaxed below) that $R(W) = R$ so that labor is supplied inelastically to the occupation.[1] Also assume that the demand for output is perfectly elastic so that second-order product market effects can be ignored.

A.   The Opportunity Locus

Risk neutral workers can band together to form a "union" which calls out a union wage, W_U. An individual firm faced with the union demand can either pay W_U and then choose to hire $d(W_U)$ workers or at some fixed cost, C_i, which varies across firms, can defeat the union and pay wage W_N, hiring $d(W_N)$ workers. C_i can be thought of as the cost of employing enough "union busters" to defeat the union or as contributions to an employee benefits fund which appease the current work force. Alternatively, if unions have beneficial effects on productivity as Freeman, and Brown and Medoff have argued, C_i is the cost of forgone productivity effects of the union. L $_i$ $C_i \sim g(C_i)$ with distribution function $G(C_i)$.[2] The union knows $G(C_i)$, but only the firms knows its particular C_i. That workers can impose a cost C_i, on a firm endows them with a property right. The National Labor Relations Act may increase the cost associated with defeating the union, but even in the absence of this law, workers impose some costs on firms by disruptive actions and thereby retain some property right.

Let the firm have a standard concave production function. The firm's profit function depends upon the price of output, price of capital and wage rate. Initially assume that demand for the product is perfectly elastic so that the first two prices are given and invariant across firms. Suppress the prices of capital and output and write $\Pi = \Pi(W)$. If the firm hires union labor, the firm's profits are $\Pi(W_U)$. If the firm hires nonunion labor, the firm's profits are $\Pi(W_N) - C_i$. The firm chooses to fight the union if

$$\Pi(W_U) < \Pi(W_N) - C_i$$

or if

$$\Pi^*(W_U, W_N) \equiv \Pi(W_N) - \Pi(W_U) > C_i.$$

For any given W_U, W_N combination then $G(\Pi^*(W_U, W_N))$ of the firms will find it more profitable to be nonunion firms.[3] Therefore the demand for labor by nonunion firms is $S[G(\Pi^*[W_U, W_N])]d(W_N)$ and the demand for labor by union firms is $S[1 - G(\Pi^*[W_U, W_N])]d(W_U)$. The market equilibrium condition is that demand for labor equal the supply of labor:

$$S[1 - G(\Pi^*[W_U, W_N])]d(W_U) + S[G(\Pi^*[W_U, W_N])]d(W_N) = R$$

or in per-firm notation,

$$[1 - G(\Pi^*[W_U, W_N])]d(W_U) + G(\Pi^*[W_U, W_N])d(W_N) = \frac{R}{S}. \quad (1)$$

In this one-period setting, the R workers are locked into the industry so Eq. (1) defines the union's "opportunity locus." For any W_U that the union chooses, a W_N will result which selects some proportion of the firms as union firms consistent with the condition that supply equals demand. A higher W_U affects W_N in two ways: First, it increases the proportion of firms that fight the union. That there are fewer union firms implies a greater supply of labor to the nonunion sector, but also a larger number of nonunion firms which means a greater demand for labor in that sector. Second, higher W_U decreases the number of workers hired by each of the union firms sending the spillover into the nonunion sector. As long as demand curves are downward sloping, the basic shape of the opportunity locus will *always* be as shown in Figure 1. In particular, it has its starting point at $[W_C, W_C]$ where W_C, the competitive wage, is given by $d(W_C) = R/S$. It is always negatively sloped initially, positively sloped as W_U gets large, below W_C so that the nonunion wage is inferior to the preexisting competitive equilibrium, and it asymptotes to W_C.[4]

Consider the last statement first. As W_U goes to infinity, $G(\Pi^*(W_U, W_N))$ goes to 1, i.e., all firms choose to fight the union. Then (1) becomes

$$d(W_N) = \frac{R}{S}$$

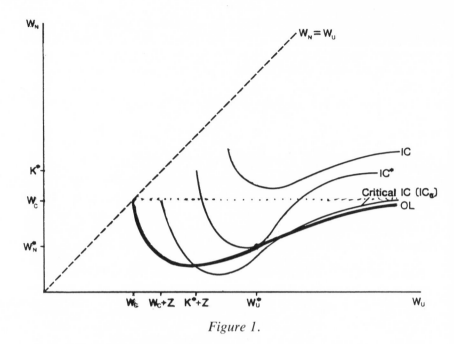

Figure 1.

so $W_N = W_C$. The intuition is clear. If the union chooses such a high wage that all firms fight the union, then all workers and all firms are in the nonunion sector so the situation there is identical to the initial competitive labor market.

It is equally clear that as W_U goes to W_C from above (no worker or union will choose $W_U < W_C$), W_N goes to W_C: From (1), we require

$$\lim_{W_U \to W_C} [1 - G(\Pi^*[W_U, W_N])]d(W_U) + G(\Pi^*[W_U, W_N])d(W_N) = \frac{R}{S}$$

or

$$[1 - G(\Pi^*[W_C, W_N])]d(W_C) + G(\Pi^*[W_C, W_N])d(W_N) = \frac{R}{S}$$

But this is just a convex combination of $d(W_C)$ and $d(W_N)$. Since $d(W_C) = R/S$, only $W_N = W_C$ will avoid a contradiction.

The intuition here is also clear. As W_U shrinks to W_C, union firms are demanding no less than their competitive share of labor and extracting workers from the nonunion sector in proportion to their numbers. Therefore, the number of workers left in the nonunion sector does not exceed the amount that these firms employ in competition and so the wage rate there must be the competitive one.

Since $W_U > W_C$ implies that union firms demand less than their proportionate share, the spillover of workers to the nonunion sector must exceed the number that those firms employ in competition. This means that $W_N < W_C$ throughout. Given that $W_N = W_C$ as W_U approaches W_C or infinity, it must be the case that $(dW_N/dW_U)\,|_{OL}$ (OL opportunity locus) starts out negative and ends up positive. This can also be seen by differentiating (1) totally to obtain $(dW_N/dW_U)\,|_{OL}$:

$$\frac{dW_N}{dW_U}\bigg|_{OL} = -\left\{\frac{d'(W_U)[1 - G(\Pi^*)] + g(\Pi^*)(\Pi_1^*)[d(W_N) - d(W_U)]}{d'(W_N)G(\Pi^*) + g(\Pi^*)\Pi_2^*[d(W_N) - d(W_U)]}\right\}$$

(2)

Recalling that $\Pi^*(W_U, W_N) = \Pi(W_N) - \Pi(W_U)$ and noting that the derivative of a profit function with respect to the price of an input is the negative of the demand for that input,

$$\Pi_1^* = -(-d(W_U)) = d(W_U) > 0$$

and

$$\Pi_2^* = -d(W_N) < 0$$

so we can rewrite (2) as

$$\frac{dW_N}{dW_U}\bigg|_{OL} =$$

$$-\left\{\frac{d'(W_U)[1 - G(\Pi^*)] + g(\Pi^*)d(W_U)[d(W_N) - d(W_U)]}{d'(W_N)G(\Pi^*) - g(\Pi^*)d(W_N)[d(W_N) - d(W_U)]}\right\}.$$ (3)

The denominator is negative since $d' < 0$, $g > 0$, $G > 0$, and the sign of the numerator changes. As $W_U \to W_C$, $G(\Pi^*) = 0$ and $d(W_N) - d(W_U) = 0$ so $dW_N/dW_U\,|_{OL} = -\infty$. As $W_U \to \infty$, $G(\Pi^*) = 1$ if we define $d(\infty) = 0$, then $dW_N/dW_U\,|_{OL} = 0$. The reason that W_N rises as W_U approaches infinity is that although more workers are being thrown into the nonunion sector, firms are switching from union to nonunion at an even more rapid rate, bidding up the price of labor there.

B.   The Indifference Curves

A potential union consisting of all R workers takes the opportunity locus as given. It can select any W_U, but this will imply a particular W_N. In addition, the choice of W_U affects the proportion of workers who will be employed in the union sector for two reasons. First, it alters the number of firms who choose to fight the union. Second, it changes the number of workers employed by each union firm. Since, in this section, all workers

are identical ex ante, the probability that a given worker will be employed
by a union firm and receive wage W_U is

$$P \equiv \frac{S(1 - G[\Pi^*(W_U, W_N)])d(W_U)}{R} \tag{4}$$

(the number of union workers divided by the total labor supply). Every
$[W_U, W_N]$ pair implies a P. However, only $[W_U, W_N]$ pairs which lie on
the opportunity locus correspond to feasible P, W_U, W_N combinations.
(The probability that a union job is obtained varies by worker characteristic, of course, and this is the subject of the last half of this paper.)

Workers are identical and risk-neutral ex ante so each has the same
objective function: maximize expected wealth. If it costs Z per union
worker to administer the union, i.e., to hire the union leader, strike or
enforce demands through other methods, then the worker's objective
function is to chose W_U so as to solve

$$\underset{W_U}{\text{Max}} \; P(W_U - Z) + (1 - P)W_N \tag{5}$$

subject to the constraint implied by (1), i.e., subject to being on the opportunity locus. Note that this answers the question as to which members
does the union represent. Ex ante, all R workers are represented. Ex
post, PR workers are union members.

The maximization of expected utility avoids the confusion that arises
when thinking about which union membership (ex ante or ex post) does
the leadership take as its constituency. It is the cleanest way to think of
the maximization problem. Although this is palatable in a one-period context, the maximization of ex ante utility becomes less obviously the only
reasonable choice in a multiperiod setting. There, one may think that
inertia creates a higher probability of union membership for those who
are already employees of the union firm and as such results in different
behavior. In the multiperiod context, allocation of union slots by age
transforms the ex ante expected utility problem into a lifetime wealth
maximization problem. Deviations between ex ante and ex post desires
are analogous to time-inconsistency problems. Perfect enforcement may
not be achievable under these circumstances. As such, a later section
entitled "Nationals and Locals" analyzes the situation where the existing
employees of the firm ignore the effects of their actions on non-employees.
Most results remain intact.[5]

That having been noted, maximization of (5) is straightforward, but
insight can be gained by considering it in two stages. We construct the
union's (i.e., each worker's) indifference curves from (5) and select W_U
such that the indifference curve is tangent to the opportunity locus.

The indifference curve corresponding to any utility (wealth) level K is

$$K = P(W_U - Z) + (1 - P)W_N \qquad (6)$$

or

$$W_N = \frac{K - P(W_U - Z)}{1 - P} \qquad (7)$$

Indifference curves are shown in Figure 1. They almost always display this shape. In particular, they start at the point $W_U = W_N + Z$, $W_N = K$ (since no workers join a union if $W_U - Z < W_N$), have negative slope initially, then positive slope, generally have no inflexion points in the negatively sloped region, one in the positively sloped region and asymptote to K. Consider each in turn.

First, if $W_U = W_N$ then (6) says $K = P(W_N - Z) + (1 - P)W_N$ or $W_N = K + Z$. Second, as W_U goes to infinity, from (4), $P = 0$; all firms fight the union and union firms demand no workers. So from (7), $\lim_{W_U \to \infty} W_N = K$.

The slope of the indifference curve is obtained by differentiating (6):

$$\left. \frac{dW_N}{dW_U} \right|_{IC} = - \left\{ \frac{P + \partial P/\partial W_U(W_U - Z - W_N)}{1 - P + \partial P/\partial W_N(W_U - Z - W_N)} \right\} \qquad (8)$$

where $\partial P/\partial W_U$, $\partial P/\partial W_N$ obtained from (4) are

$$\partial P/\partial W_U = \frac{S}{R}(1 - G(\Pi^*))d'(W_U) - \frac{S}{R}g(\Pi^*)\Pi_1^* d(W_U) \qquad (9)$$

$$= \frac{S}{R}(1 - G(\Pi^*))d'(W_U) - \frac{S}{R}g(\Pi^*)[d(W_U)]^2 < 0$$

and

$$\partial P/\partial W_N = \frac{-S}{R}g(\Pi^*)\Pi_2^* d(W_U) \qquad (10)$$

$$= \frac{S}{R}g(\Pi^*)d(W_N)d(W_U) > 0.$$

The slope on the 45° line is given by

$$-\frac{\frac{S}{R}d(W_U) - Z\left(\frac{S}{R}d'(W_U) - \frac{S}{R}g(0)d(W_U)^2\right)}{1 - \frac{S}{R}d(W_U)[1 + Zg(0)d(W_N)]} \qquad (11)$$

The numerator is positive. If Z, $g(0)$ or $d(W_U)$ is small then the denominator is positive so the slope of the indifference curve is negative.[6]
At the other extreme, as W_U approaches infinity,

$$W_N \text{ is } K, P = 0, d(W_U) = 0 \text{ so } \lim_{W_U \to \infty} \frac{dW_U}{dW_N}\bigg|_{IC} = 0.$$

The sense of the U-shaped indifference curve is this: Workers would like both higher W_U and higher W_N if nothing else were involved. But a higher W_U implies lower P. Initially, the value of an increase in W_U outweighs the loss associated with a reduction in P so indifference curves are negatively sloped. As W_U gets large and P gets small, however, the benefits to increased W_U are swamped by the loss resulting from a decreased P and workers view additional W_U as a bad, yielding positively sloped indifference curves.

C. Equilibrium

Define the "critical indifference curve" as the one that yields the same utility as the competitive equilibrium. Using (7), the critical indifference curve is the one that has $K = W_C$ or

$$W_N = \frac{W_C - P(W_U - Z)}{1 - P}. \tag{12}$$

A union equilibrium exists with certainty if the critical indifference curve crosses the opportunity locus, since this implies that there exists some feasible W_U, W_N, P combination that yields an expected utility level higher than the one offered by competition. In Figure 2, if IC_0 were the critical indifference curve, then a union equilibrium would exist. It need not exist, however. If Z were very large, for example, so that it is expensive to run the union, an equilibrium is unlikely to exist. Although the critical indifference curve and opportunity locus both asymptote to W_C, the indifference curve may well lie everywhere above the opportunity locus. In this case, workers are better off accepting the competitive wage and not forming a union.

If a union equilibrium exists, i.e., if the critical indifference curve intersects the opportunity locus, the selection of an optimum union wage is given by the first order conditions of (5) that

$$\frac{dW_N}{dW_U}\bigg|_{IC} = \frac{dW_N}{dW_U}\bigg|_{OL} \tag{13a}$$

$$[1 - G(\Pi^*)]d(W_U) + G(\Pi^*)d(W_N) = R/S. \tag{13b}$$

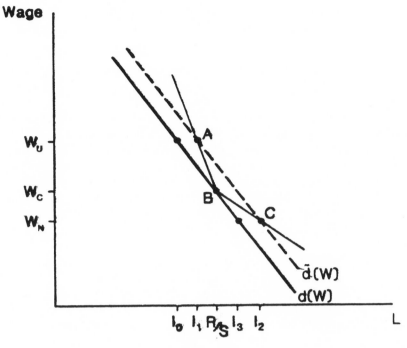

Figure 2.

Therefore, given a $G(\Pi^*)$ distribution, a $d(W)$ function and Z, the union optimum can be obtained. The solution described by (13a,b) is almost always an interior one, given the shapes of the indifference curves and opportunity locus. This implies that an occupation or industry will almost never be entirely unionized, if it is unionized at all. It always pays to leave some of those firms best able to "beat the union" out of the union sector, rather than choosing a union wage so close to W_C as to make it unprofitable for them to oppose. This seems to fit the stylized fact that unions rarely, if ever, organize all firms in an industry. (Multiple tangencies are possible. Under those circumstances, conditions for a global maximum must be checked.)

A key point is that even if ex post losers would like to bid with ex post winners for the union jobs, they are precluded from doing so freely. The firm can entertain these offers as one way to beat the union, but only at cost C_i. This model does not permit firms costlessly to accept the labor offer of a scab. Even in the absence of NLRB rules, it seems reasonable to view the hiring of scabs as carrying some real costs, perhaps larger to some firms than others.

D.   An Alternative Derivation of the Opportunity
Locus and Product Market Equilibrium

The reader may find artificial the assumption that firms are identical in all respects except for the cost of defeating the union. But the "union busting" function is easily separated from the firm and the analysis is unchanged. Let firms be identical in all respects. Let there be a group of S potential union busters whose alternative use of time is $C_i \sim g(C_i)$ across the S union busters. At any W_U, W_N pair, firms will pay up to $\Pi(W_N) - \Pi(W_U)$ to employ a union buster so the demand for union busters is perfectly elastic at price $\Pi(W_N) - \Pi(W_U)$. The number of union busters who supply their services is then $SG(\Pi(W_N) - \Pi(W_U))$ or $SG(\Pi^*(W_U, W_N))$ so $SG(\Pi^*)$ firms are nonunion and $S(1 - G(\Pi^*))$ are union and we are back to Eq. (1). All firms are identical and all earn the same profit rate equal to $\Pi(W_U)$ since nonunion firms receive $\Pi(W_N)$ but pay out $\Pi(W_N) - \Pi(W_U)$ to the union buster.

Union and nonunion firms exist in the same industry and there is no tendency for the high wage union firms to be driven out of business. Even if we think of the C_i as reflecting different costs of beating the union across firms this proposition holds. The reason is that the enterpreneur or other scarce factor that is responsible for that firm's being an effective union buster captures the rent, $(\Pi(W_N) - C_i) - \Pi(W_U)$ because union firms are willing to pay up to this amount for the scarce factor's services. So $(\Pi(W_N) - C_i) - \Pi(W_U)$ goes to the scarce factor, C_i is the direct cost of beating the union so the nonunion firm's profit is again $\Pi(W_U)$ and product market equilibrium is maintained. Union and nonunion firms exist in the same product market, each earning the same level of profit, properly measured.

E.   A Note on Labor Market Equilibrium

The labor market "clears" in the sense that aggregate supply of labor equals aggregate demand. Workers prefer the union jobs and in a multiperiod context (below) queue for them. But this market permits workers to enter the occupation in accordance with their own labor supply optimization. The wage in the nonunion sector adjusts to clear the market which allows free entry.

Incidentally, herein lies the difference between this model and the dominant firm construct found in the industrial organization literature (see Cohen and Cyert, 1975; Carlton, 1979, for examples). First, dominant firms, by restricting their supply, ensure that their own profits are maximized and second, commodities trade at the same price. In this model, the union does not have any power over the labor supply function to the entire occupation and the wage in the nonunion sector lies below the union wage. Firms, unlike customers, are not permitted costlessly to buy from the lowest price sellers of labor. In the dominant firm model, C_i is zero for all consumers, and their ability to buy from the lowest priced seller ensures that the price of the commodity is the same across sellers.

II. EXTENSIONS AND IMPLICATIONS OF THE MODEL

A. The Supply of Labor

For expositional convenience, we assumed that the supply of labor to the occupation or industry was perfectly inelastic. In this section we relax that assumption, allowing the labor force to be responsive to the actions of the union. An individual considers the expected utility from work in an occupation and compares it to the alternatives. By definition, if a union organizes an occupation, it does so because the expected utility of each member rises. Therefore let R, the number of workers in the occupation be given by R(K) where K, defined in (6), is the expected utility of entering the occupation and $R'(K) > 0$. As the expected wage in the occupation rises, those whose comparative advantage previously lay elsewhere, are now induced to acquire the requisite skills for this occupation.

The main result is that a union is less likely to exist as the supply of labor becomes more elastic. Mechanically, this is because the opportunity locus shifts downward and the critical indifference curve shifts upward making an intersection of these curves less likely. The proof of these propositions is contained in Appendix A. The intuition behind it is this: When the supply of labor is elastic, choosing a higher-than-competitive union wage induces more workers into the industry. As the result, the wage in the nonunion sector must fall more in order for nonunion firms to accommodate this larger residual labor force. This forces the opportunity locus downward. Similarly, since the probability that a given worker will obtain a union job is lower the more workers there are in the industry, a worker requires a higher nonunion wage for a given union wage to obtain the same level of expected utility. Thus, the critical indifference curve or the minimum combination of (W_U, W_N) which the worker views as preferable to the competitive wage, W_C, rises, making a union equilibrium less likely.

At the extreme, the supply of labor to the occupation is perfectly elastic. This requires a particular kind of homogeneity in ability so that no workers are relatively better at some occupations than others. Under these circumstances, no union equilibrium exists because raising the expected wage above W_C brings about an infinite sized labor force so that the probability of obtaining a union job falls to zero and all workers prefer the competitive wage. To the extent that the union can restrict entry into the occupation, it gives some inelasticity to the labor supply curve and we are back to the case just analyzed.

This may be the difference between unions organized along craft (occupational) lines and those organized along industrial lines. To the extent that the long run supply of labor to an occupation is more inelastic than to an industry, unions are more likely to be successful in crafts. As long as it is easier for an individual to switch from industry i to j than it is for him to switch from occupation k to h, the proposition holds. Heterogeneity in talents across occupations makes this feasible, even for long run labor supply. Historically, craft unions were organized before industrial unions and there is some evidence (see Lewis and Rees) that the former have been more successful than the latter.

B.   The Demand for Labor

Let us begin this section on a negative note: Although there are a number of statements that can be made about how the demand for labor affects union behavior, excluded from that set is the traditional (á la Marshall, 1922; Pigou, 1962; Hicks, 1966) and intuitive claim that unions have more power and are more likely to be successful the more inelastic is the demand for labor. The reason is quite simple. Although it is true that a given wage increase displaces a smaller number of union workers the more inelastic is the demand for labor, a given number of displaced workers drives down the nonunion wage by more, the more inelastic is the demand for labor. These spillovers must be absorbed by a nonunion sector firm with that same inelastic labor demand, implying that the wage rate in nonunion jobs must fall by more. This reduces the expected wage at the same time that the inelasticity increases it via higher union wages. The net effect is ambiguous, but in some cases, the effects are exactly offsetting so that inelasticity of labor demand does not affect the equilibrium.

Surprisingly, what is crucial is convexity of the demand curve. As the demand for labor becomes more convex, a given increase in the union wage results in a smaller displacement of workers. Also, as the demand for labor becomes more convex, a given displacement of workers into the nonunion sector reduces wages by a smaller amount there. As the result, the opportunity locus shifts upward, i.e., for a given union wage, a higher nonunion wage is available. Similarly, since the probability of obtaining a union job rises with the convexity of the labor demand curve, workers are as well off as before with a lower nonunion wage. Thus the critical indifference curve shifts down, i.e., at a given union wage, a lower nonunion wage is acceptable. Both of these forces increase the probability of obtaining a union equilibrium.[7] The proof of this proposition is contained in the last section of Appendix 2.

An increase in the demand for labor can have almost any effect depending upon the shape of the new demand curve relative to the old. However, in the simple case where demand curves are linear and the increase takes the form of a parallel shift, there will be no effect on the probability of obtaining a union equilibrium nor on the union-nonunion wage differential. The formal proof is contained in the first part of Appendix 2. This suggests that business cycle variations in union behavior and results are not caused by differences in the demand for labor per se. Findings such as those by Freeman and Medoff (1981b), and Blau and Kahn (1980) that union employment is more procyclic than nonunion employment must rely on inter-industry or interoccupational differences in product cyclical sensitivity for their explanation.[8]

C. Demand for Product

These results suggest that the analyses of Marshall (1922), Hicks (1966) and Pigou (1962) are based on an inappropriate assumption. They argued that the more inelastic is the demand for labor, the more likely it is that unions raise wage. They proceed to discuss the conditions under which the demand for labor will be more inelastic. In the last section, it was shown that the premise on which their analysis is based may be false. Yet, one of Marshall's implications, that union power increases with the inelasticity of product demand, holds. This is not because of the relationship between inelasticity of product and labor demands, but because of the relationship between inelasticity of product demand and convexity of labor demand.

The more inelastic is product demand, the more convex is the relevant labor demand curve. To see this, consider a firm that produces with labor plus one manager. In competitive equilibrium, the output price is defined by the minimum of the presumably U-shaped average cost curve.

Starting at equilibrium shown in Figure 2 by [W_C, R/S], let the union raise the wage rate to W_U. If all else were the same, the firm reduces labor demand to l_0. But the increase in the wage to W_U shifts the average cost curve upward. If all firms were unionized, this would raise the equilibrium price of output, P_Q. But even if all firms are not unionized, this must happen. Since this move raises the value of a "union buster," the salary of the manager in the nonunion firm is bid up to the point where the minimum of the average cost in the nonunion firm equals that in the union firm. (Because this is a fixed cost to the nonunion firm, output there will rise while the higher marginal cost induces output to fall in the union firm.) When output price rises to its new level, the demand for labor shifts from d(W) to d̄(W) so each union firm employs l_1 rather than l_0 of labor. Similarly, nonunion firms employ l_2 of labor and W_N is the solution to Eq. (1). The relevant demand for labor curve is then AB for union firms and BC for nonunion firms which adds convexity to the demand for labor. Further, the more inelastic is the demand for output, the larger is the increase in price P_Q which makes the labor demand even more convex. But as argued above, increased convexity increases the likelihood of a union equilibrium so less elastic product demand results in a higher probability of a union.[9]

Although the analysis suggests that there is no clear relationship between labor demand elasticity and unionization, except as influenced by product demand elasticity, some empirical evidence suggests that elasticity of substitution and the probability of unionization are inversely related. Freeman and Medoff (1982) find that in U.S. manufacturing, unionized firms seem to have lower elasticities of substitution between labor and other factors. Though not inconsistent with this model, it is a straightforward prediction of the Marshallian analysis.

D.   The Costs of Operating the Union

It has already been noted that as the cost of running the union and enforcing wage demands, Z, rises, the likelihood of a union equilibrium diminishes. Here it is shown that if a union equilibrium does exist, the observed union wage and wage differential will be larger when operating costs are higher. In addition, the proportion of workers in union jobs tends to fall as operating costs rise.

Recall that the shape of the opportunity locus is independent of Z. Consider the $[W_{U_0}, W_{N_0}]$ optimum given some Z_0. If $(dW_N)/dW_U) |_{IC}$ decreases with Z then the indifference curve for $Z_1 > Z_0$ through $[W_{U_0}, W_{N_0}]$ must cut the opportunity locus from above. This implies that $W_{U_1} > W_{U_0}$. To see this analytically, differentiate (8) with respect to Z:

$$\frac{d \left. \frac{dW_N}{dW_U} \right|_{IC}}{dZ} = \frac{\begin{array}{l}[1 - P + \partial P/\partial W_N(W_U - W_N - Z)]\partial P/\partial W_U \\ + [P + \partial P/\partial W_U(W_U - W_N - Z)](-\partial P/\partial W_N)\end{array}}{[1 - P + \partial P/\partial W_N(W_U - W_N - Z)]^2} \qquad (14)$$

$$= \frac{(1 - P)\partial P/\partial W_U - P\partial P/\partial W_N}{[1 - P + \partial P/\partial W_N(W_U - W_N - Z)]^2} < 0.$$

So as Z rises, the slope of the indifference curve through any point falls. This implies the optimal W_U increases with Z.

Further, $W_U - W_N$ increases as well since the slope of the opportunity locus is less than one (see (2)). This implies that P will tend to decline as Z rises. There will be fewer union workers, but each union worker will earn a higher union wage to compensate for the higher costs of administering the union. (See Appendix 3 for the formal discussion.)

Now consider changing the costs of opposing the union. For example, laws which make it more difficult to defeat the union would shift the $G(C_i)$

distribution rightward. Alternatively, if the shape of the G(C) distribution does not change, pro-union legislation can be thought of as lowering Z, the cost of organization. Now for a lower level of expenditures by workers on union organization, the same distribution of costs of defeating the union prevails. The implication is straightforward: Pro-union legislation, by reducing Z for a given distribution of C_i, increases the probability of obtaining a union equilibrium, increases the proportion of workers in the union, and *lowers* the union wage and wage differential. This is analogous to the situation in monopolistic product markets where cost saving technology which lowers the marginal cost function increases the firm's output and profits, but results in a decrease in price. It carries with it the somewhat paradoxical result that pro-union legislation reduces the distortion in unionized industries.

To the extent that Z is lower in occupations or industries in which firm size is relatively large, unions are more likely to exist. However, if a union equilibrium does exist in a small firm industry; other things equal, the wage differential will be larger and the proportion unionized smaller in this industry. The empirical implication is that the probability of there being any union workers in an industry and the proportion of the work force holding union jobs rises with firm size. However, among at least partially unionized industries, the union-nonunion wage differential varies inversely with average firm size.

E.   Nationals and Locals

The discussion has been in the context of a union selecting a wage for the entire industry or occupation. Thus, bargaining takes place at the "national" level where "national" is defined as the market over which workers are perfect substitutes. Now consider another possibility. Start with a competitive industry and allow each firm's R/S workers to vote separately on whether or not that firm should be unionized and then to select the union wage. The result is that locals do not maximize workers' expected wealth so that wage setting should occur at the national level. This implication is not new, but the usual reason for it relies on the relationship between bargaining power and union worker solidarity. This is not what is operating here. Because one local union's behavior affects market price and the aggregate probability that a worker obtains a union job in a way different from that perceived by the local, an inferior solution results. Also novel is that the local sometimes establishes a wage rate that is too low rather than too high. This section lays the groundwork for considering behavior by existing workers of a union firm.

Consider a wage W_N. The workers in an individual firm or local union, unlike the national, take this as given and assume that they cannot influence it. To make this applicable to existing unions, assume now that the local knows (or assumes even incorrectly) that it can install the union, i.e., that $\Pi^*(W_U, W_N) < C_i$. Then the relevant probability to that firm's workers is

$$\tilde{P} = d(W_U)/d(W_N). \tag{15}$$

The local's indifferences curves are given by

$$\tilde{W}_N = \frac{K - \tilde{P}(W_U - Z)}{1 - \tilde{P}}. \tag{16}$$

By differentiating (7) with respect to P, we obtain

$$\frac{dW_N}{dP} = \frac{K + Z - W_U}{(1 - P)^2} < 0 \tag{17}$$

since in the relevant region, $W_U > K + Z$. Note also that

$$\tilde{P} \equiv \frac{[d(W_U)]}{[d(W_C)]} \geq \frac{[d(W_U)]}{[d(W_C)]} [1 - G(\Pi^*)]$$

$$\geq \frac{d(W_U)}{R/S} [1 - G(\Pi^*)]$$

$$\geq \frac{S}{R} [1 - G(\Pi^*)]d(W_U) \equiv P.$$

Since $\tilde{P} \geq P$, $\tilde{W}_N \leq W_N$ so the critical indifference curve for myopic locals lies below that for the national. Thus, a local union might form or continue to exist even if the competitive situation were better for all workers. As such, the NLRB rules which allow the choice of union status by workers in elections generally held on a per firm basis, results in too much unionization in the sense that the procedure does not maximize workers' wealth. Because the workers in each firm do not take their effects on the market into account, they are too inclined toward unions.

This suggests the implication that the wider the definition of the voting population, the more likely is the unit to recognize market effects and therefore the less likely is the establishment of a union. So an NLRB policy that broadened the population over which it held certification elections, would make workers, as well as firms (although not necessarily union leaders), better off because it alters the prisoner's dilemma nature of the payoff structure.

Even if a union equilibrium does yield a higher expected wealth level than the competitive labor market, it is obvious that the Nash equilibrium when locals choose W_U will deviate from the equilibrium obtained when a national sets W_U. Since each local takes W_N as given and cares about $\tilde{P} = d(W_U)/d(W_C)$ rather than $P = (S/R)[1 - G(\Pi^*)]d(W_U)$, the conditions for a Nash equilibrium when locals choose wages are

$$\frac{dW_N}{dW_U}\bigg|_{IC} \equiv \frac{P + \partial P/\partial W_U[W_U - Z - W_N]}{1 - P + \partial P/\partial W_N[W_U - Z - W_N]} = \frac{dW_N}{dW_U}\bigg|_{OL} \quad (18a)$$

or

$$P + \partial P/\partial W_U[W_U - Z - W_N] = 0$$

and

$$[1 - G(\Pi^*[W_U, W_N])]d(W_U) + G(\Pi^*[W_U, W_N])d(W_N) = R/S. \quad (18b)$$

Equation (18a) says that since locals assume that they have no effect on the wage rate, the relevant opportunity locus, as they see it, is $W_N = W_N^*$ with $dW_N/dW_U\,|_{OL} = 0$. Equation (18b) merely repeats the condition that the solution, to be rational, must lie on the opportunity locus. The conditions for the national's equilibrium were given in (13a) above. Therefore, the equilibrium will differ except in the rare case when the national's optimum is located at the minimum point on the opportunity locus.

It is interesting to note that the local's choice of W_U, and W_U in equilibrium, is not always above the national's W_U equilibrium. Consider Figure 3. Suppose that the national's equilibrium were at A. Each local would try to go to B, which is unobtainable of course, and the equilibrium would

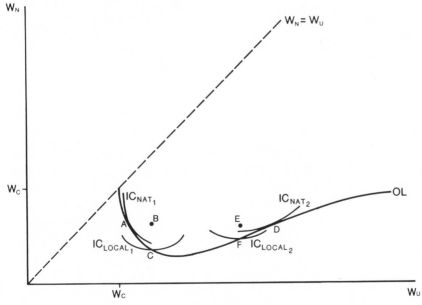

Figure 3.

be at C where

$$\frac{dW_U}{dW_N}\bigg|_{IC_{Local}} = 0, \text{ and } [W_U, W_N] \text{ are on the opportunity locus.}$$

In this case W_U would be higher if locals set wages than if nationals set wages. Alternatively, if the national's equilibrium were at D, locals would like to go to E, and equilibrium would result at F with W_U lower than the national's choice of W_U. The reason for the difference is the following: Local unions do not take into account the effect that their actions have on the nonunion wage by driving workers and firms into the nonunion sector. At A, the effect of raising W_U is to lower the nonunion wage so that by ignoring it, locals set too high a wage. At D, the effect of raising W_U is to *raise* the nonunion wage so ignoring this causes locals to set too low a wage.

Hendricks provides evidence that there is no relationship between whether bargaining takes place at the national or local levels and wage gains. Although this implication is inconsistent with naive bargaining models, it is a direct implication of the U-shaped opportunity locus, as argued in the previous paragraph.

Locals, because they ignore spillovers, choose a wage rate that does not maximize the expected wealth of workers in the entire occupation. Although any one local may be better off as the result of all unions behaving myopically, the rest are sufficiently worse off to reduce average wealth. This suggests that a national union which sets the optimal industry wage could make all workers better off ex ante. Therefore wage setting should be done at the national level. (Recall that "national" is used loosely here. It refers to the relevant labor market defined by the pool over which workers are perfect substitutes.)

To the extent that some locals may lose relative to others by this arrangement, it may be necessary to couple this with transfers from one local to another. A centralized strike or pension fund, for example, which doles out benefits in accordance with some prearranged formula, might be such a transfer mechanism.

F. Threat Effects and the Measurement of Union Power

Researchers have worried that the observed union differential may understate the true effect of the union on wage rates because nonunion firms, in attempting to discourage their workers from becoming unionized, pay more than the competitive wage.[10] As the result of the spillovers into the nonunion sector, however, it is known that the effect may go the other way. Novel is that the understatement or overstatement of the true differential bears a particular relationship to the proportion in the union.

Let us continue to think of C_i as being resources spent to hire a union buster or bribe a vote counter. Consider Figure 1. At any given wage rate, W_U, the true amount by which unions raise wages is $W_U - W_C$, measured as the vertical distance between the 45° line and the horizontal line at W_C. The observed wage differential, however, is $W_U - W_N$ or the vertical distance between the 45° line and the opportunity locus. Since OL is everywhere below W_C, the observed differential overstates rather than understates the true effect of the union on wage rates. This is because the effect of a union is to depress the nonunion wage. Further, since the difference between W_C and W_N shrinks as W_U approaches either W_C or ∞, the overstatement of the true effect is smallest when the proportion of the workers in the union is close to zero or to one.

Crucial here, of course, is the assumption that C_i does not become part of the observed wage. Thinking of C_i as salary to a union buster, a bribe for an official or even "bribes" to workers as long as these take non-pecuniary wage forms, is consistant with this. However, the standard "threat effect" approach views C_i as wages paid to nonunion workers to keep them from joining a union. It is clear, however, that even if C_i were reinterpreted as wages paid to discourage unions, for some firms, $W_U - W_N$ would overstate the effect of the union, and the average $W_U - W_N$ might also exceed $W_U - W_C$.

Kahn provides evidence on this point. He finds that the net effect of unionization is to lower the nonunion wage so that the basic characterization of the opportunity locus is supported. Threat effects are not sufficiently important to offset the depressant effect of a reduction in employment in the union sector on wages in the nonunion sector. He finds the effects smallest for clerical workers. Since clerical workers are not a highly organized occupation, this evidence is consistent with the notion that the effects are smallest at very low and very high levels of unionization, reflecting the curvature of the opportunity locus.[11]

Let us ask a more fundamental question. If the model in this paper is a reasonable description of equilibrium in a unionized industry, what can we infer from looking at the wage differential and its relationship to other variables, especially the proportion unionized? At the risk of restating a point made by Rosen in another context, consider the following. The observed W_U, W_N pair is the outcome of solving the union's optimization problem. As one moves from left to right along a given opportunity locus, $W_U - W_N$ rises and P falls yet union "power" in the sense of opportunities stays the same.

Suppose that all unions faced the same opportunity locus and differed only on Z, the costs of running a union. Recall that as Z rises, the optimal W_U rises and P falls. Occupations for which the costs of running a union are high will have high wage differentials and few union workers. From the low P, some might infer that the union is not powerful. From the high $W_U - W_N$, others might infer that it has a great deal of power. In fact, in some sense "power" is the same across occupations because the opportunity locus is unchanged. In another sense, the high Z occupation is less powerful since its costs are higher and expected wealth is lower so that union power and proportion in the union are negatively related. Finally, a regression of $W_U - W_N$ on P will yield a negative coefficient! If the opportunity locus shifts as well across occupations, then the interpretation of the relationship between $W_U - W_N$ and the proportion in the union is even more confused. This is not to imply that studies such as the classic by Lewis (1963) or that by Rosen (1969) on wage differentials tell nothing. They describe empirical regularities that models like this one should be able to explain. But inferences drawn with respect to union power on the basis of such studies, might usefully be reexamined in light of such thinking.[12]

There appears to be evidence Bloch and Kuskin (1978) that suggests that union differentials are lower when firm size is large. To the extent that part of Z (organizing costs) declines with increases in firm size, the model predicts that large firms are more likely to be organized, but that wage differentials there should be smaller. Freeman and Medoff (1981a) find a positive relationship between the proportion of an industry unionized and wage differentials. This suggests that shifts in the opportunity locus are at least as important as differences in organizing costs across industries or else the relationship would tend to be negative.

G.   Quantity Restrictions and Price Discrimination

Both Leontieff and Fellner made the point that a monopolist with the power to do so, should always set quantity equal to the efficient level. We examine that point in the context of this model. Above, it was assumed that the union as monopolist could choose only the wage, W_U. However the dead weight loss that results can be eliminated and additional rent can be captured by the union if we allow price discrimination or if we allow the union to set quantity as well as price by offering all-or-nothing contracts. This is illustrated in Figure 4.

A monopolistic union can extract more rent than it can by simply charging the monopoly price, say $\bar{W}_U$ and allowing the firm to hire $l' = d(\bar{W}_U)$ workers. The union can extract up to triangle ABC in an infinite number of ways. One is to offer the firm an all-or-nothing contract to employ R/S workers (the competitive number) at wage W_U^* each (where area FCD equals area DEB). Alternatively, the union could require that the unionized firm pay a lump sum to the union equal to area ABC. The wage rate is then free to settle to the competitive level W_C, and firms voluntarily hire R/S workers. This lump sum payment is then redistributed to workers

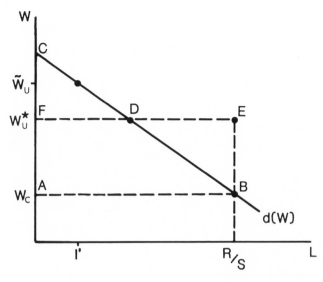

Figure 4.

who end up earning W_U^* as the result. The lump sum payment to workers may take the form of fringe benefits which are paid to workers, but are invariant with respect to number of hours worked. Freeman finds that union workers have a higher probability of receiving fringes and given that they do, they receive a higher proportion, and therefore higher absolute amount, of compensation as fringes. This is consistent with unions engaging in an optimal rent extraction policy.

The advantage of the two-part wage scheme is that since the marginal wage is free to adjust, transitory changes in supply of and demand for labor are dealt with efficiently. The number of workers employed adapts automatically to the new competitive equilibrium. The all-or-nothing contract requires explicit changes in the number of workers by the union. Adjustments made by the union are more efficient if most supply or demand changes are known by the union better than the firm. If not, the two-part wage, which allows the firm to select the number of workers, is superior. This point, best articulated by Hall and Lilien, should be coupled with another: To the extent that the lump sum transfer to the union involves the union as an intermediary, workers may prefer to avoid the possibility of skimming by the union leader through payments which come directly to workers. In a world of perfect information with respect to changes in supply and demand, this would tip the balance in favor of all-or-nothing offers. Since calling out a marginal wage necessarily implies a quantity, we conduct the following discussion in terms of the all-or-nothing offer.

It is obvious that if the firm is held captive so that it faces no alternative seller of labor, then the union's rent extracting optimum implies setting $L_U = R/S$ and wage $= W_U^*$. However, in this paper, we allow the firm to defeat the union at some cost C_i and thereby purchase labor from the nonunion firm at wage W_N. The union takes into account that higher extraction of rent implies fewer union firms from which to extract. Also since there is some probability that workers will end up in nonunion jobs, it might be preferable to select a union employment level *above* R/S and a union wage above W_C but below W_U^* so that the wage in the nonunion sector, as well as the union sector, is above W_C. (If the union firms use more than R/S workers then fewer than R/S workers are left for nonunion firms so the market clearing wage exceeds the competitive wage.)

As is proved in Appendix 4, the optimum strategy for the union remains to set $L_U = R/S$. This implies that when a union organizes a firm, it will attempt to require the firm to keep the size, although not necessarily the identity, of the labor force constant at its previous level, not pushing for higher employment but not "trading off" lower employment for higher wages. It will appear, therefore, that the relevant membership is that set of workers currently employed by the newly unionized firm even though this is exactly the number of union jobs that would have been selected if all choices were made ex ante. Further, a union that can set wage and quantity brings about an efficient allocation of labor across sectors (although not across industries or occupations).

Firms, of course, faced with paying a wage $W_U > W_C$ prefer to hire fewer than R/S workers if given the choice since the firm is off its demand curve. This has the appearance of "featherbedding," a requirement that firms hire more labor than they freely choose. Yet this featherbedding is efficient in two respects. First, it provides that a Pareto optimum is reached since the competitive number of workers are employed. Second, there is no "buy out" offer that the firm can make to the union to eliminate featherbedding which is acceptable to the union since featherbedding is an optimal rent extracting strategy. Inefficient featherbedding is discussed below.

Once we allow for quantity strategies by the union, the ambiguity in demand curve comparative statics (discussed on p. 66) disappears. Contrary to Marshall's (1922) and Hicks' (1966) assumption, it turns out that elasticity of demand affects neither the probability of obtaining a union in an occupation nor the union wage if a union does exist. The intuition is this:

Given that the union fixes quantity at $L_U = R/S$, the nonunion quantity is necessarily R/S from (1) so that $W_N = W_C$. For any given wage W_U that the union calls out, the firm's benefit from not being unionized is then $(R/S)(W_U - W_C)$. The cost of being nonunion is C_i. Neither benefit nor cost are a function of the demand for labor. Therefore, the proportion of firms that resist the union is invariant with respect to the demand for labor as is the probability of observing a union in a given occupation. Similarly, since the union fixes the amount of labor hired at R/S, the probability of obtaining a union job does not vary with the demand for labor. As such, the choice of the optimum union wage does not depend upon the elasticity of demand for labor. The formal proofs are contained in Appendix 5.

Whether or not the union can set quantity as well as price is open to debate. The factor that usually prevents a monopolist from price discriminating, namely resale of the product, does not seem to be important in this context. But both price discrimination and all-or-nothing offers give firms incentives to change their scales of operation. For example, a union which required l_U equal to $1\frac{1}{2}$ times the quantity of labor that the firm would elect to purchase at price W_U might be thwarted. The firm simply would increase all other factors of production to $1\frac{1}{2}$ times the initial amount. Lump sum requirements provide incentives for mergers. Additionally, legal restrictions, bargaining considerations, and market conditions may make it difficult for the union to set quantity as well as price. The resolution of this issue must be an empirical one.

III. AN OVERLAPPING-GENERATION MODEL

The analysis has been a static one where all workers were assumed to be identical. Yet a great deal of union activity centers on worker differences and how different preferences within the union are juggled to come out with a stable, long term, relationship. Among the most important sources of different preferences within the union are those related to the lifecycle. Old and young workers may have very different ideas about what the union should do and one wonders, for example, why such a situation does not result in one group forming its own union in competition with the other. This section proves that the multi-generational feature does not change the way in which a union behaves with respect to those issues discussed in previous sections.

What is essential about lifecycle differences within a union can be captured by a simple overlapping generation model. Assume that workers live two periods. There are Y young persons born into the occupation each period so that $R \equiv 2Y$ is the total labor supply. All workers are equally productive.

Recall that P is the proportion of workers who obtain union jobs. Before, allocation of jobs was assumed to be random. But in a two generation context the way in which jobs are assigned makes a great deal of difference. Suppose that all young workers had first claim to union jobs. If P is less than one, there will be some old workers without union jobs. They have an incentive to negotiate with the union employer, offering labor services at a wage which exceeds the nonunion wage, but is less than the union wage. The union may or may not successfully defeat such attempts at "scabbing" by older workers, but the presence of such incentives clearly raises the costs of operating the union, Z, and makes a union equilibrium less likely.

Reverse the situation. Let old workers have first claim to union jobs and the scenario is altered dramatically. Young workers, who care only about expected lifetime wealth, behave no differently. They remain loyal to the union, even as nonunion workers, because their entry into union jobs can be made contingent upon their non-disruptive behavior. Old workers, however, have no incentive to undermine the union since they are the individuals who reap the current benefits of such a scheme. As the result, no individual's ex ante lifetime wealth is reduced by a strict seniority rule for admission to the union, and the costs of operating the union are reduced, which results in a higher expected lifetime wealth for all workers.[13] Thus, union workers will tend to be older than nonunion workers. Further, if there were retired workers present in the model, they too might desire to work occasionally and their offers of labor at less than W_U to union firms would also adversely affect expected wealth. However, if these workers can be punished for this anti-union behavior, all workers can be made better off ex ante. Pensions may play an important role here. To the extent that old workers receive large pensions which are controlled at least in part by the union, scabbing can be punished by the discontinuation of pension benefits. (A union may not be able to stop pension payments to workers, but its ability to raise the uncertainty of receiving those payments has a similar, though somewhat weaker effect.) This provides another reason why union workers should receive a greater part of their lifetime compensation in the form of pensions than nonunion workers.[14] Mincer also suggests that pensions are a way to capture rents and lessen the adverse affects of the hours reduction.

Inefficient "featherbedding" too can be rationalized along these same lines. Even featherbedding which involves inefficiency and is inferior to lump sum payoffs, has the advantage that the "bought out" individual's payment is tied to the union's continued success. A bought out worker would otherwise have an incentive to undermine the union after his payoff was received.

A word on the mechanics of this market is useful. Here, young workers play a role even though they may not be in the union. Young workers' cooperation is necessary, yet they appear as nonunion workers in this market. In some situations, workers in nonunion firms may be in the union explicitly. This is extremely common in the building trades. A worker may have his union card, but is assigned to union jobs in an order often related to seniority. If he does not obtain a union job on a given day, he may work in a nonunion job at a lower wage, but obviously cannot offer his services to the union employer. His willingness to do this rests on his knowledge that someday he will be the more senior worker and will receive W_U.

In other situations, the young worker actually is outside the union, waiting for his union card. During this period, he works nonunion jobs. Yet even this worker prefers that the occupation is unionized, because his lifetime wealth is higher as a result. Further, his cooperation is necessary in order for the union to be successful in pressing its demands.

All of this implies that the probability of being in a union job will be positively related to age in the following manner: If P_0 is the probability that an old worker will be in a union and P_Y is the probability that a young worker will be in a union, then

$$P_0 = \begin{cases} 1 \text{ if } S[1 - G(\Pi^*(W_U, W_N)]d(W_U) \geq Y \\ \dfrac{S[1 - G(\Pi^*(W_U, W_N)]d(W_U)}{R - Y} \\ \text{ if } S[1 - G(\Pi^*(W_U, W_N)]d(W_U) < Y \end{cases}$$

Since $Y = R/2$, this can be rewritten as

$$P_0 = \begin{cases} 1 & \text{if } P \geq \frac{1}{2} \\ 2P & \text{if } P < \frac{1}{2} \end{cases} \tag{19}$$

where

$$P \equiv \frac{S(1 - G)d(W_U)}{R} \quad \text{as before.}$$

Similarly, since young workers claim the left-over union jobs,

$$P_Y = \begin{cases} 2P - 1 & \text{if } P \geq \frac{1}{2} \\ 0 & \text{if } P < \frac{1}{2} \end{cases} . \tag{20}$$

Except when $P = 1$, $P_0 > P_Y$ so that average age of union workers will be higher than that for nonunion workers. In this simple framework, if $\bar{A}_0$ is the average age of all old workers and $\bar{A}_Y$ is the average age of young workers (where old and young refer to their priority levels for union jobs, all being the same within the class), then the average age of union workers, $\bar{A}_U$, can be obtained. Since there are PR union workers, $(P_0)(Y)$

old workers and $(P_Y)(Y)$ young workers,

$$\bar{A}_U = \frac{P_0 Y}{PR} \bar{A}_0 + \frac{P_Y Y}{PR} \bar{A}_Y$$

or

$$\bar{A}_U = \frac{P_0}{2P} \bar{A}_0 + \frac{P_Y}{2P} \bar{A}_Y. \tag{21}$$

Analogously, for nonunion workers

$$\bar{A}_N = \frac{Y(1 - P_0)}{(1 - P)R} \bar{A}_0 + \frac{Y(1 - P_Y)}{(1 - P)R} \bar{A}_Y$$

or

$$\bar{A}_N = \frac{(1 - P_0)}{2(1 - P)} \bar{A}_0 + \frac{(1 - P_Y)}{2(1 - P)} \bar{A}_Y. \tag{22}$$

There is some evidence in the existing literature that blue-collar union workers are three to four years older than their nonunion counterparts and that they have higher levels of other variables that are positively related to human capital as well, especially education (see Brown and Medoff, 1978). The age relationship corresponds to that predicted by this model. There is no obvious reason in this why union workers should be more educated, however, unless this merely reflects a positive simple correlation between education and age. In an earlier draft, some original evidence on the age-unionization relationship was provided. It supports the predicted age-structure of union membership and is available from the author upon request.

These simple formulas yield a number of other testable empirical implications. First substituting (19) and (20) into (21), (21) can be written as

$$\bar{A}_U = \frac{P_0}{2P} A_0 = \bar{A}_0 \qquad \text{if} \quad P < \tfrac{1}{2}. \tag{23a}$$

$$\bar{A}_U = \frac{\bar{A}_0}{2P} + \frac{(2P - 1)}{2P} \bar{A}_Y \quad \text{if} \quad P \geqslant \tfrac{1}{2}. \tag{23b}$$

Similarly, (22) can be rewritten as

$$\bar{A}_N = \frac{(1 - 2P)\bar{A}_0}{2(1 - P)} + \frac{\bar{A}_Y}{2(1 - P)} \quad \text{if } P < \tfrac{1}{2} \tag{24a}$$

$$\bar{A}_N = \frac{2 - 2P}{2(1 - P)} \bar{A}_Y = \bar{A}_Y \qquad \text{if } P \geqslant \tfrac{1}{2}. \tag{24b}$$

Differentiating (23) with respect to P yields:

$$\frac{\partial \bar{A}_U}{\partial P} = 0 \qquad \text{if } P < \tfrac{1}{2} \qquad (25a)$$

$$\frac{\partial \bar{A}_U}{\partial P} = \frac{\bar{A}_Y - \bar{A}_0}{2P^2} < 0 \quad \text{if } P \geq \tfrac{1}{2}. \qquad (25b)$$

Similarly, differentiating (24) yields

$$\frac{\partial \bar{A}_N}{\partial P} = \frac{\bar{A}_Y - \bar{A}_0}{2(1 - P)^2} < 0 \quad \text{if } P < \tfrac{1}{2} \qquad (26a)$$

$$\frac{\partial \bar{A}_N}{\partial P} = 0 \qquad \text{if } P \geq \tfrac{1}{2}. \qquad (26b)$$

The sense of (25) and (26) is this: If $P < \tfrac{1}{2}$, then no young workers are in the union and some old workers are forced to work in the nonunion sector. Raising P simply brings more old workers into the union, but does not change the average age there since all union workers were and remain old. Therefore $\partial \bar{A}_U / \partial P = 0$ when $P < \tfrac{1}{2}$. The nonunion pool has all of the young workers plus some of the old. As P rises, old workers are drawn from the nonunion sector into the union sector, leaving a larger proportion of young workers left in the nonunion jobs and thereby lowering $\bar{A}_N$. Therefore $\partial \bar{A}_N / \partial P < 0$.

Alternatively, if $P \geq \tfrac{1}{2}$, all old workers and some young ones as well are the union. An increase in P brings more young workers into the union thereby lowering $\bar{A}_U$. At the same time fewer workers remain in the nonunion sector, but they remain as before, only young workers. Therefore $\bar{A}_N$ does not change.

This yields an empirically testable implication. A regression of $\bar{A}_U$ on P should yield a negative coefficient as should a regression of $\bar{A}_N$ on P.[15] Further, by using (23b) and (24a) a regression which defines as observations occupations for which $P \geq \tfrac{1}{2}$ when the relationship is (23b) and $P < \tfrac{1}{2}$ when the relationship is (24a), the coefficients of the pooled regression of $\bar{A}_U$ on $\tfrac{1}{2}P$ and $(2P - 1)/2P$ for (23b) and of $\bar{A}_N$ on $(1 - 2P)/2(1 - P)$ and $1/2(1 - P)$ for (24a) yields the estimates of $\bar{A}_0$ and $\bar{A}_U$. Since "old" workers is defined in terms of ages over which priority on entrance to the union is the same, and similarly for "young," this is a summary statistic on the age stratification of unions. For example $\hat{A}_0 = \hat{A}_Y$ implies that age is not a criterion for union membership.

It is interesting to ask how the difference between $\bar{A}_U$ and $\bar{A}_N$ varies with P. Note that from (23) and (24), one can write

$$\bar{A}_U - \bar{A}_N = \begin{matrix} (\bar{A}_0 - \bar{A}_Y)/2(1 - P) & \text{for } P < \tfrac{1}{2} \\ (\bar{A}_0 - \bar{A}_Y)/2P & \text{for } P \geq \tfrac{1}{2} \end{matrix} \qquad (27)$$

so that

$$\frac{\partial(\bar{A}_U - \bar{A}_N)}{\partial P} = \begin{array}{ll} (\bar{A}_0 - \bar{A}_Y)/2(1 - P)^2 > 0 & \text{for} \quad P < \tfrac{1}{2} \\ (\bar{A}_Y - \bar{A}_0)/2P^2 < 0 & \text{for} \quad P \geqslant \tfrac{1}{2}. \end{array} \qquad (28)$$

Since $\bar{A}_U < \bar{A}_0$, the difference between the average age of union workers and that of nonunion workers within an occupation will first rise, then fall with P. This, too, is easily verified empirically. Also note that

$$\lim_{P \to 0} \bar{A}_U - \bar{A}_N = \lim_{P \to 0} \bar{A}_U - \bar{A}_N = \frac{\bar{A}_0 - \bar{A}_Y}{2}.$$

It is obvious from (23) and (24) that

$$\frac{\partial \bar{A}_U}{\partial \bar{A}_0}, \frac{\partial \bar{A}_U}{\partial \bar{A}_Y}, \frac{\partial \bar{A}_N}{\partial \bar{A}_0}, \frac{\partial \bar{A}_N}{\partial \bar{A}_Y} \geqslant 0$$

so that an increase in the average age of the relevant labor pool will increase the average age of both union and nonunion workers. However, for a given P, an increase in $\bar{A}_0$ and $\bar{A}_Y$ which is neutral in the sense that it leaves $\bar{A}_0 - \bar{A}_Y$ unchanged will also leave $\bar{A}_U - \bar{A}_N$ unchanged. This follows directly from (27). These relationships are also empirically verifiable in the sense that they give definite predictions on the relationship between the age structure of an occupation and the age structure between union and nonunion workers within that occupation.[16]

A. Attrition

Some occupations are characterized by a more fickle labor force than others. Occupations with high turnover or attrition rates present additional difficulties for the prospective union. First, such movement makes it more difficult to keep tabs on which workers "paid their dues" when young by accepting a nonunion job without attempting to bargain away a union job from a more senior worker. This factor by itself raises Z, the costs of operating a union. As such, it will reduce the likelihood of a union equilibrium, but will *raise* the wage differential and lower the proportion of union workers in those occupations where a union equilibrium is obtained. This suggests that occupations such as secretaries and farm workers where mobility into and out of the labor force or between geographical regions is high are less likely to be unionized. It also suggests that in high attrition occupations where unions are formed, e.g., the California farm workers, only a small proportion of workers will be employed by unionized firms and the union-nonunion wage differential will be large.

Additionally, increased attrition, to the extent that it reflects ex ante known individual differences, makes a union equilibrium less likely even if it does not affect Z. The reason is that an individual who plans to leave the occupation between period one and two receives an expected wage rate in period 1 of $(W_U - Z)(P_Y) + W_N(1 - P_Y)$. He favors the union if

$$W_C < (W_U - Z)P_Y + W_N(1 - P_Y). \tag{29}$$

This is a stronger condition than the one relevant for those who plan to remain in the occupation for their entire lifetimes. That condition is

$$2W_C < (W_U - Z)(P_Y + P_0) + W_N[(1 - P_Y) + (1 - P_0)]. \tag{30}$$

It is easy to see that (29) is sufficient for (30), but that (30) can hold when (29) does not, so that young workers who plan to leave the occupation are more likely to oppose the certification of a union.[17] Further, attrition of workers between period one and two increases P_0 for a given labor force, R. This makes the stayers even more anxious for a union equilibrium. Since NLRB rules give each worker one and only one vote, strong differences in lifetime plans across workers reduces the probability of acquiring a union equilibrium.

A corollary of the previous discussion is that old workers will prefer unions before young workers do as long as their seniority is grandfathered. For old workers to prefer the union to a competitive equilibrium, we require

$$W_C < (W_U - Z)P_0 + W_N(1 - P_0) \tag{31}$$

It is easy to show that (30), the condition for the young to favor a union, is a sufficient condition for (31).[18]

B. The Relationship Between the Multi-Period Model and the One-Period Model Results

The link between the overlapping generation model and the simple period model is this: Young workers in the multiperiod world will behave exactly like single period wealth maximizers. Their "critical indifference curves" and their view of the opportunity locus is identical to that of individuals who live only a single period.[19] However, old workers may prefer a union equilibrium even when single period workers prefer the competitive equilibrium because $P_0 \geq P$. This also implies a preference by old workers for a union wage which deviates from the solutions obtained in the one-period model.

This poses no problem under a number of circumstances. The most straightforward resolution relies on the fact that the median voter is a young worker.[20] Although all young workers are not formal members of the union, their explicit or implicit acquiescence is necessary for the maintenance of a union equilibrium. Old workers would like to ignore the nonunion young workers in selecting W_U, but their persistence in following that strategy is not viable because young workers have an incentive to undermine such a union and replace it with a lifetime wealth maximizing one. In fact, the young could pay old workers enough to induce the old workers to follow the broader lifetime wealth maximizing policy. Entry fees and contributions by the current union workers to the already retired workers' pension fund might be reinterpreted as a transfer of this sort.

Since young workers behave the same as workers who live for only a single period, and since a young worker is the marginal worker, the solution, which reflects the preference of the young worker, is identical to that in the single period world. Therefore, all results of that section hold.

C.   Age-Earnings Profiles

Given the way that the union is structured so that young workers are less likely to be unionized than are old workers, there is a natural tendency for wages to grow over the lifecycle as workers move from nonunion to union jobs. This is true even if productivity does not grow over the lifecycle.

More important, is that within a union firm, age-earnings profiles will be flatter than they are in nonunion firms. The reason is that unions, in order to maintain stabilty, want the old rather than young workers to receive the benefits of the union. But in most industries and occupations, the firm, rather than the union, hires workers. A way by which the union can discourage the firm from hiring young workers is to overprice them relative to more experienced workers. This will provide the firm with incentives to hire the workers into the union firm which the union would have selected. Thus, the union can implicitly control hiring and the compensation of the firms' work force simply by calling out the appropriate wages. Block and Kushkin find that age-earnings profiles are indeed flatter for union workers than for nonunion workers using 1973 CPS data.

The same argument applies to blacks and other groups which the union wants to keep out. The wage of black union workers relative to white union workers should be higher than the wage of black nonunion workers relative to white nonunion workers. This overprices black labor by more than white labor for union firms and discourages their employment. Ashenfelter finds support for this. Blacks are somewhat less likely to be in unions than whites given occupations, but those who are, experience a smaller black-white wage differential.

A corollary is that if age and skill are positively correlated, higher quality labor will be found in union firms. Union firms, faced with flatter age-earnings profiles voluntarily select the older highly skilled workers, because they are underpriced relative to the younger, less skilled workers. An alternative is provided by Mincer who cites evidence that less on-the-job training occurs in union firms. There is no obvious theoretical reason why this should be the case.

Incidentally, if the bimodal age distribution is replaced by a continuous one, nothing is altered fundamentally but P is reinterpreted as the proportion of one's life spent in the union. Incentives remain intact and all conclusions still follow. (Of course, the formulas for the average ages of workers in union and nonunion jobs would require alteration.)

D.   Countercyclical Variations in Wage Differentials

Lewis reports that union workers do relatively better during cyclical downturns. The age-based incentive mechanism provides an explanation. Since incentive compatibility requires that old workers in unions receive benefits relative to young, we expect that seniority will be more important in determining layoff priority in union firms. As such, the average age of union workers relative to nonunion workers should rise during cyclical downturns and since age-earnings profiles are positively sloped, wage differentials will increase. This is easily tested by examining the way in which $\bar{A}_U - \bar{A}_N$ moves over the business cycle. Also, controlling for age should eliminate most of the countercyclical wage differential movement.

DEFINITION OF VARIABLES

S	Number of Firms
W	Wage rate
L	Number of workers in the firm
$R(W)$, R	Supply of labor
$d(W)$	Demand for labor per firm
W_U	Union wage
W_N	Nonunion wage
C_i	Cost of fighting union for firm i
$g(C)$	Density function
$G(C)$	Distribution function
$\Pi(W)$	Profit function
$\Pi^*(W_U, W_N)$	$\Pi(W_N) - \Pi(W_U)$
W_C	Competitive wage in the absence of unions
$dW_N/dW_U \mid_{OL}$	Slope of opportunity locus
P	Probability of obtaining a union job
$dW_N/dW_U \mid_{IC}$	Slope of indifference curve
Z	Per member cost of operating the union

Critical indifference curve	Indifference curve that yields same level of utility as available if the worker receives competitive wage, W_C.
$f(L)$	Production function of firm
$D(p_Q)$	Demand for product as function of price P_Q
Y	Number of young entrants to an occupation
p_0	Probability that an old worker is in a union
P_Y	Probability that a young worker is in a union
$\bar{A}$	Average age of all workers
$\bar{A}_0$	Average age of old workers
$\bar{A}_Y$	Average age of young workers
$\bar{A}_U$	Average age of union workers
$\bar{A}_N$	Average age of nonunion workers

APPENDICES

1: Proof that elastic labor supply shifts the opportunity locus downward.

By contradiction: Define $\tilde{W}_N$ as W_N corresponding to $R(K)$ and W_N corresponding to $R(W_C) \equiv R$. Assume that $\tilde{W}_N > W_N$. Given that $R(K) > R$, we know that

$$[1 - G(\Pi^*[W_U, \tilde{W}_N])]d(W_U) + G(\Pi^*[W_U, \tilde{W}_N])d(\tilde{W}_N)$$

$$> [1 - G(\Pi^*[W_U, W_N])]d(W_U) + G(\Pi^*[W_U, W_N])d(W_N)$$

But if $\tilde{W}_N > W_N$ then $d(W_N) > d(\tilde{W}_N)$ so

$$(1 - \tilde{G})d(W_U) + \tilde{G}d(W_N) > (1 - G)d(W_U) + Gd(W_N)$$

or

$$d(W_U)(G - \tilde{G}) > d(W_N)(G - \tilde{G}).$$

Since $W_U > W_N$, this implies $\tilde{G} > G$. But if $\tilde{W}_N > W_N$ $\tilde{G} < G$ since $\Pi_2^* < 0$ and $G' = g > 0$. This results in a contradiction.

Proof that critical indifference curve shifts upward:

Define $\tilde{P}$ as the probability of obtaining a union job if $R = R(K)$. Differentiating (7) with respect to P yields $(dW_N/dP)|_{IC} = (K + Z - W_U)/(1 - P)^2 < 0$ since $W_U > K + Z$ for a union equilibrium to exist. Therefore, if $\tilde{P} < P$ then $\tilde{W}_N > W_N$ and the indifference curve shifts up. Assume $\tilde{P} > P$. Then $S/R(K)(1 - \tilde{G})d(W_U) > (S/R)(1 - G)d(W_U)$. Since $R(K) >$

R, this implies that $1 - \tilde{G} > 1 - G$ or that $\tilde{G} < G$. But if $\tilde{P} > P$ then $\tilde{W}_N < W_N$ since $dW_N/dP < 0$. Since $\Pi_2^* < 0$, this implies $\tilde{G} > G$ which is a contradiction. Therefore the critical indifference curve shifts upward.

2: Proof that a parallel shift in demand affects neither the probability of a union equilibrium nor the wage differential selected.

It is sufficient to show that the opportunity locus and relevant indifference curves are displaced along a 45° ray. If so, all solutions will move in proportion to the new competitive wage.

Consider $\tilde{d}(W) > d(W)$ such that $\tilde{d}'(W) = d'(W) = d' \; \forall \; W$. Define $\tilde{W}_C$ such that $\tilde{d}(\tilde{W}_C) = R/S$ and $\Delta \equiv \tilde{W}_C - W_C$. Then, if $\tilde{W}_U$, $\tilde{W}_N$ are pairs on the new opportunity locus, a parallel shift of that locus requires that $\tilde{W}_N = W_N + \Delta$ if $\tilde{W}_U = W_U + \Delta$.

The equation for the opportunity locus [Eq. (1)] implies that at $\tilde{W}_U = W_U + \Delta$,

$$[1 - G(\Pi^*(W_U, W_N))]d(W_U) + G(\Pi^*(W_U, W_N))d(W_N) = R/S$$

$$= [1 - G(\tilde{\Pi}^*(W_U + \Delta, \tilde{W}_N))]\tilde{d}(W_U + \Delta) \qquad (A2.1)$$

$$+ G(\tilde{\Pi}^*(W_U + \Delta, \tilde{W}_N))\tilde{d}(\tilde{W}_N)$$

Conjecture that

$$\Pi^*(W_U, W_N) = \tilde{\Pi}^*(W_U + \Delta, \tilde{W}_N).$$

Then (A2.1) implies that

$$d(W_N) = \tilde{d}(\tilde{W}_N).$$

or

$$d(W_C) + (d')(W_N - W_C) = \tilde{d}(\tilde{W}_C) + (\tilde{d}')(\tilde{W}_N - \tilde{W}_C).$$

Since $d(W_C) = \tilde{d}(\tilde{W}_C)$, $d' = \tilde{d}'$, and $\tilde{W}_C - W_C = \Delta$, this implies that $\tilde{W}_N = W_N + \Delta$. But if $\tilde{W}_N = W_N + \Delta$ when $W_U = W_U + \Delta$, then since $\tilde{d}(W_U + \Delta) = d(W_U)$ and $\tilde{d}(W_N + \Delta) = d(W_N)$, $\Pi^*(W_U, W_N) = \tilde{\Pi}^*(W_U + \Delta, W_N + \Delta)$ so $G = \tilde{G}$ and the sufficient condition is verified. Therefore a parallel shift in the opportunity locus occurs.

Similarly, the critical indifference curve is displaced up the 45° line. Using (12),

$$\tilde{W}_N = \frac{\tilde{W}_C - \tilde{P}(\tilde{W}_U - Z)}{1 - \tilde{P}} . \qquad (A2.2)$$

Evaluating this at $\tilde{W}_U = W_U + \Delta$ and recalling that, for all points on the opportunity locus, $G = \bar{G}$, (A2.2) can be rewritten as

$$\bar{W}_N = \frac{W_C + \Delta - P(W_U + \Delta - Z)}{1 - P}$$

$$= \frac{W_C - P(W_U - Z)}{1 - P} + \Delta$$

$$= W_N + \Delta \qquad \text{(from 12)}.$$

So the critical indifference curve is displaced along the 45° line. This implies that the probability of obtaining a union equilibrium does not vary when linear demand for labor shifts out parallel.

Finally, the equilibrium wage differential does not change because the slope of the new indifference curves at the new opportunity locus exactly equals the slope of the old indifference curves at the old opportunity locus along the 45° ray. Using (8), (9), and (10),

$$\left. \frac{d(W_N + \Delta)}{d(W_U + \Delta)} \right|_{IC} = - \frac{\begin{aligned} &1 - G(\bar{\Pi}^*(W_U + \Delta, W_N + \Delta)) + (W_U + \Delta - Z - W_N - \Delta) \\ &\times \left[(1 - G(\bar{\Pi}^*(W_U + \Delta, W_N + \Delta))) \frac{\bar{d}'(W_U + \Delta)}{\bar{d}(W_U + \Delta)} \right. \\ &\left. \qquad - g(\bar{\Pi}^*(W_U + \Delta, W_N + \Delta))\bar{d}(W_U + \Delta) \right] \end{aligned}}{\begin{aligned} &\frac{R}{S} - (1 - G(\bar{\Pi}^*(W_U + \Delta, W_N + \Delta))) \\ &+ (W_U + \Delta - Z - W_N - \Delta)g(\bar{\Pi}^*(W_U + \Delta, W_N + \Delta)) \\ &\qquad\qquad\qquad\qquad\qquad\qquad\qquad \bar{d}(W_N + \Delta) \end{aligned}}$$

$$(A2.3)$$

But since $\bar{d}' = d'$, $\bar{\Pi}^*(W_U + \Delta, W_N + \Delta) = \Pi^*(W_U, W_N)$, $\bar{d}(W_U + \Delta) = d(W_U)$ and $\bar{d}(W_N + \Delta) = d(W_N)$, (A2.3) can be rewritten as

$$\left. \frac{d(W_N + \Delta)}{d(W_U + \Delta)} \right|_{IC} = - \frac{\begin{aligned} &1 - G(\Pi^*(W_U, W_N)) + (W_U - Z - W_N) \\ &\left[(1 - G(\Pi^*(W_U, W_N))) \frac{d'(W_U)}{d(W_U)} \right. \\ &\left. \qquad - g(\Pi^*(W_U, W_N))d(W_U) \right] \end{aligned}}{\begin{aligned} &\frac{R}{S} - (1 - G(\Pi^*(W_U, W_N))) \\ &+ (W_U - Z - W_N)g(\Pi^*(W_U, W_N))d(W_N) \end{aligned}}$$

Proof that the more convex the demand curve, the more likely is a union equilibrium to exist:

The formal proposition: Suppose a convex demand curve, $\tilde{d}(W)$, is tangent to a linear demand curve $d(W)$ at the competitive equilibrium $[R/S, W_C]$. If a union equilibrium exists for $\tilde{d}(W)$, then it exists for $d(W)$ although the converse is not true.

First, the opportunity locus for $\tilde{d}(W)$ lies above that for $d(W)$ (except at $W_U = W_C$). To see this, assume the opposite. Then for every given W_U, $W_N > \tilde{W}_N$. From (1),

$$[1 - G(\tilde{\Pi}^*(W_U, \tilde{W}_N))]\tilde{d}(W_U) + G(\tilde{\Pi}^*(W_U, \tilde{W}_N))\tilde{d}(\tilde{W}_N) = R/S$$

$$= [1 - G(\Pi^*(W_U, W_N))]d(W_U) + G(\Pi^*(W_U, W_N))d(W_N) \qquad \text{(A2.4)}$$

But if $W_N > \tilde{W}_N$, then $d(W_N) < d(\tilde{W}_N) < \tilde{d}(\tilde{W}_N)$ and then $G(\tilde{\Pi}^*(W_U, \tilde{W}_N)) > G(\Pi^*(W_U, W_N))$ therefore

$$G(\tilde{\Pi}^*(W_U, \tilde{W}_N))\tilde{d}(\tilde{W}_N) > G(\Pi^*(W_U, W_N))d(W_N).$$

This, along with (A2.4), implies that

$$[1 - G(\tilde{\Pi}^*(W_U, \tilde{W}_N))]\tilde{d}(W_U) < [1 - G(\Pi^*(W_U, W_N))]d(W_U)$$

or that $1 < \tilde{G} - G$ which is a contradiction since $0 \leq G, \tilde{G} \leq 1$. Also, the critical indifference curve for $\tilde{d}(W)$ lies below that for $d(W)$: Assume the opposite, $\tilde{W}_N > W_N$. Then from AI, $\tilde{P} < P$. But $\tilde{d}(W_U) > d(W_U)$ and $\tilde{W}_N > W_N$ implies that $(1 - \tilde{G}) < (1 - G)$ or $\tilde{G} > G$ which implies $\tilde{W}_N < W_N$ which is a contradiction.

3: As the cost of running the union rises, the probability of obtaining a union job tends to fall: From (4),

$$dP = \frac{-S}{R} g(\ )[\Pi_1^* dW_U + \Pi_2^* dW_N] + \frac{S}{R}[1 - G(\ )]d'(W_U)dW_U$$

$$= \frac{-S}{R} g(\ )[d(W_U)dW_U - d(W_N)dW_N]$$

$$+ \frac{S}{R}[1 - G(\ )]d'(W_U)dW_U.$$

where $dW_N = (dW_N/dW_U)\,|_{OL}\, dW_U$. The second term is always negative. For much of the opportunity locus $dW_U > 0$ implies $dW_N < 0$. For the part where $dW_N > 0$, it is smaller than dW_U so dP tends to be negative. Thus, an increase in operating costs lowers the likelihood of a union equilibrium, but if one does exist, raises the optimal union wage, wage differential, and tends to lower the proportion in the union.

4: Proof that a union that can choose price and quantity, sets quantity equal to R/S (even though this affects the wage in the nonunion sector and the probability of being beaten by the firm) and this results in $W_N = W_C$ $\forall$ W_U;

Define l_U and l_N as the labor per firm in the union and nonunion sector. Then the firm, presented with wage-quantity demand (W_U, l_U) compares the profits associated with it against that of (W_N, l_N). If this difference is smaller than C_i the firm fights (and defeats) the union. The profit function now depends upon quantity as well as price and we define

$$\Delta\Pi(W_U, W_N; l_U, l_N) \equiv \Pi(W_N; l_N) - \Pi(W_U; l_U)$$

$$= \left\{ \int_0^{l_N} [d^{-1}(l)]dl - l_N W_N - \text{fixed cost} \right\}$$

$$- \left\{ \int_0^{l_U} [d^{-1}(l)]dl - l_U W_U - \text{fixed cost} \right\} \quad \text{(A4.1)}$$

$$= \int_{l_U}^{l_N} [d^{-1}(l)]dl + l_U W_U - l_N W_N.$$

For any $[W_U, W_N; l_U, l_N]$ there will be $1 - G[\Delta\Pi(W_U, W_N; l_U, l_N)]$ union firms. The unions problem, then, is to select W_U, l_U and implicitly W_N, l_N so as to maximize

$$P(W_U - Z) + (1 - P)W_N \quad \text{(A4.2)}$$

subject to the constraint that

$$[1 - G[\Delta\Pi(W_U, W_N; l_U, l_N)]]l_U + G(\ )l_N = R/S \quad \text{(A4.3)}$$

where

$$P = \frac{S}{R}(1 - G)l_U. \quad \text{(A4.4)}$$

Forming the Lagrangean:

$$L = P(W_U - Z) + (1 - P)W_N$$

$$+ \lambda\{[1 - G(\ )]l_U + G(\ )l_N - R/S\}. \quad \text{(A4.5)}$$

Since

$$\frac{\partial \Delta \Pi}{\partial W_U} = l_U; \frac{\partial \Delta \Pi}{\partial W_U} = -l_N;$$

$$\frac{\partial \Delta \Pi}{\partial l_U} = W_U - d^{-1}(l_U); \qquad (A4.6)$$

$$\frac{\partial \Delta \Pi}{\partial l_N} = d^{-1}(l_N) - W_N,$$

The first order conditions for (A4.5) are

$$\frac{\partial L}{\partial W_U} = (W_U - Z - W_N)\frac{\partial P}{\partial W_U} + P + \lambda[(l_N - l_U)(G')l_U] = 0 \quad (A4.7a)$$

$$\frac{\partial L}{\partial W_N} = (W_U - Z - W_N)\frac{\partial P}{\partial W_N} - P - \lambda[(l_N - l_U)(G')l_N] = 0 \quad (A4.7b)$$

$$\frac{\partial L}{\partial l_U} = (W_U - Z - W_N)\frac{\partial P}{\partial l_U}$$

$$+ \lambda[1 - G + (l_N - l_U)(G')(W_U - d^{-1}(l_U)] = 0 \qquad (A4.7c)$$

$$\frac{\partial L}{\partial l_N} = (W_U - Z - W_N)\frac{\partial P}{\partial l_N}$$

$$+ \lambda[G + (l_N - l_U)(G')(d^{-1}(l_N) - W_N)] = 0 \qquad (A4.7d)$$

$$\frac{\partial L}{\partial \lambda} = (1 - G(\ ))l_U + G(\ )l_N - R/S = 0. \qquad (A4.7e)$$

Note from (A4.4) that

$$\frac{\partial P}{\partial W_U} = \frac{-S}{R} l_U(G')l_U$$

and that

$$\frac{\partial P}{\partial W_N} = \frac{S}{R} l_U(G')l_N. \qquad (A4.8)$$

Rearranging (A4.7a,b) and dividing (A4.7a) by (A4.7b) gives

$$l_U = l_N. \qquad (A4.9)$$

Using (A4.7e) implies that $l_U = l_N = R/S$. Also since $d(W_N) = R/S$, $W_N = W_C$.

5: Proof that more inelastic demand changes neither the probability of a union or the nonunion wage where unions can select price and quantity.

Consider two labor demand curves, $d(W)$ and $\tilde{d}(W)$ such that $d(W_C)$ = $\tilde{d}(W_C)$ = R/S but $|\,d'\,| < |\,\tilde{d}'\,|$ as shown. Given that $l_N = l_U = R/S$, W_N = W_C (see Appendix 4), the opportunity locus is a horizontal line at W_N = W_C. Therefore, to show that the probability of a union does not change when going from $d(W)$ to $\tilde{d}(W)$ it is sufficient to show that the indifference curves do not shift:

The equations of a indifference curve producing utility level K given demand for labor $d(W)$ and $\tilde{d}(W)$, respectively are

$$W_N = \frac{K - P(W_U - Z)}{(1 - P)} \tag{A5.1a}$$

$$\tilde{W}_N = \frac{K - \tilde{P}(W_U - Z)}{(1 - \tilde{P})} \tag{A5.2b}$$

where

$$P = \frac{S(1 - G(\Delta\Pi))R/S}{R} = 1 - G(\Delta\Pi)$$

and

$$\tilde{P} = 1 - G(\tilde{\Delta}\Pi).$$

Since $l_U = l_N = R/S$, $\Delta\Pi$ (defined in Appendix 4) is $(R/S)(W_U - W_N)$ so that (A5.1a,b) becomes

$$W_N = \frac{K - [1 - G[(R/S)(W_U - W_N)]](W_U - Z)}{G[(R/S)(W_U - W_N)]} \tag{A5.2a}$$

$$\tilde{W}_N = \frac{K - [1 - G[(R/S)(\tilde{W}_U - W_N)]](W_U - Z)}{G[(R/S)(\tilde{W}_U - W_N)]} \tag{A5.2b}$$

Substitution of (A5.2a) into (A5.2b) yields $W_N = \tilde{W}_N$ so indifference curves are identical. Profits are lower for the firm with the more elastic demand, but it is the *difference* between profits with the union and profits without and this difference is independent of demand elasticity when labor employed is held constant at the competitive equilibrium.

Corollary: Since indifference curves and opportunity locus are invariant with respect to $d(W)$, $\tilde{d}(W)$, it follows that optimal W_U is the same in both cases.

Proof: Immediate.

ACKNOWLEDGEMENTS

The author gratefully acknowledges the helpful comments of K. Abraham, G. Becker, R. Hall, V. Lazear, J. Mincer, G. Neumann, P. Pashigian, M. Reder, S. Rosen and R. Topel. Financial support was provided by the National Science Foundation.

NOTES

1. The relevant supply of labor is that pool over which employers view workers as perfect substitutes in production. This is narrower than A. M. Ross's (1948) "orbit of coercive comparison," or John Dunlop's (1944) "wage contours."

2. It is simplifying, but inessential, to assume that $g(C_i)$ does not depend upon $W_U - W_N$ directly. Workers might strive harder for the union if $W_U - W_N$, or more exactly the expected utility gain, is larger.

3. This subsumes all bargaining problems. Thus, Reder's (1952) notions of fairness and Stevens' (1958) early description of bargaining, as well as more modern bargaining models (Farber, 1978; Crawford, 1979; Atherton, 1973) are implied.

4. Johnson and Miezkowski (1970) and Diewert (1974) offer alternative two-sector models of unionism. There, the union wage is exogenous and the purpose is to trace various wage choices through the rest of the economy in a general equilibrium framework. This model is interested in the way in which spillovers affect the *choice* of a union wage.

5. Most of what has gone before, attempts to limit the relevant population to some subset of R. For example, Reder (1959) focuses on "present members." Also, Dertouzos and Pencavel (1980) estimate a wage and employment relationship using data from the International Typographical Union. This is not equivalent to my indifference curve, however, because it abstracts from spillover effects of W_U on W_N and changes in the opportunity locus over time.

6. Even in the pathological case where $g(0)$, Z, and $D(W_U)$ are sufficiently large so that the indifference curve is initially positive, it will rapidly become negative because when $W_U = W_N + Z$,

$$\frac{dW_N}{dW_U}\bigg|_{IC} = \frac{-P}{1-p} < 0.$$

7. Stiglitz (1980) obtains a similar result in a different context. He shows that convexity affects whether a random taxation scheme dominates a nonrandom one.

8. In this context, Epple, Hotz and Zelenitz (1980) formalize the argument that in high variance demand industries, the union performs a risk pooling function which reduces the necessity of formal layoffs. The union acts as the hiring hall and assigns workers accordingly. Fluctuation in an individual firm's demand does not result in a "layoff," as the result.

9. There are additional second-order effects. There is no guarante that the reduction in output by union firms plus the increase in output by nonunion firms will yield the net reduction in total output required as we move up the product demand curve. This will require a change in S, the number of firms in the industry.

10. Rosen (1969) treats this issue.

11. Freeman and Medoff (1981a) also find very small threat effects in most circumstances.

12. Recent work by Mincer (1981) makes a similar point, but exploits a different mechanism. Mincer points out that altering the probability of obtaining a job in the union sector affects the expected return to queuing for jobs in that sector and affects spillovers to the

nonunion sector. Depending upon the nature of these spillovers, the observed wage differential may overstate the true effect of unions. He, too, concludes that there is no straightforward relationship between wage differentials and power. The main difference between his approach and this one is that in this model queuing for union jobs is done while holding a nonunion job so there is never any unemployment. Mincer's queuing takes place while the worker is unemployed.

13. Lazear (1979) and Carmichael (1981) use this notion in other contexts.

14. See Freeman (19   ) for evidence in support of this prediction.

15. This assumes that $\bar{A}_0 - \bar{A}_Y$ does not vary across occupations.

16. In principle, there could be a larger number of age groups than two, and one extreme specification would allow a group for each age level, say measured in years, so that $\bar{A}_0$ and $\bar{A}_Y$ would be replaced by $A_{18}, A_{19}, \ldots A_{65}$.

17. *Proof:*

$$W_C < (W_U - Z)P_Y + W_N(1 - P_Y)$$

implies that

$$2W_C < (W_U - Z)2P_Y + W_N(2)(1 - P_Y)$$

Since $(W_U - Z) > W_N$ the convex combination $(W_U - Z)\lambda + W_N(1 - \lambda)$ increases in λ. Since $P_Y + P_0 > 2P_Y$ pt follows that $2W_C < (W_U - Z)2P_Y + W_N(2)(1 - P_Y) < (W_U - Z)(P_Y + P_0) + W_N[(1 - P_Y) + (1 - P_0)]$, so (29) is sufficient for (30).

18. *Proof:*

Equation (30) is

$$2W_C < (W_U - Z)(P_Y + P_0) + W_N[(1 - P_Y) + (1 - P_0)]$$

This implies

$$W_C < (W_U - Z)(P_Y + P_0)/2 + W_N[(1 - P_Y) + (1 - P_0)]/2$$

The r.h.s. is a convex combination of $(W_U - Z)$, W_N with $(W_U - Z) > W_N$. Now since

$$P_0 \geqslant P_Y, P_0 \geqslant (P_0 + P_Y)/2$$

therefore

$(W_U - Z)P_0 + W_N(1 - P_0)$

$$\geqslant (W_U - Z)[(P_0 + P_Y)/2] + W_N[(1 - P_0) + (1 - P_Y)]/2 > W_C$$

so (30) is sufficient for (31).

19. *Proof:*
Young vote for the union if (30) holds, i.e., if

$$2W_C < (W_U - Z)(P_Y + P_0) + W_N[(1 - P_Y) + (1 - P_0)]$$

substituting in (19) and (20) this can be rewritten as

$$2W_C < (W_U - Z)(2P) + W_N[2(1 - P)]$$

or

$$W_C < (W_U - Z)P + W_N(1 - P)$$

which is the condition for a single-period lived worker to prefer the union equilibrium [derivable from Eq. (12)].

20. See Farber (1978) for discussion of some basic aspects of union equilibrium in a median voter world.

REFERENCES

Ashenfelter, O. (1972), "Racial Discrimination and Trade Unionism." *Journal of Political Economy* 80, pt. 1(3):435–464.
——— (1976), "Union Relative Wage Effects: New Evidence and a Survey of Their-Implications for Wage Inflation," Princeton University.
Atherton, W. (1973), *Theory of Union Bargaining Goals*. Princeton, N.J.: Princeton University Press.
Blau, F., and L. Kahn (1980), "The Exit-Voice Model of Unionism: Some Further Evidence on Layoffs," University of Illinois.
Bloch, Farrell and Mark Kuskin (1978), "Wage Determination in the Union and Nonunion Sectors." *Industrial and Labor Relations Review* 31(2):183–192.
Brown, C., and J. Medoff (1978), "Trade Unions in the Production Process." *Journal of Political Economy* 86(3):355–378.
Carlton, D. (1979), "Planning and Market Structure." In J. J. McCall (ed.), *The Economics of Uncertainty*.
Carmichael, L. (1981), "Firm Specific Human Capital and Seniority Rules." Conference Paper No. 101, National Bureau of Economic Research, February.
Cohen, K. J., and R. M. Cyert (1975), *Theory of the Firm: Resource Allocation in a Market Economy,* 2nd ed. Englewood Cliffs, N.J.: Prentice-Hall.
Crawford, V. P. (1979), "On Compulsory Arbitration Schemes." *Journal of Political Economy* 87(1):131–160.
Dertouzos, J. N., and J. H. Pencavel (1980), "Wage Determinants Under Trade Unionism: The International Typographical Union," Stanford University.
Diewert, W. C. (1974), "The Effects of Unionization on Wages and Employment: A General Equilibrium Analysis." *Economic Inquiry* 12(Sept.):319–339.
Dunlop, J. C. (1944), *Wage Determination Under Trade Unions*. New York and London: Macmillan.
Epple, D., V. J. Hotz, and A. Zelenitz (1980), "Employment Contracts, Risk Sharing and the Role of Unions." Working Paper No. 70-79-80, Carnegie-Mellon University.
Farber, H. (1978), "Bargaining Theory, Wage Outcomes, and Occurrence of Strikes: An Economic Analysis." *American Economic Review* 68(June):262–271.
——— (1979), "Individual Preferences and Union Wage Determination: The Case of the United Mine Workers." *Journal of Political Economy* 86:923–942.
Fellner, W. (1947), "Prices and Wages Under Bilateral Monopoly." *Quarterly Journal of Economics* (August).
Freeman, R. (1976), "Individual Mobility and Union Voice in the Labor Market." *American Economic Review* 66 (May):361–368.
Freeman, R., and J. Medoff (1978), "The Effect of Trade Unionism on Fringe Benefits." Working Paper No. 292, National Bureau of Economic Research.
——— (1980), "The Effect of Unionism on Worker Attachment to Firms." *Journal of Labor Research* 1(Spring):29–61.
——— (1981a), "The Impact of the Percentage Organized on Union and Nonunion Wages." *Review of Economics and Statistics* 63(4):561–572.
——— (1981b), "The Impact of Collective Bargainings: Illusion or Reality?" NBER no. 258.
——— (1982), "Substitution Between Production Labor and Other Inputs in Unionized and Nonunionized Manufacturing." *Review of Economics and Statistics* 64(2):220–233.

Hall, R. E., and D. Lilien (1979), "Efficient Wage Bargains Under Uncertain Supply and Demand." *American Economic Review* 69(Dec.):868–879.

Hicks, J. R. (1966), *The Theory of Wages.* London: Macmillan.

Johnson, H. G., and P. Miezkowski (1970), "The Effects of Unionization on the Distribution of Income." *Quarterly Journal of Economics* 84(4):539–561.

Kahn, Lawrence M. (1978), "The Effect of Unions on the Earnings of Nonunion Workers." *Industrial and Labor Relations Review* 31(Jan.):205–216.

Lazear, E. (1979), "Why Is There Mandatory Retirement?" *Journal of Political Economy* (Oct.):1261–1264.

Lewis, H. G. (1963), *Unionism and Relative Wages in the U.S.* Chicago: University of Chicago Press.

Leontief, W. (1946), "The Pure Theory of the Guarranteed Annual Wage Contract." *Journal of Political Economy* 56(February):76–79.

Marshall, A. P. (1922), *Principles,* Book V, Chapter VI.

Medoff, J. (1979), "Layoffs and Alternatives Under Trade Unions in United States Manufacturing." *American Economic Review* 69(June):380–395.

Mincer, J. (1982), "The Economics of Wage Floors." *American Economic Review,* Papers and Proceedings of September 1980 Meetings.

Pigou, A. C. (1962), *Economics of Welfare,* Book IV, Chapter V.

Rees, A. (1962), *The Economics of Trade Unions.* Chicago: University of Chicago Press.

Reder, M. (1952), "A Theory of Union Wage Policy." *Review of Economics and Statistics* 34:34–45.

——— (1959), "Job Scarcity and the Nature of Union Power." *Industrial and Labor Relations Review* 13:349–362.

Rosen, S. (1969), "Trade Union Power, Threat Effects and the Extent of Organization." *Review of Economics and Statistics.*

——— (1970), "Unionism and Occupational Wage Structure in the U.S." *I.E.R.* 11(2):269–286.

——— (1974), "Hedonic Prices and Implicit Markets: Product Differentiation in Pure Competition." *Journal of Political Economy* 82(Jan./Feb.):34–55.

Ross, A. M. (1948), *Theory of Union Wage Policy.* Berkeley: University of California Press.

Sayles, L., and George Strauss (1967), *The Local Union.* New York: Harcourt Brace and World.

Stiglitz, J. (1980), "Utilitarianism and Horizontal Equity: The Case for Random Taxation." Mimeo.

Weinstein, P. A. (1964), "The Featherbedding Problem." *American Economic Review* 54:145–152

DISCUSSION

Armen Alchian

This conference is the first, so far as I know, to recognize the integration of the field of industrial and economic organization with that of the field of labor. Too long these fields have gone their separate ways. Yet each analyzes basically similar issues: how to arrange transactions among teams of inputs so as to encourage "specific" investments. In the past decade, in both fields the dominant view was that of pure competition (atomistic buyers and sellers with no individual perception of any effect on price) versus monopoly (either a seller with perceived effects on price or a seller protected from market competition by contrived restraints on potential competitors). The monopoly union and the monopolistic firm were the stereotypes. The union's contrived monopoly was often regarded as desirable to protect the employees; the firm with contrived monopoly or even with noncontrived market power was regarded as undesirable. And there matters seemed to sit.

However, recently academics in these fields have begun to look into the other field. The seminal work by Oliver Williamson, for example, on

New Approaches to Labor Unions.
Research in Labor Economics, Supplement 2, pages 97–98.

the contractual arrangements with the firm, and indeed of the meaning of the firm, has induced applications of those principles to the employee–employer relationship. Thus the union, whether a company or an independent union, is viewed as an agency for monitoring contractual performance. When employees invest in becoming more specific to an employer so that idiosyncratic situations with impacted information permit opportunistic behavior by any employer, the potential victims seek prior arrangements to avoid exploitation by expropriation of values of investments specific to the employer. The union serves that purpose. It is not to be viewed solely as a monopolizing device nor as a device protecting employees from market competition. It is a monitoring agent of investors who have made investments specific to one employer, or who would make more such investments if they have a greater assurance of protection of opportunistic expropriation of that investment value by the party to whom the investment is specific.

These bring benefits to both employers and employees—employers benefit by being able to assure employees of contractual fulfillment—that are not manifest by differences in wages between union and nonunion members. Indeed, union money wages may be lower because the non-monetary rewards, which usually are more difficult to monitor without an agent, will become a larger component of the pay package. Indeed many labor contracts can be interpreted as transactions aiding employer-specific investments by employees. For example, employment clauses like "first negotiation/first refusal" or "right of first refusal" or "tenure" or "wage rate fixity" can, under the new recognition of potential expropriation of idiosyncractic or specific investment quasi-rents, be shown to be beneficial to both employers and employees.

This conference is therefore overdue. Next time, a larger number of specialists in industrial organization will certainly be present. For now, it is gratifying to have this opportunity to speed the exchange of ideas.

PART II

THEORIES OF LABOR UNIONS IN

THE PUBLIC SECTOR

PUBLIC EMPLOYEE ORGANIZATIONS AS POLITICAL FIRMS

Michael M. Kurth

ABSTRACT

In this paper I view public employee organizations as political firms. Politicians must spend to gain votes, using some combination of direct or general services. The efficient combination will depend on the relative cost of such transactions, with public employees organized to reduce these costs. Political competition insures that efficient organizations emerge and, until the 1960s, prevented these organizations from exercising "union power." The emergence of militant unionism in the mid-sixties is explained by the intervention of state and federal politicians in the local political process: When local politicians controlled local resources, they bore the full cost of militancy; with state and federal intervention, responsibility is obfuscated and those dealing with the militants may bare only a small part of the costs. In such an environment, militant unions have the ability to (1) obtain funds otherwise unavailable to local politicians; (2) "rationalize" public administration by concentrating authority and shifting personnel functions from

New Approaches to Labor Unions.
Research in Labor Economics, Supplement 2, pages 101–125.
Copyright © 1983 by JAI Press Inc.
All rights of reproduction in any form reserved.
ISBN: 0-89232-265-9

101

civil service commissions to the bargaining process; and (3) reduce transactions costs between local employees and state or federal politicians.

I. INTRODUCTION

Perhaps the most significant development in labor relations during the
past 20 years has been the emergence of public employees as a force in
the otherwise lethargic union movement. As union penetration of the
private sector dropped to its lowest level since 1939 (approximately 20
percent), once-docile public employees flocked to join militant labor organizations. Today, public employees belong to some of the largest and
most vocal unions in the country; 3 of the AFL–CIO's 12 largest affiliates
operate primarily in the public sector; the National Education Association
(NEA) is second only to the Teamsters in size among the independent
unions; and fully one-fourth of all union members work for a government.
Making these developments even more dramatic is the suddenness with
which they took place: in just five years (1963–1968) the number of work-
days reported lost due to strikes by government employees jumped from
13,000 to almost $2\frac{1}{2}$ million.[1]

What accounts for the sudden surge of unionism in the public sector?
A potpourri of explanations have been offered, but none has gained wide
acceptance. As Lloyd G. Reynolds states in *Labor Economics and Labor
Relations*: "The reasons for rapid growth in public employee unionism
during the sixties and seventies are unclear."[2] The purpose of this paper
is to suggest a new approach to public-sector unionism which can explain
this sudden militancy and, just as important, why politicians/employers
were tolerant, even supportive, of this activity.

The present explanations can be placed in three categories. (A) those
which suggest a change in preferences, for example, a "new breed" of
public employee,[3] more enlightened politicians who rejected the doctrine
of "employer sovereignty,"[4] and/or greater acceptance of unions by the
general public;[5] (B) those which suggest cost and benefits changed in favor
of joining a union as, for instance, inflation ate into real wages,[6] the demand for public services increased,[7] or public-sector personnel practices
lagged behind those of the private sector;[8] and (C) those which rely on
a deus ex machina in the form of union organizers from the private sector,[9]
court decisions,[10] or Kennedy's executive order 10988.[11] The few empirical studies which have been done have primarily succeeded in convincing observers that private-sector models are inappropriate for explaining public-sector labor relations.[12]

In making distinctions between public- and private-sector labor relations one area has generally been overlooked. Unionism was largely im-

posed on the private sector whereas it developed spontaneously in the public sector. When the Wagner Act was passed in 1935, the union movement showed little prospect of expanding beyond its 5 percent base in the private sector;[13] in the public sector, which was not covered by federal labor legislation, it was the politician qua employer who in many cases opened the door for unionization and, in others, decided neither to prosecute nor to punish militant activity.[14] This is tantamount to coal mine operators inviting the UMW to organize their employees. Consider the maxim: "Institutions which emerge voluntarily tend to be efficient;" what is needed is an understanding of how public-sector unions can be politically efficient (in a Paretian sense), permitting both the politician and the public employees to gain.

Distinction must also be made between the different levels of government. The traditional view is that the federal government is monopolistic while state and local governments are competitive.[15] Yet it is at the local level that unions have been most influential; state employees account for only about 5 percent of all strike activity and federal employees virtually never strike. This is contrary to experience in the private sector, violating what Rees has called "probably the most important implication" of Marshall's theory of derived demand[16]—that the more competitive markets will have less successful unions. Among local governments, unionization is greatest in the older cities of the Northeast and North Central states. These areas have been declining in population and tax base, some of which can undoubtedly be attributed to the unions. But the trend was evident even before unions entered the picture, suggesting that unions in the public sector do best in declining markets.

In explaining these developments two questions need to be answered: (1) How can public employee organizations benefit both their membership and politicians? (2) What developments suddenly made unions the efficient form of organization? In Section II, I suggest that public employees are valued for the votes they generate through either direct services and political activity (patronage) or indirect, general services (the merit system). The best way to view the public employee organization is as a firm which reduces the cost of political transactions by monitoring compliance and metering performance. In section III, I apply this model to the three major forms of public employee organization: patronage, the merit system, and unionism. In examining the history of these organizations, it is clear that public employees cannot act vis-à-vis the authority of the state in the same manner that private employees, under the aegis of labor relations laws, can act vis-à-vis the private employer. In examining the turmoil of the sixties, the clearest lesson is that these organizations are competitive and must bid for their membership. Section IV examines the federal involvement in local affairs which developed during the sixties, suggesting some reasons why this might have made unions the efficient form of organization during that period. My conclusion is that unions emerged spontaneously in the public sector because they were politically efficient.

II. THE AGENCY PRINCIPLE

In labor relations it is traditional to justify unions on the basis of inherent conflict between capital and labor; union monopoly power offsetting employer monopsony power; bringing democracy to workers increasingly alienated by the division of labor; or "taking wages out of competition." But none of these concepts readily fits the public sector, where there is no capitalist, no labor monopsony, employees *do* have a voice in determining management policy (some would say an undemocratically loud one), and wages have traditionally been above the market rate. For many, including some who support private-sector unions, this reduces public-sector unionism to a simple power play by employees intent on grabbing monopoly rents.[17]

David Lewin has been critical of the "union power" thesis because it tends to deemphasize, even ignore, the "conditions that make for potentially diverse patterns of labor relations." He argues that public-sector unions display a variety of objectives: some are principally concerned with grievances, some with management decisions, some with general policy, and some with controlling the supply of labor. This suggests that "the consequences of public-sector bargaining will vary over time owing to changes in environmental conditions" (e.g., intergovernmental revenue transfers, subcontracting and statutory provisions), a possibility that seems hardly to have been entertained by advocates of the "union power" thesis.[18]

Recently more attention has been paid to the nonconflict aspects of private-sector unionism. In particular, the work of Brown, et al.[19] suggests that employee organizations can affect management structure, work relationships, and productivity, increasing the last by rationalizing the first two. Are unions a sweet-and-sour package for employers—part productivity gain, part bargaining loss? If so, one would expect unions to be popular among employers in the more competitive industries where the union's monopoly power is slight but its rationalizing power remains intact. Yet it is an inescapable observation that employers, and particularly those in competitive markets, are not fond of having their employees unionized. Does this invalidate the theory? Joe Reid says no: Employers do want unions, or at least they did until the Wagner Act forbade "company unions" in 1935. According to Reid, "there is evidence that employers who would profit most from formal hierarchical management (employers who employed many at routine jobs) did want unions. 'Company unions' were widespread in the 1920s.''[20] Such unions, sans the "right to strike," performed a valuable service by monitoring a firm's performance and communicating employee preferences. It is not unions, per se, which firms resist—it is the particular species bred of our labor laws. The public sector offers an excellent test of Reid's hypothesis because public employees were not covered by the Wagner Act and "company unions" continued to exist.

What constructive role can unions play within the firm? Modern understanding of the firm is based on the relative efficiency of different exchange relationships, not the class struggle and conflict (labor vs. capital) of classical economics. It is recognized that certain transactions can take place at lower cost if they are organized within the firm and certain arrangements, such as team production, require monitoring. Individual production, for instance, allows the payment to act as an incentive to the producer/supplier: no production, no payment. In team production it is possible for some persons to shirk, putting in little effort yet receiving their share of the payment. For efficiency wages must be equated to the marginal value of each individual's production, and setting the proper wages requires efficient monitoring. Savings within the firm also arise because information can be shared between transactors (fewer negotiations are necessary and there is less searching over price), and contracts for oft-repeated exchanges can be more readily enforced. Costs arise due to the necessity of monitoring the production and exchange agreements, with the efficient firm expanding its operations up to the point where the cost of organizing and monitoring one more transaction within the firm is greater than or equal to the cost of either going to the open market or organizing a new firm.[21]

The principals to these transactions will require the services of an agent: someone who can monitor performance and has the authority to correctly structure incentives and terminate agreements not being fulfilled. The owners of capital will require agents (managers) to look after their interests, and the owners of labor will require agents (union representatives) to look after theirs, otherwise much effort would be wasted as both principals checked the performance of the other. For an agent to properly carry out his activities either he must be a residual claimant to the savings which result from his actions or he must be in a competitive situation where failure to act properly will result in his replacement.

This model can be readily adapted to the public sector where politicians spend to gain votes. The efficient politician (i.e., the winning politician) will take only those actions which gain more votes than they cost, and government expenditures will be expanded to the point where the votes lost from an additional dollar of taxation are just equal to the votes gained from spending that dollar. Such spending can be either direct, as when transfer payments are made and direct services are provided, or indirect, as when general services are provided.[22] Public employees may be involved in both types. These exchanges—"if you vote for me, I will do this for you"—require extensive monitoring to insure that political promises are kept and that votes are cast as indicated.

The object of the political organization is to reduce the cost of making political exchanges. Both politicians and voters can use the services of an agent to monitor the other's performance and, although all such transactions need not take place within the "firm," those with the lowest cost are the most likely to be made, ceteris paribus. To realize gains for its membership, the public employee organization must reduce the cost of at least one of the two types of transactions, thus allowing the politician to also gain, or at least not be made worse off. Under perfect political competition, only such organizations will survive.

III. PUBLIC EMPLOYEE ORGANIZATIONS

In the public sector one problem the researcher encounters is the diversity of employee organizations. In the private sector, unions are often equated with "organized labor," and this may not be too far off the mark; employer assistance to a union is forbidden under Section 10(c) of the Wagner Act,[23] with the result that even weak organizations adopt confrontational tactics. In the bargaining which follows, the rights and responsibilities of both parties are carefully spelled out in the labor laws. In the absence of such legislation, public-sector organizations exhibit much more diversity and it would be a mistake to equate "organization" with unionization and collective bargaining.[24] For example, the Chicago firefighters formed the backbone of Richard Daley's political "machine" and few persons would suggest they were "unorganized," yet they had no formal agreement with the city until after Jane Byrne was elected mayor.

Nevertheless, public employee organizations can be loosely placed in one of three general categories: the political club which functions as part of a patronage system; the civil service league or association which is concerned with "professionalism;" and the union, which attempts to bargain collectively and asserts a "right to strike."

A. Patronage

Patronage has been described as an incentive system—"a political currency with which to 'purchase' political activity and political responses."[25] Jobs are the mainstay of the patronage machine, with "patronage jobs" defined as "all those posts, distributed at the discretion of political leaders, the pay for which is greater than the value of the public services performed.''[26] Employment thus becomes a "naked political quid pro quo," with persons hired and paid on the basis of how many friends and relatives they can get to the polls with the "correct" vote. Typically, machine-style politics emphasizes face-to-face contact with voters. A city is divided into wards, with a ward leader assigned to monitor and meter the political activity in each ward and a "boss" selected from among the ward leaders to supervise and coordinate the efforts of the entire machine.[27] Doorbells are rung, help is offered, and charity is dispensed along with the less innocent political favors, direct payoffs, and intimidation. Although known for corruption, some good may also be accomplished. For example, such activities are usually aimed at the lower-income ethnic groups and have been credited with facilitating the assimilation of millions of immigrants in the past.[28]

For such an organization to be successful, the cost of buying votes through it must be lower than the cost of buying votes through some other organization, special interest group, or the public at large. One explanation for the use of jobs as "currency" is that they facilitate monitoring of the political exchange. With the secret ballot, the politician has no way of knowing that the votes he pays for are actually cast and, from the perspective of the voter, campaign promises are notoriously unreliable. The patronage job acts as both a reward and an incentive in lieu of a legally enforceable contract between the buyer and the seller; it is a payoff for past performance which can only be retained through additional effort.[29] The use of this contract reduces the transaction costs associated with direct political exchange. But even with such a contract, turning out the vote remains a team effort with plenty of opportunities for free riding. The purpose of the "machine" organization of public employees is to overcome this free rider problem through close monitoring and metering of performance.

Some of the conditions under which patronage might flourish are: (1) a relatively high cost for exchanges with the public at large or special interest groups; (2) general public services have a relatively low political value; (3) there is little public accountability by public officials; and (4) individual services are highly valued. The first, the cost of exchanges with the public, will depend on the cost of assessing public preferences for services, communicating the proposed exchange, and monitoring the voting behavior of the public. Heterogeneous populations, language barriers, and secret ballots will increase these costs; the organization of special interest groups will lower them. General public services such as roads, public health and sanitation, law enforcement, and education will only have political value if voters are sufficiently concentrated and educated so that they can be easily organized to deliver blocs of votes in return for such services. Services which are difficult to measure will increase the cost of metering the politician's performance, as will language barriers and deliberate deception. Racial equality, for example, may be publicly pursued while privately eschewed, the "privacy" of the patronage machine providing more efficient channels for communicating true intent. Finally, individual services will be more highly valued by persons with special needs (i.e., immigrants, the handicapped, veterans, and minorities), where individual preferences for public goods vary widely, and where information is costly and bureaucratic "red tape" needs to be cut.

In this country, the first "spontaneous" transition in public employee organization came about in the 1820s as patronage—"the spoils system"—replaced the "semiaristocracy" and professionalism of the earlier civil service. Under Jeffersonian–Republican politics public offices were largely filled on the basis of merit. According to Leonard White, "no president before 1829 undertook to buy leadership or legislation with patronage,"[30] but there was a careful distribution of offices according to lexicographic preferences: among equally qualified candidates, those with the proper political affiliation would be chosen. One explanation for this could be that the relatively small, homogeneous electorate made it easy to organize special interest groups; voting could be closely monitored, as could political performance; and the services they wanted were relatively easy to meter: roads, canals, postal delivery, defense, and frontier-style justice.

Those advocating the "spoils system" saw themselves as champions of "the people" against "special interest" and "believed that 'the people,' to prevail against organized wealth, must be led by bosses and kept in line by the spoils system."[31] But regardless of their declarations, the fact is they were politically successful, electing Andrew Jackson as president in 1828 and holding sway in national politics until the 1890s. The Jacksonians were riding a wave of political change. The population had been expanding rapidly westward; eight new states had been admitted to the union; universal male suffrage was almost complete; property qualifications were substantially dropped and the secret ballot had been adopted. Special interest groups were dispersed, unorganized, and unable to turn out the vote in numbers equal to patronage machines such as those of Martin Van Buren in New York and James Buchanan in Pennsylvania.[32] When Jackson was elected in 1828 he was the central figure in a coalition of patronage machines whose power derived from control of local post offices, custom houses, and city halls. He defeated a man, John Quincy Adams, who sought to use federal funds for such general services as roads, canals, schools, enlarging the navy, and scientific expeditions.[33]

In the cities political power was fragmented and decentralized. It was not until the Industrial Revolution, its waves of immigrants swelling the populations of the cities, that political "machines" run by "bosses" began to consolidate urban political power. Fred Greenstein has described these political machines as being built on four conditions: (1) the requirement of organizing life in rapidly growing and industrialized cities; (2) the inability of existing governments to meet these requirements; (3) the willingness of businessmen, licit and illicit, to pay for government intervention or the lack of it; and (4) dependent voting populations, largely immigrant, "in need of security from the uncertainties of their existence."[34] It was the transactions with businessmen which provided revenue to run the machine; it was the votes of the dependent populations which made it possible for the machine to control party nominations and to remain in office.

Machine politics, however, need not rely entirely on patronage. As James Q. Wilson explains: "No city is composed exclusively of wards filled with voters responsive to organization politics and the dispensation of favors. In addition to the 'river wards' there are others, called in Chicago 'newspaper wards' and in New York 'silk-stocking' districts, which will respond much less, if at all, to the infusion of patronage."[35] The "river wards" are, of course, low-income areas with largely immigrant or minority populations. Inhabitants of the "newspaper wards" and "silk-stocking districts" are, as the terms imply, better-educated and more affluent. Patronage is not a low-cost method of conducting political exchange in the latter districts.

The political machine emerged and survived because it was efficient in the political marketplace. There was no legislation requiring boss-run machines—indeed, legislative efforts were aimed at hindering or "reforming" these organizations. It has been suggested that "more than anything else, the boss resembled a buccaneering entrepreneur" of the private sector;[36] "building on the conditions and needs of the day, the politician had mainly to supply his own ingenuity and co-ordinating ability in order to tie together the machinery of urban government. . . . the enterprising politician who could succeed in governing a city on this basis was a broker *par excellence*; generous brokers' commissions were the rule of the day."[37]

Given the intensity of political competition, public employee organizations could have little hope of extracting wage gains through militant confrontation with the boss. Disruption could jeopardize the machine's position and granting special status to one group of employees could undermine the unity and discipline essential to machine politics. Police, for example, constituted a large portion of the city's labor force, and police organizations date from pre–Civil War days. According to Sterling Spero, "these organizations, founded for the protection of the policemen and the improvement of their conditions, managed to exist with little official opposition because they functioned in such a way as to give little offense to the authorities. Many were directly controlled by the higher officials, and those which were not sought their ends either through departmental favor or through the power of the political machine."[38]

Since the turn of the century there has been a decline in patronage and a concomitant spread of the merit system (which will be discussed in the next section). Two explanations which have been offered are that the machines were starved as more and more jobs were classified under the civil service system, leaving only menial and unattractive jobs under political control; and that interest in patronage jobs declined as private-sector wages and opportunities improved. For example, in many areas recruiting census takers has become more a political pain than a political plum.[39]

But these explanations involve an apparent confusion between movement along a demand curve and a shift in that curve. Price is determined by *both* blades of Marshall's scissors: supply and demand. The effect of the changes cited above should be to shift inward the supply curve for direct political activity: civil service, which can be circumvented albeit at some cost, would do so by decreasing the exchange technology available to the machine; higher private-sector wages would increase the opportunity cost for political workers. In both cases, the price the politician pays for direct political activity—the above-market wage rate—should *rise*. The fact that it has fallen, as indicated by the lack of interest in such jobs, suggests that there has been an inward shift in the *demand* curve for direct political activity.

An explanation consistent with a decline in the demand for patronage employees is that "newspaper" and "silk-stocking" districts grew at the expense of "river wards." As the population spread to the suburbs, English became the dominant language, and mass communication improved. The cost of buying votes by exchanging general services fell relative to the cost of direct services, and as the quantity of general services demanded by the politicians increased, they began to substitute "merit" employees for patronage employees. Such changes were described by Frank Sorauf when he wrote, "first and second generation groups, traditional recipients of the attentions of the machine, are disappearing, and their children and grandchildren now luxuriate in the prosperity and conformity of the suburbs, though in many cities their place will be taken for a time by immigrants from rural areas of the United States. . . . Furthermore, party conflict since the 1930s has reflected the social and economic appeals to a greater extent. . . . American politics has become more involved with issues and less with the issueless politics of patronage, favor and preferment. Campaigning, too, has shifted from the door-to-door canvass, local rallies, and controlled blocs of votes to the mass media and advertising agencies."[40]

B. The Merit System

In a pure merit system employees would be paid strictly for services they provide the public and they would be paid market wages. The politician's task would be to adjust the mix of services so that his offerings (his "platform") receives more votes than those proposed by rival politicians, including rivals within his own party. For such exchanges to work, agents of the politician must monitor the voting behavior of the public, and the public, in turn, must be able to monitor the performance of the politician. The conditions conducive to such exchanges are (1) indentifiable and easily organized special interest groups; (2) relatively low value attached to direct services provided by the politician; (3) high public accountability; and (4) relatively high value attached to general services.

Typically, a merit system gives rise to an independent civil service commission with authority to hire, fire, pay, and promote employees on the basis of their job performance. Legislation is generally enacted giving employees "job rights," setting pay scales, and prohibiting, as the Hatch Act does, direct exchanges between the politician and public employees.

Perhaps such legislation can best be understood in the context of Tullock's middle-level politician.[41] Because most local politicians aspire to higher office, there is a dual standard of efficiency: First, there is efficiency in carrying out the responsibilities assigned the politician (police protection, for example); second, there is efficiency in promoting the political fortunes of the politician, where public employees may become part of an "entourage to assist him in his conflict with his peers for advancement." As Tullock points out, these two types of efficiency may be indistinguishable to the politician. Whereas the patronage machine may thrive on such principalities, they are inimical to a merit system which emphasizes the efficiency of the first type. Legislation such as the Hatch Act is designed to prevent the second and promote the first type of efficiency.

Of course, pure merit systems are rare, as are pure patronage systems. What we observe is politicians using combinations of merit and patronage employees; even in the heyday of the spoils system a cadre of professionals was maintained within departments to provide a modicum of public service. This is consistent with the notion of a marginal rate of technical substitution between merit and patronage employees, the marginal productivity of merit increasing and that of patronage falling as the latter are substituted for the former. Also, we observe hybrid employees whose wages have two components: a market wage for job performance and what Lentz calls a "loyalty bribe" for political activity.[42] This is consistent with the fact that merit employees can vote, and they do so disproportionately to their numbers in the population. But regardless of the mix or combination, as long as there is political competition the efficient politician will not be able to overpay on either dimension, *even if he so desires*. In such circumstances, public employees will learn that to improve their well-being they must find ways to increase productivity or "rationalize" public management. In this respect, the behavior of their organizations will be similar to the "company unions" described by Reid.

By some accounts, the spread of the merit system was the result of a series of legislated reforms beginning with the Pendleton Act (1883) which brought limited civil service classification to the federal government. But this, I believe, overlooks the endogeniety of labor legislation in the public sector. There is evidence to support Sorauf's claim that the demise of patronage was "more from its own political causes than from the campaigns of civil service reformers."[43] Several studies have recorded the change in the nature of political activity away from personal services toward more generalized services,[44] a change which occurred without the politicians being required to do so by legislation. As White noted in 1933, "much of the change [toward the merit system] has been, relatively speaking, undirected growth. Thus especially the extension of organized groups of public officials and employees, some with a highly professional point of view and others with interests primarily of an economic nature, has proceeded without much public notice and certainly without recognized leadership apart from that associated with each group."[45]

Beginning around 1890, the merit system spread gradually as successive administrations added a few more jobs to the classified lists, although such action was seldom taken until the politician had been defeated and was about to leave office. It has been suggested that extension of civil service classification was a means of increasing the value of patronage by extending "job rights."[46] The problem with this is for employees to impute future value to their present jobs they must *expect* to receive the job rights once the politician is defeated; but if this is the case, the employees have an incentive to see the politician defeated so they can lay claim to their jobs. If the employees *do not expect* the job rights, then bestowing them is simply a goodbye gift. Another explanation is that this action represents a political "scorched earth" policy: destroy the patronage so the enemy cannot use it. In this case, it is difficult to see why the incoming politician would honor such "rights."

An alternative explanation is that politicians were adjusting the mix of their employees to conform to the changing relative value of services. This can be seen in Figure 1, where VV represents an "isovote" curve

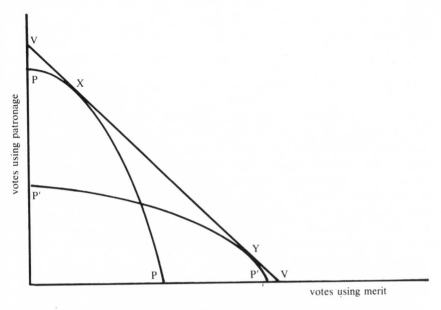

Figure 1.

(the slope of which equals −1 if politicians are indifferent to how a vote is produced) and PP represents the production possibilities curve. The efficient politician will try to equalize the values of the marginal (vote) products. If votes bought through indirect services become cheaper over time, a movement down the isovote curve would be expected—for example, from point x to point y as the production possibilities curve shifts to P'P', holding the number of votes constant.

A gradual change in the relative cost of these two types of exchange would explain the gradual spread of the merit system. Also, "job rights" differ from the patronage "contract" in that they can be a reward, but not an incentive. At the end of an administration there is no need for an incentive contract, but the politician may wish to grant promised rewards to maintain integrity for possible future campaigns. For the incoming politician, revoking such "rights" would decrease the integrity of all politicians, including himself, and he will honor them if he expects to grant similar rights and the cost is not too high, that is, if they have been applied to employees who are essentially merit employees. The role of the employees' organization is to convince the incoming politician that these costs are not too high and, for this purpose, employees may welcome "Hatch Act"–type legislation.[47]

One test of these theories would be to look at which employees were the first to be classified. If classification were either a means of capitalizing future rents or a "scorched earth" policy, then the highest-valued patronage jobs should be the first to be classified. If it were a marginal adjustment in response to changing costs, then jobs which involved general, indirect services or had little value for direct services would be classified first. At the federal level, Hoogenboom reports "the scope of the bill [the Pendleton Act] was determined not by the needs of the civil service, but by the political potential of the offices themselves. Although public opinion necessitated placing officeholders in large customhouses and post offices on a classified list to secure them against political pressure," employees in those which employed fewer than 50 persons remained under patronage.[48] In the same year (1883) the state of New York passed a civil service bill which "applied to officers employed in connection with canals, public works, prisons, asylums, and reformatories" and *authorized* mayors to adopt civil service measures in their cities.[49] "By 1884 most appointments and promotions in the fire, police, health, sanitation, and law departments [in New York cities] were based on competitive examinations and meritorious service. In the process there was a notable increase in administrative efficiency and improvement in the quality of public services."[50]

It would be wrong to assume public employees were not "organized" until the 1960s. Following classification under civil service, employee organizations sprang up to defend the new status. By 1933 Leonard White was able to report: "The large cities are now generally highly organized and formal connection with the American Federation of Labor has become common except with respect to police organizations."[51] He estimated 36 per cent of the public employees in New York City belonged to 46 organizations: 9 formed before 1900; thirty formed from 1900–20; and 7 formed during the twenties. He concluded: "The municipal services of New York have thus been progressively organized since about 1890. The movement originated with benevolent associations, unions later came on the scene, and eventually a strong federation, The Forum [the Civil Service Forum], combined the resources of a considerable number." In Chicago, employee organization was even more extensive—an estimated 78 percent of the public labor force. There he found employees such as street cleaners, garbage handlers, and bridge tenders were widely organized by 1914, "as the city council had definitely indicated that favorable consideration of wage increases could be secured only through organization—sometimes political, sometimes economic." He surmised that "Municipal unions are now firmly established in New York, Chicago, San Francisco, Detroit, Seattle, Milwaukee, and probably in other large cities. In the smaller cities there is still practically no organization except police and fire mutual aid associations."[52]

With few exceptions, these early unions did not strike because, one must suspect, strikes did not pay. For example, the International Association of Fire Fighters (IAFF) charter explicitly forbade strikes and several locals were expelled for striking or merely threatening to strike. And the AFL was in complete agreement with this policy.[53] The fact is that public employees had done quite well relying on political cooperation. It was, after all, the easy work, relatively high pay, and security from business fluctuations which made their jobs "political plums." The opportunity to demonstrate the advantages of collective bargaining existed; the American Federation of State, County, and Municipal Employees (AFSCME) had a bargaining agreement with the city of Philadelphia in 1939. Public employees for the most part were simply not interested. A 1947 survey of American Federation of Teachers (AFT) locals showed none had ever engaged in bargaining and when asked "what future part does the local feel it should play in administration and policy formation?" only 7 of 141 respondants said "bargaining agents."[54]

Typical of these early organizations was the highly successful New York Civil Service Forum which, in its statement of purpose, assured both its members and the politicians: "This association desires it to be known that it is not a striking organization and has no impertinent demands to make, but is merely a protective one and is not engaged in efforts to reduce office hours. It hopes by intelligent representation on committees and otherwise to cooperate with the various taxpayers organizations and bring about a better understanding of their part towards the people in the classified services."[55]

The success of these organizations was synchronous with reforms lowering the relative cost of political exchange using general services. Such measures included fiscal reforms which placed debt limitations on local governments; state-required budget reports following standard accounting procedures; vesting responsibility for public management in a clearly recognized executive, either a "strong" mayor or a professional city manager; nonpartisan, citywide elections; and provision for recall and referendum.[56] The tactics of the organizations were adapted to working within the reformed political structure. Their strength lay in their knowledge of the inner workings of government and their economies of scale were few. They focused their efforts on local government, relying on ad hoc coalitions when statewide lobbying was called for. As Spero observed, "organizations which did grow and thrive in this atmosphere were usually limited to a single department or class of employees. City or county-wide organizations were not uncommon, but those whose jurisdictions extended to an entire state were few. . . . They, like the large groups, functioned in alliance with the political machines, obtaining their ends through trading and log-rolling. Around budget time or during sessions of the legislature, new organizations would spring up and old ones increase in membership and activity—a tendency still present in local government services today [circa 1948]."[57]

C. Militant Unionism

In the late 1950s and early 1960s Jerry Wurf's AFSCME District Council 37, "encouraged by promulgation in 1958 of Mayor Robert E. Wagner's Executive Order 49 granting recognition to organizations of New York City employees,"[58] staged a series of successful strikes. Seeing that militancy could pay, public employees around the country began to clamor for similar tactics from their own organizations and by 1964 Wurf had been elected president of the national union. In 1966 the executive board of AFSCME issued a policy statement affirming the right of public employees to strike; in 1963 the AFT had advocated strikes; by 1967 the NEA did the same; and by 1968 even the IAFF had gone on record in support of strikes.

Yet militancy—the exercise of "union power"—does not fit easily into the simple exchange model presented in the previous sections. For a union to *force* wages up, the politician must be made to overpay for either the direct activity or indirect, general services of the employees. Under perfect political competition a politician who gives in to such union pressure will be defeated by one who stands firm, everything else being equal. Relaxing the assumption of perfect competition would allow political capital (in the form of large victory margins) to be "taxed" by a union.

What accounts for the sudden success of these unions? One possible explanation is that the political competition which had prevented earlier militancy had now slackened, but I can find no evidence of this. In fact, the opposite would appear to be true: public-sector unions do best in those states with the smallest political majorities in the state legislature (e.g., New York, Pennsylvania, Michigan, Ohio, Illinois). (The correlation coefficient is $-.49$ between the percent of local government employees covered by bargaining agreements and the size of the political majority in the state legislature.) Also, Richard Daley had huge victory margins which he hoped would lead to higher office, and he dealt very harshly with militant employees.

Contradicting the "union power" theory which would have militant employees confiscating political capital is the *favorable* action by politicians which has been a major ingredient in union success. From Jerry Wurf, president of AFSCME, we are told: "The 1960s were years of change in philosophy for many academics, lawmakers and public managers,"[59] and "there is growing acceptance of unionization and collective bargaining. This is reflected in new laws, in new legislative proposals before state legislators, and the willingness of many local employers, in particular, to bargain collectively with their employees."[60] And from Myron Lieberman, an opponent of public-sector militancy: "The supportive role of government has probably been the single most important factor associated with [the growth of] public-sector bargaining."[61] This symbiotic relationship demands closer attention.

To explain unionism, the exchange model suggests that we look at the type of political exchanges being made and the nature of the contracts used in these exchanges.

During the last 20 years technological advances in mass communication have made it easier for politicians to reach the general public; computerized mailing and word processing have made it easier for special interest groups to organize; improved public opinion polling has made estimating public preferences more accurate; and scientific methods of sampling have increased the ability to monitor voting behavior of special interest groups. These have lowered the cost of the special interest vote and made it economical to deal with more narrowly defined groups. At the same time, limitations on campaign contributions have increased the value of labor-intensive political activity. Thus we have seen the emergence of "grass roots" special interest/issue-oriented political campaigns.

Politicians, on the other hand, continue to run neck-and-neck with used-car salesmen when it comes to public trust. This is reflected in the recent development of political action committees which find it profitable to stay in business between elections solely for the purpose of monitoring the performance of elected officials, usually those officials they helped elect.

At the local level the monitoring problem has been exacerbated by federal involvement. Over the past two decades the federal government has transferred over $1 trillion (in 1980 dollars) to state and local governments, much of it in the form of categorical grants-in-aid. This has undercut local authority and obfuscated responsibility. In 1967 it was estimated that of some 68 federal grants which allowed direct payments to local governments, only 13 had the local government as the sole recipient.[62] Administrators of these programs became less responsive to local political pressures[63] as numerous special-purpose districts were created which cut across political jurisdictions.[64] Where local politicians were at odds with the federal objectives, the federal government sometimes bypassed the local political process entirely and then set up private citizen groups to monitor local compliance with the program.

Writing in 1966 when militancy was just surfacing, Edward Banfield and James Q. Wilson suggested that "[t]he political weight of organized city employees in a particular city depends largely upon the nature of the city's political structure, and especially upon the degree to which influence is centralized," and predicted that "[w]here party organization is strong, the city administration is in a relatively good position to resist the

118   MICHAEL M. KURTH

demands of organized employees. . . . [O]n the other hand, where party
organization is weak or altogether absent, the political weight of organized
employees is relatively large and might be decisive."[65] Their prediction
appears to have been quite accurate. John Burton, reporting on field work
done in about 40 cities in 1968–1969, found what he described as a "be-
wildering fragmentation of authority"[66] in the prebargaining governments, the effect of unions being to concentrate and define responsibility.
The question which must be asked is to what extent did federal intervention create an environment which was conducive to public employee
militancy?

Categorical grants-in-aid also have, as one observer put it, "the inherent
shortcoming of being categorical—[they provide] no relief for the increasing costs of basic state and city operations that do not fall within
the list of aided functions."[67] As Wes Uhlman, mayor of Seattle, com-
plained to a Senate Finance Committee, "Our [police] precinct stations
built in the 19th century have so deteriorated that they cannot be repaired.
On one floor of one station, 43 men must use an unsanitary toilet facility.
We can get Federal money to buy these men all the newest radio equip-
ment made, but we cannot get a cent to fix the plumbing of the station
so that our police can have a decent bathroom to use."[68] The situation
is made worse by the matching requirement attached to much of this aid,
which has the effect of siphoning funds away from the uses to which they
might otherwise be put. Michael Maye, president of the New York City
Uniformed Firefighters Association, was reacting to this when he ex-
claimed: "They say there's no money for us. . . . Well, fire protection
has gone from 4 percent to 3 percent of the budget. There's a drain all
right; and who's getting it? We know. Welfare has gone from 10 percent
to 22 percent—there's plenty of money for that."[69]

The cost of buying votes by promising legislation, special programs,
and funds to narrow special interest groups may be lower, but the cost
of monitoring and metering the delivery of these benefits at the local level
is higher due to the obfuscation of responsibility. If they are not delivered,
who is to be blamed?

Given local attitudes and the federal objectives, militant public employees may be able to exploit the situation. Consider a federal program
which entitles everyone named Hatfield to have their house painted free
of charge, the Hatfields being influential in national politics. Local politics, however, is dominated by the McCoys, and a Hatfield has never
voted for a McCoy. While the local politician may receive additional votes
from the housepainters he may hire, provided he has discretion over hiring, he will get no additional votes from their production. In this situation
any reduction in the housepainters' effort, holding wages constant, will
be a politically costless transfer to the painters. If one McCoy does not

permit it, another will be elected who will. If the federal government does not monitor this program, no Hatfield will have his house painted, the funds being accepted but then "shifted" to other uses. With federal monitoring, the local politicians are not given a choice over the uses for these funds and they have an incentive to support any bargaining settlement which reduces output, thereby raising the real wages of the painters. If militant employees are more successful at standing up to or circumventing federal monitors than are local politicians, a painters' union can be expected to emerge.

Why might a militant union be able to accomplish this? The federal government cannot respond to a work stoppage by local government employees the same way the local politician can, yet the strike action may be withholding more federal than local spending. A strike against an isolated government where the local politician bears all the cost is one thing, a strike in a system of subordinated governments is something else; at the extreme, where local politics are totally subordinated to "higher" levels of government, who pays for the militancy? Recent studies have suggested that mandating of local spending and performance by both federal and state governments has reached the point where little descretion is left to the local politicians. In this case, many of the costs of militancy are borne by politicians other than those dealing with the militants.

To the extent that union gains can come at the expense of programs and funds not controlled by the local politician, these unions will be viewed as symbiotic rather than parasitic by the local politician. This will also be true where federal or state administrators of these programs must choose the recipients on the basis of need and labor unrest is taken as evidence of such need.[70]

Federal funding and mandating of local government activities has quite naturally lead to federal involvement in personnel decisions as well. If local politicians place little value on the services the federal government is attempting to provide, they will be inclined to staff these positions with patronage appointees rather than merit appointees. The federal government has responded by stipulating merit standards, equal pay, affirmative action, and a host of other conditions for eligibility for over 25 programs involving over $20 billion annually in federal aid.[71]

Such mandating prevents the local politician from structuring incentives to fit his concept of political efficiency and opens up the possibility that a union may be able to structure incentives more rationally (from the local politician's view). Unions in the public sector directly attack the merit principle and the independent civil service commission. As Jerry Wurf explains, "Unions of public employees see the Civil Service agency as a recruiting organ. . . . [W]ages, hours, working conditions, rates of pay, fringe benefits, pensions—procedures for layoffs where necessary, classifications, reclassifications, appeals in the discharges or disciplinary actions and on all other work matters—all must be handled as part of the contractual relationship between the employer and the union."[72] And from another observer: "Civil service commissions may not go out of business, but more and more of their vital organs will be removed by the bargaining process until, whether officially in existence or not, they are husks of their former selves. This change is occurring not because employees are clearly dissatisfied with the existing merit systems but because they feel that unions will get more for them."[73]

One effect of this shift is to expand the set of decision variables available to the local politicians.

Finally, in the presence of such massive state and federal intervention local government employees will require the services of an agent to represent their interests at the state and federal levels of government. Earlier, local government employees had looked primarily to the local politician for any improvements and their organizations reflected this. But the last 20 years have produced an increased concentration of representation in a few large statewide or national unions. The three AFL–CIO affiliates— AFSCME, AFT, and IAFF—have been able to expand a pre-1960s toehold into a dominant position where they represent more than 80 percent of state and local union members. The NEA included, the C_4 concentration ratio for all public employee representation (unions and associations) was 70 percent in 1976. The reason, I believe, is that these national unions were best equipped to carry on exchanges between local government employees and state or federal politicians, and they had experience with militant activity.[74]

One of the best indications that federal grants matter is the competition which took place between the AFT and the NEA over creation of a Department of Education separate from the Department of Health, Education, and Welfare (HEW). The AFT, an AFL–CIO affiliate, had substantial influence within the old HEW and was able to influence the distribution of federal aid to education. The NEA, in an effort to increase their control over federal funds, endorsed Jimmy Carter for president in 1976 and worked hard for his election. The reward for their success was the creation of a separate, cabinet-level Department of Education. Clearly such political activity requires organization to prevent shirking at the polls by the members and to monitor and meter the politician's performance after the election. This is a dimension which was not present before 1960.

IV. CONCLUSION

Before the 1960s public employees were scoffed at by union organizers, and some theorists even suggested that government employees, and particularly teachers, were unorganizable because they lacked the appropriate characteristics of union members.[75] One could conclude that government employees misperceived the value of unionism all these years, suddenly awaking in the mid-sixties. I have offered an alternative explanation—that public employee organizations, under the pressure of competition, were alert to their opportunities and correctly judged them. They became militant when militancy began to pay.

One could also conclude that politicians, when they pass permissive legislation or tolerate militant activity, are acting against their own best interests. Their protests against unionism are often loud. So are my protests when I pay my electric bill each month. But such proclaimations cannot be taken as even prima facie evidence that one is made worse off by the exchange; rather, the fact that the exchange takes place is evidence that both parties gain and the trades represent, respectively, the parties' best alternatives. I have suggested the relationship between local politicians is best viewed as symbiotic rather than parasitic.

I have offered a model of public employee organizations based on Alchain and Demsetz's theory of the firm. In competitive political markets "union power" cannot be exercised to force wages up or capture political "capital," but there remains the opportunity for organizations to make their members better off by increasing their vote productivity. This model appears to fit the history of public employee organizations up to the 1960s, and I have suggested reasons why it is appropriate for militant unionism as well.

Narrowly targeted, "categorical" aid which was introduced in the late 1950s represents a significant departure from previous federal programs which had allowed local governments considerable flexibility in design, distribution, and administration. The public finance literature treats such aid as simply an income subsidy which shifts the community's budget constraint;[76] effects on the supply side are almost completely ignored.[77] My model suggests that supply-side effects are important. That intergovernmental aid, and in particular categorical aid, has contributed to the emergence of militant unionism in the public sector. Massive federal spending, combined with restrictions on the local politicians' decisions, has created an environment in which unions can (1) obtain funds not available to the local politician, either by "capturing" the value of existing federal programs or by demonstrating a "need" for additional funds; (2) "rationalize" management in the face of state and federal mandating of personnel practices by transferring control over such matters from the civil service commission to the bargaining process; and (3) organize, monitor, and meter exchanges between local government employees and state or federal politicians.

It follows from this that the most significant development in public-sector labor relations is not increased "organization" of public employees—public employees have been extensively organized for some time—rather, it is the sudden change in tactics of the existing organizations followed by an increased concentration of representation in a few, large national unions.

My conclusion is that militant unions emerged in the public sector when they became politically efficient. With employee representation competitively supplied, public employees were able to choose militant organizations once militancy became profitable. Politicians bargained with these organizations because such organizations represented the politician's best opportunities. Militancy has been most successful in declining markets because this is where most categorical aid is targeted, and federal employees have been unable to strike successfully because they work for an "isolated" government—one which is free of intervention and spending controlled by politicians at other levels of government.

ACKNOWLEDGMENTS

I would like to thank Joe Reid for his invaluable guidance and encouragement. Also, this paper benefited from comments by Roger Faith, Gordon Tullock, and Bernard Lentz. In particular, the work Lentz did in his dissertation served as a springboard for some of the ideas presented in this paper. Of course, the usual disclaimer applies.

NOTES and REFERENCES

1. U.S. Bureau of Labor Statistics, *Work Stoppages in Government, 1978*. Washington, D.C.: U.S. Government Printing Office, 1980, p. 4.

2. Lloyd G. Reynolds, *Labor Economics and Labor Relations,* 7th ed. Englewood Cliffs, N.J.: Prentice-Hall, 1978, p. 608.

3. For example, see, Everett M. Kassalow, "Trade Unionism Goes Public." *The Public Interest* 14(Winter 1969):118–130; Harry P. Cohany and Lucretia M. Dewey, "Union Membership Among Government Employees." *Monthly Labor Review* (July 1970):15–20; and John F. Burton, Jr., "The Extent of Collective Bargaining in the Public Sector." In Benjamin Aaron, Joseph R. Grodin, and James L. Stern (eds.), *Public Sector Bargaining,* Washington, D.C.: Bureau of National Affairs, 1979, pp. 1–44.

4. See Kassalow; also Abraham L. Gitlow, "Public Employee Unionism in the United States: Growth and Outlook," *Labor Law Journal,* (December, 1970) pp. 766–779.

5. See Kassalow; Gitlow; and also: Jerry Wurf and Mary L. Hennessy, "American Federation of State, County and Municipal Employees." In J. Joseph Loewenberg and Michael H. Moskow (eds.), *Collective Bargaining in Government: Readings and Cases.* Englewood Cliffs, N.J.: Prentice-Hall, 1972, pp. 60–65.

6. See, Reynolds; Cohany and Dewey; and Gitlow.

7. See, Marvin J. Levin and Eugene C. Hagburg, *Public Sector Labor Relations.* St. Paul: West Publishing, 1979, p. 69.

8. For example, see, Jack Stieber, "Collective Bargaining in the Public Sector." In Lloyd Ulman (ed.), *Challenges to Collective Bargaining.* Englewood Cliffs, N.J.: Prentice-Hall, 1967, pp. 65–88.

9. See, Stieber; Gitlow.

10. The Supreme Court's 1962 "one man–one vote" ruling which forced the reapportionment of state legislatures is often cited as contributing to the success of unions. See, Kassalow; Stieber. Also, Rees attributes union success to permissive legislation, see, Albert Rees, *The Economics of Trade Unions*. Chicago: University of Chicago Press, 1977, p. 182.

11. See, Kassalow; Stieber; Rees; and Wurf and Hennessy.

12. For a discussion, see, John F. Burton, "The Extent of Bargaining."

13. See, George E. Barnett, "American Trade Unionism and Social Insurance." *American Economic Review* 23(March):6, 1933.

14. For example, in a five-year study of public employee strikes, Cebulski "found that employers were reluctant to take action against strikers; action was initiated in only 16 cases, most of which were eventually dropped." Reported in Thomas A. Kochan, "Dynamics of Dispute Resolution in the Public Sector," in Aaron, Grodkin and Stern, p. 168.

15. For example, see, Charles M. Tiebout, "A Pure Theory of Local Expenditure." *Journal of Political Economy* 65(October):416–424, 1956.

16. Rees, p. 67.

17. This is essentially the view of Wellington and Winter. See, Harry H. Wellington and Ralph K. Winter, *The Unions and the Cities*. Washington, D.C.: The Brookings Institute, 1971.

18. David Lewin, "Public Sector Labor Relations." *Labor History* 18(Winter):133–144, 1977.

19. See, Richard Freeman and James Medoff, "Two Faces of Unionism." in *The Public Interest* (Fall 1979); Charles Brown and James Medoff, "Trade Unions in the Production Process." *Journal of Political Economy* 86(3); or Freeman and Medoff, "The Impact of Collective Bargaining: Illusion or Reality" in this volume.

20. Joseph D. Reid and Roger Faith, "The Labor Union as its Members' Agent." Working paper, Center for the Study of Public Choice, Virginia Polytechnic Institute and State University.

21. See, Robert H. Coase, "The Nature of the Firm." *Economics* 4 (November 1937) pp. 386–405; and also, Armen Alchain and Harold Demsetz, "Production, Information Costs, and Economic Organization." *American Economic Review* (December), 1972.

22. A "direct service" is a service provided directly to an individual; an indirect or "general service" is one provided to a group or community. A "private" good may be provided indirectly: for example, pensions provided through Social Security. Also, so-called "public" goods may be provided directly, as when fire or police protection is made contingent on political activity.

23. The National Labor Relations Act of 1935 can be found in 49 Stat. 449. The full text of the act with amendments is found in 28 U.S.C. 151 *et seq.*

24. Gitlow (p. 767–8) makes this distinction clear. Burton (pp. 4–5) envisions a spectrum from nonbargaining organizations to bargaining associations to unions. Militancy increases as one moves from the first to the last; unfortunately, organizations frequently do not change their names as they change their policies.

25. Frank J. Sorauf, "The Silent Revolution in Patronage." *Public Administration Review* 20(1):28, 1960.

26. James Q. Wilson, "The Economy of Patronage." *Journal of Political Economy* 69(4):370, 1961.

27. Ibid., p. 370–371.

28. In particular, see, Elmer E. Cornwell, Jr., "Bosses, Machines, and Ethnic Groups." *The Annals of the American Academy of Political and Social Science: City Bosses and Political Machines* (May):31, 1964.

29. See Wilson, p. 376–377 for a discussion of patronage as a reward and incentive.

30. Reported in Paul P. Van. Riper, *History of the United States Civil Service*. White Plains, N.Y.: Row, Peterson & Co., 1958, p. 27.

31. Samuel Eliot Morison, *The Oxford History of the American People*. New York: Oxford University Press, 1965, p. 489.

32. Ibid., pp. 416–421.

33. Ibid., p. 418.

34. Fred I. Greenstein, "The Changing Pattern of Urban Party Politics." *The Annals*, pp. 1–13.

35. Wilson, p. 374.

36. William C. Havard, "From Bossism to Cosmopolitanism: Changes in the Relationship of Urban Leadership to State Politics." *The Annals*, p. 86.

37. Greenstein, p. 5.

38. Sterling D. Spero, *Government as Employer*. Carbondale & Edwardsville, Ill.: Southern Illinois University Press, 1948, pp. 245–246.

39. For example, see, Sorauf, p. 30; Greenstein, pp. 8–9; Cornwell, p. 34.

40. Sorauf, p. 31.

41. Gordon Tullock, *The Politics of Bureaucracy*. Washington, D.C.: Public Affairs Press, 1965, pp. 120–121.

42. The term *loyalty bribe* is from Lentz, who describes two components of public employee production: "The direct (political influence) and indirect (service output demanded by voters)." See: Lentz, *Public Sector Wage Determination*. For a rigorous model, see Melvin W. Reder, "The theory of Employment and Wages in the Public Sector," ed. Daniel S. Hamermesh, (Princeton: Princeton University Press, 1975) pp. 1–48. In particular, Reder suggests, "Where public–private differences in compensation and employment per unit of output of otherwise comparable labor exist, they are due to the production in the public sector of an unmeasured output—votes" (p. 21).

43. Sorauf, p. 28.

44. For example, see, Thomas M. Guterbock, *Machine Politics in Transition*. Chicago: University of Chicago Press, 1980.

45. Leonard D. White, *Trends in Public Administration*. New York, McGraw-Hill, 1933, p. 5.

46. I am not certain as to the original source of this argument. It has been suggested to me by David Friedman and Gordon Tullock, among others.

47. Lentz, in his dissertation, suggests that these organizations represent a form of insurance for employees who wish to participate in the electoral process but avoid the risks inherent in partisan political activity.

48. Ari Hoogenboom, *Outlawing the Spoils: A History of The Civil Service Reform Movement, 1865–83*. Urbana: University of Illinois Press, 1961, p. 244.

49. Ibid., p. 257.

50. Martin J. Schiesl, *The Politics of Efficiency: Municipal Administration & Reform in America, 1800–1920*. Berkeley: University of California Press, 1977, p. 50.

51. White, p. 306.

52. Ibid., pp. 301–308.

53. Marvin J. Levine and Eugene C. Hagburg, *Public Sector Labor Relations*. New York: West Publishing Co., 1979, p. 65.

54. Philip Kochman, "The Developing Role of Teachers Union," Unpublished Ph.D. dissertation, Teachers College, Columbia University, 1939; reported in Michael H. Moskow, J. Joseph Loewenberg, and Edward Clifford Koriara, *Collective Bargaining in Public Employment*. New York: Random House, 1970, p. 144.

55. Spero, p. 206.

56. See White, *Trends*.

57. Spero, p. 204.
58. Wurf and Hennessy, "American Federation of State, County and Municipal Employees." In Lowenberg & Moskow (eds.), *Collective Bargaining in Government*, p. 62.
59. Jerry Wurf and Mary L. Hennesy, "American Federation of State, County and Municipal Employees." In J. Loewenberg and M. Moskow (eds.), *Collective Bargaining in Government*. Englewood Cliffs, N.J.: Prentice-Hall, Inc., 1972, p. 63.
60. Jerry Wurf, statement before House Special Subcommittee on Labor of the Committee on Education and Labor, in *Labor-Management Relations in the Public Sector*. Washington, D.C.: U.S. Government Printing Office, 1972, p. 31.
61. Myron Lieberman, *Public Sector Bargaining, A Reappraisal*. Lexington, Mass.: D.C. Heath & Co., 1980, p. 3.
62. Donald H. Haider, *When Governments Come to Washington*. New York: The Free Press, 1974, p. 55.
63. Ibid., p. 117.
64. Robert D. Thomas, "Implementing Federal Programs at the Local Level." *Political Science Quarterly* (Fall):425, 1979.
65. Edward E. Banfield and James Q. Wilson, *City Politics*. Cambridge, Mass.: Harvard University Press, 1963.
66. John F. Burton, Jr., "Local Government Bargaining and Management Structure."
67. Reported in: Richard E. Thompson, *A New Era in Federalism?* Washington, D.C.: Revenue Sharing Advisory Service, 1973, p. vii.
68. Ibid., p. 30.
69. Harry H. Wellington & Ralph K. Winter, Jr., *The Unions and the Cities*. Washington, D.C.: Brookings Institute, 1971, p. 202.
70. This was suggested to me by Roger Faith. It is similar to his argument in: Roger L. Faith, "Local Fiscal Crises and Intergovernmental Grants: a Suggested Hypothesis." *Public Choice* 34(4).
71. Daniel B. Smith and Donald E. Klinger, "The Erosion of Home Rule in Personnel Management." *National Civil Review* (January):26–32, 1980.
72. Jerry Wurf, in a letter to *Public Personnel Review*, January, 1966, p. 52; reported in John F. Burton, Jr., "Local Government Bargaining and Management Structure." *Industrial Relations* 11:123–40, 1972.
73. David T. Stanley, "What Are Unions Doing to Merit Systems?" *Public Personnel Review* (April 1970).
74. This is computed by dividing membership in the four largest organizations by the number of organized public employees reported by the Census Bureau (3255/4737 = 68.1 percent).
75. Clark Kerr and Aaron Siegel, "The Interindustry Propensity to Strike—An International Comparison." In A. Kornhauser, et al. (eds.), *Industrial Conflict*. New York: McGraw-Hill, 1954, pp. 189–212.
76. See: James Wilde, "The Expenditure Effects of Grants-in-Aid Programs." *National Tax Journal* 21(3):340–348, 1968.
77. For an exception, see, Jon Rasmussen, "The Allocative Effects of Grants-in-Aid: Some Extensions and Qualifications." *National Tax Journal* 29(2):211–219.

THEORETICAL PERSPECTIVES ON THE MODERN GRIEVANCE PROCEDURE

David Lewin

As a device for resolving disputes that arise at the workplace, the grievance procedure has been widely adopted and often lauded. Virtually all
written labor agreements in private industry contain a grievance procedure; by and large, the same is true of the public and nonprofit sectors
where unionism and collective bargaining have grown rapidly in recent
years (U.S. Bureau of Labor Statistics, 1964, 1975, 1981; U.S. Bureau of
the Census, 1980). Grievance procedures are commended not only for
providing a peaceful means of resolving day-to-day workplace disputes
and for enabling workers to participate in decisions that affect their work
lives, but also for the benefits that they provide to management. These
include a virtual guarantee of uninterrupted production during the life of
the labor agreement, the use by management of union resources and personnel to police the labor agreement, and a systematic source of information about problem areas in the workplace—information that can be

New Approaches to Labor Unions.
Research in Labor Economics, Supplement 2, pages 127–147.
Copyright © 1983 by JAI Press Inc.
All rights of reproduction in any form reserved.
ISBN: 0-89232-265-9

used for subsequent evaluation and corrective action (Lewin, 1978). Recognition of these benefits has apparently spurred large numbers of employers to adopt various types of appeal and due process systems for their nonunion personnel (Berenbeim, 1980).[1]

Despite its widespread use and putative benefits, the grievance procedure has received surprisingly little study, especially in the contemporary period.[2] The best-known works in the field, such as those of Kuhn (1961) and Slichter et al. (1960), are two decades old and the data on which they are based are even older. This is unfortunate because important changes have recently occurred in American industrial relations, including the growth of unionism among government employees and in the health and hospital sectors; a steady if not spectacular rise in the unionization of women, white-collar, and professional workers; and major changes in production processes, work rules, and productivity incentives in the construction, newspaper, garment, supermarket, meatpacking, and steel industries, among others.

The paucity of systematic empirical studies has retarded the development of theories of the grievance procedure; clearly, there is no overriding, generally accepted theoretical framework for the analysis of grievance procedures. Instead, the literature contains various "perspectives" on the grievance procedure, some of which will be reviewed below. As shall be evident, most of these perspectives emphasize one or another dimension of the grievance procedure or the larger labor–management relationship of which the procedure is a part. Drawing from these perspectives and from selected empirical research, a model of the grievance procedure will be developed that emphasizes grievance-handling effectiveness and its determinants. Next, the applicability of this model to public-sector as well as private-sector grievance procedures will be discussed. Finally, the relationship between grievance procedure effectiveness and some outcomes of unionism and collective bargaining, such as productivity, job tenure, and employee turnover, will be considered.[3]

I. DIMENSIONS OF THE GRIEVANCE PROCEDURE

A. Grievance Procedures as Individual Utility

A substantial literature attests to the role that the grievance procedure plays in serving the interests of individual workers and union leaders (Stagner, 1962; Thompson and Murray, 1976; Briggs, 1981). Through this procedure, the worker is able to challenge management's authority over a range of wage and working conditions issues. Moreover, it is the individual worker, not the collective of workers represented by the union, who decides which issue(s) should be taken to and through the grievance procedure. The fact that most grievances (apparently) are settled informally before being reduced to writing (Kuhn, 1961) and the additional fact that most written grievances (apparently) are settled at the lowest steps of the procedure (Slichter et al., 1960; Kuhn, 1961) in no way detract from the availability of the procedure to workers or from the opportunities that the procedure provides for the worker to exercise individual choice with respect to grievance filing and handling. Similarly, management's rejection of most worker grievances (Chamberlain and Kuhn, 1961, p. 154) does not detract from the worker's freedom to exercise choice in this regard.

In handling worker-initiated grievances, shop stewards and other union officials exercise individual choice in deciding how to respond to particular grievances and which grievances to take to the later stages of the procedure (including arbitration). In these later stages, grievance handling is subject to collective decision making, as, for example, by members of the local union grievance committee or by the committee and a national union representative. But in the earlier stages of the procedure, the shop steward or other union official exercises discretion—and thus decision-making authority—over grievances that would otherwise reside with management. Such decision-making authority presumably is sought by those who occupy union offices, and so from this perspective the grievance procedure serves their individual interests as well as those of union members.

B. Grievance Procedures as the Communication of Information

While from one perspective the grievance procedure is a mechanism for workers to express personal choice and communicate personal opinion, from another perspective the procedure is a source of information for decision making. Through the grievance procedure, the employer learns (or learns more) about actual or potential problems in the work organization, be they related to issues of pay, job assignments, technology, supervisory relations, etc. This information is provided by workers— the costs of providing it are borne by workers—and management must then decide how to respond to it. The responses can take the form of outright rejection of the grievance claim, rejection after investigation, initial acceptance, or acceptance after investigation. In cases of acceptance of grievance claims, management must take corrective action, such as the alteration of a pay rate, specification of a new job assignment, or design of a training program for first-line supervisors. (The costs of these actions are borne by the employer.) More generally, the employer receives information through the grievance procedure that can be used for decision making, first by diagnosing the problem reflected in the information and then by taking action, including corrective action. Again, this hardly means that management accepts all or most worker grievances. However, it does mean that the grievance procedure can serve management's interests through the communication of information for decision making. Further, when corrective actions are taken by management they are presumed to enhance worker productivity and commitment to the employer.[4]

C.   Grievance Procedures as Due Process

Perhaps the dominant perspective on the grievance procedure is that which emphasizes due process or adjudication of disputes (Miller and Rosen, 1957; Kuhn, 1961). Here, the arbitration step of the typical grievance procedure takes on central importance. If the direct parties to a grievance—labor and management—are unable to resolve an issue bilaterally, a third party is called upon to render a final and binding decision. The impartiality that the arbitrator is presumed to exercise, the sharing of arbitration costs equally by both sides, and the acceptance of the arbitrator's decision by both parties are, to be sure, all key aspects of this terminal step of the grievance procedure. More fundamental, however, is the existence of arbitration itself, for this component of the grievance procedure offers due process and a type of adjudication not found elsewhere; it testifies to the rights and protections that unionized workers obtain by dint of their belonging to the union.[5] From the "due process" perspective, who wins and who loses particular grievance cases, what issues are handled through the grievance procedure, and the steps at which specific grievances are settled are less significant than the fact of the grievance procedure, cum arbitration, itself. Indeed, this conclusion would hold whether few or many grievances were reduced to writing, whether management rejected few or most grievances, or whether the arbitrator more often ruled in favor of one or the other party. Moreover, being voluntarily negotiated rather than legislatively mandated, the grievance procedure permits a definition of due process and a form of adjudication that accord closely with the characteristics of the firm and the union, and of management and workers, respectively. In particular, the grievance procedure establishes precedents and sharpens workplace policies; it also tends to solidify the more formal bargaining agreement between the parties that initially gave rise to the grievance procedure (Kuhn, 1961).

D.   Grievance Procedures as Bargaining

This perspective conceptualizes the grievance procedure as an extension of the collective bargaining relationship between labor and management (Kuhn, 1961; Chamberlain and Kuhn, 1965; Briggs, 1981). The labor agreement contains specific and often quite precise provisions, but it also contains general or even (and sometimes intentionally) ambiguous provisions. The applicability of such provisions to the day-to-day workplace is, in part, determined through the resolution of disputes via the grievance procedure. In other instances, changes in workplace technologies and conditions spur foremen to adjust work rules or to negotiate at the shop level with union representatives for greater freedom to assign and reassign work and personnel. More generally, as Kuhn observes, "Special conditions . . . put the parties in the shop in positions of strength—and weakness—which provide the opportunity for them to bargain for benefits not secured in the collective agreement" (Kuhn, 1961, p. 147).

Moreover, a collective bargaining agreement will often cover large numbers of workers of different skills and interests employed in diverse conditions. The agreement tends not to address this diversity; instead, it treats the whole of the union membership as a single collective. However, specific groups of workers in the union, sharing specific skills and particular conditions and perhaps buffeted more than others by changing technologies or employment opportunities, will often seek to have their concerns addressed through the grievance procedure. Such grievance or "fractional" bargaining is thus part and parcel of the larger bargaining process, but it occurs between management and semiautonomous work groups rather than between management and the union as a whole.[6]

II. GRIEVANCE PROCEDURE EFFECTIVENESS

The aforementioned perspectives on the grievance procedure (and other perspectives not reviewed here) each contain one or more notions, often implicit, about the effectiveness of the procedure. But how can such effectiveness really be judged, given different conceptions of the grievance procedure, of effectiveness, and of the factors influencing effectiveness? To shed light on this question, a model of grievance procedure effectiveness will be developed that identifies several dimensions or components of effectiveness and several categories of independent variables.[7]

A.   Effectiveness Dimensions

The grievance rate has been most commonly used as the dependent variable in empirical studies of grievance procedure effectiveness (Weissinger, 1976). However, by itself, it is an inadequate measure. Consider that a low grievance rate may reflect effective informal resolution of labor–management disputes at the shop, office, or factory level. But it also may reflect insufficient union aggressiveness in enforcing the labor agreement or worker disillusionment with the formal grievance procedure or a weak management that feels compelled to settle grievances at the lowest possible level. Moreover, grievance rates vary by worker characteristics, workplace technology, and union and management policies (Weissinger, 1976). Thus, grievance rates may be high in some circumstances and low in others, but have little or nothing to do with the effectiveness of the grievance procedure. Consequently, other measures of grievance procedure effectiveness must be identified. A review of the (admittedly meager) literature suggests four additional measures: speed of settlement, level of settlement, extent of arbitration usage, and equity of settlement. Each of these is discussed, in turn, below.

Both labor and management spokesmen generally agree that grievances should be settled quickly, especially if the notion of due process at the workplace is to have meaning (Thompson, 1974). For example, Miller and Rosen (1957) found that union members tended to evaluate their shop stewards in part on how quickly they were able to settle worker grievances. Management regards a backlog of unsettled grievances as harmful to the larger labor–management relationship. It was to mitigate such harm that the companies studied by Kuhn (1961) sought to reduce the time limits contained in their grievance procedures. And Kennedy, a well-known arbitrator, contends that "expeditious [grievance] processing is universally recognized to be desirable, whether or not it is implemented by formal time limits" (Kennedy, 1948, p. 46).

Settlement of grievances at the lowest possible level is also frequently identified as a desirable feature of the grievance procedure. Trotta, for example, regards such lower-level settlement "as an element of an effective grievance procedure" (Trotta, 1974), and Pettefer suggests that settlement at the first step should be a formal criterion of grievance-handling effectiveness (Pettefer, 1970). In a study of five medium-size Midwestern cities, Begin (1971) found that the level of grievance settlement tended to decline as the parties obtained more negotiating experience and as more training was provided to lower-level supervisors. Despite the putative advantages of lower-level settlements, Slichter et al. (1960) warn that "it is easy to get low step settlements if the union is weak" (p. 482); thus, evidence of low-level settlements must be cautiously interpreted. Further, some unions have a policy of always appealing certain grievances to higher steps of the procedure. Nevertheless, the criterion of low-step settlement is widely acclaimed by both labor and management and should be considered in any formulation of grievance procedure effectiveness.

Similarly, labor and management appear of the same mind in believing a high rate of grievance usage to be unfavorable and indicative of an ineffective grievance procedure (Thompson, 1974).[8] The costs of arbitration and the delays in settlement associated with its use are the principal reasons underlying this view. However, as a criterion variable, arbitration rates are subject to some of the same limitations as grievance rates and levels of settlement. Thus, a grievance may be taken all the way to arbitration because of political reasons or as a result of union and management policies. Still, there is a large literature on grievance arbitration and this variable can reasonably be included in a multidimensional specification of grievance procedure effectiveness.

The equity of settlement has been identified by Kuhn (1961) and others (Anderson, 1979a; Briggs, 1981) as yet another dimension of grievance procedure effectiveness. Unlike other effectiveness criteria that can be directly measured, however, equity of settlement is an opinion or attitude and may be perceived quite differently by management, employees and union officials. Lacking a direct measure of equity or an impartial judge or basis of judgment of each grievance settlement, the view of one of the parties to a grievance may have to be selected in order to operationalize the concept of equity of settlement.[9]

In sum, grievance rates, speed of settlement, level of settlement, arbitration usage, and equity of settlement have been identified as criteria of grievance procedure effectiveness. Taken singly, each of these criteria has limitations and weaknesses as a measure of effectiveness. This suggests the desirability of simultaneously examining these criteria in order better to understand the grievance procedure and better to grasp the meaning of grievance procedure effectiveness.

III. DETERMINANTS OF GRIEVANCE PROCEDURE EFFECTIVENESS

A wide variety of independent variables have been specified in studies of grievance procedure effectiveness, with formal modeling and testing being more common to public-sector than to private-sector studies. These variables can be grouped in the following categories: (1) environmental characteristics, (2) worker characteristics, (3) working conditions characteristics, (4) management characteristics, (5) union characteristics, (6) grievance procedure characteristics, and (7) union–management relationship characteristics.[10]

A. Environmental Characteristics

Dunlop (1958) has emphasized the importance of environmental factors in labor–management conflict. More recently and more specifically, Peach and Livernash (1974), in a study set in the steel industry, found higher grievance rates to be associated with large plants located in urban areas. Similarly, Derber et al. (1965), who studied union–management relationships in 37 establishments, found community influence, as partially measured by urbanization, to be positively associated with grievance rates. And Stern (1976), who examined strike frequency in 243 cities, found a significantly higher incidence of strikes in metropolitan than non-metropolitan areas. The results of these studies are consistent with behavioral science research that finds both firm size and urbanization to be negatively related to employee morale. Consequently, among environmental characteristics, size of firm and extent of urbanization are expected to be negatively related to grievance procedure effectiveness (i.e., negatively related to perceived equity of settlement and speed of settlement, but positively related to grievance rates, arbitration rates, and level of settlement).

Technology of the workplace is commonly regarded as an important influence on grievance claims (Kuhn, 1961), although the relationship between technology and grievance procedure effectiveness has rarely, if ever, been investigated. Specifically, a technology that minimizes worker autonomy and maximizes employer control, such as an assembly line type, is considered to lead to high grievance rates. Following this proposition, we would expect such a technology also to be associated with high arbitration rates, lengthy settlements, high levels of settlement, and a perceived low equity of settlement by workers.

B. Worker Characteristics

The relationship between individual worker characteristics and grievance procedure effectiveness has not been explored by researchers, primarily because of data limitations. Other studies (Ashenfelfter, 1972; Freeman, 1980), however, underscore the importance of individual worker characteristics in various dimensions of industrial relations, and such characteristics should be incorporated into any realistic model of grievance procedure effectiveness.

For example, black and female workers may file more grievances and have relatively greater difficulty obtaining speedy and equitable settlements than white male workers. On this basis, minority and female status would be negatively associated with grievance procedure effectiveness. The relationship between worker schooling and grievance procedure effectiveness is not intuitively obvious. On the one hand, greater schooling may translate into greater knowledge of the grievance procedure, greater ability to convert a verbal grievance claim into writing, an unwillingness to settle for a quick or "bargained" outcome, and a willingness to push the grievance to higher levels. On the other hand, such schooling may bring about greater discretion in making grievance claims and using the grievance procedure, a preference for informal, speedy settlement, and greater understanding of the costs of grievance processing at higher levels. A similar set of conflicting arguments can be posited with respect to worker age, experience and on-the-job training, though some research suggests that younger workers are generally more militant than other workers, other things constant, and hence are more likely to file grievances and press them through to upper steps of the procedure. In sum, while it is important to incorporate worker characteristics into a model of grievance procedure effectiveness, the relationships between most of these characteristics and effectiveness cannot be specified *a priori*.[11]

C. Working Conditions

There has been remarkably little investigation of the relationship between working conditions and grievance processing—probably because so much of the literature in this area is of the case study type. The working conditions that can be expected to be related to grievance procedure effectiveness include pay, fringe benefits, and work schedule. More highly paid workers might be expected to file fewer grievances, pursue quicker and lower-level settlements, and resort to arbitration less frequently than relatively low paid workers. For unionized workers in particular, job satisfaction bears (a slight) positive relationship to pay, and the opportunity to use the grievance procedure may offer comparatively more "rewards" to those who are less well paid. A similar rationale can be applied to the relationships between fringe benefits and grievance rates, speed of settlement, level of settlement, and arbitration usage. The relationship between pay or fringe benefits and perceived equity of settlement is indeterminate *a priori*.

Those on full-time work schedules can perhaps be expected to use the grievance procedure more often than those on part-time schedules. However, the latter may be more likely than the former to pursue grievances to higher levels of the procedure, including arbitration, to accept slower settlements, and to have perceptions of less equity in grievance settlement. Hence, the relationship between work schedule and grievance procedure effectiveness depends upon the effectiveness dimension in question.

D. Management Characteristics

On the management side of industrial relations, first-line supervision is generally regarded as of paramount importance to the grievance procedure. In almost all cases, the first-line supervisor is the first step in the grievance procedure and hence should be an important determinant of the procedure's effectiveness. Empirical research (Peach, 1972; Stagner,

1962; Fleishman and Harris, 1962; Weissinger, 1976) has focused on the relationship between various characteristics of supervisors—leadership style, personality, time worked with same union steward—and grievance rates (but not other measures of effectiveness). Researchers and practitioners commonly stress the importance of supervisor quality and training in labor relations affairs (Slichter et al., 1961). Therefore, grievance and arbitration rates should be lower and settlements should be quicker, occur at lower steps of the procedure, and be perceived as more equitable the higher the quality of first-line supervision.

The structure of the labor relations function is also expected to influence grievance procedure effectiveness. Peach and Livernash (1974), for example, found grievance rates and settlement levels to be highest in plants with highly centralized decision-making structures. Gantz (1978) obtained similar results in a study of 118 private-sector bargaining relationships in Canada. Consequently, the centralization of decision making within management is expected to have a negative influence on grievance procedure effectiveness.

Management policies are often cited as important determinants of grievance procedure effectiveness. Some authors posit that the formalization and consistent application of management policies lead to lower grievance rates (Peach and Livernash, 1961). Others, however, note that management may follow a policy of pressing certain categories of grievances to higher steps in the procedure, including arbitration (Slichter et al., 1961). Further, management's commitment to the industrial relations function, and thus its impact on grievance procedure effectiveness, may be reflected in a specific policy, such as whether or not it compensates union officials for the time required to investigate and resolve grievances. Consequently, management policies may have a negative or positive impact on grievance procedure effectiveness.

E.   Union Characteristics

The internal structure and governance of unions and the tactics unions employ are potentially important determinants of grievance procedure effectiveness (Anderson, 1979a). For example, Bok and Dunlop (1970) propose that unions become more effective in grievance processing as they develop administrative bureaucracies. Analogous to management, however, a decentralized decision-making structure may serve to quicken grievance processing and to bring about lower-level settlements. Another dimension of structure that may influence grievance processing is the employment of professional staff by the union. Presumably, a paid staff invests time in contract administration and should improve the effectiveness of the grievance procedure.

Other aspects of union structure and governance have also been found (or been posited) to effect grievance procedure effectiveness. Specifically, the higher the ratio of union stewards to union members, the more likely are grievances to be settled quickly and at lower levels of the procedure (Anderson, 1979a). A high ratio of union stewards to members is also associated with grievants' perceptions of equitable grievance settlements. Further, various authors have identified the presence of a union grievance screening committee as a determinant of "successful" grievance processing (Peach, 1972; Kuhn, 1961). Presumably, such a committee gives the union an opportunity to assess the merits of grievances and, when grievances are processed, to increase the likelihood of their being settled quickly and at lower steps of the procedure. Moreover, as with their management counterparts, the more skilled and experienced the union stewards, the more likely is the grievance procedure to operate effectively.

Peach (1972), Kuhn (1961), and others have proposed that political stability within the union makes for more effective grievance processing. The grievance procedure is more likely to be used to bring pressure on management or to prove the union leaders' competence when new leaders are elected or when established leaders face an election challenge. Additionally, political factors that form within the union typically act to increase the volume of grievance claims. Thus, political stability within the union should increase the effectiveness of the grievance procedure— perhaps in part by increasing the probability of a stable labor–management relationship.

Militant tactics employed by the union in grievance processing have received considerable attention in the literature on this topic. Tactics such as slowdowns and walkouts are thought by some to provide the motivation for management to settle grievances on the union's terms (Chamberlain and Kuhn, 1961); others have proposed that such tactics serve to stiffen management's resistance and thus move grievances to higher steps of the procedure (Slichter et al., 1961). Glassman and Belasco (1975), who studied local public schools, found that the chapter chairman's attitudes toward militance were positively related to the grievance rate but negatively associated with the appeal of grievances to higher levels. In a Canadian study, Anderson (1979a) found that union pressure tactics in grievance processing significantly increased the time to settlement and the percentage of grievances settled in favor of the grievant, but had no effect on grievance and arbitration rates or settlement steps. Therefore, militant tactics may have differential influences on specific criteria of grievance procedure effectiveness.

F.   Grievance Procedure Characteristics

Most discussions of the grievance procedure per se are descriptive and occupied largely with the workings of arbitration as the final step. A subset

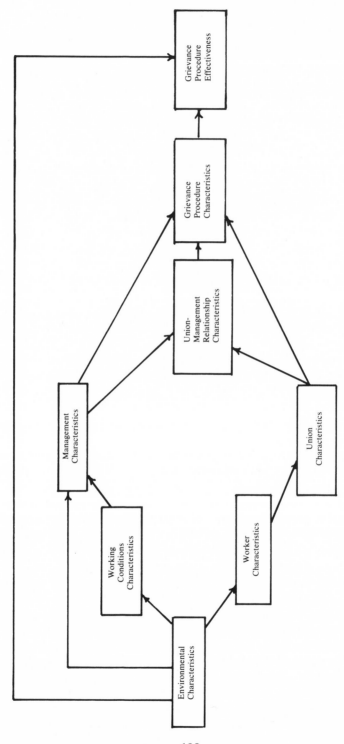

Figure 1. A Model of Grievance Procedure Effectiveness.

of the literature (Walton and McKersie, 1965) deals with the use of adversarial versus problem-solving approaches to grievance handling, and also with informal versus formal grievance processing (Thompson and Murray, 1976). From one perspective, the more formal the procedure, the more likely it is to be associated with effective grievance handling. Alternatively, the high rate of informal grievance settlement that apparently occurs in American industry suggests that informality is positively associated with grievance procedure effectiveness. The latter hypothesis received some support from Anderson's (1979a) study (of Canadian local governments) which found informal grievance settlement to be associated with lower-level settlements, quick settlements, and low grievance and arbitration rates. Further, the presence of an elected union official in the grievance procedure could be expected to be associated with more effective grievance handling.

G.   Union–Management Relationship
Characteristics

Among the characteristics of the union–management relationship that may affect grievance procedure effectiveness are the age or maturity of the relationship and the level of trust or cooperation between the parties. The literature is replete with statements to the effect that, as the labor relationship matures, the parties move from hostility to cooperation and develop higher levels of intergroup trust (Turner and Robinson, 1978). Following these hypotheses, the age of the labor–management relationship and the degree of trust between the parties can be expected to be positively related to grievance procedure effectiveness.

This model of grievance procedure effectiveness, which incorporates the seven sets of independent variables discussed above, is summarized in Figure 1.

IV.   GRIEVANCE PROCEDURE EFFECTIVENESS IN THE PUBLIC SECTOR

How would this model of grievance procedure effectiveness be modified when applied to the public sector? Relatively little, it would seem. Consider, first, that a substantial portion of the research on grievance procedures, especially research of recent vintage, has been done in the public sector, typically in local government (Anderson, 1979a; Briggs, 1981). The model takes account of this research as well as that conducted in the private sector. Second, there is little evidence of behavioral differences between public-sector and private-sector unions or of differences in their internal structures, governance mechanisms, and policies (Lewin et al., 1979; Kochan, 1980). Hence, no separate set of public-sector union characteristics is presently identifiable. Third, grievance procedures, though somewhat less comprehensive in the public than the private sector, operate similarly in the two sectors, featuring common steps and forms of representation (Ullman and Begin, 1970; U.S. Bureau of Labor Statistics, 1975, 1981; U.S. Bureau of the Census, 1980).[12]

The differences that do exist between the public and private sectors and that may be relevant to grievance procedure effectiveness pertain primarily to management characteristics. With respect to the structure of government, for example, several studies have found city manager–type governments to be associated with relatively high pay levels and rates of employee unionization (Ehrenberg and Goldstein, 1975; Lewin et al., 1979; Bartel and Lewin, 1981). This suggests the propriety of including a government structure variable in a model of public-sector grievance procedure effectiveness. Similarly, many governments maintain civil service systems that often contain appeals procedures which bear some— but only some—similarity to grievance procedures. Where these exist and where employees have the choice of using one or the other procedure, a civil service variable can be incorporated into the model of grievance procedure effectiveness.[13]

Perhaps the most important difference between the public and private sectors insofar as industrial relations is concerned has to do with the nature of bargaining in the two sectors. In brief, and unlike bilateral bargaining in the private sector, public-sector bargaining has been found to be multilateral in nature in that there are more than two distinct parties to negotiations (Kochan, 1974; Feuille, 1974). Decision-making authority typically is widely dispersed within a government, and this fragmentation is not necessarily overcome for bargaining purposes by creating a labor relations office or by designating a chief management spokesman for negotiations. In a city government, for example, a mayor, a city council, individual department heads, a chief administrative officer, a city attorney, and others may play roles in labor relations, even if none of them "negotiates" directly with organized employees. The presence and persistence of such diverse decision-making authorities means that there is a large amount of internal conflict on the management side of the public-sector bargaining table—considerably more conflict than is presumed to exist within the management structure of the firm (Kochan, 1980). Not only does such conflict tend to induce certain bargaining tactics on the part of public sector unions, such as "end runs," that are less common to or nonexistent in the private sector, it also may reduce the effectiveness of grievance procedures in the public sector. Following the latter proposition, an internal management conflict variable should be added to other management characteristics when modeling and testing for grievance procedure effectiveness in the public sector.

V. GRIEVANCE PROCEDURE EFFECTIVENESS AND SOME OUTCOMES OF UNIONISM

Empirical research on grievance procedures has been conducted largely by behavioral scientists and "institutional" economists. This work reflects a central interest in the labor relations process and only a subsidiary interest in labor relations outcomes. Until recently, most "outcome" research in industrial relations was concerned with the impact of unions on relative wages, a subject that received a boost from the development of human capital theory and the construction of new data sets on individual workers. However, several newer studies, including those of Freeman (1980), Freeman and Medoff (1979), Clarke (1980), and Cooke (1981), have employed the exit-voice model of the social system developed by Hirschman (1970) to analyze some of the nonwage consequences of unionism and collective bargaining.

To summarize briefly, these studies propose that "voice" in the labor market is principally reflected in the institutions of unionism and collective bargaining. When such institutions exist, "workers have a voice . . . for expressing discontent [and] they should use the exit option less frequently and thus exhibit lower quit rates and longer spells of job tenure with firms" (Freeman, 1980, p. 643). Empirical tests of these hypotheses find that "*with wages and other measures of pecurinary reward held fixed,* trade unionism is associated with significant large reductions in exit behavior" (Freeman, 1980, p. 644, italics in original); such reductions are key to the union-induced productivity gains that have also been identified in this type of research (Brown and Medoff, 1978; Freeman and Medoff, 1979; Clarke, 1980).[14] But, while the exit-reducing tendencies of unionism seem relatively clear, the "interpretation of the impact of unionism in terms of 'voice' is open to some question" (Freeman, 1980, p. 644).

Why is this so? Why is the union effect on exit behavior more evident and identifiable than the union effect on voice? One reason, perhaps, is that their are more and better data for assessing the union impact on worker exit (and productivity) than for assessing the union impact on worker exercise of voice. Specifically, data on output per work hour, separations, quits, and job tenure are readily available and pertain to actual worker (and firm) behavior. In contrast, data on voice are much less readily available *and tend not to reflect actual behavior.* For example, with the level of job satisfaction (an attitudinal measure) held constant, unionized workers have been shown to have lower quit rates than nonunion workers (Freeman, 1980). The commonly accepted interpretation of this finding is that unionized workers have more opportunity to exercise voice than nonunion workers. But there is no direct evidence on this point and, indeed, one might expect that the comparative advantage of unionized workers in exercising such voice would result in higher levels of job satisfaction than exist among nonunion workers. However, this supposition is not supported by surveys of worker job satisfaction (Survey Research Center, 1978).

Another (indirect) method of assessing the union impact on workers' exercise of voice is to compare quit rates under grievance procedures of varying scope and dimension. The results show that quit rates are lowest where the most comprehensive grievance provisions prevail, and the interpretation, once again, is that such procedural comprehensiveness is a reflection of the exercise of voice (Freeman, 1980). But in these studies, there is no direct evidence of grievances actually filed, handled, or resolved under existing procedures!

Finally, the voice-inducing properties of unionism are often inferred from the behavior of firms that adopt grievancelike appeals systems for their nonunion personnel. The standard interpretation is that, through these systems, employers are attempting to provide a substitute for unions, thereby hopefully preventing the unionization of their (nonunion) work forces (Freeman, 1980, Berenbeim, 1980). Of course, if such nonunion appeals systems were as widely prevalent as negotiated grievance procedures, it would be difficult to explain why quit rates should differ so substantially (other variables held constant) between organized and unorganized workers. This point aside, it is apparent that even the most closely reasoned analyses of exit-voice behavior in the labor market tend to rely on inferrential evidence in associating unionism with workers' exercise of voice.

VI. CONCLUSION

If unionism reduces exit behavior, lengthens job tenure, and increases productivity; if these consequences stem from the voice that unions provide to organized workers in the employment relationship; and if the grievance procedure is the principal forum for exercising voice, then the concept of grievance procedure effectiveness takes on new importance. Such effectiveness can now be modeled not as a dependent variable, but as an intervening variable, linking the major independent variables described above with the outcomes of unionism and collective bargaining (this is shown in Figure 2). Specifically a more effective grievance procedure, by which is meant a procedure that features low grievance and arbitration rates, speedy and low-level settlements, and settlements that workers perceive to be highly equitable, should be associated with low quit rates, long job tenure, and high output per work hour. Empirical testing of this model (which will commence shortly and be reported in another set of papers) should provide direct, behavioral evidence about workers' ex-

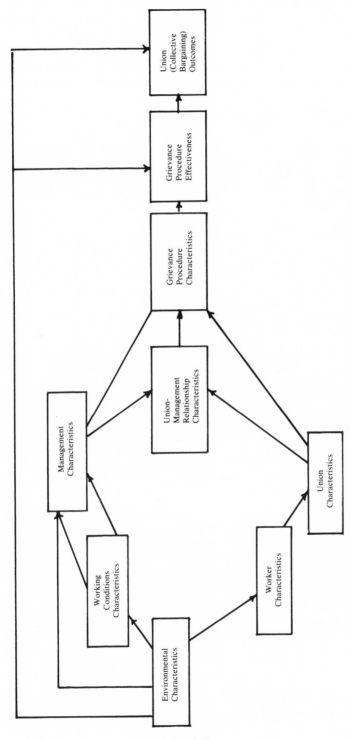

Figure 2. A Model of Grievance Procedure Effectiveness and Union Outcomes.

143

ercise of voice and illuminate the linkages between the processes and outcomes that are commonly, if separately, associated with labor unions (see Lewin, 1980; Peterson and Lewin, 1982; Lewin and Feuille, 1983).

ACKNOWLEDGMENTS

The comments on an earlier version of this manuscript of participants in the Conference on New Approaches to Labor Unions, held at Virginia Polytechnic Institute and State University, Blacksburg, Virginia, October 1981, are gratefully acknowledged, as are the comments of an anonymous referee.

NOTES

1. The more highly unionized the firm, the lower the probability that it will have an appeals system for its nonunion employees (Berenbeim, 1980, pp. 3–5). Avoidance of unionism is among the leading reasons given by employers for adopting nonunion appeals systems. Unlike grievance procedures in unionized contexts, nonunion appeals systems rarely incorporate arbitration as the last step of the procedure.

2. But see Peach and Livernash (1974), Thompson and Murray (1976), Gandz (1978), and Anderson (1979a).

3. Thus, this paper is an attempt to develop a theoretical framework for the analysis of grievance procedures; it does not report new empirical evidence. The empirical testing of the model will be carried out over the 1982–1983 period under a grant from the National Science Foundation (see Lewin (1980) for further detail).

4. This interpretation is consistent with the view that unions can "shock" management to improve personnel policies (see Rees, 1977, pp. 92–94). Note that union officials also use grievance information for decision making in connection with the enforcement of the labor agreement.

5. Farber and Saks (1980) found that "if individuals felt that they were being treated unfairly . . . they would be more likely to vote for unionization" (p. 384).

6. For further analysis of such work groups, see Sayles (1958).

7. These effectiveness criteria are also discussed by Anderson (1979a) and Briggs (1981). Also see Peterson and Lewin (1982). The concept of effectiveness is treated very differently by economists and industrial relations–organizational behavior scholars. The former associate the concept with a "final outcome," represented, for example, by the notion of Pareto optimality, while the latter treat the concept in "process" or "intermediate" terms. For a systematic analysis of these different research perspectives on industrial relations more broadly, see Lewin and Feuille (1983).

8. Arbitration is the final step in all but about 4 percent of grievance procedures in American industry (U.S. Bureau of Labor Statistics, 1981). For discussion and examples of the structure of these procedures, see Chamberlain et al. (1980), Chapter 5.

9. Both Anderson (1979a) and Briggs (1980) operationalize equity of settlement as the proportion of grievances settled in the grievant's favor.

10. The model developed here is similar to those which have recently been formulated to examine collective bargaining outcomes, especially nonwage outcomes. See Kochan and Wheeler (1975), Gerhart (1976), Kochan and Block (1977), Anderson (1979b), and Lewin et al. (1981).

11. Occupation is another important worker characteristic that may affect grievance procedure effectiveness. However, in subsequent empirical work, this model will be tested

against cross-sectional data, with occupation entering the analysis as a control variable. Hence, occupation is not discussed here.

12.   Note, however, that the scope of issues treated under grievance procedures is generally narrower in the public than the private sector.

13.   In some governments, unionized employees can choose between filing grievance claims under a negotiated grievance procedure or a civil service–type appeals system. In other governments, only nonunion employees may use the civil service appeals system.

14.   Note that the effects described here are associated with unionism per se. These studies *do not* attempt to differentiate the effects of unions that have and *have not* obtained collective bargaining agreements with employers. Other research—for example, that conducted on the wage effects of unionism (Ehrenberg, 1971)—shows that such effects are larger and/or more significant where unions have achieved collective bargaining agreements with employers.

REFERENCES

Anderson, John C. (1979), "The Grievance Process in Canadian Municipal Labor Relations." Paper presented to the 39th Annual Meeting of the Academy of Management, Atlanta, Georgia, August.

——— (1979b), "Bargaining Outcomes: An IR Systems Approach." *Industrial Relations* 18(Spring):127–143.

Ashenfelter, Orley, "Racial Discrimination and Trade Unionism." *Journal of Political Economy* 80(May/June):435–464.

Bartel, Ann, and David Lewin (1981), "Wages and Unionism In The Public Sector: The Case of Police." *The Review of Economics and Statistics* 63(February):153–159.

Begin, James P. (1971). "The Private Grievance Model in the Public Sector." *Industrial Relations* 10(February):21–35.

Berenbeim, Ronald (1980), *Non Union Complaint Systems: A Corporate Approach.* Report No. 770. New York: The Conference Board.

Bok, Derek C., and John T. Dunlop (1970), *Labor and the American Community.* New York: Simon and Schuster.

Briggs, Steven (1981), *The Municipal Grievance Process In California.* Unpublished Ph.D. dissertation. Los Angeles: University of California.

Brown, Charles, and James Medoff (1978), "Trade Unions in the Production Process." *Journal of Political Economy* 86(June):335–378.

Chamberlain, Neil W., and James W. Kuhn (1965), *Collective Bargaining,* 2nd ed. New York: McGraw-Hill.

Chamberlain, Neil W., Donald E. Cullen, and David Lewin (1980), *The Labor Sector,* 3rd ed. New York: McGraw-Hill.

Clark, Kim B. (1980), "The Impact of Unionization on Productivity: A Case Study." *Industrial and Labor Relations Review* 33(July):451–459.

Cooke, William N. (1981), "The Collective Decision to Unionize: Theory and Evidence." *Industrial and Labor Relations Review* 36(April):forthcoming.

Derber, Milton, et al. (1965), *Plant Union-Management Relations.* Urbana, Ill.: University of Illinois Press.

Dunlop, John T. (1958), *Industrial Relations Systems.* New York: Holt.

Ehrenberg, Ronald G. (1973), "Municipal Government Structure, Unionization and the Wages of Firefighters." *Industrial and Labor Relations Review* 27(October):36–48.

Ehrenberg, Ronald G., and Gerald S. Goldstein (1975), "A Model of Public Sector Wage Determination." *Journal of Urban Economics* 2(July):223–245.

Farber, Henry S., and Daniel H. Saks (1980), "Why Workers Want Unions: The Role of Relative Wages and Job Characteristics." *Journal of Political Economy* 88(April):349–369.

Feuille, Peter (1974), "Police Labor Relations and Multilateralism." *Proceedings of the Twenty-Sixth Annual Meeting of the Industrial Relations Research Association, 1973.* Madison, Wis.: IRRA, pp. 170–177.

Fleishman, Edwin A., and Edwin F. Harris (1962), "Patterns of Leadership Behavior Related to Employee Grievances and Turnover." *Personnel Psychology* 15(Winter):43–55.

Freeman, Richard B. (1976), "Individual Mobility and Union Voice in the Labor Market." *American Economic Review* 66(May):361–368.

——— (1980), "The Exit-Voice Tradeoff in the Labor Market: Unionism, Job Tenure, Quits, and Separations." *The Quarterly Journal of Economics* 94(June):643–673.

Freeman, Richard B., and James Medoff (1979), "The Two Faces of Unionism." *The Public Interest* 57(Fall):69–93.

Gandz, Jeffrey (1978), "Union-Management Relationships, Grievance Rates and Arbitration." Working Paper Series No. 203, School of Business Administration, University of Western Ontario, London, Canada, July.

Gerhart, Paul F. (1976), "Determinants of Bargaining Outcomes in Local Government Labor Negotiations." *Industrial and Labor Relations Review* 29(April):331–351.

Glassman, Alan, and James Belasco (1975), "The Chapter Chairman and School Grievances." *Industrial Relations* 14(May):233–241.

Hirschman, Albert O. (1970), *Exit, Voice and Loyalty.* Cambridge, Mass.: Harvard University Press.

Kennedy, Thomas (1948), *Effective Labor Arbitration: The Impartial Chairmanship of the Full-fashioned Hosiery Industry.* Philadelphia: University of Pennsylvania Press.

Knight, Thomas (1978), *Factors Affecting the Arbitration Submission Rate: A Comparative Case Study.* Unpublished Master's Thesis. Ithaca, New York: Cornell University.

Kochan, Thomas A. (1974), "A Theory of Multilateral Collective Bargaining in City Government." *Industrial and Labor Relations Review* 27(July):525–542.

——— (1980), *Collective Bargaining and Industrial Relations: From Theory to Policy and Practice.* Homewood, Ill.: Irwin.

Kochan, Thomas A., and Hoyt N. Wheeler (1975), "Municipal Collective Bargaining: A Model and Analysis of Bargaining Outcomes." *Industrial and Labor Relations Review* 29(October):46–66.

Kochan, Thomas A., and Richard N. Block (1977), "An Interindustry Analysis of Bargaining Outcomes: Preliminary Evidence From Two-Digit Industries." *Quarterly Journal of Economics* 91(August):431–452.

Kuhn, James W. (1961), *Bargaining In Grievance Settlement.* New York: Columbia University Press.

Lewin, David (1978), "The Impact of Unionism On American Business: Evidence For An Assessment." *Columbia Journal of World Business* 13(Spring):89–104.

——— (1980), "The Grievance Procedure in Private and Public Sector Labor Relations: A Theoretical and Empirical Analysis." Proposal submitted to the National Science Foundation. New York: Columbia University, processed July.

Lewin, David, Raymond D. Horton, and James W. Kuhn (1979), *Collective Bargaining and Manpower Utilization in Big City Governments.* Montclair, N.J.: Allanheld Osmun.

Lewin, David, Peter Feuille, and Thomas A. Kochan (1981), *Public Sector Labor Relations: Analysis and Readings,* 2nd ed. Sun City, Ariz.: Horton and Daughters.

Lewin, David, and Peter Feuille (1983), "Behavioral Research in Industrial Relations." *Industrial and Labor Relations Review* 36(April):forthcoming.

McKersie, Robert B., and William W. Shropshire (1962), "Avoiding Written Grievances: A Successful Program." *Journal of Business* 35(April):133–147.

Miller, Glen W., and Ned Rosen (1957), "Members' Attitudes Toward the Shop Steward." *Industrial and Labor Relations Review* 10(July):516–531.

Peach, David A. (1972), "Union and Management Decision-Making in the Grievance Process." *Relations Industrielles* 27(Fall):757–767.

Peach, David A., and E. Robert Livernash (1974), *Grievance Initiation and Resolution: A Study in Basic Steel.* Cambridge, Mass.: Graduate School of Business, Harvard University.

Peterson, Richard B., and David Lewin (1982), "A Model for Research and Analysis of the Grievance Process." *Proceedings of the Thirty-Fourth Annual Meeting of the Industrial Relations Research Association, 1981.* Madison, Wisc.: IRRA, pp. 303–312.

Pettefer, J. C. (1970), "Effective Grievance Administration." *California Management Review* 13(Winter):12–18.

Rees, Albert (1977), *The Economics of Trade Unions,* rev. ed. Chicago: University of Chicago Press.

Sayles, Leonard R. (1958), *Behavior of Industrial Work Groups.* New York: McGraw-Hill.

Slichter, Sumner, James H. Healy, and E. Robert Livernash (1960), *The Impact of Collective Bargaining On Management.* Washington, D.C.: Brookings Institution.

Stagner, Ross (1962), "Personality Variables in Union-Management Relations." *Journal of Applied Psychology* 46(October):350–357.

Stern, Robert N. (1976), "Intermetropolitan Patterns of Strike Frequency." *Industrial and Labor Relations Review* 29(January):218–235.

Survey Research Center, University of Michigan (1978), *The 1977 Quality of Employment Survey.* Ann Arbor.

Thompson, Andrew J. W. (1974), *The Grievance Procedure In The Private Sector.* Ithaca, New York: New York State School of Industrial and Labor Relations, Cornell University.

Thompson, Andrew J. W., and Victor F. Murray (1976), *Grievance Procedures.* Westmead, England: Saxon House.

Trotta, Maurice (1974), *The Arbitration of Labor-Management Disputes.* New York: American Management Association.

Turner, James T., and James W. Robinson (1972), "A Pilot Study of the Validity of Grievance Settlement Rates as a Predictor of Union Management Relationships." *Journal of Industrial Relations* 14(December):314–322.

Ullman, Joseph C., and James P. Begin (1970), "The Structure and Scope of Appeals Procedures for Public Employees." *Industrial and Labor Relations Review* 23(April):323–334.

U.S. Bureau of Labor Statistics (1964), *Major Collective Bargaining Agreements: Grievance Procedures.* Bulletin No. 1425-1. Washington, D.C.: U.S. Government Printing Office.

——— (1975), *Grievance and Arbitration Procedures in State and Local Agreements.* Bulletin No. 1833. Washington, D.C.: U.S. Government Printing Office.

——— (1981), *Characteristics of Major Collective Bargaining Agreements.* Washington, D.C.: U.S. Government Printing Office.

U.S. Bureau of the Census (1980), *Labor-Management Relations In State and Local Governments: 1978.* State and Local Government, Special Studies No. 95. Washington, D.C.: U.S. Government Printing Office.

Walton, Richard E., and Robert B. McKersie (1965), *A Behavioral Theory of Labor Negotiations.* New York: McGraw-Hill.

Weissinger, William J. (1976), *The Determinants of Grievance Rates: A Case Study.* Unpublished Master's Thesis. Ithaca, New York: Cornell University.

DISCUSSION

Bernard F. Lentz

The two papers by Michael Kurth and David Lewin produce some interesting conjectures that strongly suggest the need for empirical testing of their models of the role of public-sector unions and grievance procedures. Still, a fundamental difference exists in their basic conception of the public employer. Kurth argues that public-sector unions serve the interests of local elected officials, who therefore often have welcomed unionism among their employees. Lewin suggests that there is little difference between grievance procedures in the public and private sectors. It is clear that private employers have resisted unions, despite any presumed benefits from grievance procedures. Thus, that public-sector and private-sector unions differ because of differences in the objective function of the employers with whom they deal is essential. This fact can be shown to have a substantial bearing on the modeling of grievance processes in both sectors.

At the base of the distinction between public-sector and private-sector employers are the methods by which they are chosen and the ownership

New Approaches to Labor Unions.
Research in Labor Economics, Supplement 2, pages 149–153.
Copyright © 1983 by JAI Press Inc.
All rights of reproduction in any form reserved.
ISBN: 0-89232-265-9

rights of the persons who chose the employer. Crudely, private-sector employers are chosen by the stockholders of firms who are seeking financial return on their capital invested. These shareholders, through a combination of capital market and shareholders actions, attempt to select employers who act so as to maximize the expected returns on stockholder capital. Public employers are elected periodically by voters who have attenuated rights over any returns that may be produced by the public sector and who derive utility from a wide variety of government actions. Indeed, voters may look to government for a good-paying job! This reliance of the public employer on being elected or reelected suggests that employees in the public sector will be compensated not only for their public service output, but also for the votes they have themselves or may produce by direct political activity. In sum, public employers have expected vote objectives and private employers have expected profit objectives.

Of perhaps equal importance as this difference between objective functions of public-sector and private-sector employers are the changes in objective functions that occur with changes in individual public employers. One may argue that the electoral objective function really does not change from one administration to the next. On the other hand, the fact that the political coalition supporting one administration has different policy goals (and workers with which it wishes to achieve those goals) from those of the previous administration is a recurring fact of life for workers in the public sector. While it is true that takeovers in private industry will sometimes witness a housecleaning of top management, the degree of employment instability in the public sector under the patronage system is enormous, and often the housecleaning reaches down to the level of janitors and part-time summer employees (Ranzal, 1977). Cannot unionization of public employees be a response to such employment instability? Others have found adverse market or technological changes to give rise to unions in the private sector.

Kurth argues that the destabilizing influences of federal government intergovernmental transfers led to a disruption of local government political equilibria and to the militant unionism and strikes of the 1960s. However, one could argue the importance of other changes that occurred in the 1960s or shortly before and that upset the electoral coalitions in which public employees participated. In particular, the vast changes in the underlying electorate of most major northern cities, which resulted from the flight to the suburbs of white ethnics, plausibly could have induced elected officials radically to alter traditional compensation and employment schemes of public employee groups drawn largely from the now-absent white ethnic population. As perhaps the most blatant example, the New York State Civil Service Commission and the New York State Department of Civil Service attempted to grant preference in appointment to applicants "who are successful in the examination and who have recognizable identification with Black and Spanish-speaking minority communities" (*Jackson* v. *Poston*, 1971, 68 Misc2d 590, 328 N.Y.S. 279). In the same vein, contrast the heavily unionized city of New York, where Mayor Lindsay walked through the riot-torn streets of Harlem, with the largely nonunion city of Chicago, where charges of segregation still are heard and Mayor Daley issued his famous "shoot to kill" order to the police handling the West Side riots. The first major strike in New York City occurred the day that Lindsay took office, a strike that was conducted by a union characterized as having substantial racial conflicts (Horton, 1973).

It is not easy to present evidence of the sources of political instability in general. But evidence of the impact on public unions of potential changes in elected officials-employer is available at the state government level. Of the 35 state employee organizations surveyed by Lelchook (1973) which were not founded as spinoff associations, 82.35 percent were founded in either a gubernatorial election year or the year following a gubernatorial election. These associations cited protection of retirement systems or civil service systems as major reasons for their formation. Thus, we see that even if the patronage system has been reduced, so that public employers are compelled by law to continue employees in their current positions, a change of employer-elected official is likely to disadvantage public employees and thus cause them to organize or strike.

One might consider the payment of dues to a union or association as the insurance premium that the public employee spends to make more certain his income from government employment. The general perception of public employees is that they are highly risk-averse. If true, it is surprising that public employers historically have resisted granting public employees coverage under unemployment insurance laws: in 1971, only 7.19 percent of all state and local government were covered by state unemployment insurance laws, according to the Manpower Administration (1972). One can only guess that public employers, who have been frequently shown to pay substantial wage premia on average, sought to elicit electoral activity of their employees, who were adverse to the possible loss of their jobs and who therefore sought to insure themselves by a higher level of campaign activity and the resultant greater likelihood of the relection of their current employer.

IMPACT OF EMPLOYER OBJECTIVE FUNCTION CHANGES ON GRIEVANCE PROCEDURES

Frequently, it has been asserted that the reason that unions place such emphasis on grievance procedures and that unions themselves come into being is the desire of employees to avoid arbitrary and capricious behavior on the part of their employer. Most neoclassical economists, however, would argue that no profit-maximizing employer would ever allow any truly arbitrary and capricious behavior by his agents, for it would assuredly raise his labor costs through increased quits and decreased recruits. The above discussion suggests that "arbitrary and capricious" may take on a new meaning in public-sector grievance proceedings, when there is a change of public employers. For example, if a conservative administration is elected to a state house, it would slow processing of welfare and unemployment insurance claims to keep down costs and make potential workers search more in the labor market. A liberal administration probably would increase the speed with which these transfer payments are made, to increase the level of needed services provided by state government. Public workers in either the unemployment office or the welfare department could argue that the change of administration led to an arbitrary and capricious change in the basis of measuring their productivity for purposes of pay increases, promotions, and the like. Just this sort of change in management philosophy caused a great increase in grievances in mental health departments in the states of Ohio, Michigan, New York, and Massachusetts (Crane et al., 1976).

I have been emphasizing changes of employer in the public sector, for it seems that these changes more likely will produce great shifts in employer objective functions. But these changes may also occur outside government when individual output is hard to measure, as with team production, or when supervisors take personnel actions which serve their own interests and not the goals of the firm. A new foreman may produce great friction with the supervised workers, due to his ignorance of the implicit (as opposed to explicit) contracts that his predecessor had made. Thus, it is even possible in the for-profit sector that changes of employer will lead to increased worker dissatisfaction and increased grievances or moves toward unionization. The actions of employers and workers evidenced in the Howard Johnson [Supreme Court, 73-631 (1974)] and Burns Security [406 U.S. 272 (1972)] cases are ample evidence that employer changes can create labor relations problems.

In summary, unionization or increased utilization of union services via the grievance procedure may be the result of changes in employers or supervisors and consequent breaches of implicit contracts. Indeed, this sort of logic perhaps is related to the recent work on strikes of Reder and Neuman (1980), who argue that a shorter bargaining history leads to more breakdowns in union–management negotiations. What I am arguing is that the human capital accumulated in labor relations likely is not only firm-specific, but perhaps team- or individual-specific. Thus, Lewin's concern with the level of training of supervisors must go far beyond considerations of number of training courses in labor relations. Similarly, I believe that Kurth's analysis of unionization and strikes in the public sector must take account of disruptions of public worker–public employer implicit contracts that are due to the all-too-frequent changes and potential changes in public employers. In fact, one could see the advent of public-employee associations and their support for civil service likewise as emanating from public-employer instability.

REFERENCES

Crane, Edgar G., Bernard F. Lentz, and Jay M. Shafritz (1976), *State Government Productivity: The Environment for Improvement*. New York: Praeger Publishers, Inc.

Horton, Raymond D. (1973), *Municipal Labor Relations in New York City: The Lessons of the Lindsay-Wagner Years*. New York: Praeger Publishers, Inc.

Lelchook, Jerry (1973), *State Civil Service Employee Associations: An LMSA Staff Study*. Washington, D.C.: U.S. Department of Labor, Labor-Management Services Administration.

Lentz, Bernard F. (1976), *Public Sector Wage Determination: A Democratic Theory of Economics*. Unpublished dissertation, Yale University.

Ranzal, Edward (1977), "Summer Job List of 200 Youths With Political Ties is Canceled." *New York Times*, May 4, 1977, D-D15.

Reder, Melvin W., and George Neumann (1980), "Conflict and Contract: The Case of Strikes." *Journal of Political Economy* 88:867–86.

Smith, Sharon P. (1977), "Government Wage Differential." *Journal of Urban Economics* 4:521–34.

U.S. Department of Labor, Manpower Administration (1972), *Employment and Wages of Workers Covered by State Unemployment Insurance Laws, First Quarter, 1971*, 55.

PART III

EMPIRICAL ANALYSIS OF

LABOR UNIONS

THE EFFECT OF UNIONIZATION AND CIVIL SERVICE ON THE SALARIES AND PRODUCTIVITY OF REGULATORS

Eli M. Noam

A large number of recent studies have investigated the effect of unionization on the *compensation* of private and public employees.[1] Other analyses, noticeably smaller in number and concentrating exclusively on the private sector, have looked at the effects of unionization on *productivity* (Clark, 1980a,b; Brown and Medoff, 1978; Ehrenberg and Schwarz, 1981). Their focus is on the question of whether union protection reduces the incentives for employee performance or whether it leads to a workforce with higher morale and lower turnover, and hence to greater labor productivity. Surprisingly, no study has yet integrated the simultaneous effects of unionization on compensation and on productivity, even though they are plainly two sides of the same coin. A salary increase may attract a better and more productive quality of employee, while more productive

New Approaches to Labor Unions.
Research in Labor Economics, Supplement 2, pages 157–170.
Copyright © 1983 by JAI Press Inc.
All rights of reproduction in any form reserved.
ISBN: 0-89232-265-9

employees may command higher salaries. Because of this simultaneity, an analysis of the effect of unionization on compensation is not conclusive without an investigation of the effects of unionization on productivity, and vice versa. Quite possibly, changes in wages that are attributed to unions are overestimated because they partly reflect changes in productivity due to an upgraded work force.

The aim of this paper is threefold: (1) to provide a simultaneous analysis of the salary and productivity effects of unionization, an approach that has not been taken by any previous study; (2) to investigate the relation of unionization (and of civil service tenure) to the productivity of public employees, since past work on unions and their impact on productivity has dealt with the private sector only;[2] and (3) to look at the effects of unionization (and civil service) on *regulators,* since regulation is a public service that has not yet been investigated at all for its sensitivity to unionization.

The paper proceeds by developing a brief model of productivity and salary under a union and a nonunion state, showing that the direction of a union effect is ambiguous theoretically and dependent on the parameters of the model. It then estimates these relations empirically for local building departments, finding significantly higher salaries but no higher productivity where unionization and civil service exist.

I. THE MODEL

Assume a production function for a fixed-capital service of public administration, such as regulatory oversight, of a Cobb–Douglas form

$$\phi = \alpha(QL)^\beta, \tag{1}$$

where ϕ = units of output;
       L = units of labor in hours;
       Q = quality of labor; and
       $\alpha > 0, \quad 0 < \beta < 1.$

The supply of labor is perfectly elastic at the prevailing wage. Only one type of labor is hired. The quality of labor Q that is hired is a function of wage rate paid

$$S = M + Q^\gamma \tag{2}$$

where S = wage rate
       M = minimum wage rate
and[3] $\gamma > 1.$

Also assumed is a fixed budget B for the public service, which is spent on salaries for its employees. We assume a purely administrative program without transfer payments, and without new capital outlays. For many established regulatory agencies, this is a fairly realistic budget structure. Over the past decade their budgets have increased very little in real terms. Thus

$$B = S \cdot L \tag{3}$$

Let us now consider two situations, one with a union and one without it. In state U an employee union and civil service exist and protect employees' jobs at hiring level $\hat{L}$ (or, alternatively, wage level $\hat{S}$), while in state N these numbers are variable. For both states it is assumed that the agency's objective is, within its constraints, to maximize its activity level, i.e., output.[4]

In the no-unions situation N, the head of an agency can hire any combination of labor quantity and quality, subject only to his budget constraint B. We thus have a constrained maximization problem given by the Lagrangean function Z:

$$Z = \alpha(QL)^\beta + \lambda(B - L(M + Q^\gamma)), \tag{4}$$

which can be solved for the optimal quantity of labor L, in the nonunion situation N, by meeting the conditions

$$\frac{\partial Z}{\partial L} = \alpha\beta Q^\beta L^{\beta-1} + \lambda(M + Q^\gamma) = 0 \tag{5}$$

$$\frac{\partial Z}{\partial Q} = \alpha\beta Q^{\beta-1} L^\beta + \lambda\gamma L Q^{\gamma-1} = 0 \tag{6}$$

$$\frac{\partial Z}{\partial \lambda} = B - L(M + Q^\gamma) = 0. \tag{7}$$

This solves to the optimal labor hired

$$L_N = \frac{B(\gamma - 1)}{M\gamma}. \tag{8}$$

Second order conditions for a maximum are satisfied at that point.

With L_N known, average wages can be found by simply dividing the budget by the units of labor $S = B/L_N$ so that optimal salary paid is

$$S_N = \frac{M\gamma}{\gamma - 1} \tag{9}$$

Hence, the relation of the actual salary S_N to minimum wages M is determined by the size of γ (the elasticity of the salary addition to minimum wages with respect to the quality of labor). Where γ is large, S_N

approaches M, because it would be too expensive to hire highly qualified labor.

From Eq. (9) the optimal labor quality Q_N, via Eq. (2), is

$$Q_N = (S - M)^{1/\gamma} = \left(\frac{M}{\gamma - 1}\right)^{1/\gamma} \tag{10}$$

and the quantity of output produced is

$$\phi_N = \alpha(QL)^\beta = \alpha \left[\left(\frac{M}{\gamma - 1}\right)^{[(1/\gamma) - 1]} \frac{B}{\gamma}\right]^\beta . \tag{11}$$

In the alternative situation U, an employee union and a civil service status exist and define an inflexible "civil service" employment level $\hat{L}$. Given a budget B, the average salary is then

$$S_U = \frac{B}{\hat{L}} . \tag{12}$$

We can also make the alternative assumption that the union fixes salaries at a level $\hat{S}$. This is merely the other side of the same coin.[5] With quality and salary related, from before, by the function

$$S_U = M + Q^\gamma, \tag{13}$$

the quality of labor is then determined at

$$Q_U = \left(\frac{B}{\hat{L}} - M\right)^{1/\gamma} \tag{14}$$

and the output of the agency is

$$\phi_U = \alpha(LQ)^\beta = \alpha\hat{L}^\beta \left(\frac{B}{\hat{L}} - M\right)^{\beta/\gamma} . \tag{15}$$

If we define average productivity per employee as ϕ/L, we find that in the nonunion situation productivity is

$$\left(\frac{\phi}{L}\right)_N = \alpha \left(\frac{M}{\gamma - 1}\right)^{\beta[(1/\gamma) - 1] + 1} \left(\frac{B}{\gamma}\right)^{\beta - 1} \tag{16}$$

and with unions it is

$$\left(\frac{\phi}{L}\right)_U = \alpha\hat{L}^{\beta - 1} \left(\frac{B}{\hat{L}} - M\right)^{\beta/\gamma} . \tag{17}$$

When the two sets of results are compared, one can predict the direction of the union effect on salaries and on the quality of employees. A higher salary and greater labor quality exist under a union whenever the condition holds

$$\hat{L} < \frac{B}{M} \frac{\gamma - 1}{\gamma} \tag{18}$$

This is equivalent to the condition

$$\frac{S}{M} > \frac{\gamma}{\gamma - 1} . \tag{18'}$$

The direction of the union effect on productivity depends on the parameters and cannot be predicted unambiguously. Productivity is higher (lower) under a unionized system when

$$\left(\frac{B}{\hat{L}} - M\right)^{\beta/\gamma} \gtreqless \left(\frac{M}{\gamma - 1}\right)^{(\beta/\gamma) - \beta + 1} \left(\frac{B}{\gamma L}\right)^{\beta - 1} . \tag{19}$$

The next section will empirically test the relations of salaries and productivity with and without unions.

II. EMPIRICAL ANALYSIS

The regulatory bodies which are analyzed are local building departments, the agencies that administer building codes. Building departments formulate and update the construction standards under which builders must operate (building codes); they pass judgment on technical construction plans by granting building permits; and they inspect construction sites for compliance. Information for more than 1100 building departments is available from the 1970 survey.[6]

Let the average productivity be given by the functional relationship

$$\frac{\phi}{L} = f_1(U, C, Q_i, X_j), \tag{20}$$

where ϕ = labor output;
    L = number of employees;
    U = employee unionization;
    C = civil service status;
    Q_i = quality variables for employees; and
    X_j = local characteristics that affect primarily productivity.

Since Eq. (2) defines salaries as a function of employee quality, the productivity equation is also estimated, in the alternative, as a function of salaries

$$\frac{\phi}{L} = f_2(U, C, S, X_j). \tag{20'}$$

Salary S of building department employees (defined as the midpoint between starting salaries and that of the highest official next to the chief himself) is affected—by hypothesis—by unionization, civil service, and, from Eq. (2), by the quality of employees. It may also be a function of the prevailing level of compensation in the area, of the local tax base, the political attitude toward regulation in general, and the conformity of the agency's activities to the local political balance. Hence, we write the effects of unionization on salaries as

$$S = g(U, C, \phi/L, Q_i, I, Y, A, F), \tag{21}$$

where S, U, C, and ϕ/L are defined as above, and
  Q_i = quality variables of employees;
  I = prevailing private industry wages;
  Y = local tax base;
  A = local attitude towards public spending; and
  F = conformity of agency policy relative to local interest groups'
       strengths.

Thus, we have a system of equations describing interactions of productivity and salary. This system can be estimated empirically. Let us begin by defining the variables.

For output ϕ we use two alternative measures: the number of building permits granted and the total construction volume supervised. It is not obvious a priori which measure is the better one. The first gives the number of decision processes, but without regard to their complexity. The second aggregates the total volume of activity that is regulated, without regard to the number of decisions involved.

The other variables are defined as follows: Q_i, the quality variables for manpower, is the number of years of schooling of entry-level employees, and the prior job experience, in years, of these employees. U and C are dummy variables for an employee union and civil service.

For I, the prevailing private wages, the average hourly manufacturing wages in the SMSA is used;[7] Y, the local ability to pay, is measured by median household income and the median value of houses; A, the attitude toward government spending, is assumed to be reflected in local "conservative" voting;[8] F, the variable for conformity in policy, is a measure of the strictness of regulation relative to the prevailing strength of interest groups. Underlying F is the observation that regulatory policy, if not conforming to the relative strength of competing interest groups that favor or oppose the regulatory policy, leads to a reduction of political support for the agency and thus to a reduced budget and salaries (Noam, 1981).[9] This can be expressed by a relation between regulatory strictness[10] r to the balance of affected groups [construction unions (G_1) and construction firms (G_2)].[11]

Among the local characteristics included is size (by population); housing market conditions (using rates of vacancy and increase of population as proxies for demand preferences); form of government (city manager vs. elected chief executive), which may affect efficiency; qualifications of the agency chief (as a proxy for managerial ability); and the existence of a national code, i.e., of regulation standards that are fairly easy to apply.

III. ESTIMATION

First, we estimate the effects of unionization on productivity and on salaries in a separate fashion by using ordinary least squares (OLS) over logarithmic functions of (20), (20'), and (21). The results are given in columns 1 and 3 of Tables 1, 2, 3, and 4.

Table 1. Elasticities of Salary[a]
(Recursive Model with Quality Variables)

Dependent Variables	(Output by Units) OLS Estimation	2-SLS Estimation	(Output by Volume) OLS Estimation	2-SLS Estimation
Employee Union	.1626 (3.3063)	.1764 (2.1394)	.1686 (3.4095)	.1707 (2.9094)
Civil Service Status	.0381 (1.1794)	.0190 (.3543)	.0389 (1.2260)	.0356 (.9670)
Productivity per Employee	−.0153 (.7363)	.1838 (1.3635)	−.0167 (1.0000)	.0730 (1.1321)
Employee Schooling	.1716 (2.3069)	.7992 (1.2805)	.1642 (2.2117)	.4562 (1.2662)
Prior Job Experience	.0143 (.2421)	−.3588 (.9970)	.0056 (.0955)	−.0343 (.1337)
Median Housing Value	.1595 (4.0477)	.1818 (2.6327)	.1622 (4.2084)	.1455 (3.0211)
Private Industry Wages	.0314 (1.4021)	−.0399 (.6824)	.0274 (1.2754)	.0202 (.7871)
Non-Conformity in Regulation	−.0228 (1.9529)	−.0299 (1.4613)	−.0221 (1.9209)	−.0234 (1.6288)
Political Conservatism	.0299 (.2771)	.0512 (.2723)	.0350 (.3248)	.0052 (.0359)
R^2	.3336	.1625	.3350	.2663

Notes: (t − statistics in parentheses)
[a] For employee unions and civil service, the coefficients are shift parameters.

Table 2. Elasticities of Salary[a]
(Simultaneous Model with Salary Variables)

Dependent Variables	(Output by Units)		(Output by Volume)	
	OLS Estimation	2-SLS Estimation	OLS Estimation	2-SLS Estimation
Employee Union	.1626	.1512	.1686	.1479
	(3.3063)	(2.8101)	(3.4095)	(2.7249)
Civil Service Status	.0381	.0295	.0389	.0334
	(1.1794)	(.8415)	(1.2260)	(.9642)
Productivity per	−.0153	.0839	−.0167	.0661
Employee	(.7363)	(1.2539)	(1.0000)	(1.2668)
Required Schooling	.1716	.1570	.1642	.2049
	(2.3069)	(1.9399)	(2.2117)	(2.4356)
Prior Job Experience	.0143	−.0208	.0056	.0167
	(.2421)	(.3072)	(.0955)	(.2613)
Median Housing Value	.1595	.1855	.1622	.1563
	(4.0477)	(4.0635)	(4.2084)	(3.7197)
Private Industry	.0314	.0031	.0274	.0238
Wages	(1.4021)	(.1049)	(1.2754)	(1.0136)
Non-Conformity in	−.0228	−.0250	−.0221	−.0242
Regulation	(1.9529)	(2.0371)	(1.9209)	(1.9253)
Political Conservatism	.0299	.1289	.0350	−.0044
	(.2771)	(.1098)	(.3248)	(.0370)
R^2	.3336	.3040	.3350	.3016

Notes: (t − statistics in parentheses)
[a] For employee unions and civil service, the coefficients are shift parameters.

More interesting, however, are the results for the systems (20) and (21), and (20') and (21), obtained by 2SLS. These results are given in columns 2 and 4 of the tables, with Tables 1 and 2 corresponding to the set of Eqs. (20) and (21) (the recursive model) and Tables 2 and 4 to (20') and (21) (the simultaneous model). For both tables, the results are obtained for two different definitions of output, namely the volume of economic activity (i.e., of construction) that is regulated and, alternatively, the number of cases (building permits) that the agency acted upon. The results are reported on the right and the left sides of the tables. As can be seen, the coefficients and statistical significance are fairly similar for both definitions of the output. Similarly, the results for the simultaneous model are close to those of the recursive model.

First described are the results of the salary equation. Looking at the top row of Table 1, we can see a fairly strong and statistically significant positive association of employee unions and salaries. Both the size and significance of the coefficients are large in the simultaneous equations. In percentage terms, the results suggests about an 18.6 percent higher salary level where unions exist. (The antilog of the union coefficient of .1707, when the recursive model is chosen, is 1.1861; this number is the multiplying factor for the salary equation, in the presence of an employee union.) For civil service status the results show a higher salary, but without statistical significance.

Table 3. Elasticities of Productivity per Employee[a]
(Recursive Model with Quality Variables)

Dependent Variables	*(Output by Units)*		*(Output by Volume)*	
	OLS Estimation	2-SLS Estimation	OLS Estimation	2-SLS Estimation
Employee Union	−.0824 (.4012)	−.1145 (.1932)	.0451 (1.0901)	.0023 (.7318)
Civil Service Status	.0805 (.5891)	.0640 (.1601)	.0451 (.2728)	.0023 (.0099)
Employee Schooling	.3739 (1.1887)	8.8104 (.5309)	−.2972 (.7782)	3.9415 (.3328)
Prior Job Experience	.2734 (1.1105)	−2.2982 (.5292)	.0612 (.2055)	.6517 (.2481)
Population Increase	.0579 (.3888)	−.0733 (.1294)	.2484 (1.5283)	.0887 (.1798)
Vacancy Rate	.1198 (1.4396)	.3684 (.5964)	.0787 (.7786)	.2402 (.5662)
City Manager Form of Government	−.0280 (.1937)	−.5894 (.4322)	.0274 (.1560)	−.3471 (.3719)
Land Area	.1871 (3.1157)	.3150 (1.0853)	.2027 (2.8071)	.2524 (1.4612)
Experience of Agency Chief	.5884 (1.6646)	1.8738 (.8619)	−.5239 (1.2268)	−.6292 (.4810)
National Code	−.0785 (1.6161)	−.2134 (.6619)	−.0418 (.7097)	−.1208 (.5592)
Structures of Regulation	−.6372 (1.5216)	−.0722 (.0477)	−.2358 (.4719)	−.0216 (.0186)
R^2	.1438	.2010	.1199	.0652

Notes: (t − statistics in parentheses)
[a] For employee union, civil service, city manager and national code, the coefficients are shift parameters.

Table 4. Elasticities of Productivity Per Employee[a]
(Simultaneous Model with Salary Variables)

	(Output by Units)		(Output by Volume)	
Dependent Variables	OLS Estimation	2-SLS Estimation	OLS Estimation	2-SLS Estimation
Employee Union	−.0125	−.0858	.3057	.1914
	(.0581)	(.4061)	(1.1723)	(.7353)
Civil Service Status	.0989	.0691	.0412	−.0071
	(.7201)	(.4915)	(.2503)	(.0417)
Salary	−.2085	.4283	−.2547	.9173
	(.6626)	(.7315)	(.6717)	(1.2768)
Population Increase	−.0805	.0693	.2377	.2326
	(.5397)	(.4572)	(1.4758)	(1.3940)
Vacancy Rate	.0987	.1098	.0831	.0973
	(1.1951)	(1.2585)	(.8337)	(.9393)
City Manager Form of Government	.0388	−.0052	.0243	−.0514
	(.2693)	(.0357)	(.1399)	(.2971)
Land Area	.1801	.1875	.2035	.2184
	(2.9929)	(3.0601)	(2.8249)	(2.9170)
Experience of Agency Chief	.6949	.6708	−.4866	−.5221
	(2.0277)	(1.9264)	(1.1804)	(1.2221)
National Code	−.0066	−.0741	−.0428	−.0575
	(1.3627)	(1.4971)	(−.7319)	(.9450)
Strictness of Regulation	−.6767	−.5633	−.2629	−.0708
	(1.9565)	(1.2839)	(.5238)	(.1338)
R^2	.1319	.1290	.1181	.1180

Notes: (t − statistics in parentheses)
[a] For employee union, civil service, city manager and national code, the coefficients are shift parameters.

The usefulness of the interactive approach manifests itself in looking at the relation of productivity increase to salaries. In the nonsimultaneous estimation, this relation appears to be negative, a counterintuitive result. However, when the 2SLS approach is taken, we find that the sign reverses itself and becomes positive,[12] though the statistical significance is not high.

Of the variables for labor quality, we also find a good-sized positive association of schooling. Prior job experience, on the other hand, shows an only limited relation to salaries.

Because the salaries of public employees' reflect a community's ability to pay, we also take them into account. The results show a strong association of wealth (using as a proxy for wealth the median value of houses) with salaries.

Interestingly, the relation of regional wages with those of public employees is fairly insignificant.[13]

Some thought-provoking results are the good-sized and fairly significant coefficients for conformity of regulation. This variable, it may be recalled, shows the strictness of the regulation in relation to the interest group strengths in the community. For example, one expects a restrictive building code regulation in a city with strong construction unions. Where this is not the case, the results show that the regulatory agency has smaller salaries, ceteris paribus, which may be explained by a mechanism of incentives and punishment for an agency.

We next turn to Table 3 and the productivity equation. A first observation is that the existence of unions and of civil service is not associated with higher productivity. Coefficients for the union variable are actually often negative, though they are not statistically significant. For civil service, the coefficients are positive, but also not significant. Neither are the coefficients of employee quality on productivity particularly significant. Other factors that seem to contribute to productivity are the job experience—in years—of the agency chief, and the size of the jurisdiction, suggesting some economies of scale in building regulation.

What do these results tell us? First, higher labor quality is associated with higher salaries of public employees in building agencies. Second, the wealth of a community affects the salaries of these public employees. Third, when the regulatory strictness which would "conform" to the local balance of interest group strengths is not in fact provided by building agencies, one also finds reduced salaries. More importantly, however, the analysis shows the relation between unionization and civil service status on the one side and productivity and compensation on the other. The results show that employee unions, but not civil service, are associated with higher salaries in a good sized and statistically significant way. Productivity, on the other hand, is not found to be higher where unionization and civil service exist, for both definitions of productivity.

IV. CONCLUSION

This paper constructed two simple models of salaries and productivity under unions and without them. It then tested these relations empirically by using the data for building departments of 1100 American cities and towns and applied them in two interactive models. The results show that where public employee unions exist, the salaries of public employees in local regulatory agencies are higher, while productivity is not found to be increased.

ACKNOWLEDGMENTS

The author wishes to thank John Addison, Ann Bartel, Charles Brown, Eugene Kroch, and David Lewin for helpful comments. Financial assistance by the Columbia University Center for Law and Economic Studies towards the computer expenses is gratefully acknowledged.

NOTES

1. See survey in Parsley (1980) and many of the references of this paper.
2. A concurrent paper by Ehrenberg and Schwarz (1981) is the only exception. That study, however, is methodologically quite distinct, and draws on a limited data base; it is viewed by the authors as preliminary to their further work (p. 18 f).
3. Quality increases require rising salary augmentations, as the progressivity of salaries over hierarchical ranks suggests. This may be caused by supply elasticity with respect to quality increases that is smaller than that of demand.
4. Some commentators of administrative agencies instead believe that an agency maximizes the number of its employees (Parkinson, 1960), its budget (Niskanen, 1971), its political support (Tullock and Buchanan, 1967), or public benefits (Bator, 1958). The optimization criterion of this paper accommodates both public-benefit and agency self-interest hypotheses, as long as the supply of the public service is below its optimal level in terms of public benefits. Beyond that point, only the agency's self-interest is operative, provided that affected interest groups could compensate each other for a lower activity level.
5. The assumption implies that the union can alter the quantity of labor demanded, but not the demand curve itself.
6. International Association of City Managers. Data made available by R. Ventre, Bureau of Standards, and Oster and Quigley (1977). Unless otherwise noted data is from the IACM set.
7. Index of hourly wage of "maintenance men," U.S. Department of Commerce, Bureau of Labor Statistics (1975), and regional data in same source. Data provided by J. Quigley and gratefully acknowledged.
8. As measured by voting for Barry Goldwater in the 1964 presidential election. The code survey data is for the year 1970 and reflects the codification, budgeting, and hiring that were undertaken in the preceding years; thus the 1964 voting figure—in an election where the political philosophies of the candidates were distinct—seems to be a good proxy for the attitudes toward regulation that existed in a locality.
9. See E. Noam, "The Demand and Supply of Local Regulation," Research Working Paper No. 366A (1981), Columbia University, Graduate School of Business.
10. Higher-quality standards in construction or greater frequency of prohibitions of building techniques do not by themselves require a costlier process of regulation. For example, a rule that completely prohibits plastic pipes is not more expensive to administer than one that permits agency discretion on the basis of quality demonstrations.
11. One would expect an above average interest group strength ratio G_1/G_2 to be associated with a high restrictiveness of regulation r, and a low rate to be associated with a low interest group strength ratio. Hence, the expression $D = r/(G_1G_2)$ (with all measures normalized over national averages) should be close to 1 if the regulatory policy of an agency conforms to the relative strength of interest groups. Nonconforming agency behavior is denoted by $F = |1 - D|$.
12. This is analogous to Bartel and Lewin's (1981) findings on unionism as a cause and effect of compensation.
13. A multicollinearity issue may exist for this variable, however.

REFERENCES

Ashenfelter, Orley (1971), "The Effect of Unionization on Wages in the Public Sector: The Case of Firefighters." *Industrial and Labor Relations Review* (January).

Ashenfelter, Orley, and George E. Johnson (1972), "Unionism, Relative Wages and Labor Quality in U.S. Manufacturing Industries." *International Economic Review* (October).

Baird, Robert N., and John H. Landon (1972), "The Effects of Collective Bargaining on Public School Teachers' Salaries: Comment." *Industrial and Labor Relations Review* (April).

Bartel, Ann, and David Lewin (1981), "Wages and Unionism in the Public Sector: The Case of Police." *Review of Economics and Statistics* 93.

Bator, Francis M. (1958), "The Anatomy of Market Failure." *Quarterly Journal of Economics* (August).

Brown, Charles, and James Medoff (1978), "Trade Unions in the Production Process." *Journal of Political Economy* 86(June).

Clark, Kim B. (1980), "The Impact of Unionization on Productivity: A Case Study." *Industrial and Labor Relations Review* 30.

——— (1980), "Unionization and Productivity: Micro-Economic Evidence." *Quarterly Journal of Economics*.

Edwards, Franklin, and Linda N. Edwards (1980), "The Effect of Unionism on the Money and Fringe Compensation of Public Employees: The Case of Municipal Sanitation Workers." Columbia University, Graduate School of Business, Research Paper No. 267A.

——— (1980), "Wellington-Winter Revisited: Public and Private Unionism in Municipal Sanitation Collection." Columbia University, Graduate School of Business, Research Working Paper No. 386A.

Edwards, Linda N. (1978), "An Empirical Analysis of Compulsory Schooling Legislation, 1940–1960." *Journal of Law and Economics* 21(April).

Ehrenberg, Ronald G. (1973), "Municipal Government Structure, Unionization and the Wages of Firefighters." *Industrial and Labor Relations Review* (October).

Ehrenberg, Ronald G., and Joshua L. Schwartz (1981), "The Effect of Unions on Productivity in the Public Sector: The Case of Libraries." NBER Working Paper #717, July.

Ehrenberg, Ronald G., and Gerald Goldstein (1975), "A Model of Public Sector Wage Determination." *Journal of Urban Economics* (July).

Fottler, Myron D. (1977), "The Union Impact on Hospital Wages." *Industrial Labor Relations Review* (April).

Freeman, Richard B. (1980), "The Exit-Voice Tradeoff in the Labor Market: Unionism, Job Tenure, Quits and Separations." *Quarterly Journal of Economics* 94(June):643–673.

Freeman, Richard B., and James L. Medoff (1979), "The Two Faces of Unionism." *Public Interest* (Fall):69–93.

Freund, James L. (1974), "Market and Union Influences on Municipal Employee Wages." *Industrial and Labor Relations Review* (April).

Frey, Donald E. (1975), "Wage Determination in Public Schools and the Effects of Unionization." In Daniel Hamermesh (ed.), *Labor in the Public and Nonprofit Sector*. Princeton, N.J.: Princeton University Press.

Hall, W. Clayton, and Norman E. Carroll (1973), "The Effects of Teachers' Organizations on Salaries and Class Size." *Industrial and Labor Relations Review* (January).

Hamermesh, Daniel S. (1970), "Wage Bargains, Threshold Effects and the Phillips Curve." *Quarterly Journal of Economics* 84(3):501–507.

Jorgenson, Dale, and Zvi Griliches (1967), "The Explanation of Productivity Change." *Review of Economic Studies* 34(July).

Kasper, Hirschel (1970), "The Effects of Collective Bargaining on Public School Teachers' Salaries." *Industrial and Labor Relations Review* (October).

Lee, Lung-Fei (1978), "Unionism and Wage Rates: A Simultaneous Equations Model with Qualitative and Limited Dependent Variables." *International Economic Journal* (June).

Lewin, David (1977), "Public Sector Labor Relations: A Review Essay." *Labor History* 18(Winter).

Lewin, David, and John H. Keith, Jr. (1976), "Managerial Responses to Perceived Labor Shortages: The Case of Police." *Criminology* (May).

Lewis, H. Gregg (1963), *Unionism and Relative Wages in the United States*. Chicago: University of Chicago Press.

—— (1959), "Competitive and Monopoly Unionism." In P. D. Bradley (ed.), *The Stake in Union Power*. Charlottesville: University of Virginia Press, pp. 181–208.

Lipsey, David B., and John E. Drotning (1973), "The Influence of Collective Bargaining on Teachers' Salaries in New York State." *Industrial and Labor Relations Review* (October).

Niskanen, William A. (1971), *Bureaucracy and Representative Governments*. Chicago: Aldine, Atherton.

Noam, Eli (1981), "Rewards to Conformity in Regulation." Columbia University, Graduate School of Business, Research Working Paper.

Oster, Sharon, and John Quigley (1977), "Regulatory Barriers of the Diffusion of Innovation: Some Evidence from Building Codes." *Bell Journal of Economics* (8):361.

Parsley, C. J. (1980), "Labor Union Effects on Wage Gains: A Survey of Recent Literature." *Journal of Economic Literature* 18.

Parkinson, Cyril Northcote (1960), *The Law and the Profits*. Boston: Houghton Mifflin.

Pencavel, John H. (1977), "The Distributional and Efficiency Effects of Trade Unions in Britain." *British Journal of Industrial Relations* 15(2):137–156.

Rede, Melvin W. (1965), "Unions and Wages: The Problems of Measurement." *Journal of Political Economics* 77(April):188–196.

Schmenner, Roger W. (1973), "The Determination of Municipal Employee Wages." *Review of Economics and Statistics* (February).

Schmidt, Peter, and Robert Strauss (1976), "The Effect of Unions on Earnings and Earnings on Unions: A Mixed Logit Approach." *International Economic Review* 17(February).

Shapiro, David (1978), "Relative Wage Effects of Unionism in the Public and Private Sectors." *Industrial and Labor Relations Review* (January).

Tullock, Gordon, and James N. Buchanan (1967), *The Calculus of Consent, Logical Foundations of Constitutional Democracy*. Ann Arbor: University of Michigan Press.

Victor, Richard B. (1977), "The Effects of Unionism on the Wage and Employment Levels of Police and Firefighters." Rand Corporation Report, August.

WORKER PREFERENCES FOR UNION REPRESENTATION

Henry S. Farber

ABSTRACT

A model of the determinants of worker preferences for union representation as distinct from their actual union status is developed and estimated using data from the Quality of Employment Survey. In order to implement the model, a pair of econometric issues were addressed. First, the worker preferences were available only for nonunion workers. After correcting for this censoring, it was found that preference for union representation was higher among the workforce in general than among the nonunion workforce. In addition, preferences for representation vary much more by worker characteristics among the workforce in general than they do among the nonunion workforce. This is undoubtedly due to sorting based on worker preferences. The second problem regarded proper estimation of the union–nonunion wage differential, which was hypothesized to be a positive determinant of worker's preferences for union representation. Three different measures were used and, while there was some variation between them, they all showed a similar relationship with worker preferences.

New Approaches to Labor Unions.
Research in Labor Economics, Supplement 2, pages 171–205.
Copyright © 1983 by JAI Press Inc.
All rights of reproduction in any form reserved.
ISBN: 0-89232-265-9

I. INTRODUCTION

A relatively neglected area of research on labor unions is the determination of the union status of workers. In order to understand the process through which labor unions developed, what their future holds, and what their effects on workers, the workplace, and compensation are, it is crucial that a thorough understanding of this issue be gained. In most studies which develop structural models of the determination of the union status of workers (e.g., Ashenfelter and Johnson, 1972; Lee, 1978), it is argued that union status is determined strictly as a result of worker preferences for unionization. However, as Kochan and Helfman (1981) point out, this is only part of the story. A worker's preference for a unionized job will only translate into such a job if a unionized employer is willing to hire that worker, and it is likely that there will be excess demand for vacancies in existing union jobs.[1] Hence, the employer's criteria for selection of workers from the queue need to be modeled along with worker preferences in order to model adequately the determination of union status.

Abowd and Farber (1982) attempt an analysis of the determination of a worker's union status in which a distinction is drawn between worker preferences and employer choice criteria. However, their analysis is hampered by the fact that only the final outcome (union status) is observed, and it is impossible to determine whether nonunion workers did not want a union job, could not get a union job, or both. This difficulty is compounded by the problem that a worker's current preference for a union job, given accrued seniority, may be different than it was at the time the worker took his current job. For example, a nonunion worker with 10 years seniority may not want a union job even if one were offered at that point. However, the worker may have preferred a union job 10 years earlier but was not offered one.

In this study, a rather unique data set is employed which can be used to identify for nonunion workers their preferences for unionization *holding seniority fixed*. Thus, one-half of the process through which worker union status is determined can be investigated. However, these data do not permit investigation of the employer selection process, and a satisfactory solution of the entire puzzle must await future research.

In the next section, a simple structural model of worker preferences for unionization is developed based on utility maximization by individual workers. Section III contains a discussion of the data set from the 1977 Quality of Employment Survey (QES) developed by the Survey Research Center at the University of Michigan. Particular attention is paid to the interpretation of the question, "If an election were held with secret ballots, would you vote for or against having a union or employees' association represent you?'' The response to this question (VFU) serves as the basis for the analysis of this study.

Empirical implementation of the model developed in Section II is hampered by two problems. First, the crucial question (VFU) was asked only of nonunion workers. Analysis of the responses in this context is interesting in that insight can be gained into the characteristics of nonunion workers which lead them to desire union representation *conditional* on their nonunion status.[2] However, for an analysis of preferences for union representation *unconditional* on union status, the data are censored on the basis of an obviously related variable. An econometric model which takes account of this censoring and yields consistent estimates of unconditional preferences for union representation is developed in Section IV.

The second problem which hampers the empirical implementation of the model is that a crucial element of the structural model is the union–nonunion wage differential (ΔW) facing a worker. Potential problems of sample selection bias in estimating ΔW, while solved from a technical standpoint, are notoriously difficult to handle in a convincing fashion from a practical point of view.[3] For this reason, the analysis of the structural version of the model is deferred until a later section, and a reduced form version of the model is derived in Section IV which does not require estimates of ΔW. This reduced-form model is then estimated in Section V both with and without accounting for the censored sample problem noted above. The estimates suggest that preferences for union representation among the nonunion workforce are relatively flat across most individual characteristics, while among the workforce as a whole there are sharp distinctions. This result is consistent with sorting in the sense that many workers who desire union representation on the basis of both their observed and their unobserved characteristics are already working on union jobs, leaving a group of nonunion workers whose preferences for union representation show little systematic variation with characteristics.

In Section VI, separate union and nonunion earnings functions are estimated by a number of different techniques in order to derive estimates of ΔW for the structural version of the union preference model. First, ordinary least squares (OLS) estimates are derived. However, these are potentially biased and inconsistent due to the fact that the sample censoring of wage rates based on union status may be correlated with the wage differentials. A not completely satisfactory attempt to account for this sample selection bias is made by estimating the union and nonunion earnings functions by two additional methods. The first of these is to use OLS augmented by the hazard rate (inverse Mill's ratio) derived from a reduced-form probit union status model. This technique is described by Lee (1979). The second method is to estimate a maximum-likelihood switching regression model consisting of the union and nonunion earnings functions plus an equation explaining union status. The union–nonunion wage differentials implied by these various methods are then evaluated and compared but, while the results differ, it cannot be concluded that any particular measure is clearly superior.

In Section VII the structural version of the preferences for the union representation model is estimated both conditional on nonunion status and accounting for sample censoring. All three measures of ΔW derived in Section V are used due to the ambiguity concerning the correct measure, and the results are compared. The results are remarkably similar, particularly in light of the substantial differences in the estimated wage differentials. Overall, the analysis in this section confirms the predictions of the theory developed in Section II in that a positive, though insignificant, relationship is found between ΔW and worker preferences for union representation.

The final section of the paper contains a synthesis of the results along with conclusions which can be drawn from the analysis.

II. A SIMPLE MODEL OF WORKER PREFERENCES FOR UNION REPRESENTATION

At its simplest level, a worker's preference for union representation on a job versus no such representation can be modeled as a comparison by the worker of the utilities yielded to him by his job in each case. His preference will be for that case which yields him the largest utility. A worker's utility on the job is affected by many factors—wages, fringe benefits, safety, job security, comfort, etc. In addition, there are subjective factors such as satisfaction with supervision, perceived fairness of treatment, equitable comparisons with others, and perceived chances for promotion. In the absence of explicit measures of most of these factors for each worker in both a union and a nonunion environment, it is argued that these utilities vary across workers as functions of their personal and occupational characteristics as well as the measurable characteristics of the union and nonunion jobs.

In order to examine this argument more carefully, assume, as is done below, that the only explicit job characteristic which can be measured for each worker in both a union and a nonunion context is the wage rate. More formally, it is argued that

$$V_u = V_u(Z, W_u) \tag{1}$$

and

$$V_n = V_n(Z, W_n), \tag{2}$$

where V_u and V_n represent the worker's union and nonunion utilities, respectively; Z represents a vector of personal and occupational characteristics; and W_u and W_n represent the worker's union and nonunion wage rates, respectively. The worker's preference for union representation can be expressed by computing $y = V_u - V_n$. If this difference in utilities (y) is positive, then the worker will opt for union representation. If y is negative, then the worker will not opt for union representation. It is clear that this difference in utilities can be expressed as

$$y = y(Z, W_u, W_n), \qquad (3)$$

where variations in Z measure variations in the difference between the worker's union and nonunion utilities.

Examples of such variations are not hard to come by. For instance, it is well known that fringe benefits are substantially more generous on union jobs in such dimensions as medical insurance, pensions, and vacation pay.[4] Those workers who place a greater value on these fringe benefits are more likely to have a positive y and hence desire union representation. For example, older workers are likely to value their potential pension benefits more than younger workers, while workers with young families are likely to value medical insurance relatively highly. In another dimension, the prevalence of layoff by inverse seniority rules in unionized establishments may lead workers with relatively more seniority to desire union representation due to the increased job security such seniority confers in union settings.[5]

In order to derive the empirical analogue of this model, a specific functional form must be elected for y. This is

$$y = Z\gamma + \delta(\ln W_u - \ln W_n) + \epsilon_1, \qquad (4)$$

where γ is a vector of parameters, δ is a parameter expected to be positive, and ϵ_1 represents unmeasured components of the utility difference. Clearly, if y, Z, W_u, and W_n were observable for all workers, the parameters in Eq. (4) could be estimated using straightforward linear methods. However, this is not the case, and the discussion turns to an examination of the data and their limitations.

III. THE DATA

The data used are from the 1977 cross section of the Quality of Employment Survey (QES) developed by the Survey Research Center of the University of Michigan. The QES contains data for approximately 1500 randomly selected workers (both union and nonunion) on their personal characteristics and job attributes.[6] The crucial bit of information for this study is the response to the question asked only of nonunion workers,

"If an election were held with secret ballots, would you vote for or against having a union or employee's association represent you?" This variable is called "vote for union?" or VFU. It is interpreted here as the preference of a worker for union representation on his current job. Thus, it holds all job characteristics fixed except those which the worker expects the union

Table 1.   Means (Standard Deviations) of Data Quality of Employment Survey, 1977

Variable	Description (Dichotomous variables = 0 otherwise)	Combined Sample (n = 880)	Union Sub-Sample (n = 327)	Non-Union Sub-Sample (n = 553)
U	= 1 if works on union job	.372	—	—
VFU	= 1 if desires union represent.	—	—	0.376
Age	age in years	36.4 (12.9)	38.1 (12.5)	35.4 (13.0)
Exp	labor market experience in years	16.9 (12.4)	19.1 (12.4)	15.6 (12.2)
Sen	firm seniority in years	6.81 (7.46)	9.50 (8.22)	5.22 (6.45)
Fe	= 1 if female	.420	.324	.477
Marr	= 1 if married w/spouse present	.636	.703	.597
Marr*Fe	= 1 if Fe = 1 and Marr = 1	.200	.174	.215
NW	= 1 if nonwhite	.139	.162	.125
South	= 1 if worker resides in South	.353	.235	.423
Ed < 12	= 1 if <12 years education	.220	.257	.199
12 < Ed < 16	= 1 if >12 years & <16 years educ.	.213	.165	.241
Ed ≥ 16	= 1 if ≥16 years education	.199	.199	.199
ln (wage)	natural logarithm of wage	1.58 (.859)	1.83 (.983)	1.43 (.737)
Cler	= 1 if occupation is clerical	.208	.116	.262
Serv	= 1 if occupation is service	.153	.113	.177
Prof & Tech	= 1 if occupation is professional or technical	.230	.205	.244

to affect. It is assumed that the worker's response is based on his current utility as compared with what the worker's utility is expected to be were the job to be unionized.[7]

A sample of workers was derived from QES by selecting those workers for whom the survey contained valid information on the variables listed in Table 1. Self-employed workers, managers, salesworkers, and construction workers were deleted from the sample. The remaining sample contains 880 workers. Table 1 contains descriptions of the variables used in the study as well as their means and standard deviations for both the entire sample and the union and nonunion subsamples. The base group for the dichotomous variables are white, nonsouthern, single, male blue-collar workers with 12 years of education. On average, the 37 percent of the sample who are unionized are slightly older, earn substantially more, have somewhat more experience, and are more likely to be male, married, nonwhite, nonsouthern, and in a blue-collar occupation.

Thirty-eight percent of the nonunion sample expressed a preference for union representation (VFU = 1). It is unfortunate that the analogous question was not asked of union members ("If an election were held by secret ballot, would you vote to continue union representation?"). This would make information available for all workers about worker preferences for unionization of their current job at the current time.[8] The lack of this information poses some important problems of econometrics and interpretation. It is to this and related problems that the next section is addressed.

IV. ECONOMETRIC ISSUES AND OPTIONS

A number of problems arise in the estimation of the parameters of the worker preference model specified in Eq. (4). The first problem is that y, which represents the differences in a worker's utility between union and nonunion status on the job, is not observed. All that is observed is the sign of y through the worker's response to the VFU question ($y > 0$ $\Leftrightarrow$ VFU = 1, $y < 0$ $\Leftrightarrow$ VFU = 0). The limited nature of the dependent variable implies that $\Pr(\text{VFU} = 1) = \Pr(y > 0)$, yielding from Eq. (4) that

$$\Pr(\text{VFU} = 1) = \Pr(\epsilon_1 > -Z\gamma - \delta(\ln W_u - \ln W_n)). \quad (5)$$

If ϵ_1 is assumed to be distributed normally with zero mean and unit variance, then Eq. (5) implies a probit specification for a likelihood function.[9] The contribution of any individual to the log-likelihood function is

$$L = \text{VFU} \ln[\Phi(Z\gamma + \delta(\ln W_u - \ln W_n))] \quad (6)$$
$$+ (1 - \text{VFU}) \ln[1 - \Phi(Z\gamma + \delta(\ln W_u + \ln W_n))]$$

where $\Phi(\cdot)$ represents the standard normal cumulative distribution function.[10]

If all of the elements of Eq. (6) were observed for all workers, it would be a straightforward exercise to maximize the appropriate likelihood function to obtain estimates of Z and γ. Unfortunately, our task is not so simple. As mentioned above, VFU is observed only for nonunion workers. If the question of interest is the estimation of a model of nonunion worker preferences for union representation and if the assumption is made that ϵ_1 has a standard normal distribution conditional on the workers being nonunion, then maximum-likelihood estimation applied to the likelihood function implied by Eq. (6) over all of the nonunion workers in the sample will lead to consistent estimates of γ and δ. However, these estimates cannot be interpreted as those which describe a model applicable to all workers regardless of union status unless a particular (testable) restriction described below is imposed.

In order to continue the analysis, an empirical model of the determination of the union status of workers is required. A simple model is specified of the form

$$S = C\alpha + \epsilon_2, \qquad (7)$$

where S is an unobservable latent variable determining union status, C is a vector of worker and job characteristics, α is a vector of parameters, and ϵ_2 is a random component with a standard normal distribution which captures unmeasured aspects of the union status determination process. If S is positive, then the worker works on a union job (U = 1), and if S is negative, then there is no union representation on the job (U = 0). Thus, $\Pr(U = 1) = \Pr(S > 0)$, which implies that

$$\Pr(U = 1) = \Pr(\epsilon_2 > -C\alpha). \qquad (8)$$

Given the normality assumption regarding ϵ_2, the contribution to the log-likelihood function regarding union status is a probit of the form

$$L = U \ln [\Phi(C\alpha)] + (1 - U) \ln[1 - \Phi(C\alpha)]. \qquad (9)$$

In light of the introductory discussion of the process by which union status is determined through separate decisions by workers and employers, the behavioral underpinnings of this probit model are left deliberately vague. It is to be interpreted as a reduced-form empirical relationship describing the union status of a worker. However, a note of caution is required. It is difficult (if not impossible) to think of a structural model of the determination of the union status of a worker where both the worker and employer make separate decisions which would have a reduced form which could be described as a simple univariate probit. In fact, this study is motivated, at least in part, by a desire to model the union status determination of workers in a manner which is consistent with separate worker and employer decisions in order to move away from the behaviorally naive structural model which is implicit in the simple probit model described here. Nonetheless, with this potential problem in mind, the analysis proceeds using this model.

If the random components in the VFU and U functions (ϵ_1 and ϵ_2) are correlated [e.g., they have a standardized bivariate normal density function $b(\epsilon_1, \epsilon_2; \rho_{12})$], then estimation of the likelihood of VFU from Eq. (6) is incorrect if the goal is to estimate γ and δ for workers unconditional on their union status. In particular, ϵ_1 was assumed to have a normal distribution with zero mean unconditional on union status, but the ϵ_1 are observed only for nonunion workers. The condition for a worker being nonunion from Eq. (8) is that $\epsilon_2 < -C\alpha$ so that ϵ_1 is observed only if $\epsilon_2 < -C\alpha$, and the likelihood must be written in terms of this conditional distribution. Using Bayes's rule and assuming joint normality of ϵ_1 and ϵ_2, the conditional distribution of ϵ_1 given $\epsilon_2 < -C\alpha$ is

$$f(\epsilon_1 \mid \epsilon_2 < -C\alpha) = \frac{\int_{-\infty}^{-C\alpha} b(\epsilon_1, \epsilon_2; \rho_{12}) \, d\epsilon_2}{\Phi(-C\alpha)}. \qquad (10)$$

This conditional distribution is nonnormal and involves the parameters α and ρ_{12}.

Two points are worth noting here. First, if ϵ_1 and ϵ_2 are uncorrelated so that $\rho_{12} = 0$, then $\epsilon_1 \mid \epsilon_2 < -C\alpha$ is distributed as a standard normal and the likelihood function on VFU implied by Eq. (6) and estimated over the sample of nonunion workers can be interpreted correctly as that relevant to all workers unconditional on their union status. However, it seems likely that unmeasured determinants of the union status of a worker and of the worker's preference for union representation are correlated with each other so that $\rho_{12} \neq 0$. This potential restriction will be tested in succeeding sections. The second point to note is that where $\rho_{12} \neq 0$, the conditional interpretation given to the probit VFU likelihood function derived from Eq. (6) and the conditional-likelihood function for VFU derived from the bivariate normal model in Eq. (10) are inconsistent with each other because $f(\epsilon_1 \mid \epsilon_2 < -C\alpha)$ is nonnormal. Nonetheless, estimates from the simple probit VFU likelihood function will be interpreted as estimates of worker preferences for union representation conditional on being nonunion.

While the appropriate conditional-likelihood function for VFU could be derived from Eq. (10), a much more efficient approach is to use information from the whole sample to write the joint likelihood of preferences for union representation and union status while noting that VFU is censored for union workers. For nonunion workers who desire union

representation the appropriate contribution to the likelihood function is
$\Pr[\epsilon_1 > -Z\gamma - \delta(\ln W_u - \ln W_n), \epsilon_2 < -C\alpha]$. Given the distributional
assumption, this is

$$\Pr(VFU = 1, U = 0) = \int_{\infty}^{-C\alpha} \int_{\kappa_1}^{\infty} b(\epsilon_1, \epsilon_2; \rho) \, d\epsilon_1 \, d\epsilon_2, \qquad (11)$$

where $\kappa_1 = -Z\gamma - \delta(\ln W_u - \ln W_n)$. Similarly, for nonunion workers
who do not desire union representation, the appropriate contribution is
$\Pr[\epsilon_1 < -Z\gamma - \delta(\ln W_u - W_n), \epsilon_2 < -C\alpha]$, which yields

$$\Pr(VFU = 0, U = 0) = \int_{-\infty}^{-C\alpha} \int_{-\infty}^{\kappa_1} b(\epsilon_1, \epsilon_2; \rho) \, d\epsilon_1 \, d\epsilon_2. \qquad (12)$$

Finally, for union workers no information regarding VFU is known, so
that ϵ_1 is integrated out and the contribution of these workers to the likelihood function is a univariate normal CDF representing $\Pr(\epsilon_2 > -C\alpha)$,
which yields

$$\Pr(U = 1) = \Phi(C\alpha). \qquad (13)$$

Using these results, the contribution of a worker to the structural log-
likelihood function accounting for the sample censoring is

$$L = (VFU)(1 - U) \ln[\Pr(VFU = 1, U = 0)]$$
$$+ (1 - VFU)(1 - U) \ln[\Pr(VFU = 0, U = 0)] \qquad (14)$$
$$+ U \ln[\Pr(U = 1)],$$

where the relevant probabilities are defined in Eqs. (11)–(13).

One more hurdle must be overcome before the model can be estimated.
Two important variables required for all nonunion workers are those
workers' union and nonunion wage rates. However, only the nonunion
wage is observed, and a question arises as to how to handle this problem.
The difficulty is that it is likely that the union–nonunion wage differential,
and hence the union and nonunion wage rates, are important determinants
of ultimate union status (in a structural version of the model) as well as
of worker preferences for union representation. This raises potentially
serious problems of selection bias in estimating union and nonunion earnings functions which will be addressed in Section VI. In addition, the fact
that the observed nonunion wage is likely to be correlated with union
status makes it improper to estimate the model conditional on this wage
rate. The correlation must be accounted for.

One approach toward solution of this problem is to specify union and
nonunion individual earnings functions respectively as

$$\ln W_u = X\beta_u + \epsilon_u \qquad (15)$$
$$\ln W_n = X\beta_n + \epsilon_n,$$

where X is a vector of exogenous characteristics, β_u and β_n are vectors of parameters, and ϵ_u and ϵ_n are normally distributed unobserved elements. The difficulties stem from the possibility that ϵ_u and/or ϵ_n are correlated with ϵ_1 and ϵ_2. If the representations of ln W_u and ln W_n from Eqs. (15) are substituted into Eq. (4), the resulting union–nonunion utility difference can be expressed as

$$y = Z\gamma + \delta X(\beta_u - \beta_n) + \epsilon_3 \qquad (16)$$

where $\epsilon_3 = \epsilon_1 + \delta(\epsilon_u - \epsilon_n)$ and is distributed normally unconditional on union status.

Substituting into Eq. (6), the individual contribution to the log-likelihood function for VFU which is interpreted conditionally on nonunion status is

$$L_1 = \text{VFU} \ln[\Phi(Z\gamma + \delta X(\beta_u - \beta_n))]$$
$$+ (1 - \text{VFU}) \ln[1 - \Phi(Z\gamma + \delta X(\beta_u - \beta_n))] \qquad (17)$$

under the normalization that the variance of ϵ_3 is 1.[11] Similarly, the relevant probabilities for the joint likelihood function defined in Eq. (14) can be rewritten as

$$\Pr(\text{VFU} = 1, U = 0) = \int_{-\infty}^{-c\alpha} \int_{\kappa_3}^{\infty} b(\epsilon_3, \epsilon_2; \rho_{23}) \, d\epsilon_3 \, d\epsilon_2 \qquad (18)$$

and

$$\Pr(\text{VFU} = 0, U = 0) = \int_{-\infty}^{-c\alpha} \int_{-\infty}^{\kappa_3} b(\epsilon_3, \epsilon_2; \rho_{23}) \, d\epsilon_3 \, d\epsilon_2, \qquad (19)$$

where $\kappa_3 = -Z\gamma - \delta X(\beta_u - \beta_n)$ and ρ_{23} is the correlation between ϵ_2 and ϵ_3. The $\Pr(U = 1)$ is unchanged.

The structure of Eq. (16) raises some serious identification problems because only for those elements of Z which are not included in X can the associated γ terms be estimated. Similarly, only the product of $\delta(\beta_u - \beta_n)$ can be estimated, and then only for elements of X which are not included in Z. What can be identified is a reduced-form version of Eq. (16) which is specified by substituting $Z^*\gamma^* = Z\gamma + \delta X(\beta_u - \beta_n)$ into Eqs. (16) through (19). The vector Z^* contains all of the variables which are in either Z or X, and γ^* is the vector of reduced-form coefficients. This reduced-form model is estimated in the next section.

The entire structural model can be identified and estimated by using data on the union and nonunion wage rates to derive estimates of β_u and β_n which can then be substituted into the model to estimate γ and δ conditional on these estimates of β_u and β_n. However, there is some question as to the best technique to estimate these vectors, and three different methods are used in Section VI. Finally, in Section VII the structural version of the model is estimated.

V. ESTIMATION OF THE REDUCED-FORM MODEL

Substitution of $Z^*\gamma^*$ for $Z\gamma + \delta X(\beta_u - \beta_n)$ in Eq. (17) yields the reduced form probit contribution to the log-likelihood function for VFU interpreted conditionally on nonunion status of

$$L = VFU \ln[\Phi(Z^*\gamma^*)] + (1 - VFU \ln[1 - \Phi(Z^*\gamma^*)]. \quad (20)$$

The vector Z^* includes all variables which appear either in the structural union preference function (Z) or in the earnings functions (X). Those variables assumed to be in the earnings function are three dichotomous variables for different levels of education, labor market experience and its square, seniority with current employer and its square, and dichotomous variables for nonwhite, female, and southern residence. The labor market experience measure is actual years worked for pay since age 16 rather than the standard age − education − 6. The variables assumed to be in the preference for union representation function (Z) include seniority with current employer and its square, and the dichotomous variables for nonwhite, female, and southern residence. In addition, the Z function includes age, dichotomous variables for married with spouse present and the product of female and marital status, and three dichotomous variables for broad occupational groupings. The union of these sets of variables contain the 16 variables plus a constant which make up Z^*. All variables are defined in Table 1 along with their means and standard deviations. The base group for the sample consists of white, nonsouthern, single males with 12 years of education working in a blue-collar occupation.

Note that there are two sets of constraints implicit in this formulation. The first is that 5 variables are excluded from the structural VFU function while they are included in the earnings functions. These are the 3 education and 2 experience variables. The set of 4 overidentifying constraints is testable in the structural version, and such a test is performed in Section VII.[12] Second, 5 variables are also excluded from each earnings function, and these 10 constraints are also theoretically testable. However, as discussed in the next section, difficulties in estimation and interpretation hinder the actual performance of an appropriate test.

The estimates derived for γ^* by maximizing the likelihood function implied by Eq. (20) over the 553 nonunion workers are contained in the first column of Table 2. At first glance the only variable which has a substantial effect on a nonunion worker's preference for union representation is race. No other variable is asymptotically significantly different from zero at conventional levels, and only 6 of the 16 coefficients have estimates whose absolute values exceed their asymptotic standard errors.[13] While the relationship looks relatively flat, a likelihood ratio test of the hypothesis that all of the coefficients except the constant equal zero rejects the hypothesis at any reasonable level of significance.[14] This

Table 2. Estimates of Pr (VFU) and Pr (U) Univariate and Bivariate Probit Models

Variables	Pr (VFU = 1 | U = 0) Univariate (1)	Pr (U = 1) Univariate (2)	Pr (VFU = 1) Bivariate (3)	Pr (U = 1) Bivariate (4)
Constant	−.151 (.271)	−.0852 (.253)	.444 (.358)	−.0933 (.254)
Ed < 12	.0530 (.172)	.0538 (.133)	.0641 (.150)	.0467 (.134)
12 < Ed < 16	−.190 (.150)	−.0942 (.130)	−.187 (.136)	−.120 (.129)
Ed ≥ 16	.129 (.200)	.231 (.174)	.188 (.180)	.267 (.172)
Exp	.0142 (.0226)	.0151 (.0194)	.0169 (.0207)	.0147 (.0195)
Exp^2	−.000368 (.000398)	−.000316 (.000331)	−.000401 (.000371)	−.000336 (.000330)
Sen	.000255 (.0302)	.105 (.0232)	.0431 (.0362)	.110 (.0232)
Sen^2	−.00143 (.00129)	−.00224 (.000908)	−.00186 (.00111)	−.00239 (.000919)
NW	.827 (.180)	.295 (.141)	.787 (.192)	.303 (.142)
Fe	.221 (.197)	−.0513 (.167)	.187 (.178)	−.0394 (.168)
South	−.00481 (.118)	−.530 (.102)	−.218 (.167)	−.547 (.102)
Age	−.00469 (.0109)	−.0123 (.0104)	−.00936 (.00994)	−.0115 (.0105)
Marr	−.117 (.180)	.0777 (.142)	−.0436 (.169)	.0789 (.144)
Marr*Fe	−.273 (.243)	.00253 (.212)	−.260 (.219)	−.0331 (.213)
Cler	−.154 (.174)	−.738 (.151)	−.433 (.209)	−.749 (.151)
Serv	.121 (.181)	−.499 (.144)	−.128 (.221)	−.491 (.145)
Prof & Tech	−.209 (.193)	−.656 (.171)	−.446 (.216)	−.719 (.169)
ρ_{23}	0		.778 (.366)	
ln L	−337.8	−496.7	−833.1	
n	553	880	880	

Note: (Numbers in parentheses are asymptotic standard errors.)

suggests that there is some collinearity in the set of explanatory variables, which is not surprising in light of the presence of five time-trending variables (Age, Sen, Sen^2, Exp, Exp^2).

In order to investigate how sensitive nonunion worker preferences for union representation are in a number of dimensions, Table 3 contains values of Pr(VFU = 1 | U = 0) at the point estimates of the parameters contained in the first column of Table 2 for 30-year-old single males with 12 years of education, 10 years of experience, 5 years of seniority, and various occupations, race, and regions. It is clear that for any occupation and region, nonwhites are substantially more likely to desire union representation than are whites.[15] On the other hand, region has a trivial effect, while the occupational variation is moderate.

The second column of Table 2 contains maximum-likelihood estimates over the sample of 880 workers of the simple probit model of the union status of workers based on the likelihood function derived from Eq. (9) where the vector of variables (C) is the same set as Z*. These are consistent estimates of the reduced-form empirical relationship described earlier and, given the ambiguity regarding its behavioral underpinnings, not much space will be allocated to evaluation of these results. Suffice it to say that nonwhites and nonsoutherners are more likely to be union mem-

Table 3. Predicted Pr (VFU = 1) for Workers Varying by Race, Region, and Occupation

	Pr (VFU = 1 | U = 0)		Pr (VFU = 1)	
	Non-South	*South*	*Non-South*	*South*
Blue Collar				
white	.413	.411	.678	.596
nonwhite	.728	.726	.894	.848
Clerical				
white	.354	.352	.511	.425
nonwhite	.674	.673	.792	.725
Service				
white	.460	.458	.630	.546
nonwhite	.766	.765	.869	.839
Professional and Technical				
white	.334	.332	.398	.350
nonwhite	.654	.653	.702	.656

Notes: Computed for 30-year-old single males with 12 years education, ten years experience, and five years seniority. Pr (VFU = 1 | U = 0) was computed from estimates in column (1), Table 2. Pr (VFU = 1) was computed from estimates in column (3), Table 2.

bers, as are younger workers and those with more seniority.[16] In addition, there are rather sharp occupational breaks which imply that blue-collar workers are most likely to be unionized, while clerical workers are least likely, holding other factors fixed. A likelihood ratio test of the hypothesis that all coefficients except the constant term are zero can be rejected at any reasonable level of significance.[17] This relationship regarding Pr(U) is reestimated as a piece of each succeeding analysis and, as is expected, the results do not change substantially. Hence, no further discussion of $Pr(U = 1)$ will take place.

Estimation of the reduced form joint union preference–union status model proceeds by substituting $Z^*\gamma^*$ for $Z\gamma + \delta X(\beta_u - \beta_n)$ in Eqs. (18) and (19), yielding

$$Pr(VFU = 1, U = 0) = \int_{-\infty}^{-C\alpha} \int_{-Z^*\gamma^*}^{\infty} b(\epsilon_3, \epsilon_2; \rho_{23}) \, d\epsilon_3 \, d\epsilon_2 \qquad (21)$$

and

$$Pr(VFU = 0, U = 0) = \int_{-\infty}^{-C\alpha} \int_{-\infty}^{-Z^*\gamma^*} b(\epsilon_3, \epsilon_2; \rho_{23}) \, d\epsilon_3 \, d\epsilon_2. \qquad (22)$$

The $Pr(U = 1)$ is unchanged from Eq. (13). These expressions are combined with Eq. (14) to form the appropriate likelihood function. The maximum-likelihood estimates of this model are contained in columns 3 and 4 of Table 2. Note that the estimates contained in the first two columns of this table relate to a constrained version of the joint model where $\rho_{23} = 0$. The estimated value of ρ_{23} is .778 with an asymptotic standard error of .366. The hypothesis that $\rho_{23} = 0$ can be rejected at the 5 percent level of significance using a two-tailed asymptotic t-test. The asymptotically equivalent likelihood ratio test can be performed by summing the log-likelihoods for the first two columns of Table 2 and comparing the constrained log-likelihood to the unconstrained value. Using this test, the hypothesis that $\rho = 0$ can be rejected at the 10 percent level of significance.[18] The positive value estimated for ρ_{23} suggests that unobserved factors which make workers more likely to work on union jobs also make these workers more likely to prefer union representation.

The estimates on the $Pr(VFU = 1)$ function unconditional on union status contained in the third column of Table 2 are much better determined than those for the conditional model (column 1). While only 3 of the 16 coefficients are significantly different from zero at conventional levels, fully 11 of the 16 coefficient estimates exceed their asymptotic standard error in absolute value. The effect of race on worker preferences for union representation is significantly different from zero at conventional levels, as are two of the three occupational variables. Both clerical and professional/technical workers are less likely than blue-collar workers to prefer union representation. Southern workers are significantly less likely at the 10 percent level to prefer union representation than nonsouthern workers.

Table 3 contains values of $\Pr(\text{VFU} = 1)$ at the point estimates of γ^* contained in the third column of Table 2 for 30-year-old single males with 12 years of education, 10 years experience, and 5 years seniority. The hypothetical worker's occupation, race, and region are varied in order to investigage the sensitivity of $\Pr(\text{VFU} = 1)$ to these factors. It is clear that race and occupation have large effects on workers' preferences for union representation. Nonwhites are substantially more likely to prefer union representation. Professional and technical workers are the least likely in terms of occupation to prefer union representation, while blue-collar workers are most likely. Southern workers are somewhat less likely than nonsouthern workers to desire union representation.

It is interesting to contrast the preferences of nonunion workers for union representation to workers' preferences unconditional on union status. The calculated probabilities contained in Table 3 facilitate this comparison. It is clear that workers in general are more likely to desire union representation than nonunion workers. For example, for the four types of blue-collar workers listed in Table 3 (combinations of race and region), the probability that workers in general desire union representation is on average 37 percent higher than the probability that workers desire union representation conditional on being nonunion. The difference is positive but less pronounced for the other listed occupations. While this result is not unexpected, there is nothing in the specification which guarantees it, and finding this result is evidence of the "reasonableness" of the estimates.

Two other differences are that region plays a much greater role in determining overall preferences for unionization than it does among the nonunion workforce. In addition, the occupational distinctions are much greater among the workforce in general than among the nonunion workforce. These results are consistent with the notion that workers with a given set of observable characteristics have been "sorted" into union and nonunion jobs at least partially on the basis of unobservable characteristics related to their preferences. Thus, the remaining nonunion workers with *differing* observable characteristics are relatively homogeneous in their preferences for union representation. This will be discussed in more detail below in the context of estimation of the structural model.

VI. ESTIMATION OF THE UNION–NONUNION WAGE DIFFERENTIAL

In order to estimate the parameters of the structural model, consistent estimates of the parameters of the union and nonunion earnings functions

$$\ln W_u = X\beta_u + \epsilon_u$$

and (15)

$$\ln W_n = X\beta_n + \epsilon_n$$

must be derived. However, W_u is observed only for union workers, while W_n is observed only for nonunion workers. The reduced form empirical model which described the union status of workers was specified as

$$S = C\alpha + \epsilon_2, \qquad (7)$$

where $\Pr(U = 1) = \Pr(S > 0) = \Pr(\epsilon_2 > -C\alpha)$. It is straightforward to show that if the random component of the union status decision (ϵ_2) is correlated with the random components of earnings (ϵ_u and ϵ_n), then ordinary least squares (OLS) applied to the two equations in (15) separately will yield biased and inconsistent estimates for β_u and β_n. This so-called sample selection bias is due to the same sort of data censoring which was described above in relation to the missing data for union workers on their preferences for union representation. Given this problem, two alternative estimation procedures are developed.

The bias is introduced by the fact that the union and nonunion earnings functions are estimated only over their respective subsamples. This causes the expectations of ϵ_u and ϵ_n to vary by observation because they are only observed conditionally on union status. More formally, $E(\epsilon_u \mid U = 1) = E(\epsilon_u \mid \epsilon_2 > -C\alpha)$ and $E(\epsilon_n \mid U = 0) = E(\epsilon_n \mid \epsilon_2 < -C\alpha)$. If ϵ_u and ϵ_n are not independent of ϵ_2, then these conditional expectations vary with $C\alpha$. Assuming joint normality of ϵ_u, ϵ_n, and ϵ_2 results in

$$E(\epsilon_u \mid \epsilon_2 > -C\alpha) = \sigma_u \rho_{2u} \frac{\phi(C\alpha)}{\Phi(C\alpha)} \qquad (23)$$

and

$$E(\epsilon_n \mid \epsilon_2 < -C\alpha) = -\sigma_n \rho_{2n} \frac{\phi(C\alpha)}{1 - \Phi(C\alpha)}. \qquad (24)$$

where σ_u and σ_n are the standard deviations of ϵ_u and ϵ_n, respectively; ρ_{2u} and ρ_{2n} are the correlations between ϵ_2 and ϵ_u and between ϵ_2 and ϵ_n, respectively; and $\phi(\cdot)$ is the standard normal density function. The quantities $\phi(\cdot)/\Phi(\cdot)$ and $\phi(\cdot)/[1 - \Phi(\cdot)]$ are the "hazard rates" or inverse "Mill's ratios" of union and nonunion status, respectively. They will be called HR_u and HR_n.

The first approach to consistent estimation of β_u and β_n is a two-step procedure described in detail by Lee (1979). Write the earnings functions conditional on union status as

$$\ln W_u = X\beta_u + (\epsilon_u \mid U = 1) \qquad (25)$$

and

$$\ln W_n = X\beta_n + (\epsilon_n \mid U = 0). \qquad (26)$$

The conditional error terms can be written as

$$(\epsilon_u \mid U = 1) = E(\epsilon_u \mid U = 1) + \theta_u \tag{27}$$

and

$$(\epsilon_n \mid U = 0) = E(\epsilon_n \mid U = 0) + \theta_n, \tag{28}$$

where θ_u and θ_n are random components with zero mean. Substitution for the error terms in Eqs. (25) and (26) yields

$$\ln W_u = X\beta_u + \lambda_u HR_u + \theta_u \tag{29}$$

and

$$\ln W_n = X\beta_n + \lambda_n HR_n + \theta_n \tag{30}$$

using the conditional expectations derived in Eqs. (23) and (24) and the definitions of HR_u and HR_n. The parameters λ_u and λ_n represent $\sigma_u\rho_{2u}$ and $-\sigma_n\rho_{2n}$, respectively. If HR_u and HR_n are observed for union and nonunion workers, respectively, then OLS can be applied to these conditional earnings functions, and consistent estimates of β_u, β_n, λ_u, and λ_n will be obtained.

Although HR_u and HR_n are not observed directly, they are strictly functions of $C\alpha$, and the latter can be estimated consistently from the simple probit model of union status derived earlier. The maximum-likelihood estimates of α from the model are contained in the second column of Table 2. They were used to compute consistent estimates of HR_u and HR_n which can then be used to compute consistent estimates of β_u and β_n by OLS as described above.

The second and more efficient approach to consistent estimation of β_u and β_n is to derive the likelihood function of the switching regression model defined by the two earnings functions and the union status function, and to use the likelihood function to derive the maximum-likelihood estimates of the parameters. The contribution to the appropriate log-likelihood function for an individual is[19]

$$L = U \ln\left[\int_{-C\alpha}^{\infty} f_{2u}(\ln W_u - X_u\beta_u, \epsilon_2)\, d\epsilon_2\right]$$
$$+ (1 - U) \ln\left[\int_{-\infty}^{-C\alpha} f_{2n}(\ln W_n - X_n\beta_n, \epsilon_2)\, d\epsilon_2\right], \tag{31}$$

where $f_{2u}(\cdot, \cdot)$ and $f_{2n}(\cdot, \cdot)$ represent the bivariate normal densities of ϵ_2 and ϵ_u and of ϵ_2 and ϵ_n, respectively. The parameters of the model are β_u, β_n, α, ρ_{2u}, ρ_{2n}, σ_u^2, and σ_n^2.

The OLS estimates of β_u and β_n are contained in columns (1) and (3) of Table 4. These results are atypical in a number of respects. Although

Table 4.   Estimate of Union and Nonunion Earnings Functions

Variable	$\ln W_u$ (1)	$\ln W_u$ (2)	$\ln W_n$ (3)	$\ln W_n$ (4)
Constant	1.27 (.175)	1.38 (.331)	1.19 (.0872)	1.24 (.127)
Ed < 12	.0490 (.141)	.0413 (.140)	−.195 (.0796)	−.189 (.076)
12 < Ed < 16	.135 (.151)	.156 (.158)	.184 (.0737)	.177 (.0771)
Ed ≥ 16	.562 (.143)	.573 (.144)	.337 (.0788)	.335 (.0746)
Exp	.0480 (.0177)	.0480 (.0173)	.0244 (.00847)	.0243 (.00802)
Exp^2	−.000923 (.000346)	−.000905 (.000344)	−.000470 (.000180)	−.000479 (.000171)
Sen	.0416 (.0255)	.0343 (.0311)	.0523 (.0144)	.0571 (.0166)
Sen^2	−.00150 (.000925)	−.00134 (.000992)	−.00167 (.000623)	−.00177 (.000619)
NW	−.337 (.147)	−.352 (.150)	−.175 (.0862)	−.162 (.0854)
Fe	−.429 (.114)	−.405 (.128)	−.354 (.0585)	−.371 (.0645)
South	.0261 (.123)	.0657 (.157)	.0130 (.0568)	−.00909 (.0726)
HR_u	—	−.112 (.283)	—	—
HR_n	—	—	—	−.0911 (.176)
SEE	.918	.904	.652	.617
n	327	327	553	533

Notes:

HR_u = Hazard Rate (inverse Mills' ratio) for union workers computed from estimates in column (2) of Table 2.

HR_n = Hazard Rate (inverse Mills' ratio) for nonunion workers computed from estimates in column (2) of Table 2.

The numbers in parentheses are standard errors. These are asymptotic and corrected in columns (2) and (4).

the average union–nonunion differential computed for these estimates $(\bar{X}(\beta_u - \beta_n))$ is positive (.264), previous evidence and experience with other data sets suggests that the union earnings function (even conditional on union status) ought to be flatter in virtually every dimension.[20] In addition, the previous evidence suggests that the unexplained variance in earnings is larger in the nonunion sector than in the union sector. The common explanation is that unions standardize wage rates by attaching wages to jobs rather than to workers. This reduces a union employer's discretion to vary wages according to individual characteristics.[21] However, the estimates presented here do not indicate this standardization, and it suggests that caution be exercised in interpreting the results derived from these data.

Closer examination of the results and comparison with the results obtained with other data sets suggests that it is the estimates of β_u which are "odd" rather than those of β_n. One approach to solving this problem might be to use a more "representative" group of union workers. However, the well-known difficulties involved with choice-based sampling preclude such an approach. Hence, the analysis continues with the current data.[22]

Consistent estimates of β_u, β_n, λ_u, and λ_n obtained by applying OLS to Eqs. (29) and (30) are contained in columns (2) and (4) of Table 4. The asymptotic standard errors and the standard error of estimation (SEE) are corrected through use of the consistent estimates of σ_u^2 and σ_n^2 rather than those printed by the OLS program.[23] The first thing to note is that the estimate of both λ_u and λ_n have relatively large asymptotic standard errors so that, although the hypotheses that λ_u and λ_n are zero cannot be rejected at conventional levels of significance, it is not possible to determine the potential for selection bias very precisely. The point estimates of the parameter vectors β_u and β_n are virtually identical to those derived using OLS without including the "selectivity regressors." The predicted average union–nonunion wage differential is $\bar{X}(\beta_u - \beta_n) = .325$, which is somewhat higher than that derived using OLS without HR_u and HR_n.

The maximum-likelihood estimates of the switching regression model defined in Eq. (31) are contained in Table 5. The estimates of β_u and β_n differ substantially from those contained in Table 4, but the results are, if anything, less intuitively appealing than the earlier estimates. The union earnings function still does not exhibit the sort of standardization of rates expected of it and, in adddition, the average union–nonunion wage differential is $\bar{X}(\beta_u - \beta_n) = -1.01$. This large negative differential suggests that an average worker earns in a union job only 36 percent of what could be earned in a nonunion job. This, of course, does not acccord with any reasonable view of the union–nonunion wage differential debate.

Another somewhat surprising aspect of the results, particularly given

Table 5. Maximum Likelihood Estimates of Switching Regression Model

Variable	$\ln W_u$ (1)	$\ln W_n$ (2)	$Pr\ (U)$ (3)
Constant	.438 (.323)	1.50 (.130)	−.155 (.280)
Ed < 12	.143 (.288)	−.156 (.109)	.0282 (.149)
12 < Ed < 16	−.0327 (.300)	.130 (.111)	−.154 (.149)
Ed ≥ 16	.367 (.294)	.359 (.105)	.293 (.172)
Exp	.0414 (.0270)	.0247 (.0115)	.0109 (.0198)
Exp^2	−.00101 (.000481)	−.000537 (.000232)	−.000258 (.000358)
Sen	.110 (.0480)	.0799 (.0197)	.103 (.0253)
Sen^2	−.00306 (.00183)	−.00215 (.000833)	−.00231 (.00101)
NW	−.313 (.247)	−.0488 (.120)	.231 (.167)
Fe	−.654 (.169)	−.453 (.0855)	.250 (.185)
South	−.265 (.173)	−.142 (.0868)	−.400 (.108)
Age	—	—	−.0114 (.0104)
Marr	—	—	−.00799 (.147)
Marr*Fe	—	—	.150 (.221)
Cler	—	—	−.314 (.156)
Serv	—	—	.137 (.153)
Professional & Technical	—	—	−.481 (.153)

ρ_{2u} = .841 (.0272) ρ_{2n} = .833 (.0182) $\ln L$ = −1417.6

σ_{u^2} = 1.30 (.101) σ_{n^2} = .564 (.0171)   n = 880

Note: (Numbers in parentheses are asymptotic standard errors.)

the lack of significance of λ_u and λ_n in the "selectivity regressor" model, are the maximum-likelihood estimates of ρ_{2u} and ρ_{2n}. These are estimated to be large (.841 and .833, respectively) with very small standard errors (.0272 and .0182, respectively). The hypothesis that both correlations are zero can be rejected at any reasonable level of significance using a likelihood ratio test.[24] Note that the estimated correlations are so close to each other as to be virtually identical. The hypothesis that $\rho_{2u} = \rho_{2n}$

Table 6. Estimates of Determinants of ΔW ($\beta_u - \beta_n$)

	ΔW^a OLS (1)	ΔW^b OLS with Hazard Rate (2)	ΔW^c MLE (3)
Constant	.080 (.20)	.140 (.355)	−1.06 (.346)
Ed < 12	.244 (.162)	.230 (.159)	.299 (.292)
12 < Ed < 16	−.049 (.168)	−.021 (.176)	−.163 (.309)
Ed ≥ 16	.225 (.163)	.238 (.162)	.008 (.295)
Exp	.0236 (.0196)	.0237 (.0191)	.0167 (.0282)
Exp^2	−.000453 (.000390)	−.000426 (.000384)	−.000473 (.000508)
Sen	−.0107 (.0293)	−.0228 (.0353)	.0301 (.0488)
Sen^2	.00017 (.00112)	.00043 (.00117)	−.00091 (.00188)
NW	−.162 (.170)	−.190 (.173)	−.264 (.270)
Fe	−.075 (.128)	−.034 (.143)	−.201 (.185)
South	.0131 (.135)	.0566 (.173)	−.123 (.184)

Notes:
[a] Computed from estimates contained in columns (1) and (3) of Table 4. Standard errors are in parentheses.
[b] Computed from estimates contained in columns (2) and (4) of Table 4. Corrected asymptotic standard errors calculated assuming no covariances between estimates of β_u and β_n are in parentheses.
[c] Computed from estimates contained in Columns (1) and (2) of Table 5. Asymptotic standard errors are in parentheses.

cannot be rejected at any reasonable level of significance using an asymptotic t-test.[25] The identity of these correlations is what would be expected if the earnings function errors (ϵ_u and ϵ_n) for an individual were perfectly correlated with each other. However, in the absence of longitudinal data it is impossible to identify ρ_{un}, so this must remain conjecture.

Since the estimated wage differential (ΔW) is what is of importance for the model of worker preferences for union representation, it is interesting to compare the three sets of estimates of β_u and β_n with regard to their implications of ΔW. Toward this end, Table 6 contains the coefficients of ΔW ($\beta_u - \beta_n$) for each of the three sets of estimates along with their standard errors. As expected, the estimates from the OLS and OLS augmented with the "selectivity regressors" are very similar. The estimates for the maximum-likelihood model differ somewhat from the first two sets, but the major difference is in the sharply negative constant term. This is what yields the large negative average differential mentioned above, and it suggests that the lower average differential estimated using the maximum-likelihood estimates (MLEs) is an "across-the-board" reduction rather than associated primarily with particular groups, although some groups (nonwhites, females, and southerners) do have somewhat lower estimates of $\beta_u - \beta_n$ using MLEs than using the two OLS techniques.

Overall, none of the results presented here offers much help in choosing a "best" measure of ΔW to use in the structural estimation. The maximum-likelihood estimates are theoretically the best, but the large negative differentials estimated using MLEs are counterintuitive. In addition, the two sets of "consistent" estimates are likely to be sensitive to distributional and other specification assumptions. Finally, the reduced-form probit relationship for union status used in the analysis may be inadequate for the purpose of correcting for selection bias in wage equations due to its shortcomings outlined above. Given the lack of a clear guide to the right set of estimates of ΔW, the analysis continues using all three measures so that their performance can be compared.

VII. ESTIMATION OF THE STRUCTURAL MODEL

Given the estimates of ΔW derived in the last section, the structural version of the model of worker preference for union representation can be estimated. This allows estimation of the effects of individual characteristics on worker preferences after controlling for variation in the union–nonunion wage differential. Both the model conditional on nonunion status and the unconditional model are estimated.

Consistent estimates of the parameters of the structural version of the conditional model can be derived by maximizing the simple probit likelihood function derived from Eq. (17) over the sample of 553 nonunion workers. Unfortunately, the asymptotic standard errors derived from the matrix of second derivatives of the log-likelihood function are inconsistent in this case because they do not account for the fact that the predicted wage differentials are random variables themselves. While it is possible to derive corrected asymptotic standard errors for these estimates, a more straightforward technique is to use these consistent parameter estimates as starting values for one Newton step on the likelihood function relating to the overall model consisting of the two earnings functions, the worker preference function, and the union status function.

The contribution to this log-likelihood function is

$$L = U \ln \left(\int_{-C\alpha}^{\infty} f_{2u}(\ln W_u - X_u\beta_u, \epsilon_2) \, d\epsilon_2 \right)$$

$$+ (1 - U) \, VFU \ln \left(\int_{-\infty}^{-C\alpha} \int_{\kappa_3}^{\infty} h(\epsilon_3, \epsilon_2, \ln W_n - X_n\beta_n) \, d\epsilon_3 \, d\epsilon_2 \right) \quad (32)$$

$$+ (1 - U)(1 - VFU) \ln \left(\int_{-\infty}^{-C\alpha} \int_{-\infty}^{\kappa_3} h(\epsilon_3, \epsilon_2, \ln W_n - X_n\beta_n) \, d\epsilon_3 \, d\epsilon_2 \right),$$

where $f_{2u}(\cdot, \cdot)$ represents the bivariate normal density function of ϵ_2 and ϵ_u; $h(\cdot, \cdot, \cdot)$ represents the trivariate normal density function of ϵ_3, ϵ_2, and ϵ_n; and the quantity $\kappa_3 = -Z\gamma - \delta X(\beta_u - \beta_n)$. For any individual, this contribution represents the joint probability density of observing their preference for union representation, union status, and wage rate. A critical element of this likelihood function is the covariance matrix of the four errors. This is

$$\text{cov} \begin{pmatrix} \epsilon_3 \\ \epsilon_2 \\ \epsilon_u \\ \epsilon_n \end{pmatrix} = \begin{pmatrix} \sigma_3^2 & \sigma_{23} & \sigma_{3u} & \sigma_{3n} \\ \sigma_{23} & \sigma_2^2 & \sigma_{2u} & \sigma_{2n} \\ \sigma_{3u} & \sigma_{2u} & \sigma_u^2 & \sigma_{un} \\ \sigma_{3n} & \sigma_{2n} & \sigma_{un} & \sigma_n^2 \end{pmatrix}.$$

Of the 10 unique elements of this covariance matrix, two (σ_{3u} and σ_{un}) do not appear in the likelihood function and hence are not estimable. Two elements (σ_3^2 and σ_2^2) are normalized to one in order to fix the scale of the probit parameters (C, γ, and δ). This leaves six elements of the covariance matrix which must be estimated (σ_{23}, σ_{3n}, σ_{2u}, σ_{2n}, σ_u^2, and σ_n^2).

As it is written, this model is not conditional on nonunion status. However, given the joint normality of the errors, the conditional model is equivalent to the constrained version of the joint model where $\rho_{23} = 0$. Imposing this constraint and taking one Newton step on the entire sample from the appropriate consistent estimates yields consistent and asymptotically efficient estimates with consistent asymptotic standard errors. These estimates of the Pr(VFU) function are contained in Table 7 for the

three different measures of ΔW.[26] Examination of the point estimates of
the structural parameter (δ), which is the coefficient of the wage differential, yields the result that a nonunion worker's union–nonunion wage
differential has a positive effect on preference for union representation.
However, the effect is not asymptotically significantly greater than zero
at conventional levels of significances for any of the three measures of
ΔW.[27] Given the large difference between the estimated ΔW derived from
the MLE switching regression and the other two measures, it is interesting
that they yield roughly the same result. This is likely due to the fact that
the major differences in the three measures of ΔW lay in the constant
term (see Table 6), and this would explain the differences in the constant
term between the three preference models estimated using the three measures of ΔW. The relatively large constant in the ΔW_{MLE} model is due to
the relatively large negative mean of ΔW_{MLE}.

Table 7. Two-Step Estimates of Structural Probit Likelihood Function
on Pr (VFU = 1 | U = 0) with Different Measures of ΔW

Variable	(1)	(2)	(3)
Constant	−.210	−.00173	.333
	(.389)	(.602)	(.537)
Sen	.00847	.0116	−.0155
	(.0534)	(.0605)	(.0434)
Sen^2	−.00155	−.00160	−.000875
	(.00213)	(.00217)	(.00174)
NW	.919	.957	.973
	(.323)	(.332)	(.264)
Fe	.297	.289	.348
	(.246)	(.262)	(.239)
Marr	−.104	−.0985	−.0880
	(.188)	(.188)	(.188)
Marr*Fe	−.272	−.272	−.313
	(.251)	(.252)	(.250)
South	−.0194	−.0389	.0392
	(.189)	(.270)	(.158)
Age	−.00882	−.00945	−.00531
	(.00732)	(.00781)	(.00618)
Cler	−.134	−.134	−.139
	(.173)	(.174)	(.177)
Serv	.117	.105	.114
	(.187)	(.188)	(.194)

(continued)

Table 7.   (*Continued*)

Variable	(1)	(2)	(3)
Prof & Tech	−.186 (.183)	−.186 (.185)	−.0848 (.175)
ΔW_{OLS}	.701 (.775)	—	—
ΔW_{HR}	—	.737 (.794)	—
ΔW_{MLE}	—	—	.532 (.487)
ln L	−338.5	−338.7	−338.7

Notes: Estimates computed by taking one Newton step on full four equation likelihood function from initial consistent estimates derived assuming $\rho_{23} = 0$.

Initial consistent estimates of γ and δ were derived by maximizing the likelihood function in equation (17). Consistent estimates of α are contained in column (2) of Table 2. An initial consistent estimate of ρ_{3n}, which only appears in the full likelihood function, was derived by grid search using consistent estimates of the other parameters. Initial consistent estimates of the other parameters were derived as follows:

Column 1:   Initial consistent estimates of β_u, β_n, σ_u^2 and σ_n^2 were computed from the estimates in columns (1) and (3) of Table 4. The parameters ρ_{2u} and ρ_{2n} were constrained to zero.

Column 2:   Initial consistent estimates of β_u, β_n, σ_u^2, σ_n^2, ρ_{2u}, and ρ_{2n} were computed from estimates in columns (2) and (4) of Table 4.

Column 3:   Initial consistent estimates of β_u β_n σ_u^2, σ_n^2, σ_{2u} , and ρ_{2n} were computed from estimates in columns (1) and (2) of Table 5.

The values of the log-likelihood function are based on the initial consistent estimates of Pr (VFU = 1 | U = 0).

These estimates are asymptotically efficient. The numbers in parentheses are asymptotic standard errors.

n = 880

The estimates of the other parameters are virtually identical across the three versions. Nonwhite nonunion workers have a much larger probability of preferring union representation after controlling for the wage effect of unions. However, this result must be interpreted with caution due to the fact that the union–nonunion wage differential is estimated to be smaller for nonwhites than for whites. This is contrary to previous evidence, which suggests that nonwhites receive a larger wage advantage than whites from unionization (Ashenfelter, 1972).

An interesting relationship is found between sex and marital status and the desire for union representation among nonunion workers. Using the estimates contained in the first column of Table 7, nonunion single females are significantly more likely at the 12 percent level to prefer union representation than are nonunion single males, and they are significantly more likely at the 5 percent level to prefer union representation than are nonunion married males. However, married nonunion females behave in the opposite manner. Their preferences for union representation is significantly less than that of nonunion single females at the 2 percent level. In addition, the preference of married nonunion females for union representation does not differ significantly from either single or married nonunion males.

The overidentifying restrictions embedded in the structural model can be tested by noting that the reduced-form estimates contained in column 1 of Table 2 represent an unconstrained version of the structural model. The relevant likelihood ratio test has four restrictions (representing the five variables included in the earnings functions but excluded from the preference function less one for ΔW). For none of the three measures of ΔW can the constrained structural model be rejected at conventional levels of significance.[28]

Consistent estimates of the structural version of the union preference model unconditional on union status can be derived based on the likelihood function defined by Eqs. (18), (19), (13), and (14). However, as in the case described above, the estimated asymptotic standard errors are inconsistent due to the randomness of the predicted wage differentials. Asymptotically efficient two-step estimates of the parameters of the structural model are derived with corrected standard errors by taking one Newton step on the log-likelihood function defined in Eq. (32) from the initial consistent estimates without the constraint that $\rho_{23} = 0$. These estimates of the parameters of the Pr(VFU) and Pr(U) functions for the three measures of ΔW are contained in Tables 8 and 9.

The estimates contained in Table 7 when combined with the estimates of Pr(U = 1) contained in the second column of Table 2 relate to a constrained version of the joint model where $\rho_{23} = 0$. The point estimates, contained in Table 8, for ρ_{23} are all significantly different from zero at conventional levels so that the constrained model can be rejected. The estimated positive correlation suggests that workers who are more likely for unobserved reasons to desire union representation are also more likely to work on a union job.

The central hypothesis of the structural model is that workers with high union–nonunion wage differentials will be more likely to desire union representation. While the point estimates of the coefficients of ΔW are positive for all three measures, in no case are they significantly greater than zero at conventional levels.[29] However, for the ΔW_{MLE} version the coefficient is significantly greater than zero at the .13 level.

The estimates of the parameters of the Pr(VFU) function are similar across the three measures of ΔW. Thus, in order to facilitate the discussion, only the parameters derived using ΔW_{OLS} will be examined explicitly.

Table 8. Two-Step Estimates of Structural Bivariate Probit
Likelihood Function on Pr (VFU) with Different Measures of ΔW

Variable	(1)	(2)	(3)
Constant	.405	.545	.874
	(.474)	(.681)	(.558)
Sen	.0547	.0530	.0213
	(.0593)	(.0677)	(.0403)
Sen^2	−.00200	−.00194	−.00139
	(.00215)	(.00227)	(.00159)
NW	.890	.923	1.04
	(.358)	(.373)	(.280)
Fe	.260	.246	.246
	(.240)	(.264)	(.241)
Marr	−.0284	−.0353	−.0499
	(.172)	(.171)	(.164)
Marr*Fe	−.260	−.256	−.285
	(.223)	(.223)	(.224)
South	−.247	−.259	−.139
	(.228)	(.298)	(.159)
Age	−.0131	−.0133	−.00767
	(.00714)	(.00760)	(.00600)
Cler	−.425	−.412	−.352
	(.201)	(.197)	(.164)
Serv	−.146	−.136	−.0591
	(.214)	(.209)	(.174)
Prof & Tech	−.412	−.404	−.225
	(.201)	(.200)	(.164)
ΔW_{OLS}	.790	—	—
	(.811)		
ΔW_{HR}	—	.815	—
		(.834)	
ΔW_{MLE}	—	—	.597
			(.513)
ρ_{23}	.814	.771	.654
	(.323)	(.308)	(.0953)
ln L	−834.0	−834.2	−834.6

Notes: Estimates computed by taking one Newton step on full four equation likelihood function from
initial consistent estimates derived from maximizing the likelihood function defined by Eqs. (18),
(19), (13), and (14), and using the appropriate estimate of β_u, β_n, and the covariance parameters.
An initial consistent estimate of ρ_{3n}, which appears only in the full likelihood function, was derived
by grid search using consistent estimates of the other parameters. The numbers in parentheses
are asymptotic standard errors.

See notes to Table 7 for the sources of the consistent estimates of β_u, β_n, and covariance parameters.
Ln L is computed based on the initial consistent estimates.
n = 880

Table 9. Two-Step Estimates of Structural Bivariate Probit
Likelihood Function of Pr (U) with Different Measures of ΔW

Variable	(1) ΔW_{OLS}	(2) ΔW_{HR}	(3) ΔW_{MLE}
Constant	−.0898 (.258)	−.0972 (.257)	−.161 (.226)
Ed < 12	.0856 (.136)	.0865 (.136)	.114 (.146)
12 < Ed < 16	−.0782 (.130)	−.0687 (.129)	−.0828 (.133)
Ed ≥ 16	.270 (.180)	.280 (.181)	.198 (.171)
Exp	.0151 (.0195)	.0150 (.0194)	.0141 (.0173)
Exp^2	−.000319 (.000333)	−.000329 (.000326)	−.000362 (.000321)
Sen	.111 (.0238)	.112 (.0240)	116 (.0243)
Sen^2	−.00244 (.000935)	−.00250 (.000940)	−.00265 (.000944)
NW	.297 (.147)	.297 (.148)	.303 (.155)
Fe	−.0376 (.174)	−.0459 (.174)	−439 (.150)
South	−.550 (.103)	−.552 (.103)	−.555 (.0973)
Age	−.0125 (.0103)	−.0121 (.0104)	−.0108 (.00715)
Marr	.0738 (.148)	.0666 (.148)	.0638 (.126)
Marr*Fe	−.0276 (.218)	−.0215 (.217)	.0121 (.165)
Cler	−.746 (.154)	−.747 (.154)	−.640 (.132)
Serv	−.493 (.151)	−.486 (.151)	−.358 (.131)
Prof & Tech	−.709 (.171)	−.725 (.172)	−.578 (.140)

Note: Estimates of Pr (VFU), ρ_{23}, and the value of ln L are in Table 8. See notes to Tables 7 and 8.
n = 880

Southern workers are significantly less likely to desire union representation than are nonsouthern workers at the 15 percent level. This contrasts with the result that southern nonunion workers are no less likely than nonsouthern nonunion workers to desire union representation. This could explain in part the relatively low level of unionization which coexists with currently comparable levels of new organization in the two regions.[30] Specifically, the relatively more numerous nonsouthern workers who desire union representation are already union members, leaving in the nonunion sector a group of workers who are less likely to desire union representation and hence comparable to their nonunion southern brethren.

Older workers are significantly less likely to desire union representation than are younger workers after controlling for seniority. Marital status has an insignificant effect on male worker's preferences for union representation. On the other hand, single females are significantly more likely to desire union representation than are either males or married females. Married females are indistinguishable from males on this basis.

Sharp occupational distinctions arise in worker preferences for union representation. Clerical and professional and technical workers are significantly less likely to desire union representation than are either blue-collar or service workers. Again, these distinctions do not exist conditional on nonunion status, and the same sorting argument which was made above for southern versus nonsouthern workers can be made here.

The overidentifying restrictions used to identify the coefficient of ΔW can be tested by noting that the structural model is a constrained version of the reduced-form model whose estimates are contained in Table 2. A likelihood ratio test of these four overidentifying restrictions fails to reject the constrained model at reasonable levels of significance.[31]

Overall, the results concerning the structural model are mixed. For all three measures of ΔW, the effect of the wage differential on worker preferences for union representation is positive but not significantly greater than zero at conventional levels. However, this may be due more to imprecision in estimating ΔW rather than a problem with the structural specification itself. Evidence of sorting was found in a number of dimensions, including region, occupation, and age. Among nonunion workers, little distinction in preferences for union representation could be found along these dimensions. However, after correcting for the sample censoring on union status, differences in preferences were defined quite sharply along these dimensions.

VIII. SUMMARY AND CONCLUSIONS

A model of the determination of worker preferences for union representation was developed which led to the hypothesis of a positive relationship between a worker's preference in this area and the worker's union–nonunion wage differential. A distinction was drawn between the observed union status of workers and their current preferences for union representation, which was based on costs of job mobility and the existence of queues for union jobs. A rather unique set of data, the Quality of Employment Survey, was used because it contained a question the response to which indicated directly a worker's preference for union representation. Unfortunately, this particular bit of information was available only for nonunion workers.

A pair of econometric issues were raised. One had to do with techniques for handling the censored nature of the union preference information. The second had to do with appropriate techniques for estimating the central explanatory variable: the union–nonunion wage differential.

The censored data problem was handled by developing a reduced-form empirical model to explain union status and hence the censoring under the assumption of joint normality of latent variables determining union status and preference for union representation. The union preference function was estimated using both the model conditional on nonunion status and, by accounting for the censored data, the model unconditional on union status. A comparison of the general nature of the results both yields some insight into the determination of the extent and locus of unionization and has important implications for prospects for organizing currently unorganized workers.

Overall, worker preferences for unionization among nonunion workers are rather flat in that there is little variation across workers with different characteristics.[32] On the other hand, a number of relatively sharp delinations in worker preferences for union representation along such dimensions as region and occupation occur in the model unconditional on union status. This suggests that many workers with those characteristics (both observed and unobserved) which make them likely to desire union representation are, in fact, union workers. The nonunion workers who are left are relatively homogeneous in their lack of interest in union representation. This interpretation is supported by the positive correlation estimated between the unobservable factors affecting preference for union representation and actual union status. In terms of the prospects for union organizing, this sorting suggests both that current nonunion workers will be less receptive to organizing efforts and that effective targeting of campaign efforts on the basis of gross characteristics such as region will not be terribly useful in light of the flatness of preferences.

The problem of the appropriate estimates of the union–nonunion wage differential (ΔW) arose because, as must be true in the absence of longitudinal data, only one wage or the other is observed for any individual. Apart from OLS applied separately to the two subsamples, two techniques were used to derive "consistent" estimates of ΔW under the assumption of joint normality of ln W and the latent variable determining union status. One technique (Mill's ratio or selectivity regressors) gave results similar to the OLS estimates. The other technique (maximum-likelihood switching regression) gave vastly different and unreasonable results in that a large negative average differential was estimated. The sensitivity of these techniques to the particular sample and specification is well known, and as a result the analysis of the structural model was carried out using all three measures.

The results of the estimation were remarkably similar across all three measures of ΔW. The central hypothesis was weakly supported in that the effect of ΔW on the propensity to desire union representation was positive in all cases, though only significantly so in one case. This weakness may be due to problems in estimating ΔW rather than to problems with the structural model.

In closing, two cautions are necessary. First, all of the results presented here were derived under the assumption of joint normality largely for computational convenience. The results may be sensitive to alternative distributional assumptions. Second, as was discussed earlier, the reduced-form empirical probit model used to explain union status and hence to correct for sample censoring has rather ambiguous behavioral underpinnings. Indeed, part of the reason for carrying out this study was to improve our understanding of union status determination. Some progress has been made but more is yet to be done.

ACKNOWLEDGMENTS

This research was supported by the National Science Foundation under Grant No. SES-7924880.

NOTES

1. There is reason to believe that there are advantages to union employment which are not offset completely by union dues and initiation fees paid by workers. This results in an excess demand for vacancies in existing union jobs. See Abowd and Farber (1982) for a more detailed discussion of this point.

2. See Farber and Saks (1980) for an analysis which focuses on the preferences of non-union workers for union representation.

3. See Freeman and Medoff (1981) for a convincing discussion of the problems with standard sample selection correction techniques in the union wage effect context.

4. Freeman (1981) presents evidence on the relationship between unionization and fringe benefits.

5. It must be cautioned that these examples are not meant to imply specific empirical hypotheses. Any particular personal characteristic can be correlated with these utilities in a number of dimensions. The effect of these characteristics in Eq. (3) is the net effect of all of these dimensions.

6. See Quinn and Staines (1979) for a detailed description of the survey design.

7. The question of how workers form their expectations about what unions do is interesting and important. However, it is left to future research. Kochan (1979) presents an analysis of worker perceptions of unions based on the QES.

8. It is fallacious to argue that since union workers are in fact union workers voluntarily, they desire union representation. While it is true that they desired union representation when they took the job in the sense that it was part of a package of job characteristics which was preferred to any other package, the accumulation of seniority can reduce mobility so that a union worker may desire to retain his job but eliminate unionization. This does *not* mean that the worker will desire to quit.

9. The assumption of unit variance is a normalization required by the dichotomous nature of VFU in order to fix the scale of γ and δ.

10. The identity that $\Phi(a) = 1 - \Phi(-a)$ is used in deriving this expression.

11. Note that this is a different normalization than the one used above ($\text{var}(\epsilon_1) = 1$). This will result in a different scaling for the parameters, but the initial scaling was arbitrary to begin with.

12. The full set is not testable because X must contain at least one variable which is not contained in Z in order to identify δ. Thus, the test carried out in Section VII embodies only four restrictions.

13. This represents a level of significance of 32 percent with a two-tailed test or 16 percent with a one-tailed test using an asymptotic t-test.

14. The constrained log-likelihood is -366.1, while the unconstrained log-likelihood is -337.8. The test statistic is $-2(-366.1 - (-337.8)) = 56.8 > 34.3 = \chi^2_{.005}$ (16).

15. There is redundant information in these results because there is not a complete analysis of variance. In other words, a complete set of interaction variables was not included. The analysis is done because of the nonlinearity inherent in the relationship between $Z^*\gamma^*$ and $\text{Pr}(\text{VFU} = 1 \mid U = 0)$ and the resulting difficulty in interpreting the parameter estimates from probit models.

16. The estimated effect of seniority may be more the result of union status than an explanatory factor. It is well known that seniority is higher on union jobs through lower quit rates. See Table 1 for union and nonunion means on seniority as well as Freeman (1980) for an analysis of the relationship between union status and quit rates.

17. The constrained log-likelihood is -580.6, while the unconstrained log-likelihood is -496.7. The test statistic is $-2(-580.6 - (-496.7)) = 167.8 > 34.3 = \chi^2_{.005}$ (16).

18. The constrained log-likelihood is -834.5, while the unconstrained log-likelihood is -833.1. The test statistic is $-2(-834.5 - (-833.1)) = 2.8 > 2.71 = \chi^2_{.1}$ (1).

19. See Lee (1979) for a more detailed discussion of this likelihood function.

20. This can be verified using samples from the Panel Study of Income Dynamics (PSID), the National Longitudinal Survey (NLS), and the Current Population Survey (CPS). See, for example, Bloch and Kuskin (1978) and Abowd and Farber (1982).

21. See Webb and Webb (1920) for a classic discussion of the standard rate.

22. See Cosslett (1981) and Manski and Lerman (1977) for discussions of the choice-based sampling problem.

23. The technique for deriving the consistent estimates of σ_u^2 and σ_n^2 is described by Lee (1979). Briefly, the estimated residuals in each sector are regressed on a constant and the appropriate hazard rate multiplied by the estimated $C\alpha$. The estimated constant terms are consistent estimates of the residual variances.

24. The constrained log-likelihood, derived from the OLS estimates of β_u and β_n and the simple probit estimates of α, is -1470.0. The unconstrained log-likelihood is -1417.6. The test statistic is $-2(-1470.0 - (-1417.6)) = 104.8 > 10.6 = \chi^2_{.005}$ (2).

25. The quantity $\rho_{2u} - \rho_{2n} = .008$ with an asymptotic standard error of .0313. The t-statistic is .256, which is marginally significant only at the 60 percent level.

26. See the note to Table 7 for sources of the initial consistent estimates of the parameters in each of the three cases.

27. It is interesting that examination of the inconsistent asymptotic standard errors derived from the initial consistent estimates suggests that for all three measures of ΔW the effect of the wage difference on Pr(VFU) is significantly greater than zero at the .06 level. Since these estimated standard errors would be correct under the assumption that the estimated differentials were in fact the actual differentials, this implies that the lack of precision in estimation of ΔW is what is causing the relatively large standard errors on δ.

28. The unconstrained model has a log-likelihood of -337.8. The three versions of the constrained model have log-likelihoods computed using the initial consistent estimates of -338.5, -338.7, and -338.7. The test statistic is minus twice the difference in the log-likelihoods, which yields values of 1.4, 1.8, and 1.8. The critical value of a χ^2 distribution with four degrees of freedom at the .75 level of significance is 1.92. This test is not strictly valid due to the unaccounted-for randomness of ΔW. However, the results are suggestive.

29. Once again, the inconsistent standard errors were small enough to allow rejection of the hypothesis that the coefficient of ΔW equals zero at the 5 percent level of significance. This suggests that it is the imprecision in the estimation of ΔW which is the cause of the relatively large standard errors. See note 27.

30. Evidence from the U.S. Bureau of Labor Statistics (1975, 1978) and from the National Labor Relations Board (1974) indicate that 1.2 percent of nonunion workers in the south were eligible to vote in NLRB-supervised representation elections in 1974. Outside the southern region, only 0.9 percent of nonunion workers were eligible to vote in such elections. (Eligibility refers to working in a potential bargaining unit where an election was held.) Of those workers who voted, 46 percent of workers in the South voted for union representation compared with 50 percent of nonsouthern workers. Similarly, union representation rights were won in 46 percent of the southern elections and in 51 percent of the nonsouthern elections. In both regions approximately 0.3 percent of nonunion workers were newly organized in 1974 as a result of NLRB-supervised elections.

31. The unconstrained model has a log-likelihood of -833.1. The three versions of the constrained model have log-likelihoods computed from the initial consistent estimates of -834.0, -834.2, and -834.6. The likelihood ratio test statistics are 1.8, 2.2, and 3.0. The critical value of a χ^2 distribution with four degrees of freedom at the 50 percent level is 3.36. Again, this test is not strictly valid due to the unaccounted-for randomness of ΔW. However, the results are suggestive.

32. An exception to this is that nonunion nonwhites are substantially less likely than nonunion whites to desire union representation.

REFERENCES

Abowd, John M., and Henry S. Farber (1982), "Job Queues and the Union Status of Workers." *Industrial and Labor Relations Review* 35(3).

Ashenfelter, Orley (1972), "Racial Discrimination and Trade Unionism." *Journal of Political Economy* 80(3, Pt. 1):435–464.

Ashenfelter, Orley, and George E. Johnson (1972), "Unionism, Relative Wages, and Labor Quality in the U.S. Manufacturing Industries." *International Economic Review* 13(3):488–509.

Bloch, Farrell E., and Mark S. Kuskin (1978), "Wage Determination in the Union and Non-Union Sectors." *Industrial and Labor Relations Review* 31(2):183–192.

Cosslett, Stephen R. (1981), "Maximum Likelihood Estimator for Choice-Based Samples." *Econometrica* 49(5):1289–1316.

Farber, Henry S., and Daniel H. Saks (1980), "Why Workers Want Unions: The Role of Relative Wages and Job Characteristics." *Journal of Political Economy* 88(2):349–369.

Freeman, Richard B. (1980), "The Exit-Voice Tradeoff in the Labor Market, Unionism, Job Tenure, Quits, and Separations." *Quarterly Journal of Economics* 94(June):643–673.

———— (1981), "The Effect of Trade Unionism on Fringe Benefits." *Industrial and Labor Relations Review* 34(4):489–509.

Freeman, Richard B., and James L. Medoff (1981), "The Impact of Collective Bargaining: Illusion or Reality?" In Stieber, McKersie, and Mills (eds.), *U.S. Industrial Relations 1950–1980: A Critical Assessment.* Madison, Wisc.: Industrial Relations Research Association.

Kochan, Thomas A. (1979), "How American Workers View Labor Unions." *Monthly Labor Review* (April):23–31.

Kochan, Thomas A., and David E. Helfman (1981), "The Effects of Collective Bargaining on Economic and Behavioral Job Outcomes." Working Paper No. 1181–81, Alfred P. Sloan School of Management, M.I.T., January.

Lee, Lung-Fei (1978), "Unionism and Wage Rates: Simultaneous Equations Model with Qualitative and Limited Dependent Variables." *International Economic Review* 19:415–433.

———— (1979), "Identification and Estimation in Binary Choice Models with Limited (Censored) Dependent Variables." *Econometrica* 47(4):977–996.

Manski, Charles F., and Steven R. Lerman (1977), "The Estimation of Choice Probabilities from Choice Based Samples." *Econometrica* 45(8):1977–1988.

National Labor Relations Board (1974), *Annual Report, 1974.* Washington, D.C.: U.S. Government Printing Office.

Quinn, Robert P., and Graham L. Staines (1979), *The 1977 Quality of Employment Survey: Descriptive Statistics, with Comparison Data from the 1969–70 and the 1972–1973 Surveys.* Ann Arbor, Mich.: Institute for Social Research.

U.S. Bureau of Labor Statistics (1975), *Directory of National Unions and Employee Associations, 1975,* Bulletin No. 1937. Washington, D.C.: U.S. Government Printing Office.

———— (1978), *Handbook of Labor Statistics, 1978.* Bulletin No. 2000. Washington, D.C.: U.S. Government Printing Office.

Webb, Sidney, and Beatrice Webb (1965), *Industrial Democracy, 1920,* reprint ed. New York: Augustus M. Kelley.

COMMENT ON NOAM AND FARBER

John T. Addison

The paper by Noam is a brave attempt to investigate the effect of unionism on salaries and productivity within a "public-sector" sample of 1100 building departments. Although the author claims that his particular (two-stage least-squares) approach is a novel treatment, I think he rather misinterprets the "Harvard school" literature (see below). That literature employs a production function test of unionism's *net* impact on productivity. The capital/labor ratio figures explicitly in the production function and controls for the spurious effect of unionism on productivity resulting from an employer moving up his demand curve in response to a positive union–nonunion relative wage differential. Also, the labor input in the production function is adjusted/weighted for labor quality via an auxiliary earnings function—or the extent of quality bias otherwise analyzed. In short, Harvard analysts do recognize the need to obtain estimates of unionism's impact on productivity purged of these two "productivity effects" which have nothing to do with unionism per se. I would argue therefore that the simultaneity issue *as articulated by Noam* (and there

New Approaches to Labor Unions.
Research in Labor Economics, Supplement 2, pages 207–215.
Copyright © 1983 by JAI Press Inc.
All rights of reproduction in any form reserved.
ISBN: 0-89232-265-9

is some real ambiguity here) *is* incorporated in the new literature on unionism.

The key question is whether the author's approach represents an improvement on the Harvard school literature since he, too, has a theoretically ambiguous sign on the unionism coefficient. Here, I have to say that I do not regard the partial regression coefficients on salaries in the estimated form of (20) and on productivity in (21) as terribly meaningful. The problem in a nutshell is that the specification of the quasi-reduced-form equations is ad hoc. There is some suggestion of an embryonic "economy of high wages" argument in the specification, although the relevance of this to the public sector is I think rather tenuous.

I also have problems with the underlying model of the bureaucracy/administrative agency in question. First, the reconciliation of the author's optimization criteria with other theoretical models is left hazy. Second, and related, I am not sufficiently informed of the relevant structural equations. Third, there is the standard problem of measuring the "output" of the bureaucracy. Noam uses two measures, namely number of building permits granted and volume of construction output supervised. Output might alternatively have been assessed in terms of compliance. Furthermore, we are surely in some sense speaking of "voter productivity" in all of this.

My reservations concerning the salary variable in the productivity equation and with the productivity variable in the salary equation are such that I do not propose to comment on the empirical findings of this paper although I did find a number of the arguments (e.g., "nonconformity in regulation") of interest. Consider, for example, Eq. (21). According to Eq. (2), salary is simply a function of the minimum wage rate (M) plus quality of labor (Q^γ). Are we to assume that the other nonquality arguments in (21) are a proxy for M? Accordingly, I cannot agree with the author that "we have a system of equations describing interactions of productivity and salary."

I would argue that the study does not really achieve its stated aim, though it is an enterprising attempt. (A similar criticism will be leveled at the Harvard analyses.) Perhaps a less ambitious goal might have been set, focusing on, say, the determinants of the demand for labor in this particular agency.

I conclude this comment on Noam's paper with some final reflections on the Harvard school literature referred to above and amplified somewhat in Freeman and Medoff's survey paper in this volume.[1] Some six studies have reported strongly positive union coefficients in the production function test that roughly correspond in magnitude to parallel union relative wage effects reported in the relevant auxiliary earnings functions (Frantz, 1976; Brown and Medoff, 1978; Allen, 1979; Clark 1980a, 1980b;

Freeman et al., 1982). While the various authors interpret their results as suggesting that union and nonunion plants may after all be able to compete in the same product market because of the productivity-enhancing nature of unionism, considerable doubt must attach to the estimated net productivity effect of unionism.[2]

Focusing first on the narrower empirical issues, four problems of the literature might usefully be identified. First, the use of value added per unit of labor as the dependent variable in three of the studies (Frantz, Brown and Medoff, and Allen) runs into an acknowledged problem of compounding price and productivity effects. However, Gregg Lewis has suggested to me that what the unionism coefficient is actually picking up in this specification is a crude measure of the union–nonunion wage differential.[3] (In consequence, we should not be terribly surprised to learn that unionism's spurious "productivity effect" exceeds the earnings function estimate of the wage differential since the latter is computed with more care!) I now find this argument the stronger of the two. Second, the absence of controls for "firm effects" in all studies except those of Clark is unhelpful in a literature that purports to argue that "internal organization matters." Third, the assumption that production functions are identical as between the union and nonunion sectors, except for the productivity of labor parameter in the union sector, is unsatisfactory.[4] Again, only Clark relaxes this assumption. Fourth, the hedonic wage equation correction for labor quality may lead to upward biases in the unionism effect because observable characteristics may be poor indicators of the true attribute of interest (e.g., mechanical aptitude).

In fact, only Clark has attempted to come to grips with the above specification problems. We note here that his cross-section study (Clark, 1980b) should properly be interpreted as finding that unions have *no* effect either way on productivity (Addison and Barnett, 1981). And while his innovative time-series study of unionism's impact (Clark, 1980a) *does* consistently point to positive union effects under a variety of assumptions and alternative model specifications, the author interprets some of his statistics in a rather puzzling manner. Thus his use of one-tail test procedures seems singularly inappropriate given the theoretical uncertainty (see below) surrounding the sign of the union effect. Again, the employment of .10 significance levels coupled with this procedure provides excessively generous rejection intervals. Furthermore, with each additional specification the reported DW statistics offer strong evidence of first-order autocorrelation; and when the author corrects for this, estimated t-values for the union coefficients are rather low, ranging from 1.48 to 1.60 in the three relevant equations. These reservations are reinforced by the fact that Clark draws his data from only six plants (namely those changing their union status over the sample period, 1950–1973). The sample is sufficiently small and the correction for time trends sufficiently crude to cast doubt on the reliability of the author's results. Clearly, Clark's study does not resolve the union versus nonunion productivity issue.

Despite these negative comments, I would conjecture that Harvard analysts are essentially correct if they are arguing that the *static* allocative and X-inefficiency consequences of unionism have been overplayed in conventional analysis, at least insofar as we are speaking of industrial type labor markets.

Finally, consider the theoretical content of the unions-raise-productivity thesis. What theory there is rests upon a collective-voice model (Freeman, 1976), exploiting the public goods dimension of the workplace. Interestingly, since Freeman draws heavily on the efficient contract literature, it is curious that Harvard analysts have failed to consider unionism as being jointly determined with the degree of internal labor market structuring (productivity?). This is perhaps the principal lacuna of the model: Unions simply exist in some settings with associated productivity effects, but not others.

It is a rather unsatisfactory aspect of the "model" that the coefficient in unionism is theoretically ambiguous. Here, the optimal procedure would appear to lie in the development of a public choice theoretic model of unionism à la Pencavel (1982) and Farber (1978). In other words, there is no specific story of what it is that unions do.

Of course, the general story advanced by Harvard analysts would be more compelling were it possible to identify the mechanisms by which productivity is improved. With the exception of Brown and Medoff (1978), who use a turnover test, we are simply presented with a black box of productivity-enhancing mechanisms. The crude turnover test is basically flawed because of the absence of controls for the propensity to quit. Though Freeman (1980a) has presented an interesting analysis of turnover suggesting that reduced quits are due to actual changes in behavior (rather than selectivity) caused by the specific work relations associated with the union institution, other researchers also using panel data have argued cogently that the impact of unions on work stability has been much exaggerated (Polachek and McCutcheon, 1981). Without the turnover test, the model collapses to a shock-effect argument. Unions indirectly cause higher productivity by inducing management to introduce more efficient working practices. The problem with the shock theory is that it has no dynamic intent, is not estimated directly, and coexists uneasily with the efficient contracts literature.

Interestingly, Duncan and Stafford (1980) have recently argued that adverse working conditions might on public goods grounds give rise to unionism at the same time as being conducive to higher productivity.

Accordingly, one could regard unionism as an intervening variable in a recursive model after the authors or as an endogenous variable within a full simultaneous-equations model. Thus unionized and nonunionized plants could compete in the same market despite the higher relative wages associated with unionism for reasons other than those described if not measured by Harvard analysts. Specifically, Duncan and Stafford report that the male blue-collar worker union differential shrinks from 20.4 to 6.4 percent once allowance is made for such adverse working condition variables. In other words, almost 70 percent of the wage difference is compensating differential.

However, I do not wish to trade off empirical result against empirical result. My point here is that the results of the new literature on unions are subject to specification error while consistent with a variety of interpretations.

The bottom line is, unfortunately, that our knowledge of what it is that unions do is not greatly advanced by this literature. Moreover, we cannot tell whether managements in response to unionization are moved from non–cost-minimizing behavior to cost-minimizing behavior or more generally whether the type of behavior that is cost-minimizing differs in union and nonunion plants.

The paper by Farber addresses the important issue of what determines union status. The key assumption underpinning his analysis is that union status is determined by worker preferences for unionism, subject only to a likely excess demand for union jobs and hence (unionized) employer selection from a queue. While sympathetic to this approach, I enter the caveat that it may be unrealistic to view union status as determined by employee demand, even if qualified in the above manner.

Farber's empirical analysis exploits nonunion workers' responses to the following question: "If an election were held with secret ballots, would you vote for or against having a union or employees' association represent you." From this "vote-for-union?" (VFU) response conditional on nonunion status, Farber erects a simple model of the determinants of worker preferences for union representation unconditional on actual union status which is estimated using a 1977 cross section of the Quality of Employment Survey (on which more below). The model depicts union preference as a function of worker characteristics and the magnitude of the union–nonunion wage differential. Since worker preferences as revealed by the QES are conditional on nonunion status and since wages are observed in dichotomous situations, much of Farber's paper is given over to enterprising technical "solutions" to the respective problems of censored data and selectivity bias.

In his reduced-form specification, Farber can sidestep the wage selectivity bias problem. Rather interesting differences are revealed between the determinants of $Pr(VFU = 1, U = 0)$ and $Pr(VFU = 1)$. Specifically, not only is the latter function better determined than the conditional model, but also occupation and region emerge as significant determinants in addition to race. Apparently, blue-collar workers are on average 37 percent more likely to desire union representation than are nonunion workers, which points to a sorting phenomenon.

In order to test the structural variant, Farber has to come to grips with sample selection bias. Accordingly, supplemental to running a simple OLS earnings equation over the union and nonunion samples, the author also employs OLS augmented by the hazard rate derived from a reduced-form probit union status model *and* a maximum-likelihood switching regression model consisting of the union and nonunion functions plus an equation explaining union status. Perhaps not surprisingly in the light of Freeman and Medoff's contribution in this volume, Farber obtains very different estimates of the logarithmic differential ranging from .325 through .264 to -1.01. Each estimate of the differential is subsequently incorporated in estimating the structural model. Two comments might be made on Tables 4 and 5. Farber is evidently concerned that his earnings functions for the union sector is not flatter than that of the nonunion sector. He notes that the common "explanation" for the widely observed flatter union function (Block and Kuskin, 1978; Borjas, 1979; Freeman, 1980b; Duncan and Leigh, 1980) is that unions standardize wage rates by attaching wages to jobs rather than to individuals. Ergo, characteristics should be less important in the union earnings function. Too much can be made of this. While the seniority principle may reduce the employer's discretion to vary wages according to individual characteristics, this result does not necessarily follow. Here I would draw the author's attention to the idiosyncratic exchange/efficient contract model of Williamson et al. (1975) and the theoretical elaboration supplied by Miyazaki (1977) both of which stress the role of the promotion apparatus as a continuous screening mechanism. The results obtained by Farber need not necessarily be surprising because of uncontrolled differences in firms (i.e., their degree of internal labor market structuring) that potentially underpin differences in union status. This harks back to the assumption that employee preferences solely determine union status.

In fact, the most recent empirical research using panel data has suggested that unions may not after all flatten earnings profiles and that unions may organize where age–earnings profiles are relatively flat (the causality point) (Hutchins and Polachek, 1981). This material is able to reconcile the generally opposing cross-section and longitudinal data findings which would seem to suggest that we cannot be sanguine about Farber's (three) wage variables employed in the full structural model.

Turning to the structural model, Farber finds that workers with high union–nonunion differentials will be more likely to desire union representation and that workers whose characteristics make them likely to desire union representation are already union members—a sorting phenomenon already hinted at in the reduced-form estimates—leaving nonunion workers relatively homogeneous in their lack of interest in union membership. I have no substantive comments to make on the actual equations themselves, other than the point noted in the previous paragraph, except to note that I, too, am puzzled by the result for blacks given the small order of magnitude of the black worker union–nonunion wage differential. I am inclined to regard this as an empirical *curiosum*.

My final comment centers on what I see as an important omission in Farber's study. I refer to the role of working conditions, both as a determinant of the wage differential and as influencing the demand for unionism. In other words, unionism may be an intervening variable between working conditions and wages. (This possibility harks back to the issue of whether the union differential is an equilibrium or a disequilibrium phenomenon. Here I detect a certain ambiguity in Farber's treatment.)

I single out working conditions because a recent study by Duncan and Stafford estimates a union membership function using QES data—like Farber they ignore union supply effects. Although they are unable to obtain sophisticated measures of working conditions from QES data (comparable with those constructed from the Time Use Study in their main study) some interesting findings emerge. The QES data contain measures of overtime hours flexibility and the extent to which the respondent (n = 570) characterized his job as "allowing freedom as to how to do work, requiring hard work, physical effort, allowing decision making, or being repetitive." Duncan and Stafford report that when these variables (plus demographic controls) were related to a dichotomous measure of union status in a linear probability regression for their blue-collar worker sample, several proved to be statistically significant and of the expected sign. Among the significant variables reported by the authors were two dummy overtime hours flexibility variables, respectively measuring whether overtime work was set by a supervisor and, if so, whether it could be refused without penalty. Those who would be penalized for refusing overtime work were 17 percent more likely to belong to a union than those who could set their own overtime hours, while those who were not subject to penalty but did not have control over their overtime hours were 13 percent more likely to be union members than those with freedom to determine their own overtime hours. Also, those workers who reported having jobs which allowed freedom "as to how you do your work" were significantly less likely to be union members. Only one working condition variable ran counter to expectations, namely that denoting "very hard" working conditions. Here those reporting such conditions were significantly *less* likely to be union members. On the other hand, respondents reporting jobs which "require a lot of physical effort" were more likely to be union members. As noted above, this particular work effort variable was considerably less refined than the proxy constructed from Time Use Survey data.

The working conditions variables are suppressed in Farber's treatment though they clearly have a bearing on his findings both with respect to the wage differential (and the interpretation of that differential) and in amplifying the role of occupational variables. While white-collar workers are much less likely to be unionized than their blue-collar counterparts, it appears from Duncan and Stafford's study that white-collar workers whose jobs had working conditions earlier found by the authors to be important predictors of blue-collar unionism (working with machines, being constrained with free time, and work effort) were also the most likely to be unionized. Interestingly, the authors are unable to report any evidence of compensating wage differentials for these nonpecuniary aspects of work. They attribute this result to an omitted variable problem and conjecture that white-collar workers with high potential earnings choose to buy better working conditions.

These findings qualify but do not of course overturn Farber's results. I sympathize with the author's particular preoccupations given the considerable data-censoring and sample selection bias problems that he has to tackle even in testing a relatively simple model. My point is that we should turn to a behavioral model. Farber concedes this point in his own paper, which he evidently views as a first step along the road of modeling adequately the determination of union status. He sees the next stage presumably as tackling what is to him the other half of the process, namely employer selection from the queue of aspiring union workers. I personally do not see that objective as necessarily constituting an urgent research agenda.

NOTES

1. A fuller discussion is given in Addison (1982).
2. Not least because the actual values reported suggest that unionized plants will outcompete their nonunion counterparts—a result that is prima facie at odds with Freeman and Medoff's (this volume) own statement that profits (the rate of return on capital) are consistently lower in unionized plants.
3. The "working" is available from the author on request.
4. Brown and Medoff (1978) themselves provide an illustration of the ambiguity introduced by potential differences in technology.

REFERENCES

Addison, J. T. (1982), "Are Unions Good for Productivity?" *Journal of Labor Research* 3(2):125–138.

Addison, J. T., and A. H. Barnett (1981), "Unionization and Productivity." Department of Economics, University of South Carolina, mimeographed.

Allen, S. G. (1979), *Unionized Construction Workers Are More Productive*. Washington, D.C.: Center to Protect Workers' Rights, November.

Bloch, F., and M. Kuskin (1978), "Wage Determination in the Union and Nonunion Sectors." *Industrial and Labor Relations Review* 31(2):183–192.

Borjas, G. (1979), "Job Satisfaction, Wages and Unions." *Journal of Human Resources* 14(1):21–40.

Brown, C., and J. L. Medoff (1978), "Trade Unions in the Production Process." *Journal of Political Economy* 86(3):355–378.

Clark, K. B. (1980a), "The Impact of Unionization on Productivity: A Case Study." *Industrial and Labor Relations Review* 33(4):451–469.

——— (1980b), "Unionization and Productivity: Micro-Econometric Evidence." *Quarterly Journal of Economics* 95(4):613–639.

Duncan, G. J., and F. P. Stafford (1980), "Do Union Members Receive Compensating Differentials?" *American Economic Review* 70(3):355–371.

Duncan, G., and D. Leigh (1980), "Wage Determination in the Union and Nonunion Sectors." *Industrial and Labor Relations Review* 34(1):24–36.

Farber, H. S. (1978), "Individual Preferences and Union Wage Determination: The Case of the United Mineworkers." *Journal of Political Economy* 86(5):923–942.

Frantz, J. R. (1976), "The Impact of Trade Unions on Production in the Wooden Household Furniture Industry." Senior Honors Thesis, Harvard University, March.

Freeman, R. B. (1976), "Individual Mobility and Union Voice in the Labor Market." *American Economic Review, Papers and Proceedings* 66(2):361–368.

——— (1980a), "The Exit-Voice Tradeoff in the Labor Market: Unionism, Job Tenure, Quits and Separations." *Quarterly Journal of Economics* 94(4):643–673.

——— (1980b), "Unionism and the Dispersion of Wages." *Industrial and Labor Relations Review* 34(1):3–23.

Freeman, R. B., J. L. Medoff, and M. L. Connerton (1982), "Industrial Relations and Productivity: A Study of the U.S. Bituminous Coal Industry." Harvard University, mimeographed.

Hutchins, M. T., and S. W. Polachek (1981), "Do Unions Really Flatten the Age-Earnings Profile?: New Estimates Using Panel Data." University of North Carolina at Chapel Hill, mimeographed.

Miyazaki, H. (1927), "The Rat Race and Internal Labor Markets." *Bell Journal of Economics* 8(2):394–418.

Pencavel, J. H. (1981), "The Empirical Performance of a Model of Trade Union Behavior." Department of Economics, Stanford University, mimeographed.

Polachek, S. W., and E. P. McCutcheon (1981), "Union Effects on Employment Stability: A Comparison of Panel Versus Cross-Sectional Data." University of North Carolina at Chapel Hill, mimeographed.

Wachter, M. L., and O. E. Williamson (1978), "Obligational Markets and the Mechanics of Inflation." *Bell Journal of Economics* 9(2):549–571.

Williamson, O. E., M. L. Wachter, and J. E. Harris (1975), "Understanding the Employment Relation: The Analysis of Idiosyncratic Exchange." *Bell Journal of Economics* 6(2):250–278.

UNION EFFECTS:

WAGES, TURNOVER, AND JOB TRAINING

Jacob Mincer

I. INTRODUCTION

Growing numbers of empirical studies confirm the prevalence of the following features which distinguish unionized from nonunionized labor markets: (1) higher wages, (2) a larger share of fringe benefits in total compensation, (3) lower quit rates and lesser turnover, and (4) flatter age profiles of wages. These findings appear to hold both in the aggregate, as when more unionized industries are compared with less unionized or nonunionized, and in micro data where a variety of variables are used to control for personal and, less frequently, firm characteristics which might affect these differences.

Traditionally, economists have been concerned with the relative wage and much less the employment impact of unionism, just as they have been concerned with price-quantity impacts of product monopolies. On the other hand, students of industrial relations tend to emphasize nonwage

New Approaches to Labor Unions.
Research in Labor Economics, Supplement 2, pages 217–252.
Copyright © 1983 by JAI Press Inc.
All rights of reproduction in any form reserved.
ISBN: 0-89232-265-9

aspects of unionism in the work setting. Some time ago (1958) H. G. Lewis dichotomized aspects of unionism into "monopolistic" and "competitive." In the first category are the imposition of wages above competitive levels, either by union restriction of supply or by threats of strikes implicit in collective bargaining. In the second are all those activities of unions and work rules espoused by unions which need not be inconsistent with competitive wage setting. However, these "two faces" of unionism do not correspond to wage and nonwage aspects of unionism: union-induced nonwage conditions may also impose higher costs on employers, inconsistent with competition. Conversely, union–nonunion wage differentials need not reflect monopoly rents, but may be merely compensatory, reflecting a faster and more regimented pace of work (Duncan and Stafford, 1980) or higher quality of workers in unionized jobs.

The wage-push hypothesis receives little or no attention in analyses of other features of unionized labor markets listed in the first paragraph. Thus with "voice," as a substitute for "exit," unionized workers quit less frequently than others. With longer expected stay, the probability of receiving initially nonvested pensions increases; hence larger pensions (a major part of fringe benefits) are demanded by union workers. Other explanations of larger union fringes run from union democracy which favors the older worker to union management of pension funds as an instrument of power. Finally, the flatter union wage profile is seen as a result of union egalitarian or bureaucratic compression of the wage structure.

Although some or all of these hypotheses may be valid, it is possible to view the union wage pressure as a source, if not necessarily an exclusive one, of all of the features I have enumerated. It is the purpose of the present study to test this proposition empirically.

II. UNION WAGE GAINS

Before I proceed to explore the effects of union wage pressure on turnover, fringe benefits, and wage profiles, it is necessary to establish that unions indeed succeed in pushing their wages above competitive levels. A large literature (see review by Parsley, 1980) answers this question positively by observing a differential in favor of union members after controlling for a large number of worker personal characteristics in wage level regressions. However, unmeasured differences in labor quality may still be responsible for part or all of the wage gap. The question is whether, indeed, the same worker, and not merely his statistical surrogate, receives higher wages in union than in nonunion employment.

If the existence of a net union wage gain is confirmed in this fashion, we would expect its size to be smaller than the cross-sectionally observed union wage differential. This is because above equilibrium wages imply queues on the supply side which must be rationed.[1] Only in the case of probabilistic rationing ("first come, first served") and of rationing by price (union dues) or by discrimination and nepotism would the observed net wage gain equal the gross wage differential observed in the cross section. But employers have incentives to reduce the increase in labor costs imposed by the union by systematic rationing, that is, by hiring more productive workers from the queue. The increase in labor costs cannot, however, be completely offset in this fashion partly because the marginal cost of screening for quality is positive and because of technological constraints in the production function. Moreover, where unions have a voice in hiring, as in the closed shop and in union hiring halls, there are no obvious incentives for upgrading of labor quality, and rationing is largely probabilistic. Rationing by price (in corrupt unions) or by discrimination and nepotism is outlawed, in principle, but its existence cannot be excluded.

The empirical analysis described below relies on observing wages received by the same worker before and after his change of union status. This approach was used most recently by Duncan and Stafford (1980)[2] and, thus far, most comprehensively by Wesley Mellow (1981). Duncan and Stafford observed wage changes of a small sample of union joiners between 1968 and 1971 in the Michigan Panel Survey of Income Dynamics (MID), and Mellow in two 1-year intervals (1974–1975 and 1977–1978) in the much larger sample of the Current Population Survey (CPS). Large data sets, like the CPS sample, are needed to observe adequate numbers of workers who change union status, since their proportion is quite small. An alternative to using the CPS is pooling of the longitudinal samples. Although the annually surveyed samples in the MID and NLS (National Longitudinal Surveys) are much smaller than the CPS, their advantage lies in some of the information not available in the CPS. Especially useful in this context is information on job mobility and job tenure.

In the work to be described I pooled the MID sample in order to relate annual changes in wages of white men over the 10-year period 1968–1978 to changes in their union status. Since the NLS panels contain information on union status in the years 1969 and 1971,[3] I utilized this single interval for the same analysis on the two NLS panels of young white men (who were 17–27 years old in 1969) and older white men (who were 48–64 in 1969). The MID contains all ages, but as in the NLS, I limited the sample to nonstudents and to a maximum age of 64. For (partial) comparability with the NLS, I also stratified the MID panel into young (less-than-30) and older (30–64) subsamples.

The statistical analysis relies on wage functions, where the dependent variable is the logarithm of hourly earnings, and the independent variables are education (Ed), experience (x) and its square (x^2), length of job tenure (T) and its square (T^2), marital status (Mar), health status (Hlth), local (Lun) and national unemployment rate (Nun). These are the "standardizing" variables. The main focus is on the additional (dummy) variables U_{ij}, where i and j index the first and second period, and have values (0, 1), 0 denoting nonunion status and 1 union membership. Thus U_{00} means nonunion both years, U_{01} = union joiner (between the first and second survey), U_{10} = union leaver, and U_{11} = union stayer. These four union status categories were also cross-classified by mover–stayer status, and for movers by form of separation (quit, layoff) and whether moved within or between industries.

Wage level equations were used separately for the first and second year bracketing the changes.[4] Both equations contain the same union dummies. Thus in "year 1" equations, the dummies indicate prospective changes (or continuation) of union status, while in "year 2" they indicate recent change. Both are useful in exploring selectivity in hiring. The specification of *wage change* equations is derived by taking first differences of the variables in the level equations. Thus the experience variable becomes $\Delta x = 1$ for all, and its coefficient enters the intercept, but Δx^2 differs with the level of experience. The tenure variable ΔT equals 1 for job stayers but becomes negative $(-T$, where T is length of job tenure on the *preceding* job). Correspondingly, ΔT^2 is positive for stayers, but is negative and equals $-T^2$ for movers. Standardization for tenure is important: Since wages grow with tenure (experience held fixed), wage change estimates from regressions which omit tenure depend on how long recent movers stayed on the previous job. Put another way, estimates which omit tenure indicate the immediate wage change in moving from one job to another, while the present specification estimates the wage change from the prior to the current job, at comparable tenure levels. This is clearly a more appropriate measure of returns to job mobility or to change in union status.

Although the pooling of 10 periods provides an effectively much larger sample of the MID observations, the smaller NLS sample is in some respects superior: Fewer observations are lost due to incomplete responses, and hourly wage refers to the current job rather than to the calendar year as in the MID. The NLS also contains an alternative union status definition in addition to union membership (UM), a question on whether the job is covered by collective bargaining (CB).[5]

In the MID, job and union status changed between surveys, which were taken in the second quarter of each year. Wage changes, however, refer to calendar years. Since we bracketed status changers by adjacent years, if the reported wages are indeed weighted annual figures, they could underestimate the true change by as much as 33 percent. We checked on

the degree of bias in several periods (1976, 1977, 1978) when the question
on wages was asked for the current job. The so estimated bias was on
average 21 percent. The bias could be removed by leaving out 2 years
between "year 1" and "year 2." But this would have eliminated a large
fraction of job changers, whose tenure at moving is short.

Table 1 shows sample means (i.e., proportions) of the union status
categories for the young and old men panels by alternative definition of
union status in NLS and in MID. Here 28.3 percent of the young men
and 36.3 percent of the old men were union members in 1969. Somewhat
larger proportions (33.2 percent and 39 percent, respectively) were covered by collective bargaining agreements. Union–nonunion turnover is
quite large among the young and much smaller among older job movers.
A surprising and somewhat puzzling statistic is the number of union status

Table 1. Sample Proportions in Union Status Categories NLS and MID

	Young Men, n = 1160		Old Men, n = 1588	
	UM	CB	UM	CB
Movers	%	%	%	%
(A) *NLS*				
Movers				
U_{00}	24.3	21.9	6.5	5.9
U_{01}	4.6	4.9	.8	1.0
U_{10}	4.4	5.2	.5	.8
U_{11}	4.4	5.7	2.6	2.7
Stayers				
U_{00}	38.6	36.0	52.2	49.4
U_{01}	4.2	4.0	4.2	4.7
U_{10}	1.5	2.0	2.0	2.8
U_{11}	18.0	20.3	31.2	32.7
	All, n = 9,987	*Age <30, n = 3,069*	*Age ≥ 30, = 6,905*	
(B) *MID*				
Movers				
U_{00}	7.3	13.4	4.6	
U_{01}	1.0	2.0	.5	
U_{10}	0.9	1.8	.5	
U_{11}	1.3	2.0	1.0	
Stayers				
U_{00}	56.8	53.6	58.3	
U_{01}	2.6	2.7	2.5	
U_{10}	2.3	2.4	2.3	
U_{11}	27.8	22.1	30.3	

changers who do not change jobs (firms)—it is as large as the number of union joiners who are movers among the young and even larger among the old. The preponderance of stayers who are union status changers is even stronger in MID, in which the proportion of all movers appears to be smaller than in the NLS.

Although some stayers may become union members, after a short period in the union shop, or by switching jobs within the firm, or by the firm becoming unionized, the figures for job stayers who change union status appear to be inflated by misreporting or misclassification. This is especially likely in the MID samples, where wages of union status changers who are job stayers are about the same (relative to the base group) before and after the change (see Table 5).

Table 2 presents estimates of the 1969 to 1971 wage changes in the NLS by union change category, net of the other variables (these are shown in Appendix Table A1), classified by mobility status, age, and definition of union sector (UM: union membership; CB: coverage of wage by collective bargaining agreement). Numbers in Table 2 are regression coefficients, with t-statistics shown in parentheses.

Using point estimates and the union membership criterion, young men who joined unions by changing firms got a 17.6 percent increase in wages, while older men gained 7.4 percent. However, by the collective bargaining criterion, the gain was similar for young and old (13.5 percent vs. 11.6 percent). The figures for the older men are barely significant. The wage changes are adjusted for inflation and are net of the wage change experienced by the base group of nonunion stayers. Firm stayers who report joining unions show smaller gains, with lesser statistical significance. Although it may be advisable to discount (or ignore?) the estimates for stay-

Table 2.   Wage Growth 1969 to 1971 in the NLS

	Young		Old	
	(UM)	*(CB)*	*(UM)*	*(CB)*
Movers				
U_{01}	17.6 (4.0)	13.5 (3.2)	7.4 (1.5)	11.6 (1.2)
U_{10}	−26.0 (5.7)	−28.7 (6.8)	−8.2 (.6)	−20.4 (1.8)
U_{11}	7.7 (1.8)	7.9 (2.0)	6.9 (1.1)	6.6 (1.1)
U_{00}	3.5 (1.2)	6.4 (2.3)	−3.2 (.7)	−3.9 (.8)
Stayers				
U_{01}	10.6 (2.4)	6.3 (1.4)	4.7 (.4)	6.2 (1.3)
U_{10}	−6.6 (1.0)	−6.3 (1.0)	2.6 (.4)	1.6 (.3)
U_{11}	4.0 (1.7)	4.3 (1.9)	5.2 (2.4)	4.6 (2.1)
U_{00} (Base)				

ers, there is still a question whether the figures for job movers should be viewed as the net union premium: even if they did not join a union, young movers between nonunion firms (U_{00}) gained 3.5 to 6.4 percent. If such gains measure the return on costs of mobility, the net profit of joining unions by moving is reduced to between 7 and 14 percent for the young movers, and is comparable for the older union joiners, although the statistical reliability of the estimates for the older group is much weaker.

When the movers' separation is distinguished by quit and layoff (see Table A3, upper panel), the gain from joining a union is about the same regardless of manner of separation, though for movers within the nonunion sector (U_{00}) the gain is a positive 5–6 percent for quitters and near zero for those laid off. These distinctions are not perceptible for the older union joiners whose sample further divided into quit and layoff becomes miniscule. However, old nonunion movers (U_{00}) experience zero gains in quitting and significant losses by layoff.

In turn, when movers are distinguished by moves between or within industry (Table A3, lower panel) (at the two-digit level), gains to young union joiners were observed only for interindustry movers. They are not significant for within-industry movers, but the latter comprise no more than 20 percent of young movers who join unions. Again, no significant differences can be observed in the small samples of older movers.

Movers who left unions (U_{10} in Table 2) suffered losses which exceeded the gains of movers who joined unions. The losses were even greater when the separation from the union job was by layoff and when the move was between industries. Again less confidence should be attached to such findings for the older men. If the loss of union leavers is to be viewed as another measure of the union premium (with a negative sign), it is not clear why it is so much larger than the positive measure. The discrepancy may reflect further sorting by layoff from union firms, but the basis for such speculation is weak.

Table 3 presents estimates of annual wage change equations, pooled over the period 1968 to 1978 in the MID. Only one definition of union status (union membership) is available for all the years. The findings, coefficients of union dummies, are shown for all ages and for the two age groups, below age 30 and 30–64, separately. The complete wage equations are shown in Table A2.

Young men who join the union by changing firms gain about 13 percent in wages; the older men's gain of 4 percent is not statistically significant. The average gain for all is 9 percent. This reduces to 6 percent for the young and less than 5 percent for all, if the union premium is viewed as net of the return to mobility into a nonunion job. However, when the moves of union joiners are classified by quit and by layoff (Table A4, upper panel), the gain by quitting was significantly larger: 19.8 percent

Table 3. Annual Wage Growth 1968–1978, MLD, Pooled

	All	*Age <30*	*Age ≧30*
Movers			
U_{01}	9.0 (3.2)	12.9 (3.4)	4.0 (1.0)
U_{10}	−1.8 (.6)	−.3 (.2)	−1.6 (.3)
U_{11}	6.4 (2.4)	5.3 (1.4)	8.2 (2.4)
U_{00}	4.3 (3.2)	7.0 (3.6)	.7 (.4)
Stayers			
U_{01}	1.7 (1.0)	4.5 (1.7)	−.4 (.2)
U_{10}	−2.7 (1.5)	−3.9 (1.0)	−2.1 (1.0)
U_{11}	−.6 (.9)	−.8 (.5)	−.6 (1.0)
U_{00} (Base)			

for the younger and 11.8 percent for the older group. The nonunion quitters had gains of 12.4 percent and 4.6 percent, respectively. A net premium which would take into account the returns to mobility makes the net differential about 7 percent for quitters in both age groups. Again, as in the NLS, the gain for union joiners who are movers shows up in interindustry mobility.

Compared to the NLS, MID estimates of the average union premium appear to be somewhat smaller.[6] A major difference is in the estimate of losses of union leavers: They are larger than the gains of joiners in the NLS, but insignificant in MID. However, the insignificance in the MID sample applies only to the young group. Among those over 30, union leavers who quit gain 12 percent while those laid off lose 8.6 percent. No significant wage changes are observed for persons who did not change jobs. Reported changes of union status in this group are more questionable than in the NLS sample.

To summarize the findings in both the NLS and MID:

(1) Estimates of wage changes of union joiners are near 15 percent for young (<30) white men and 4–12 percent for older men. If gains from (nonunion) mobility are subtracted from these estimates, the net union premium is reduced to between 6 and 14 percent for the young joiners.

(2) The union premium appears to be larger for the young than for the older men. This is not true if collective bargaining rather than union membership is a criterion (in the NLS). Nor is it true in MID if union joiners quit from the preceding job.

(3) The union premium is clear and significant mainly if union joiners quit the preceding job and moved between (two-digit) industries, as 80 percent of them did.

(4)   Union leavers lose more than union joiners gain in the NLS. In the MID sample, only union leavers over 30 who were laid off lose as much or more than joiners gain. There is no evidence of losses for the younger union leavers.

III.   CROSS-SECTION DIFFERENTIALS AND SELECTIVITY IN HIRING

Table 4 (for NLS) and Table 5 (for MID) present coefficients on union status dummies in two cross-section wage regressions, year 1, prior to the change in union status, and year 2 after the change. Thus for job movers the coefficient in U_{01} in the "prospective" regression (year 1) estimates the wage of prospective movers from nonunion to union jobs

Table 4.   Wage Level Equations NLS

	Young		Old	
	(UM)	*(CB)*	*(UM)*	*(CB)*
1969 = year 1				
Movers				
U_{01}	1.2 (.3)	−2.6 (.6)	−3.4 (.2)	−4.5 (.7)
U_{10}	20.8 (4.6)	20.7 (4.9)	3.1 (.2)	−2.9 (1.0)
U_{11}	33.3 (7.4)	27.2 (6.6)	42.9 (6.1)	43.7 (6.4)
U_{00}	−9.7 (4.0)	−10.2 (4.0)	−11.6 (2.6)	−11.0 (2.3)
Stayers				
U_{01}	6.1 (1.3)	7.2 (1.5)	−9.8 (1.8)	−9.4 (1.8)
U_{10}	11.7 (1.6)	6.9 (1.0)	−6.4 (.8)	−6.3 (1.0)
U_{11}	16.0 (6.2)	15.2 (6.0)	.2 (.1)	.3 (.1)
U_{00} (Base)				
1971 = year 2				
Movers				
U_{01}	22.0 (4.0)	14.4 (2.6)	7.6 (.5)	9.5 (.8)
U_{10}	1.8 (.3)	−4.5 (.1)	.2 (0)	−27.0 (2.0)
U_{11}	43.4 (7.9)	38.7 (7.6)	55.5 (7.6)	56.2 (7.1)
U_{00}	−3.2 (1.6)	− .5 (.2)	−9.2 (1.6)	−8.6 (1.5)
Stayers				
U_{01}	−1.5 (.2)	14.1 (2.6)	−1.5 (.3)	−3.5 (.6)
U_{10}	−2.8 (.3)	3.7 (.5)	−2.8 (.3)	−4.0 (.6)
U_{11}	20.0 (7.2)	19.6 (7.0)	4.5 (1.6)	3.4 (1.2)
U_{00} (Base)				

(e.g., a coefficient of 1.2 means 1.2 percentage points larger than the wage of the base group, nonunion stayers). The coefficient of U_{01} in the "retrospective" regression (year 2) estimates the wage on the new union job of these recent union joiners, again relative to the base group in year 2.

If the existence of a union premium induces employers to select more productive labor, we would expect prospective union joiners to have higher wages in the prior, nonunion job than other nonunion workers. We have to be careful, however, to compare wages of new hires into union jobs with wages of new hires into nonunion jobs: employers select among new hires. Thus the difference between the coefficients of U_{01} and U_{00} of job movers in the prospective regression (year 1) measures the upgrading in hiring into union jobs. Although union joiners had a prior nonunion wage about the same as the base group of nonunion stayers, their wages were significantly higher (about 10 percent) than the prior nonunion wage of new hires into nonunion jobs. This selectivity differential appears

Table 5. Wage Level Estimates, MID—Pooled

	All	Age <30	Age ≧30
Year 1			
Movers			
U_{01}	−12.9 (3.9)	−6.2 (1.8)	−24.2 (3.8)
U_{10}	−8.6 (2.3)	2.2 (.5)	−17.2 (3.0)
U_{11}	17.6 (5.6)	21.5 (4.4)	13.7 (3.2)
U_{00}	−16.0 (11.3)	−14.1 (7.5)	−15.2 (7.2)
Stayers			
U_{01}	5.5 (2.3)	10.4 (2.6)	2.7 (.9)
U_{10}	3.5 (1.6)	4.4 (1.2)	3.1 (1.1)
U_{11}	17.8 (19.9)	22.8 (13.8)	15.4 (14.5)
U_{00} (Base)			
Year 2			
Movers			
U_{01}	−1.4 (.4)	13.2 (2.8)	−10.5 (1.8)
U_{10}	−4.7 (1.1)	1.0 (.2)	−2.6 (.4)
U_{11}	26.1 (7.4)	32.7 (6.2)	23.7 (5.7)
U_{00}	−14.2 (8.9)	−4.9 (2.0)	−15.2 (6.5)
Stayers			
U_{01}	5.3 (2.1)	10.7 (2.3)	3.7 (1.2)
U_{10}	1.9 (.7)	3.5 (.8)	1.8 (.5)
(U_{11}	16.7 (17.3)	22.4 (11.2)	14.8 (13.1)
U_{00} (Base)			

Table 6.

	Wage Differentials New Hires $(\beta_{01}-\beta_{00})_2$	Selectivity in Hiring $(\beta_{01}-\beta_{00})_1$	Implicit Wage Gain (1) − (2)	Estimated Net Gain of Joiners (Tables 2 & 3)	Wage Differential of Stayers
	(1)	(2)	(3)	(4)	(5)
NLS					
Young (UM)	25.2	10.9	14.3	14.1	20.0
(CB)	14.9	7.6	7.3	7.1	19.6
Old (UM)	16.8	8.2	8.6	10.6	4.5
(CB)	18.1	6.5	11.6	15.5	3.4
MID (UM)					
Young	18.1	7.9	10.2	5.9	22.4
Older	4.7	− 9.0	13.7	3.3	14.8
All	12.8	3.1	9.7	4.7	16.7

to be similar for the young and old NLS samples and is roughly comparable in size to (a bit smaller than) the net union premium estimated from the wage changes.

The comparison of coefficients on U_{01} and U_{00} of MID movers (Table 5) in year 1 yields the conclusion that workers newly hired into union jobs had, on average, higher wages on the preceding job in the nonunion sector than nonunion workers hired into nonunion jobs. The difference is smaller in the Michigan Panel than it was in the NLS. But this is a result of two opposite differentials by age. The young workers hired into union jobs had 8 percent higher wages than the prospective nonunion hires, a figure comparable to the selectivity differential estimated for young NLS workers. However, the older group of new hires (30 +) had lower wages than the comparison group of nonunion hires.

Inspection of year 2 wages of new hires in their new jobs shows that the wage differential between nonunion workers (in year 1) who moved to union and nonunion jobs, respectively (in year 2), has just about doubled (roughly from 10 to 20 percent) between year 1 and year 2 in both NLS and MID samples of young workers. Thus the union–nonunion differentials (among new hires in year 2) reflect selectivity in hiring and a net union wage premium in about equal measure. For the older worker the results are mixed: In the NLS the union–nonunion differential among new hires (year 2) more than doubled compared to year 1, while in the MID the differential changed from negative in year 1 to positive in year 2.

A sharper view of these comparisons is shown in Table 6. A little arithmetic is helpful in inspecting the table. First, it is clear that the *increment* in the wage differential between union and nonunion new hires from year 1 (on the old jobs, both nonunion) to year 2 (on the new jobs, one union, the other nonunion) is in principle[7] equivalent to the wage change regressions estimate of the union wage premium, net of selectivity, since

$$[(\beta_{01} - \beta_{00})_2] - [(\beta_{01} - \beta_{00})_1] = [(\beta_{01})_2 - (\beta_{01})_1] - [(\beta_{00})_2 - (\beta_{00})_1].$$
$$(1)$$

The β_{ij} are the regression coefficients on the respective union dummies U_{ij}. The first term on the left-hand side is the cross-sectional union–nonunion wage differential for new hires; the second term measures upgrading in union hiring; and the right-hand term is the implicit union wage premium $(\Delta\beta_{01} - \Delta\beta_{00})_1$, with returns on costs of mobility netted out.

The interpretation expressed on the left-hand side of Eq. (1) justifies the use of the second term on the right-hand side: Emphasis on new hires coming from the nonunion sector, where wages may be assumed to reflect the marginal value product, justifies the netting out of returns to mobility of workers moving within the nonunion sector only.

Column 1 of Table 6 shows the cross-section union–nonunion differential for new hires. Column 2 shows the selectivity (upgrading) differential, which is a component of the union–nonunion wage gap (1). Column 3 is the difference between columns 1 and 2, the implicit net union wage premium obtained by new hires. For comparison, column 4 shows the net union wage premium estimated from the wage-change regressions, and column 5 the cross-section union–nonunion wage differential among stayers (coefficients of U_{11} of stayers in year 2), which comes closest to the usual regression estimates of the union–nonunion differential in the cross section.

Judging by the first two columns of Table 6, selectivity in hiring, as measured by prior wages, accounts for almost one-half of the union–nonunion wage differential among young new hires in the NLS, but less in the MID. The time series estimates of the net wage premium (column 4) are comparable to the implicit cross-section estimates (column 3) in NLS, but they are smaller in the MID. For the older group in MID, selectivity into the union (column 2) appears to be perverse, that is, negative.

The analysis summarized in Table 6 contains several innovations: (1) It relies on estimates of wage changes of workers whose union status changes as they move between firms. This is because reports of changes in union status while staying in the firm appear to be less reliable and show small or no effects. Previous studies which do not contain information on job mobility therefore probably attenuate the effects of unions on wages. (2) Information on mobility also permits more direct estimates of selectivity in hiring, as shown in column 2 of Table 6. (3) Finally, the information on tenure makes possible estimates of gains from mobility as upward shifts of the whole tenure profile of wages from the old to the new job. Usually observed instantaneous wage changes may be negative, as is often found, but the longer-run effects obtained in the present analysis are more likely to be positive.[8]

As to numerical results, it appears that estimates of net union gains in wages, as seen in new hires, range from 7 to 15 percent in the NLS and from 3 to 14 percent in the MID. Since the latter is biased downward, upward adjustments would put the central tendency of both NLS and MID a little over 10 percent. Selectivity accounts for almost as much in the NLS and the young workers in MID, but not so in the over-30 group in MID.

IV. TURNOVER IN UNION EMPLOYMENT

If the wage received in union employment exceeds the worker's opportunity wage in nonunion employment, he is less likely to quit a union job than a nonunion job.

As Table 7 indicates, quit rates in the union sector are about half as large as in the nonunion sector for young workers and are about one-third as large for men over 30 (in MID), and one-seventh as large for men over 48 (in NLS). The differences are smaller for separations, since layoffs are somewhat larger in the union, at least in the NLS.

Although one-third of the white male workers are unionized (somewhat less among the young), less than 10 percent of nonunionized jobseekers find employment in the union sector, while a half of the young and two-

Table 7. Turnover Rates (Percent), by Union Status and Age

		NLS		MID	
		Young	*Old*	*Age <30*	*Age ≥30*
(a)	*Quits*				
	NU	26.7	6.5	14.6	4.7
	U	14.3	.9	7.5	1.7
(b)	*Layoffs*				
	NU	13.5	5.0	7.0	3.0
	U	17.7	7.0	6.6	2.7
(c)	*Separation*				
	NU	40.2	11.5	21.6	7.7
	U	32.0	7.9	14.1	4.4

third of the older unionized job movers find employment in the union sector. Since these statistics apply to "unstandardized" workers, they may reflect differences in tastes and in geography, industry, and occupation. At face value, at any rate, the differences are consistent with our findings: nonunion workers could get a bigger wage gain by moving to union jobs, but are evidently prevented by fewer vacancies and non-probabilistic rationing (stricter hiring standards, nepotism, etc.) resulting from the wage premium in the union sector. Union workers, however, can gain from mobility within the union sector, but face a wage loss when they leave the union sector (Tables 2 and 3, above). Thus they tend not to leave the firm unless there is a good chance of landing another union job.[9]

If unionization reduces job mobility, this reduction should be observed on the same individual by comparing his mobility before and after joining a union firm. And if the wage premium gained by moving to a union firm matters, the reduction in mobility should be greater the greater the wage gain.

According to Table 8, young NLS men who joined unions between 1969 and 1971 have prior quit frequency (in 1967–1969) which was not smaller than the quit of other nonunionized workers at that time.[10] This is based on regressions with quit as a dependent variable (0, 1) and 1969 values of the same standardizing variables as used in the wage level regressions. However, the frequency of quit was lower by about 13 percentage points in 1971–1973 after joining a union (coefficient of U_{01}) in the interval 1969–1971. This reduction is as large as the unstandardized cross-section difference in Table 7. In 1971–1973 union stayers (U_{11} in 1969–1971) had about the same low quit rates as union joiners.[11]

No significant results were obtained for the older NLS men who joined

Table 8. Quits and Layoffs, Before and After Change in Union Status, NLS

	1967–69		1971–73	
	Young	*Old*	*Young*	*Old*
Quits				
U_{01}	−1.8 (.9)	+.9 (.4)	−12.7 (2.8)	−1.1 (.5)
U_{10}	2.9 (.6)	−.8 (.2)	−4.9 (.9)	−2.3 (.8)
U_{11}	−4.4 (1.5)	−2.2 (1.7)	−16.4 (5.2)	−2.7 (2.7)
Layoffs				
U_{01}	6.0 (1.2)	3.4 (1.1)	10.3 (2.7)	−1.0 (.4)
U_{10}	16.5 (3.2)	7.8 (1.8)	4.8 (1.1)	3.6 (.9)
U_{11}	−9.4 (3.3)	−.7 (.5)	4.1 (1.6)	2.6 (1.9)

Table 9. Changes in Quits Related to Changes in Union Status and in Wages (MID)

	Changes in Quits	Changes in Mobility Rates (Sample restricted to movers prior to 1974)		
	ΔQ		$\Delta \ln M$	ΔM
U_{01}	-6.1 (3.5)	U_{01}	$-.24$ (4.4)	$-.01$ (.3)
U_{10}	.7 (.4)	$\Delta \ln W_{01}$	$-.27$ (2.0)	$-.20$ (2.4)
U_{11}	1.2 (1.3)	$\Delta \ln W_{00}$	$-.05$ (1.7)	$-.07$ (1.6)
$\Delta \ln W$	-4.9 (3.4)			

unions, but union stayers had significantly lower quit rates than nonunion workers both in 1967–1969 and in 1971–1973.

A comparable analysis was performed on the full MID sample (including movers and stayers) using all ages and changes in quit (ΔQ) as the dependent variable which assumes values (-1, 0, $+1$). Again, the standardizing variables were the same as in the $\Delta \ln$ wage equations. The results are shown in column 1 of Table 9.

Union joiners experienced significant reductions in quit rates compared to all other groups. Larger wage gains (for all movers and stayers) also reduced quits in the next period. Here we do not distinguish wage gains of union joiners from those of everyone else.

To observe this distinction we restricted the sample to job movers (about two-thirds of the sample had at least one move during the 10-year panel period). We constructed a mobility index (M), which is a count of numbers of firms in which the person worked up to the current job (i.e., number of separations + 1) divided by the time interval over which mobility was recorded. The denominator of the index is the interval since entry into the labor force, or since 1958 if entry into the labor force was before this date. Wage changes associated with job moves were recorded separately for union joiners and for others between 1968 and 1973, and their effects estimated on the change in M (and in ln M) between the move and 1978, the last year of the panel.

The numerator of the mobility rate includes permanent layoffs in addition to quits, but is dominated by quits. We could not restrict the index to quits, since the pre-1968 mobility is reported as separations. However, as Table 8 showed, although (permanent) layoffs are somewhat larger in the union sector in the NLS, they are not larger in the MID sample. But even in the NLS differences in separations are dominated by differences in quits.

A preliminary cross-section analysis [Table A5, panel (a)] showed that the mobility rate (M and ln M) declines with experience in a decelerating fashion and is reduced by education, marital status, union status, and economywide unemployment.

The dependent variable (ΔM or $\Delta \ln M$) in columns 2 and 3 of Table 9 is the difference between the index in 1978 and the first move observed between 1968 and 1973 (inclusive) for nonunion people (for most of them this was not the first move, since they moved also before 1968) or the move at which they joined a union. The union dummy U_{01} distinguishes union joiners from nonunion movers, and wage gains of joiners ($\Delta \ln W_{01}$) are distinguished from wage gain of nonunion movers. The standardizing variables are in the form of differences between 1978 and levels at the time of the move. Dummies were added to account for entry into the labor force before 1968 and 1958 and years observed in the panel.

The results show that union joiners reduce their mobility more the larger the wage gain from joining a union. A similar, but much smaller and barely significant, effect is observed for wage gains of movers in the nonunion sector. This is true whether the index or the changes in wages are logarithmic or arithmetical.

The weak effect of an episode of mobility among nonunion jobs is not surprising: Unless the rate of return on the cost of moving is unusually high, there are no disincentives to future job search. However, the larger the wage premium for union joiners the greater the potential loss from future mobility. This reasoning applies more clearly to quit behavior, but the effects on total separations, if weaker, are similar.

Whether mere unionization without a wage premium produces a reduction in mobility is not as clear in Table 9. The union dummy has a strong effect on the change in the logarithmic, but not arithmetical, mobility index. It is also strong in column 1, where the wage gain of union joiners was not separated from others. Undoubtedly it represents a response to other union benefits, in fringes and in working conditions, including the more certain advantages of seniority. Nevertheless, our findings support the inference that the union wage gain is not merely a compensatory differential for quality of labor, or costs of mobility, or for inferior conditions in union jobs. Union rents appear to be real, although relatively small (closer to 10 percent than to 20 percent).

Although cross-section union–nonunion wage differentials (gross) overstate the size of the (net) union premium, it may be useful to explore their effects on differentials in quit rates in the cross section, on the assumption that the gross and net wage differentials are positively correlated. Again the purpose is to find out whether it is not merely union status but the size of the differential that affects mobility.

The companion analysis whose results are shown in Table 10 exploits the large size of the MID panel in another way: We explore whether union–nonunion wage differentials affect quit rates *within*, alternatively,

Table 10. Quit Differentials within Groups
MID, 1968–1978

Group*	U	U × β
Industry	− .032 (3.5)	.002 (.1)
State	− .024 (3.0)	− .080 (1.8)
Occupation	− .002 (.2)	− .21 (4.1)

Note:
* Listed in Table A6.

industries, regions (states), and occupations. The analysis proceeds in two steps: First we added industry (or state, or occupation), union, and industry × union membership dummies to the cross-section wage function. The coefficients of the cross-product dummies (β_i) are estimates of within-group union–nonunion (relative) wage differentials (estimates shown in Table A6). In the second step we included industry (or other groups) and a union dummy as well as its cross-product with the estimated union–nonunion wage differentials (β_i from the wage regressions) in quit regressions. We ruled out groups for which we had too few (less than 20) observations in the union or nonunion sector. Thus we utilized 22 industries, 31 states, and 27 occupational categories (Table A6).

The intragroup union–nonunion wage differentials β_i amounted, on average, to 15–20 percent. They ranged from 0 to over 40 percent and were most prominent (larger and more significant) in the occupational category, less so within states, and least within industries.

Table 10, which reports the results of step 2, shows respectively the effects of union status (U) and of wage differentials (β) on differences in quit rates between unionized and nonunionized workers within the various groups of workers. Effects of wage differentials are not significant *within* industries (at a level higher than one-digit for workers with the same measured characteristics), but they are significant within regions and occupations. Union status alone (the U dummy) is sufficient to affect the intraindustry differences, but plays no role other than via wage differentials inside occupations. Both variables are significant within states. Note also that U is significant in all three groups when β is dropped, and conversely.

V. FRINGE BENEFITS AND HOURS OF WORK

If numbers employed (N) and hours per worker (H) are viewed as separate factors of production, cost-minimizing employers will determine their demand for N and H at the point where the ratio of marginal factor costs is equal to the ratio of marginal productivities, that is, to the slope of the optimal production isoquant.

Following Rosen (1968), the equilibrium marginal factor cost ratio is[12]

$$\frac{MC_N}{MC_H} = \frac{H}{N} + \frac{F(r + q)}{NW}, \tag{2}$$

where F is the fixed cost of employment per worker, amortized per period by r, the interest cost of capital, and by q, the worker quit probability which depreciates the capital sum creating a capital loss Fq per period.

To the extent that F is positive an increase in the wage rate W reduces the factor cost ratio, shifting the relative demand away from hours toward numbers.[13] In the minimum wage case it may be argued that F is significant at most in terms of training expenses, but that minimum wages tend to reduce or eliminate such expenses, so that the predicted effects on hours may be observed only in the short run before the adjustment is completed, or it may be indeterminate.

In contrast to the minimum wage, union pressure on wages extends to most components of the wage package. Indeed, union push on components other than directly paid-out wages appears to be even stronger. Union fringe benefits exceed nonunion benefits not only in dollar value but also as a proportion of the wage package (by about 30 percent). A number of possible explanations have been conjectured, running from union democracy which favors the older worker to union management of pension funds as an instrument of power. One economic argument relies on reduced turnover, which is a result of union wage push and of other gains. In the presence of incomplete vesting of pensions in the worker, longer tenure of union members means that the probability of ultimately receiving the pension is higher in union than in nonunion jobs. Hence the incentive to push for larger pensions[14] (Freeman, 1981). But why increase fringe benefits by a larger percentage than the increase in the paid-out wage? One reason is the higher marginal income tax rate, if the income elasticity of worker demand for fringes is otherwise unitary (Rice, 1966). But this may explain only a small part of the proportional increase (Donsimoni and Shakotko, 1979).[15] Even when the value of the wage package is the same in union and nonunion jobs, the share of fringes is greater in union jobs.

The analysis of effects of wage push on hours may provide one rationale for union pressure on fringes: An increase in union wages W, with F unchanged, would lower the ratio of marginal factor costs both by raising the denominator in the second right-hand component of Eq. (2) and by reducing q in the numerator. If hours are reduced, weekly earnings may not increase much even if wage rates rise significantly. To blunt the adverse effect on hours, more specifically, to prevent their reduction which would limit union gains in earnings, quasi-fixed costs, such as fringes, must be increased by a larger percentage than the paid out wage (W), since quits (q) decline when both W and F are increased.

In contrast to hypotheses which rely on nonwage aspects of unionism to explain the larger ratio of fringe benefits to paid out wages in union employment, this analysis predicts a positive link between the percent union wage premium and the relative increase in fringe benefits (F). Moreover, the percent increase in F is expected to exceed the percent increase in the wage, since the larger the latter, the bigger is the decrease in the quit rate. Thus unions which achieve the biggest gain in paid out wages would also want the largest *proportion* of their total compensation in fringe benefits.

This proposition is tested on a sample of over 4000 firms in 70 (two-digit) industries. Average paid out wages in union firms were 21 percent higher than in nonunion firms within the industry (a simple average of 70 wage ratios), while average fringe benefits were 60 percent higher. The first regression (Table 11, panel A) relates the ratios of fringes $(F_u/F_n)_i$, where u is union, n is nonunion, and i is industry, to ratios of money wages, standardizing for age of employees, size of firm, geographic region, and union coverage of the industry.

As predicted, the coefficient on the wage ratio in Table 11 is significantly larger than unity (1.62). This implies that a 10 percent increase in the union wage premium would create a 16 percent increase in the union–nonunion ratio of fringe benefits. This ratio was, on average, 32 percent in the unstandardized data.

A second test was performed, at the firm level on union firms alone. First a wage and fringe function was estimated on nonunion firms in order to impute nonunion levels of wages and fringes to union firms. Thus the denominators of the wage ratio and the fringe ratio are imputed values which workers in union firms would receive if they were not unionized. This is a more stringent test because it relates fringes to wages in union firms only, and because errors in imputation bias the coefficients against the hypotheses (downward). The results (Table 11, panel B) nevertheless are once again as predicted, although the coefficient on the wage ratio is, indeed, smaller than in panel A.

In the data analyzed in Table 11 the value of union fringes is 80 percent higher than of nonunion fringes, while wages are 30 percent higher. Assuming that the net union effect is a half of this figure (i.e., 15 percent) and that quit rates are half as large in the nonunion sector (as observed in Table 7), we can calculate the required *ratio of fixed costs* F_u/F_n which would remove employer incentives to cut hours schedules of union workers. Given N (numbers employed), the condition is, by Eq. (2),

$$\frac{F_u(r + q_u)}{W_u} = \frac{F_n(r + q_n)}{W_n} .$$

Table 11.   Fringe Benefits and Wages, Regressions on Industry (A)
and Firm (B) Levels

(A) *Industry Level—Panel A*		(B) *Firm Level—Panel B*	
Variables	*T-Stat*	*Variables*	*T-Stat*
F-BRAT	—Dep. Variable—	HFBRAT U	—Dep. Variable—
MWRAT	1.6183	6.0	HTWRAT-U	1.5167	41.3
TWRAT	—	—	HMWRAT-U	—	—
SIZE-N	−0.0422	−0.8	COVER	−0.4483	−6.6
SIZE-U	0.0575	1.1	C4	0.2748	3.2
SOUTH-N	0.1750	0.9	EDUCATION	−0.0503	−2.0
SOUTH-U	0.0315	0.1	MALE	0.1217	1.7
URBAN-N	−0.0638	−0.3	URBAN	0.0485	2.2
URBAN-U	−0.0212	−0.1	SOUTH	−0.0642	−2.4
Y1-N	0.9546	3.6	SIZE	−0.0172	−2.2
Y1-U	−0.6160	−2.2	YOUNG	0.0001	0.1
Y2-N	0.0161	0.1	OLD	−0.0018	−0.7
OLD	0.0052	0.9	Y1	0.0150	0.6
COVER	0.3413	1.8	INTERCEPT	−0.4607	−1.4
INTERCEPT	−0.9640	−1.7			
DFE		56	DFE		2551
F-RATIO		6.7	F-RATIO		146.6
R-SQUARE		.61	R-SQUARE		0.46

Variables and Sources:

Dependent Variable: F-BRAT, union/non-union fringe benefit ratio.

Independent Variables:

INDUSTRY-LEVEL REGRESSIONS: Panel (A)

MWRAT	—union/nonunion money wage ratio
SIZE	—size of establishments measured by the logarithm of the total number of employees, industry average. *Source:* a.
SOUTH	—proportion of establishments in the south. *Source:* a.
URBAN	—proportion of establishments in urban areas. *Source:* a.
Y1, Y2	—proportion of firms surveyed in 1967–1968 wave and 1969–1970 wave respectively. Reference group was 1971–1972 wave. *Source:* a.
OLD	—industry average of the proportion of workers over age 50. *Source:* a.
COVER	—proportion of workers covered by collective bargaining agreements. *Note:* the industry definition for this variable is slightly different from the industry definition used in the main part of the study, but no industries are more broadly defined in the COVER variable. *Source:* c.

Table 11. (*Continued*)

FIRM-LEVEL REGRESSIONS: Panel (B)

COVER	—see above.
C4	—Four-firm sellers' concentration. Weighted sum of 4-digit level concentration figures with value of shipment used as weight, and raw data corrected to account for regional and national markets. *Source:* b.
EDUCATION	—average years of education of blue-collar workers. *Source:* b.
MALE	—proportion of male blue-collar workers. *Source:* b.
URBAN	—dummy, 1 if firm is in an urban area. *Source:* a.
SOUTH	—dummy, 1 if firm is in the south. *Source:* a.
SIZE	—see above, log of number of employees in firm. *Source:* a.
YOUNG	—percentage of firm employees under age 35. *Source:* b.
OLD	—percentage of firm employees over age 40. *Source:* b.
Y1, Y2	—see above, dummy form. *Source:* a.

Sources: a. Expenditures for Employee Compensation. Three surveys conducted by the Bureau of Labor Statistics in 1968, 1970, and 1972 have been pooled. They include 4,073 establishments, 2,580 unionized and 1,493 nonunionized.
   b. May Current Population Survey. Three surveys conducted 1973, 1974, and 1975 have been pooled. They include 50,000 households with 49 percent of union members.
   c. Richard Freeman and James Medoff. "New Estimates of the Industrial Unionism in the U.S." *Industrial and Labor Relations Review,* January 1979, 143–174.

Assuming r = 10 percent and q_n = 10 percent,

$$\frac{F_u}{F_n} = \frac{W_u(r + q_n)}{W_n(r + q_u)} = 1.15 \times \frac{4}{3} = 1.53.$$

The actual *ratio of fringe benefits* is larger (1.80), presumably because fringes represent only a part, although a major one, of fixed labor costs.

An important consequence of higher fixed costs (in hiring and in fringes) imposed on union employers is greater stability of employment—reduced fluctuations in N, when labor demand fluctuates (see Rosen, 1968). As a result, the major means of adjustment to fluctuating demand in union employment are the use of overtime when labor is short and the use of temporary layoffs (recall unemployment) in slack times. Temporary layoff is favored by union workers, as it implies lesser income loss than corresponding reductions in weekly hours, because of unemployment compensation and other unemployment benefits. For their part, employers can expect less attrition, since temporarily laid-off union workers are less likely to look for other jobs than comparable nonunion workers.

The evidence that average weekly hours are not less in the union than in the nonunion sector, that overtime is more prominent, and that temporary layoffs are more frequent and a larger porportion of total layoffs in the union sector is available[16] and consistent with our hypothesis. In this light, union pressure on fringe benefits is not merely a trade-off for higher wages, but a policy which increases both earnings and job security of union workers.

VI. UNION WAGE PROFILES AND JOB TRAINING

The cross-section union–nonunion differentials in wages diminish with age. They are reduced from over 22 percent to about 15 percent between ages less than and more than 30 for union stayers (U_{11}) in MID (Table 5), and reduced further to a little over zero for those over 48 in NLS (Table 4). The implication is that the typical union age (experience)–wage profile, although higher in level, is flatter than the typical nonunion profile. The difference could, in part, be due to differential union gains in fringes, as workers age. But such age effects were not observed in Table 11. The difference in wage profiles has been found in other studies and has been ascribed to union policy of compressing wage differentials across firms and workers, who may differ in sex, education, race, and age.

The policy of wage compression has been attributed to union pursuit of equity, to administrative convenience in collective bargaining, and to union efforts to reduce competition from lower-wage firms. However, a more direct explanation of flatter wage profiles involves union emphasis on wage progression by seniority rules: Within the firm, the wage structure and other rules of collective bargaining agreements are specified in terms of seniority or job tenure. Although wages grow as tenure lengthens in nonunion jobs as well as in union jobs (Table 12), the explicit seniority

Table 12.   Union and Non-union Wage Functions MID, Pooled, 1968–1978

	(A) Wage Level (lnW)			(B) Wage Growth (lnW)	
	Union	Nonunion		Union	Nonunion
Ed	5.0 (22.4)	9.6 (46.4)		.1 (.5)	−.2 (1.1)
X	1.7 (10.6)	3.7 (21.2)		2.0 (.5)	6.5 (1.9)
X^2	−0.2 (7.4)	−0.6 (17.9)		−.04 (1.7)	−.06 (2.3)
T	2.4 (12.5)	2.1 (9.3)	1.6 (6.5)	1.0 (1.5)	1.0 (2.2)
T^2	−.06 (8.1)	−.03 (3.2)	−.02 (2.2)	−.03 (.9)	−.02 (.3)
Mar	.4 (.2)	13.1 (7.1)		−.3 (.2)	−.4 (.3)
Hlth	−7.3 (4.4)	−12.7 (6.1)		−4.2 (2.5)	2.6 (1.3)
LocUn	1.2 (6.1)	2.7 (11.1)		.1 (.7)	.1 (.7)
M	−.8 (.9)		−5.5 (5.1)	.2 (.3)	−1.3 (1.6)

rules in union firms are a great deal more rigid: Seniority is the necessary condition for promotion in most union firms. If the higher job level requires additional training, union clauses often provide that senior employees are to be trained in order to fill the higher-level vacancies.[17] Such provisions limit the supply of trained workers from the outside. At the same time they severely reduce the benefits from transferable training. Consequently, incentives for general (transferable) training are reduced for union workers, both because such training is not adequately rewarded within the union firm and because union workers are less likely to move in the first place.

This helps to explain the declining with age proportion of job movers who join union firms (Table 1) and the smaller coefficient of experience[18] at fixed levels in the wage function of union compared to nonunion workers (Table 12).

Whatever training exists in union firms—and certainly some initial (apprentice) training exists in crafts—and is provided for the purposes of filling more skilled vacancies from within, almost by definition all of it is specific to the firm. If wage growth with tenure at fixed levels of experience reflects the growth of specific capital, tenure–wage profiles in union firms need not be flatter and may even be steeper than in nonunion firms.

This is, indeed, found in Table 12, where the coefficient on tenure in the union wage equation is no smaller than in the nonunion equation. Table 12 is restricted to MID data because estimates of experience and tenure coefficients in NLS are sensitive to truncation by age. The nonunion tenure coefficient in the wage level equation (left-hand panel) is smaller in column 3, where an attempt was made to adjust the estimate for heterogenity bias[19] by introducing the (prior) mobility rate variable. This variable (M) has a negative and significant effect in the nonunion equation, where it also reduces the tenure coefficient, but has no effect in the union equation. The right-hand panel of the table shows separate wage growth equations for union and nonunion workers. The comparative results are similar to the results in wage levels, but all coefficients are smaller and less significant.

The experience coefficient is much smaller in the union equation. Thus the flatness of gross union wage profiles (by age or experience) when tenure is ignored, or by tenure when experience (or age) is ignored, is due solely to lesser worker investments in general training.

The flatter gross union profile also suggests that the total volume of training is smaller in union firms. In principle, this need not be the case, since the wage profile measures returns to workers but not returns on costs borne by employers. The reluctance of union workers to quit should provide incentives for union employers to invest in specific training of their workers, since the risk of a capital loss by worker quit is smaller. Union workers have a corresponding insurance against capital losses only to the extent that seniority rules reduce layoffs. This is true at higher levels of seniority at the expense of low-tenured workers. Thus, in contrast to the usual (competitive) analysis (Becker, 1975) where worker turnover—both quits and layoffs—is a result of investments in specific human capital shared by workers and employers, such investments are the result, rather than cause, of turnover patterns induced by union pressure.

Because of lower quit, we might expect employer investments in specific training of union workers to exceed the corresponding investments of nonunion employers. But the fact that *permanent* layoff rates of union workers are no smaller than in the nonunion sector raises doubts about such expectations. However, higher rates of union layoffs concentrated at low tenure levels may both reflect additional screening of new hires and may be a substitute form of adjustment for reduced quit.[20] If the volume of specific training is not clearly larger in union firms, total training, including the general component, is likely to be smaller. This is apparently confirmed by the more direct evidence on reported training, to which we proceed.

In the NLS, training was reported in response to questions: "Do you receive or use additional training (other than school training) on your job?" In MID, different questions were used in different surveys; the most appropriate for our purposes is the question asked in 1976–1978: "Are you learning skills on the current job which could lead to a better job or to promotion?"

In a recent paper (Mincer and Leighton, 1981) these questions were used to explore the effects of minimum wage laws on training on the job. Training so reported was used as a dependent variable[21] in the NLS and MID equations (the same set of independent variables was used as in the wage equations). A union dummy included in those equations was significantly negative in all periods in the MID and in the older NLS sample.

In the current study, we further classified the union status variable as joiners (U_{01}), leavers (U_{10}), and stayers (U_{11}), and explored the incidence of training before and after the change of union status.

In the NLS samples (Table 13, panel A) the old union stayers and union joiners show significantly less training than nonunion stayers. The signs on coefficients of the young union joiners are negative, not significant before joining and almost significant after. Old union leavers show positive but not significant coefficients.

The MID results (Table 13, panel B) similarly show significantly less training among union stayers (U_{11}). They also show that less training is required on union jobs, though not as a precondition for hiring (coefficient U_{01} is not significant in year 1, panel C). The coefficients of union joiners

Table 13.

(A) Union Effects on Training, NLS 1969–1971				
	Training in 1969 Job		Training in 1971 Job	
	Young	Old	Young	Old
U_{01}	−3.1 (.7)	−6.5 (1.8)	−5.5 (1.3)	−4.9 (1.4)
U_{10}	−1.3 (.3)	4.6 (1.1)	− .3 (.1)	2.7 (.6)
U_{11}	− .4 (.1)	−5.1 (2.9)	−3.6 (1.3)	−7.4 (4.1)

(B) Union Effects on Training, MID 1976–1978 (Ages ≤45)		
	Year 1 (1976)	Year 2 (1978)
U_{01}	−6.3 (1.2)	−11.5 (3.0)
U_{10}	−14.4 (2.4)	−3.8 (.9)
U_{11}	−15.0 (5.3)	−12.9 (5.8)

(C) Is Non-School Training Required for Current Job? (MID, Education ≤12)		
	Year 1 (1976)	Year 2 (1978)
U_{01}	−3.9 (.6)	−6.8 (1.7)
U_{10}	−7.5 (1.1)	3.6 (.8)
U_{11}	−6.7 (2.1)	−9.7 (4.2)

are negative and not significant before but significant after joining the union (year 1 and year 2 regressions). Inferentially, they received more training than union stayers before the start of the union job. Conversely, union leavers appear to receive more training than before on the nonunion job to which they moved.

The findings on workers who *changed* union status are not very secure, but they suggest that selectivity in hiring may involve prior training (in addition to some concentration of it at the outset of some of the union jobs, such as in crafts). This may explain the results for the very young NLS workers where union effects on training were not significant.

The finding that union workers receive less training on the job than nonunion workers is also confirmed in the Michigan Time Study, as reported by Duncan and Stafford (1980). They report that while nonunion workers spend on average 6.1 hours per week on job training, comparable union workers spend 4.2 weekly hours on such training.

VII. SUMMARY

Among a number of features that distinguish unionized from nonunionized labor markets, at least four have been repeatedly observed in empirical studies: (1) higher wages; (2) larger fringes, more than in proportion to wages; (3) lesser turnover, reflecting lesser quit, though not less layoffs;

and (4) flatter age–wage profiles. Although the labor monopoly hypothesis has been used (and disputed) as an explanation of higher union wages, it does not receive much, if any, attention in analyses of features other than wages.

This study explores the existence of a net union premium and of the extent of rationing by quality of the resulting excess supply. The net union premium was estimated in Section II by relating changes in wages to changes in union status of the same worker in longitudinal panels (NLS and MID). In Section III, two cross-section wage level regressions, a "prospective" and "retrospective," permit more direct observation of selectivity in hiring. Over half of the cross-section differential of over 20 percent for the "same" (standardized) worker is a net union rent, and much of the rest reflects a quality adjustment in hiring, as measured by wages. This conclusion was less reliable for older workers.

The next step (Section IV) was to ascertain whether the net union wage premium is responsible, together with other advantages secured by the union such as fringes and seniority rules, for the lesser turnover, especially quit of union workers. The answer is positive: The reduction in quit depends on the size of the net wage premium in an individual analysis, and is also positively related to the gross, cross-section wage differentials within groups of workers, classified by location and occupation, though not by industry. Fringes and seniority rules or other union advantages did not explicitly enter this analysis, but they are likely to be embodied in the union membership variable.

In Section V, it is hypothesized that the imposition of larger fixed labor costs (such as fringes) helps to deter employers from preferring reductions in hours to reductions in men, and it helps to stabilize employment in the face of fluctuating demand, more frequent use of overtime, and temporary layoffs in the union sector. This hypothesis links the size of fringe benefits to the union wage gain. An analysis of firms in 70 industries confirms this link.

Section VI explored the consequences of union pressure on the tenure profile of wages by the rather rigid linking of wage levels to seniority in the job. The consequently reduced incentives for worker investment in general (transferable) training, even if no such reduction needs to apply to specific training, is consistent with observed flatter experience (or age) profile of wages of union workers. In sum, total training is likely to be less frequent in union firms, and this is confirmed by direct responses in survey reports.

ACKNOWLEDGMENTS

Research was supported by a National Science Foundation grant SES-7812878 AO2 to the NBER and by a Sloan Foundation grant to Columbia University's

Workshop in Labor Economics. The usual disclaimers apply. The comments of H. Gregg Lewis have been most helpful. Thanks are due also to Reuben Gronau, Nori Hashimoto, and John Pencavel. I am grateful to Robert Shakotko for helpful discussions and for the supply of data on firms, to Dan Friedlander for able and conscientious research assistance, and to Annette Fisch for competent and devoted secretarial help.

NOTES

1. The existence of union-induced queues has been inferred in an econometric analysis of Farber and Abowd (1981).

2. Other references are Brown (1980), Duncan (1979), Chamberlain (1978), Kenny (1978), and Raisian (1981).

3. I did not use the less adequate telephone survey of 1970 which also contained questions on union status.

4. In the NLS the first year is 1969, the second 1971. In the MID the pairs of years are adjacent.

5. However, UM is, in effect, a subset of CB, since only those reporting collective bargaining coverage were asked whether they are union members. The CB definition is available in MID only for a few periods, so it could not be utilized in the pooled sample.

6. Recall that MID estimates of wage changes tend to be understated.

7. In practice, the estimates differ largely because of a differing structure of errors in levels and in changes.

8. Even though superior as measures of gains from mobility, the shifts in tenure wage profiles are not fully commensurate with gains in present values. It can be shown that in order to secure the same gain in the present value of wages, moves after longer tenure require a larger shift in the tenure profile on the new job. This was confirmed empirically by positive and significant coefficients on a job change $\times$ prior tenure interaction variable in the wage change estimates (not included in the present study).

9. If the existence of grievance procedures ("voice" instead of "exit") were the major force that ties groups of workers with similar preferences to a firm, we would expect lesser quit from firms with such labor relations. We would, therefore, expect such procedures to exist in many nonunion firms. If so, in the absence of a wage premium in unionized firms, workers who separate from such firms would be indifferent whether they moved to a union or nonunion firm.

10. For a similar finding, based on other data, see Freeman (1980a).

11. Recall that union status was not reported in 1967, so many of the young union stayers in 1969–1971 were likely to have been joiners in 1967–1969.

12. Let total labor costs be $C = NHW + NF (r + q)$, Then $MC_n = dC/dN = HW + F(r + q)$ and $MC_H = dC/dH = NW$.

13. This analysis of substitution between H and N ignores scale effects. The qualitative conclusions, however, remain valid so long as the elasticity of demand for numbers (N) with respect to wages (including fringes) is less than unitary.

14. For the same reasons, more vesting is less costly to union than nonunion employers.

15. They found that fringe benefits were substantially larger for union workers whose total compensation (wages + fringes) was the same as the total compensation of nonunion workers.

16. In MID, straight time in weekly hours is about 4 percent shorter in union jobs, but total hours are no less in union than in nonunion jobs. See also Blau and Kahn (1981) and Raisian (1981).

17. See BLS Bulletin, "Union Status and Benefits of Retirees," July 1973.

18. And of education, if job training is complementary.
19. For an introduction of this approach, see Mincer and Jovanovic (1978).
20. Blau and Kahn find that unionism increases permanent layoffs among the young, not among the old NLS. Our own research (not presented here) shows that while quits and layoffs decline with tenure at about the same rate for nonunion workers, layoffs decline more steeply than quits for union workers.
21. As an independent variable, the training dummies are positive and significant in both wage level and wage growth equations (not reported here).

REFERENCES

Abowd, John, and Henry Farber (1981), "Job Queues and the Union Status of Workers." Unpublished.

Ashenfelter, Orley, and George E. Johnson (1972), "Unionism, Relative Wages, and Labor Quality in U.S. Manufacturing Industries." *International Economic Review* 12(October):488–507.

Becker, Gary (1975), *Human Capital.* New York: Columbia University Press.

Blau, Francine D., and Lawrence M. Kahn (1981), "The Exit-Voice Tradeoff in the Labor Market: Some Additional Evidence." Mimeograph.

Bloch, Farrell E., and Mark S. Kuskin (1978), "Wage Determination in the Union and Non-Union Sectors." *Industrial and Labor Relations Review* 31(January):183–192.

Brown, Charles (1980), "Equalizing Differences in the Labor Market." *Quarterly Journal of Economics* 94(February):113–134.

Brown, Charles, and James Medoff (1978), "Trade Unions in the Production Process." *Journal of Political Economy* 86(June):355–378.

Chamberlain, Gary (1978), "On the Use of Panel Data." Unpublished.

Clark, Kim B. (1980a), "The Impact of Unionization on Productivity: A Case Study." *Industrial and Labor Relations Review* 33(July):451–469.

——— (1980b), "Unionization and Productivity: Micro-Econometric Evidence." *Quarterly Journal of Economics* 95(December):613–639.

Donsimoni, Marie-Paule, and Robert A. Shakotko (1979), "Unionism and the Structure of Total Compensation." Mimeograph.

Duncan, Gregg (1979), in *Five Thousand American Families,* Vol. VIII.

Duncan, Gregg, and Frank P. Stafford (1980), "Do Union Members Receive Compensating Wage Differentials?" *American Economic Review* 70(June):355–371.

Farber, Henry S. (1979), "Unionism, Labor Turnover, and Wages of Young Men." Mimeograph.

Freeman, Richard B. (1980a), "The Exit-Voice Tradeoff in the Labor Market, Unionism, Job Tenure, Quits, and Separations." *Quarterly Journal of Economics* 94(June):643–673.

——— (1980b), "Unionism and the Dispersion of Wages." *Industrial and Labor Relations Review* 34(October):3–23.

——— (1981), "The Effect of Trade Unionism on Fringe Benefits." *Industrial and Labor Relations Review* 34(July).

Johnson, George E. (1975), "Economic Analysis of Trade Unionism." *American Economic Review* 65(May):23–28.

Johnson, George E., and Kenneth Youmams (1971), "Union Relative Wage Effects by Age and Education." *Industrial and Labor Relations Review* (January):171–180.

Jovanovic, Boyan, and Jacob Mincer (1981), "Labor Mobility and Wages." In S. Rosen (ed.), *Studies in Labor Markets* University of Chicago Press, pp. 21–64.

Kalachek, Edward, and Frederick Raines (1980), "Trade Unions and Hiring Standards." *Journal of Labor Research* (Spring):63–75.

Kenny, Lawrence W. (1978), "Male Wage Rates and Marital Status." Unpublished.

Leighton, Linda, and Jacob Mincer (1981), "The Effects of Minimum Wages on Human Capital Formation." In R. Rottenberg (ed.), *The Economics of Legal Minimum Wages* AEI, Washington, D.C., pp. 155–173.

Lewis, H. Gregg (1959), "Competitive and Monopoly Unionism." In P. Bradley (ed.), *Public Stake in Union Power.* Charlottesville: University of Virginia Press.

────── (1963), *Unionism and Relative Wages in the United States.* Chicago: University of Chicago Press.

Medoff, James L. (1979), "Layoffs and Alternatives under Trade Unionism in U.S. Manufacturing." *American Economic Review* 69(June):380–395.

Mellow, Wesley (1981), "Unionism and Wages: A Longitudinal Analysis." *Review of Economics and Statistics* 63(February):43–52.

Mincer, Jacob (1980), "The Economics of Wage Floors." Paper delivered at the AEA Meetings, September.

Mitchell, Daniel J. D. (1980), "Some Empirical Observations of Relevance to the Analysis of Union Wage Determination." *Journal of Labor Research* (Fall):193–216.

Parsley, C. J. (1980), "Labor Unions and Wages: A Survey." *Journal of Economic Literature* (March):1–32.

Pencavel, John (1980), *An Analysis of the Quit Rate in American Manufacturing Industry.* Princeton, N.J.: Industrial Relations Section, Princeton University.

Raisian, John (1981), "Contracts, Tenure, and Cyclical Variability in Wages and Hours." BLS, mimeograph, April.

Rice, Robert G. (1966), "Skill, Earnings, and the Growth of Wage Supplements." *American Economic Review* 56(May):583–593.

Rosen, Sherwin (1968), "Short-run Employment Variation on Class I Railroads in the U.S." *Econometrica* (July):511–529

Appendix follows

APPENDIX

Table A1. NLS Wage Equations

	$\Delta \ln W$ (1969 to 1971)					
	Young Men			Old Men		
	Mean	β	t	Mean	β	t
(a) Wage Growth						
$\Delta \ln W$	8.2			2.6		
Intercept		.10	(5.5)		.038	(.9)
ΔX^2	22.8	−.002	(2.7)	152.0	.0005	(1.3)
ΔT	1.19	.018	(2.4)	1.22	−.0004	(.6)
ΔT^2	8.11	−.001	(.8)	46.22	.0002	(1.0)
Mar	.63	−.007	(.4)	.92	−.017	(.7)
Hlth	.09	−.034	(1.2)	.21	−.0006	(.9)
Lun	3.7	−.0003	(.5)	3.8	−.0002	(.5)
		$R^2 = .35$			$R^2 = .10$	
(b) Wage Level (69)						
$\ln W$	1.12			1.34		
Intercept		−.19	(2.4)		1.21	(2.5)
Educ	12.2	.078	(15.6)	10.3	.053	(11.5)
X	6.7	.045	(4.5)	39.0	.033	(1.4)
X^2	57.8	−.001	(1.3)	1551.4	−.0003	(1.0)
T	1.65	.024	(2.2)	14.8	.003	(1.1)
T^2	7.12	−.002	(1.5)	342.2	−.0001	(1.4)
Mar	.63	.096	(4.5)	.92	.238	(5.9)
Hlth	.09	−.024	(.8)	.21	.043	(1.5)
Lun	3.7	−.002	(.4)	3.8	.001	(1.5)
		$R^2 = .36$			$R^2 = .28$	

Table A2. MID Wage Equations 1968–1978, Annual, Pooled

	All			Age <30			Age ≧30		
	Mean	β	t	Mean	β	t	Mean	β	t
(a) Wage Growth									
$\Delta \ln W$	2.25			4.91			1.06		
Educ	12.5	−.001	(1.1)	13.0	.001	(.4)	12.2	−.001	(1.1)
ΔX	1.0	.048	(2.3)	1.0	.021	(.4)	1.0	.042	(1.6)
ΔX^2	40.2	−.0005	(3.5)	13.1	−.002	(1.4)	52.2	−.0002	(1.2)
ΔT	.64	.010	(2.7)	.57	.021	(2.1)	.68	.007	(1.9)
$\Delta T;2$	12.8	−.0002	(1.2)	3.6	−.001	(1.5)	16.8	−.0007	(.4)
Mar	.92	−.005	(.5)	.88	.017	(.9)	.94	−.02	(1.5)
Hlth	.08	.004	(.4)	.06	−.013	(.5)	.09	.009	(.8)
Lun	5.6	.001	(.8)	5.6	−.002	(1.0)	5.6	.0015	(1.2)
Nun	.3	−.004	(1.8)	.3	−.013	(2.8)	.3	−.0003	(.1)
		$R^2 = .007$			$R^2 = .012$			$R^2 = .003$	

(*continued*)

Table A2. (Continued)

	All			Age <30			Age ≧30		
	Mean	β	t	Mean	β	t	Mean	β	t
			(b) *Wage Level (year 1)*						
ln W	1.68			1.53			1.76		
Intercept		.522	(18.5)		.563	(9.3)		.541	(12.0)
Educ	12.5	.073	(51.0)	13.1	.062	(18.3)	12.2	.075	(44.2)
X	19.5	.028	(23.9)	6.1	.058	(7.5)	25.8	.025	(11.4)
X^2	542.6	− .0005	(19.7)	46.2	− .003	(5.4)	771.4	− .0004	(11.0)
T	7.4	.022	(14.6)	2.2	.056	(10.9)	9.8	.018	(10.9)
T^2	118.5	− .0004	(7.0)	11.1	− .003	(5.9)	168.0	− .0002	(4.2)
Mar	.91	.083	(6.2)	.86	.065	(3.4)	.94	.086	(4.5)
Hlth	.08	− .108	(7.9)	.06	− .076	(2.8)	.09	− .119	(7.5)
Lun	5.6	.021	(13.2)	5.6	.023	(8.5)	5.6	.020	(10.2)
Nun	4.8	− .022	(4.6)	4.8	− .024	(4.5)	4.8	− .019	(4.1)
	$R^2 = .43$			$R^2 = .37$			$R^2 = .43$		

Table A3.

	Young Men				Old Men			
	(UM)		(CB)		(UM)		(CB)	
(a) *Wage Gains (Percent) of Movers, by Union Status, and by Quit (Q) and Layoff (L)* NLS, 1967–1969								
$U_{01}Q$	17.3	(2.8)	13.1	(2.6)	5.5	(.4)	16.7	(1.1)
$U_{01}L$	15.1	(2.5)	10.1	(1.6)	−8.1	(.4)	4.2	(.3)
$U_{10}Q$	−24.4	(4.3)	−23.6	(4.4)	−9.4	(.6)	−17.6	(1.0)
$U_{10}L$	−31.4	(5.0)	−37.0	(6.7)	−16.7	(.6)	−27.9	(1.8)
$U_{11}Q$	10.6	(1.6)	11.4	(2.0)	10.6	(.5)	10.2	(.5)
$U_{11}L$	3.4	(.6)	3.0	(.6)	3.8	(.6)	3.4	(.5)
$U_{00}Q$	5.1	(1.8)	6.0	(2.0)	−1.9	(.4)	−3.9	(.7)
$U_{00}L$	−4.8	(1.4)	2.3	(.6)	−12.0	(1.7)	−10.9	(1.5)
(b) *Wage Gain of Movers, by Union Status and by Industry* Change* (B = moved between industries; W = moved within industries)								
$U_{01}B$	18.8	(4.0)	13.4	(2.9)	2.4	(.1)	8.1	(.7)
$U_{01}W$	4.3	(1.5)	5.6	(1.7)	2.3	(0)	7.7	(.5)
$U_{10}B$	−33.5	(6.4)	−35.0	(7.7)	−9.1	(1.4)	−35.7	(2.4)
$U_{10}W$	−12.9	(1.7)	−13.0	(1.7)	−17.9	(.9)	−10.0	(.6)
$U_{11}B$	5.7	(.8)	6.9	(1.2)	3.7	(.3)	3.4	(.3)
$U_{11}W$	6.1	(1.2)	6.0	(1.1)	3.2	(.4)	2.9	(.4)
$U_{00}B$	− .8	(.3)	3.2	(1.3)	−28.9	(4.8)	−30.7	(4.8)
$U_{00}W$	7.2	(2.0)	8.0	(2.2)	15.1	(2.6)	13.9	(2.4)

Table A4. Wage Gains in MID

	All		Age <30		Age >30	
(a) Movers, by Union Status and by Quit and Layoff MID, Pooled						
$U_{01}Q$	17.2	(4.4)	19.8	(3.6)	11.8	(1.8)
$U_{01}L$	−2.8	(.6)	−1.9	(.3)	−3.3	(.5)
$U_{10}Q$	.4	(.1)	−9.9	(1.6)	12.1	(3.0)
$U_{10}L$	−2.8	(.4)	−7.4	(1.0)	5.2	(1.0)
$U_{11}Q$	10.6	(2.7)	10.9	(1.8)	11.6	(2.0)
$U_{11}L$	5.6	(1.6)	−2.3	(.3)	10.7	(2.6)
$U_{00}Q$	9.0	(5.6)	12.4	(4.6)	4.6	(2.0)
$U_{00}L$	.7	(.3)	2.4	(.7)	−.8	(.3)
(b) Movers, by Union Status, and Industry Change						
$U_{01}B$	10.1	(2.1)	11.2	(3.4)	4.2	(.6)
$U_{01}W$	−.4	(.7)	5.6	(.7)	−6.9	(2.0)
$U_{10}B$	−7.2	(1.7)	−10.1	(1.5)	−5.6	(.9)
$U_{10}W$	−.2	(.4)	−.6	(.1)	4.5	(.9)
$U_{11}B$	12.1	(2.7)	15.2	(2.0)	12.4	(2.1)
$U_{11}W$	3.0	(.8)	1.3	(.2)	5.5	(1.1)
$U_{00}B$	6.9	(3.8)	8.7	(3.0)	7.3	(2.8)
$U_{00}W$	3.2	(1.5)	8.5	(2.4)	−1.4	(.4)

Table A5.

	ln M		M	
(a) Mobility Rate Regression, MID, Cross-section pooled				
Educ	−.050	(7.3)	−.015	(4.8)
X	−.048	(7.0)	−.031	(9.9)
X^2	.0004	(3.0)	.0002	(1.2)
Mar	−.092	(12.8)	−.050	(15.1)
Hlth	.001	(.3)	−.001	(.2)
Nun	−.454	(9.2)	−.421	(18.5)
Union	−.093	(2.5)	−.042	(2.6)
	$R^2 = .62$		$R^2 = .55$	

	Union			Non-union		
	Mean	β	t	Mean	β	t
(b) Quit Rate Regressions, MID, Cross-section						
Q	.039			.083		
Intercept		.157	(6.2)		.275	(13.1)
Educ	11.4	−.0016	(1.1)	13.0	−.0053	(4.5)
X	22.4	−.0040	(3.5)	18.6	−.0068	(6.8)
X^2	666.2	.00004	(2.0)	500.0	.00007	(3.6)
T	9.0	−.0036	(2.5)	6.6	−.0080	(5.4)
T^2	151.8	.0001	(2.2)	99.4	.00027	(5.1)
Mar	.94	−.027	(2.0)	.91	−.012	(1.1)
Hlth	.09	.018	(1.6)	.08	.023	(1.9)
ln M*	−.0048	.010	(1.7)	.0038	.043	(6.8)
		$R^2 = .03$			$R^2 = .06$	

Note:
* Prior mobility rate.

Table A6.   Estimates of Group Wage Differentials, MID, Pooled

I.   A category was excluded if the number of union observations in it was less than 20 in
the full sample.

   The coefficients reported below represent the percent union differential for each category. The dependent variable is log defalted average hourly earnings. No intercept was
used so that levels rather than contrasts could be read for the group dummies (not
reported here).

(1)   The first set of dummies refers to detailed industries:

VARIABLE	PARAMETER ESTIMATE	T RATIO	
IU01	0.192876	2.6447	mining and extraction
IU02	0.030812	0.8054	metal industries (manuf.)
IU03	−0.027250	−0.9070	machinery, incl. electric (manuf.)
IU04	0.098406	3.2413	motor vehicles, other transportation equipment (manuf.)
IU05	0.120014	3.4501	other durables (manuf.)
IU06	0.117478	2.5718	food and kindred products (manuf.)
IU07	0.281642	4.1110	textiles, apparel, shoes (manuf.)
IU08	0.028735	0.3106	paper and allied products (manuf.)
IU09	−0.110420	−2.5741	chemical, allied products (manuf.)
IU10	0.349179	12.4312	construction
IU11	0.130612	3.9211	transportation
IU12	0.084606	1.4231	communication
IU13	0.168903	3.5534	other public utilities
IU14	0.273232	7.1365	retail trade
IU15	−0.043016	−0.8688	wholesale trade
IU16	0.110787	1.2200	repair service
IU17	0.142907	1.4794	personal services
IU18	0.184840	2.7868	printing, publishing, allied services
IU19	−0.073909	−0.9493	medical and dental and health services, public or private
IU20	0.136501	3.9973	educational services, public or private
IU21	0.219599	2.7867	professional and related services other than medical or dental
IU22	0.138157	4.3291	government, other than medical or educational services; NA whether other

	R RATIO	4701.32
	DFE	8463
	R-SQUARE	0.9682

(2)   The second set of dummies referes to states of the continental U.S.A. These states
were dropped:

Alabama	Nevada
Colorado	New Hampshire
Delware	New Mexico
District of Columbia	North Dakota
Idaho	Rhode Island
Kansas	South Carolina
Louisiana	Vermont
Montana	West Virginia
Nebraska	Wyoming

(continued)

Table A6. (Continued)

VARIABLE	PARAMETER ESTIMATE	T RATIO	
SU01	0.132901	1.7058	Arizona
SU02	0.268430	4.3792	Arkansas
SU03	0.177617	6.6824	California
SU04	−0.105243	−1.1892	Connecticut
SU05	0.106447	1.4246	Florida
SU06	0.005364501	0.0696	Georgia
SU07	0.004690769	0.1242	Illinois
SU08	0.029036	0.7859	Indiana
SU09	0.367906	8.0557	Iowa
SU10	0.062387	1.4132	Kentucky
SU11	0.283081	3.1941	Maine
SU12	0.160142	1.7876	Maryland
SU13	0.089620	1.8404	Massachusetts
SU14	0.026547	0.8876	Michigan
SU15	0.081187	1.8014	Minnesota
SU16	0.101594	1.3480	Mississippi
SU17	0.275612	7.9395	Missouri
SU18	−0.073130	−2.0036	New Jersey
SU19	0.083717	3.0567	New York
SU20	0.419438	5.6320	North Carolina
SU21	0.185828	6.9361	Ohio
SU22	−0.114174	−1.3375	Oklahoma
SU23	0.134037	3.1064	Oregon
SU24	0.105055	3.6566	Pennsylvania
SU25	0.454598	6.2741	South Dakota
SU26	0.407114	8.3154	Tennessee
SU27	0.149538	2.5615	Texas
SU28	0.165572	1.8644	Utah
SU29	0.184553	4.7105	Virginia
SU30	0.218756	4.3970	Washington
SU31	0.107793	2.1447	Wisconsin

F RATIO 4633.36
DFE 11758
R-SQUARE 0.9655 NOTE: NO INTERCEPT TERM IS USED.

(3) The third set of dummies refers to aggregate occupations cross-classified by aggregate industries:

VARIABLE	PARAMETER ESTIMATE	T RATIO	
Durable manufacturing			
IOU01	−0.161345	−2.7482	professional or managerial
IOU02	0.017291	0.2213	clerical and sales
IOU03	0.106036	3.9576	craftsmen, foremen and kindred
IOU04	0.223627	8.1542	operatives and kindred
IOU05	0.153847	1.9201	laborers and service workers

Table A6. (*Continued*)

Non-durables manufacturing			
IOU06	− 0.222012	− 2.4278	professional or managerial
IOU07	0.020362	0.2382	clerical and sales
IOU08	0.102038	1.7847	craftsmen, foremen and kindred
IOU09	0.258602	6.3823	operatives and kindred
IOU10	0.136277	1.2682	laborers and service workers
Construction			
IOU11	0.380947	4.0230	professional or managerial
IOU12	0.394693	11.8224	craftsmen, foremen and kindred
IOU13	0.341520	3.8748	laborers and service workers
Transportation, communication, public utilities			
IOU14	0.035351	0.5346	professional or managerial
IOU15	− 0.00629608	− 0.0954	clerical and sales
IOU16	0.184263	4.2493	craftsmen, foremen and kindred
IOU17	0.201402	4.0272	operatives and kindred
IOU18	0.318112	3.1273	laborers and service workers
Wholesale and retail trade			
IOU19	0.073211	1.0787	professional or managerial
IOU20	0.123114	2.2794	clerical and sales
IOU21	0.359201	5.9317	operatives and kindred
IOU22	0.412222	5.1120	laborers and service workers
Educational services, private or public			
IOU23	0.171116	4.3852	professional or managerial
Those and all other services			
IOU24	0.068333	2.3846	all occupational categories, except IO23
Government, excl medical or educational services; NA whether other			
IOU25	0.148524	2.3907	professional or managerial
IOU26	0.145901	1.9485	clerical and sales
IOU27	0.247951	3.7062	craftsmen, foremen and kindred
	F RATIO	4083.84	
	DFE	8284	
	R-SQUARE	0.9688	

Table A7.   Determinants of In-Firm Training on Current Job

Variable	NLS Young Men, 1969–1971 White, Educ ≦12				MID, All Men, 1973–1975 White, Educ ≦12	
	β	t			β	t
Educ	.013	(7.2)	.039	(6.0)	−.0007	(.01)
X	.009	(1.4)	.015	(1.1)	−.001	(0)
X²	−.001	(.9)	−.0005	(.5)	−.001	(0)
T	.055	(3.4) ⎱?			−.005	(.7)
T²	−.005	(2.1) ⎰			.00	(.3)
Mar	.018	(1.1)			.014	(.1)
Hlth	−.044	(1.3)			.005	(.1)
Union	.014	(.7)			−.164	(26.8)
Min. Wage*	−.196	(2.7)			−.220	(2.4)
		R² = .06			R² = .08	

Note:
* Inverse of one plus state wage differential, multiplied by coverage (see Leighton and Mincer, 1980).

EMPLOYER SIZE, UNIONISM, AND WAGES

Wesley Mellow

Studies have indicated that wages are higher in large firms or establishments. However, theoretical and empirical considerations have resulted in some uncertainty about how this finding should be interpreted.

Proposed theoretical linkages between employer size and wages are varied and sometimes contradictory. Some researchers take a neutral position. Rees and Shultz (1970), for instance, note "there is no particular basis in theory for expecting such a relationship" (p. 7). Most argue for a positive relationship. Among the arguments are: (1) a compensating payment in response to the requirement of large employers for "workers who are more dependable and more willing to be regimented" (Masters, 1969, p. 342); (2) a greater ability to pay due to product market structure—"many of the arguments for the monopoly wage hypothesis can be used to argue for higher earnings in large shops" (Weiss, 1966, p. 99); (3) an offset against other factors in the employer's cost function, particularly monitoring—"wage rates are less in small plants than in large, and the

New Approaches to Labor Unions.
Research in Labor Economics, Supplement 2, pages 253–282.
Copyright © 1983 by JAI Press Inc.
All rights of reproduction in any form reserved.
ISBN: 0-89232-265-9

difference reflects at least in part (and perhaps in whole) the lower cost to the small employer of judging quality" (Stigler, 1962, p. 102; also see 0i, 1983)—and turnover—premiums reduce turnover and protect investments in firm-specific skills associated with greater specialization in large firms; and (4) finally there is the public scrutiny that is concomitant with bigness (Lester, 1967). On the other hand, Lester also notes that one might expect a negative relationship if large employers "use their monopoly power to depress wage scales" (p. 65).

Empirically, isolating the independent effect employer size has on wages is difficult because size is interrelated with many other factors that influence wages, including unionization, the extent of product market competition, size of location, and labor quality. As Reynolds (1978) notes, "large plant size, a high concentration ratio and strong unionization tend to go together. Thus it takes a careful statistical analysis to separate out the effect of each factor" (p. 187). Lester (1967) provides an extended discussion of many of the problems associated with estimating the impact employer size has on wages.

Most estimates of the employer size wage effect are based on industry data (Masters, 1969; Rosen, 1970; Haworth and Reuther, 1980; Pugel, 1980). A critical limitation of using industry data in this context is that only very limited controls for labor quality are available. Consequently, to the extent employer size is correlated with labor quality the estimated wage effect will be biased.

A second approach has been to analyze data on individual workers matched with industry data on product market structure, unionization, and employer size (Weiss, 1966; Freeman and Medoff, 1981). The major shortcoming associated with this approach is the imprecision of the matching process. Ideally, employer size should be measured at the worker level instead of being imputed on the basis of industry averages. A further limitation of both approaches is that reliance on industry data, which are generally available only for manufacturing, effectively limits the analysis to specific sectors of the economy.

This paper presents new estimates of the employer size wage relation using data from the Current Population Surveys for May and June 1979. In contrast to the data used in prior studies, these data cover the entire work force and provide worker-specific information on personal characteristics, union status, wages, *and* employer size. By analyzing economywide data on both worker and job characteristics collected at the individual worker level, I obtain better estimates of the impact that employer size has on wages and how size interacts with other factors important in the wage determination process, particularly unionism.

The principal findings of the analysis are that gross employer size wage premiums are quite substantial; that controlling for labor quality reduces estimated premiums by about 50 percent; that also controlling for union status reduces estimated premiums still further; but that even when factors such as location and occupational/industrial status are included in the wage equation there is still a large estimated employer size wage premium. In addition to the basic analysis, the interaction between size and union membership is extensively examined and several extensions are considered in an attempt to discriminate among specific arguments supporting an employer size wage premium.

I. ESTIMATING FRAMEWORK AND DATA

To isolate the effect of employer size on wages it is necessary to control for the many other factors that also influence wages. One way to accomplish this standardization of the wage comparison is by estimating an equation of the form

$$\ln W_i = \alpha ESIZE_i + X_i\beta + e_i, \tag{1}$$

where for the ith individual, W is the wage rate, ESIZE is a measure of employer size, and X is is a vector of personal and job characteristics that influence wages (education, experience, race, sex, union status, location, etc.). With a log-linear regression specification, the estimate of α provides an indication of the proportionate employer size wage effect.

Equation (1) can be estimated with data taken from the Current Population Survey (CPS). The CPS is the monthly survey of 56,000 households used by the Bureau of Labor Statistics to calculate the official unemployment rate. In addition to questions on labor force status and personal characteristics, each monthly survey obtains information on hourly earnings (for those paid by the hour), usual weekly earnings, and usual hours worked at the primary job from approximately one-fourth of the employed survey participants. A special supplement to the May 1979 survey obtained information on a wide range of additional worker and job characteristics, including current job tenure, union membership status, employer size, and selected fringe benefits. For this analysis, the sample is limited to the 18,551 wage and salary workers providing responses to the earnings questions in either the May or June survey and the employer size questions in the May survey.[1]

The hourly wage variable is either reported as hourly earnings for workers paid by the hour, or usual weekly earnings divided by usual weekly hours for other workers. Employer size was determined by the question: "About how many persons are employed by your employer at all locations?" The survey allowed respondents to indicate one of five exclusive and exhaustive categories: less than 25, 25–99, 100–499, 500–999, 1000 and over. Dummy variables were constructed indicating each of the four

Table 1. Employer Size and Sample Means.

Variable	Definition	Mean Value by Employer Size Category					
		1–24	*25–99*	*100–499*	*500–1000*	*1000+*	*Total*
WAGE	Hourly earnings	4.97	5.59	6.24	6.38	7.33	6.23
RACE	1 if nonwhite, 0 otherwise	.10	.09	.09	.09	.10	.10
SEX	1 if female, 0 otherwise	.48	.44	.48	.50	.38	.44
EDUCATION	Years of formal education	11.96	12.28	12.88	13.22	13.08	12.64
JOB TENURE	Years at current job	3.95	5.13	6.40	6.96	8.77	6.51
OTHER EXPERIENCE	Age-EDUCATION-JOB TENURE-6	13.89	13.28	11.59	10.37	9.48	11.57
PART-TIME	1 if works fewer than 35 hours per week, 0 otherwise	.34	.20	.14	.17	.11	.20
UNION MEMBER	1 if union member at current job, 0 otherwise	.06	.18	.26	.29	.35	.23
PERCENT UNION	percent union in worker's 3-digit industry	.14	.18	.19	.18	.26	.20
Sample Size		5,043	2,650	2,608	1,011	7,239	18,551

Note: Data are from a matched file of the May and June Current Population Surveys for 1979. Included in the sample are all wage and salary workers responding to questions on employer size and earnings. Employer size is number of persons employed by employer at all locations.

largest size categories. The less-than-25 category is omitted in estimation and thus serves as the reference group. It should be noted that measuring employer size at the firm or enterprise level differs from most earlier studies, where size has been measured at the establishment or plant level.[2]

Two union variables are included in the analysis. First, a dummy indicating union membership was determined by the question: "On this [the primary] job is . . . a member of a labor union or of an employee association similar to a union?" A second dimension of unionism was captured by a variable indicating the percent of the worker's three-digit industry that is unionized.[3] Other elements of the X vector were constructed in straightforward fashion from responses to specific survey questions.

Table 1 summarizes the data by providing mean values of selected worker and job characteristics with the sample stratified into the five employer-size categories. Some significant variations in the distribution of characteristics are readily apparent. Wages, education, job tenure, and union membership all increase sharply with employer size. On the other hand, the percent of workers who are part-time falls dramatically. Perhaps because it is related to the part-time pattern, the percent of workers who are female decreases markedly when moving from the penultimate to final size category.

II. EMPIRICAL RESULTS

A. Initial Estimates

Estimates from alternative log-linear wage regressions are presented in Table 2. From an initial specification containing only employer size, the explanatory vector is expanded by sequentially adding variables that control for other determinants of wages, including personal characteristics, union status, and location and occupational/industrial status. The reduction in the estimated effect of employer size as the specification changes indicates the extent to which the newly added variables account for the estimated employer-size wage premium.

When only the employer-size dummies are included as explanatory variables, estimated wage differentials are significant and increase monotonically with employer size. Compared to the excluded size category (less than 25 workers), wages are 51 percent higher when employer size exceeds 1000 workers.[4]

The inclusion of personal characteristics are explanatory variables cuts the estimated effect of employer size in half. The estimated wage premium for the largest size category is now 25 percent.[5] Estimated coefficients on the personal characteristic variables are consistent with those obtained in many other studies. Note that the experience measure is segmented

Table 2. Regression Estimates of the Impact of Employer Size, Union, and Other Variables on Log Hourly Earnings (absolute values of t-statistics are in parentheses).

Explanatory Variable	Regression						
	1	2	3	4	5	6	7
Employer Size:							
SMALL (25–99)	.134 (11.49)	.064 (6.88)	.043 (4.66)	.015 (1.77)		.032 (2.44)	.013 (1.47)
MED (100–499)	.247 (21.01)	.126 (13.30)	.093 (9.82)	.060 (6.60)		.062 (4.35)	.055 (6.04)
LG (500–999)	.278 (16.59)	.142 (10.44)	.109 (8.07)	.080 (6.36)		.074 (3.47)	.075 (5.89)
XLG (1000+)	.415 (46.41)	.221 (29.21)	.159 (20.44)	.124 (16.19)		.150 (12.08)	.134 (16.48)
RACE		−.070 (7.14)	−.072 (7.46)	−.040 (4.30)	−.038 (4.10)	−.073 (5.24)	−.040 (4.29)
SEX		−.343 (57.44)	−.295 (48.11)	−.240 (35.78)	−.239 (35.43)	−.262 (21.86)	−.240 (35.76)
EDUCATION		.047 (5.73)	.033 (4.11)	.022 (2.85)	.027 (3.42)	.045 (3.46)	.022 (2.88)
(EDUCATION/10)^2		.084 (2.98)	.161 (5.80)	.083 (3.05)	.073 (2.67)	.035 (.69)	.081 (3.00)
JOB TENURE		.021 (10.60)	.017 (8.66)	.013 (7.12)	.015 (8.20)	.012 (4.42)	.013 (7.19)
(JOB TENURE/10)^2		−.043 (12.73)	−.041 (12.28)	−.036 (11.62)	−.041 (12.95)	−.029 (6.26)	−.036 (11.62)

	(1)	(2)	(3)	(4)	(5)	(6)	(7)
OTHER EXPERIENCE		.022 (11.96)	.022 (11.79)	.014 (8.28)	.014 (8.18)	.014 (4.88)	.014 (8.19)
(OTHER EXPERIENCE/10)^2		-.033 (15.84)	-.031 (15.23)	-.021 (11.36)	-.022 (11.18)	-.042 (6.73)	-.022 (11.28)
(EDUCATION × JOB TENURE)/100		.038 (2.98)	.057 (4.60)	.061 (5.28)	.062 (5.25)	.026 (1.25)	.060 (5.19)
(EDUCATION × OTHER EXPERIENCE)/100		-.069 (6.31)	-.064 (6.01)	-.035 (3.52)	-.039 (3.89)	-.042 (2.23)	-.035 (3.45)
UNION MEMBER			.058 (7.91)	.075 (10.32)	.093 (12.96)	.151 (15.19)	.099 (9.90)
PERCENT UNION			.408 (23.09)	.262 (10.36)	.311 (12.30)	.219 (6.39)	.273 (10.72)
UNION MEMBER × EMPLOYER SIZE (XLG)							-.046 (3.51)
PART-TIME				-.076 (10.19)	-.086 (11.53)	-.124 (8.59)	-.076 (10.11)
Marital Status Dummies (3)		yes	yes	yes	yes	yes	yes
SMSA (2), Region (3), Occupation (8), and Industry (8) Dummies		yes	yes	yes	yes	yes	yes
Sample	all	all	all	all	all	blue-collar	all
Sample Size	18551	18551	18551	18551	18551	5980	18551
R^2	.109	.436	.458	.532	.524	.525	.532

Note: Data and variables are described in table 1.

259

into current job tenure and a residual measure of other potential labor force exposure. Taking account of the interaction terms, the estimated coefficients indicate that at sample means the marginal return to a year at the current job is roughly three times greater than to a year of imputed general experience. Given the measurement error inherent in the residual calculation of potential experience and the selectivity problem associated with current tenure, this difference is not surprising. Moreover, to the extent that wages and job tenure are jointly determined, the inclusion of current job tenure as an explanatory variable has the added effect of reducing the estimated impact of employer size.[6]

B. Employer Size and Unionism

Much research suggests that unions are successful in obtaining wage gains for their members (see Lewis, 1963; Johnson, 1975; and Parsley, 1980, for discussion and reviews of the evidence). In addition, a range of arguments, including substantial fixed costs associated with organizational activities, the structure of industries with large employers, and the nature of the work setting, would imply that the proportion of workers who are union members increases with employer size.[7] Taken together, these two observations suggest that understanding how employer size and unionism interact in the wage determination process is important in attempting to isolate the wage effect of either factor.

When in regression 3 the union member and percent union variables are included in the wage regression, the estimated employer-size premium takes another sharp drop; the estimated wage premium for the largest size category is now 17 percent. Regression 4 adds part-time status, location and occupational/industrial status variables resulting in an additional modest decline in the estimated size effect—to 13 percent for the largest size category. Regression 5 reverses the sequencing and excludes the employer size variables, while regression 6 limits the sample to blue-collar workers. These latter two changes have the effect of increasing the estimated impact of the union member variable.

The estimated coefficient on the union member variable in regression 4 indicates that the estimated union–nonunion relative wage differential is 8 percent.[8] To see if the wage gains associated with union membership are greater among large employers,[9] regression 7 adds an interaction term indicating that the worker is a union member and employer size is 1000 or more. The estimated coefficients on the union member variable and the interaction term indicate that on average the union–nonunion relative wage differential is 10 percent for employer size less than 1000 and 5 percent for employer size of 1000 or more. With the size–union interaction term included in the regression, the estimated wage gain from working in a large firm (1000 +) is 14 percent for a nonunion worker.

A second dimension of unionism is indicated by the estimated impact of percent union, where an increase from 20 to 50 percent is associated with an 8 percent wage increase.[10] Of course, to determine fully the impact that percent union has on union–nonunion wage differences it is necessary to account for the fact that union workers are on average located in more organized settings and for the possibility that the impact of percent union varies with union status.[11] To investigate these issues and to understand better the size–union interaction, separate wage equations are estimated for union and nonunion workers. Table 3 summarizes the results.

Consistent with the earlier findings using the size–union interaction term, employer size has a greater wage impact in the nonunion sector. The estimated wage premium for workers in firms of 1000 or more is 6 percent in the union sector and rises to 13 percent in the nonunion sector. As in earlier studies, the returns to education and job tenure are greater in the nonunion sector (Bloch and Kuskin, 1978; Duncan and Leigh, 1980). The impact of percent union is greater in the union sector.

As an alternative to calculating the union–nonunion relative wage differential directly from the full sample regressions, the disaggregated results can be used to estimate the union wage premium. Assuming that the union wage structure is applicable for all workers, an estimate of the union wage premium is obtained by applying the nonunion means to the union coefficients (to determine predicted log wage if the nonunion worker were paid according to the union structure) and then subtracting the actual nonunion mean log wage. This approach yields an estimated premium of 10 percent. Additionally, if percent union for the average nonunion worker is raised to the economywide average rate (from .16 to .20) the estimated union wage premium is 11 percent.

C. Expanding the Wage Measure: Health and Pension Benefits

Thus far the comparisons have involved wages. In principle one would like to make comparisons on the basis of some measure of total compensation. A partial move in this direction is possible since the supplement to the May 1979 CPS also obtained information on the worker's receipt of two specific fringe benefits: participation in an employer-provided group health plan and participation in an employer-supported pension plan.

Logit analysis is used to estimate equations indicating the worker's likelihood of receiving health or pension benefits. Explanatory variables are the employer size, personal characteristic and union, part-time, locational, occupational and industrial status variables used in the wage analysis, plus hourly wage. Wage is included as an explanatory variable even though it is jointly determined with fringes in order to net out of the

Table 3. Regression Estimates of the Determinants of Log Hourly Earnings: Union and Nonunion Samples (absolute values of t-statistics are in parentheses)

Explanatory Variable	Means		Union Sample	Nonunion Sample
	Union Sample	Nonunion Sample		
Employer Size:				
SMALL (25–99)	.11	.15	−.033 (1.41)	.011 (1.14)
MED (100–499)	.16	.14	−.008 (.37)	.061 (5.96)
LG (500–999)	.07	.05	−.001 (.00)	.085 (5.74)
XLG (1000+)	.59	.33	.056 (2.78)	.119 (13.96)
RACE	.12	.09	−.041 (2.58)	−.033 (3.02)
SEX	.30	.48	−.201 (16.01)	−.246 (31.81)
EDUCATION	12.49	12.68	.001 (.06)	.021 (2.35)
$(\text{EDUCATION}/10)^2$	1.64	1.68	.108 (2.00)	.091 (2.90)
JOB TENURE	9.75	5.54	.007 (2.24)	.012 (5.48)
$(\text{JOB TENURE}/10)^2$	1.75	.87	−.029 (5.23)	−.038 (10.68)
OTHER EXPERIENCE	10.73	11.82	.009 (2.32)	.014 (7.22)
$(\text{OTHER EXPERIENCE}/10)^2$	2.19	2.87	−.017 (3.47)	−.022 (9.96)
(EDUCATION × JOB TENURE)/100	1.19	.71	.062 (2.98)	.085 (5.98)
(EDUCATION × OTHER EXPERIENCE)/100	1.23	1.39	−.020 (.84)	−.034 (3.07)
PERCENT UNION	.33	.16	.331 (8.72)	.203 (6.17)
PART-TIME	.09	.23	.026 (1.45)	−.088 (10.64)
Sample Size			4265	14286
R^2			.399	.535

Note: Data and variables are described in table 1. Also included as explanatory variables are marital status (3), SMSA (2), region (3), occupation (8), and industry (8) dummies.

estimated size and union coefficients any impact attributable to size or union-related wage premiums. Maximum-likelihood estimates of the two fringe benefit equations are summarized in Table 4.

The estimates indicate that employer size and union membership have strong positive impacts on the receipt of both health and pension benefits.

Table 4. Logit Estimates of the Effect of Employer Size, Union and Other Variables on the Receipt of Health and Pension Benefits

	Dependent Variable	
Explanatory Variable	*Health Insurance (= 1 if included in a group health insurance plan at the current job, 0 otherwise; mean = .66)*	*Pension Plan (= 1 if included in a private pension plan at the current job, 0 otherwise; mean = .50)*
Employer Size:		
SMALL	1.107 (17.66) .200	.092 (13.53) .229
MED (100–499)	1.142 (21.35) .264	1.500 (22.00) .375
LG (500–999)	1.696 (16.74) .317	1.868 (20.01) .469
XLG (1000+)	1.689 (21.71) .316	2.223 (36.61) .557
UNION MEMBER	.711 (11.67) .144	1.284 (21.96) .321
PERCENT UNION	−.220 (.93) −.041	−1.144 (5.61) .286
WAGE	.126 (13.69) .024	.094 (11.77) .024
χ^2	8,711(43)	10,654(42)
Likelihood Ratio Index	.367	.414

Note: Reported coefficients are maximum likelihood estimates of the parameters of a logit model. Also reported are the asymptotic t-statistics and derivatives (at sample means) respectively. The estimated coefficients indicate the change in the odds of receiving the indicated fringe benefit for a one unit change in an explanatory variable, and the derivatives reveal the marginal effect of a change in the explanatory variable on the absolute probability of receiving the benefit. Data and variables are described in Table 1. In addition to the indicated variables, each equation includes race, sex, education, job tenure, other experience and part-time, locational, occupational and industrial status variables.

Based on the calculated derivatives, there is an increase of .20 in the absolute probability of health benefits associated with the first size category (25–99); moving to the largest size category increases the absolute probability of benefits by .32. For pensions the increase in the probability of benefits also shows up in the first size category and increases through the remaining ones; the absolute probability of benefits is .56 higher in the largest size category. Because the mean of the pension variable is smaller than that of the health variable (.50 versus .66), the relative impact of employer size on the probability of receiving benefits is greater for pensions. Taking an expanded view of the compensation package thus leaves unaltered the basic conclusion: employer size has a strong independent impact on compensation, however measured. The estimates also indicate that union membership has a strong positive influence on the receipt of the two fringes.[12]

III. EXTENSIONS

A. Why Does Employer Size Influence Wages?

The basic estimates indicate a substantial employer-size wage premium, but they are not especially informative as to what factors might be responsible for the estimated effect. To consider some of the arguments supporting a positive employer-size wage effect, alternative size variables and sample specifications are examined. In general, the evidence generated in these experiments should be viewed as at best suggestive in answering the question: "Why does employer size influences wages?" On a more positive note, the experiments do surface a lot of interesting issues related to the structure of wages. In particular, disaggregating the data by industrial status or alternatively by firm size and union status illuminates important structural differences in the wage determination process.

Alternative Size Measures

In the earlier analysis employer size is measured at the firm or enterprise level instead of at the plant or establishment level. Although neither size concept is unambigously superior, a good case can be made that plant size is more closely related to working conditions. Thus if the size premium is related to compensating payments for working conditions, a plant-level measure should be of importance. Several experiments conducted using plant-level measures of employer size are summarized in Table 5.

Regression 1 includes plant- instead of firm-level size dummies in a regression specification that is otherwise identical to regression 4 in Table

Table 5. Regression Estimates of the Impact of Alternative Size Variables: Membership on Log of Hourly Earnings (absolute values of t-statistics are in parentheses)

Explanatory Variable	Mean	Regression		
		1	2	3
Establishment/Plant Size:				
Small (25–99)	.24	.033 (4.69)	.026 (3.58)	.015 (1.48)
MED (100–499)	.19	.076 (9.61)	.065 (8.12)	.035 (3.36)
LG (500–999)	.06	.118 (9.98)	.105 (8.84)	.068 (4.85)
XLG (1000+)	.13	.160 (16.67)	.143 (14.59)	.102 (8.56)
Multi-location Employer	.57		.045 (7.51)	
Firm/Enterprise Size:				
Small (25–99)	.14			.007 (.62)
MED (100–499)	.14			.042 (3.64)
LG (500–999)	.06			.048 (3.29)
XLG (1000+)	.39			.079 (7.99)
UNION MEMBER	.23	.085 (11.82)	.078 (10.86)	.077 (10.65)
PERCENT UNION	.20	.268 (10.62)	.260 (10.31)	.252 (9.98)
R^2		.532	.533	.534

Note: Establishment/plant size is number of persons employed by employer at the worker's location; multi-location employer is a dummy assuming the value 1 if the employer operates at more than one location, 0 otherwise; and firm/enterprise size is number of persons employed by employer at all locations. Data and other variables are defined in Table 1. The sample size is 18,551 in all regressions. In addition to the indicated variables each regression includes race, sex, education, job tenure, other experience, and part-time, location, occupation, and industrial status variables.

2. The estimates are quite similar. Because of the arguably stronger relation between plant size and working conditions, it is also noteworthy that the estimated union effect is slightly larger than that obtained using the firm-level size measures. Adding a dummy indicating that the worker's employer operates in more than one location, regression 2 finds that, holding plant size constant, multilocation employers provide wage premiums of 5 percent. But when the multilocation dummy is replaced with the firm-size measures used earlier, regression 3 indicates that both plant and firm size are associated with increased wages.

To the extent size is a proxy for working conditions, the earlier Table 2 results also have implications for the relation between unions and working conditions. Recently, several researchers have suggested that part of the union wage premium actually represents a compensating payment for adverse working conditions. A clear statement of the argument is the "interdependencies" hypothesis advanced by Duncan and Stafford (1980): "shared levels of work effort and working conditions give rise to the need for compensating wage differentials and unions" (p. 361).[13] To test the hypothesis, Duncan and Stafford estimate wage equations with and without subjective measures of working conditions and compare the estimated union wage effects. Their estimates indicate that about 40 percent of the union wage premium represents a compensating payment for adverse working conditions.[14]

If one views size as a good proxy for working conditions, then the change in the estimated union wage effect between regressions 5 and 4 in Table 2 (or any of the regressions in Table 5) provides an alternative test (that does not rely on responses to subjective questions) of the hypothesis. Adding employer size to the equation results in a decline in the estimated union wage effect—from 9.7 percent in regression 5 to 7.9 percent in regression 4. These estimates are thus qualitatively consistent with those of Duncan and Stafford, but indicate a smaller compensating wage component.[15]

Industry-Stratified Results

In contrast to prior studies, the results reported thus far are based on economywide data. While comprehensiveness has advantages, it also may have the disadvantage of obscuring important differences across sectors. Stratifying the sample by major industry group is one way to gain additional insight, particularly on the interaction of employer size and market structure in the wage determination process.

Table 6 summarizes earnings regressions estimated for workers in specific major industry groups. Three interesting groups to consider are construction/mining (where unionism rather than a concentration of large

Table 6. Regression Estimates of the Impact of Employer Size and Union Variables on Log of Hourly Earnings in Selected Industries

(absolute values of t-statistics are in parentheses)

Explanatory Variable	Industry Group						
	Construction and Mining	Durable Goods Manufacturing	Non-Dur. Goods Manufacturing	Transport., Comm. and Publ. Utilities	Wholesale and Retail Trade	Finance, Insurance and Real Estate	Personal Services (ex. hh)
Employer Size:							
SMALL (25–99)	.051	−.005	−.014	.005	.041	−.019	−.015
	(1.83)	(.77)	(.44)	(.12)	(2.49)	(.49)	(.81)
MED (100–499)	.058	.010	.032	.119	.098	.017	.049
	(1.77)	(.01)	(1.00)	(2.94)	(4.88)	(0.42)	(2.86)
LG (500–999)	.103	.047	.081	.067	.083	.085	.068
	(1.83)	(1.47)	(2.01)	(1.14)	(2.55)	(1.48)	(3.17)
XLG (1000+)	.206	.162	.137	.318	.096	.035	.094
	(5.71)	(6.92)	(4.47)	(8.69)	(6.12)	(1.00)	(5.68)
UNION MEMBER	.364	.080	.095	.159	.163	.019	.019
	(13.23)	(6.91)	(3.40)	(4.25)	(5.58)	(.23)	(.99)
UNION MEMBER × EMPLOYER SIZE (XLG)	−.244	−.050	−.001	−.187	−.040	−.243	−.0006
	(4.76)	(1.92)	(.00)	(4.14)	(.94)	(1.82)	(.00)
PERCENT UNION	.047	.267	.207	.273	.376	−.971	−.147
	(.54)	(7.36)	(3.01)	(4.02)	(5.22)	(1.48)	(1.38)
Sample Size	1256	2707	1638	1286	3640	1108	4632
R^2	.478	.566	.579	.422	.529	.454	.447

Note: Data and variables are described in Table 1. In addition to the indicated variables, each regression includes race, sex, education, job tenure, other experience, and part-time, location, and occupational status variables.

267

employers is the primary source of monopoly power on product markets); durable goods manufacturing (where significant monopoly power as a result of a concentration of large employers would exist independent of unionism); and transportation, communications, and public utilities (where market organization is dominated by government regulation).[16] The percentage wage effects of employer size and union membership for these industries are computed in Table 7 for two illustrative size categories and union and nonunion members.

For nonunion workers, size is consistently important. In construction/ mining and durable goods manufacturing, wages are respectively 23 and 18 percent higher in the largest employer size category, while in trans- portation, communications, and public utilities, wages are 37 percent higher in the largest size category.[17] For union workers the estimated size impacts show more variability across industries. In construction/mining union workers receive roughly a 40 percent wage premium in both large and small firms. In durable goods manufacturing the wage premium of union workers is only 8 percent in small firms but increases to 21 percent in large ones, while in transportation, communications, and public utilities the corresponding premiums of union workers are 17 and 34 percent.

The results for nondurable manufacturing are qualitatively similar to durable manufacturing. In wholesale and retail trade both size and un- ionism have significant positive independent impacts, but the two factors have no combined effect. In personal services size matters but unionism does not, while in finance, insurance, and real estate neither factor mat- ters. The consistently positive impact of employer size across industry groups characterized by divergent product market structures suggests that size does not derive the major portion of its observed impact by serving as a proxy for product market conditions.[18]

Table 7. Percentage Wage Premiums by Employer Size and Union Status: Selected Industries

	Union Status	
Employer Size	*Nonmember*	*Member*
less than 25	0	44 (CM)
		8 (DGM)
		17 (TCPU)
1000 and over	23 (CM)	39 (CM)
	18 (GDM)	21 (GDM)
	37 (TCPU)	34 (TCPU)

Note: Computations based on the estimated coefficients reported in Table 3. Industry groups shown are: construction and mining (CM); durable goods manufacturing (DGM); and transportation, communications and public utilities (TCPU).

Table 8.   Regression Estimates of the Impact of Employer Size, Union and Concentration Variables on Log Hourly Earnings in Manufacturing (absolute values of t-statistics are in parentheses)

Explanatory Variable	Mean	Regression			
		1	*2*	*3*	*4*
Employer Size:					
SMALL (25–99)	.13	−.012	−.015		−.017
		(.58)	(.77)		(.77)
MED (100–499)	.15	.023	.016		.012
		(1.17)	(.81)		(.55)
LG (500–999)	.06	.066	.057		.026
		(2.67)	(2.31)		(.91)
XLG (1000+)	.58	.147	.127		.115
		(8.32)	(7.04)		(5.69)
UNION MEMBER	.34	.065	.113	.131	.149
		(5.65)	(5.21)	(6.02)	(5.12)
PERCENT UNION	.37	.250	.189	.141	.219
		(7.96)	(5.39)	(3.85)	(5.12)
CON RATIO (4-firm concentration ratio)	.36		.199	.174	.219
			(5.61)	(3.94)	(4.66)
UNION MEMBER × CON RATIO	.14		−.128	−.121	−.182
			(2.53)	(2.38)	(3.13)
ln (average value of shipments)	1.29			.026	
				(4.55)	
R^2		.574	.577	.566	.547
Sample Size		4345	4345	4345	2767

Note: Data and variables unless otherwise noted are described in Table 1. In addition to the indicated variables, each regression includes race, sex, education, job tenure, other experience, and part-time, locational and occupational status variables. The sample for regressions 1–3 is all workers in manufacturing; regression 4 further limits the sample to blue-collar workers.

The employer-size–market-structure relation can be considered more directly by explicitly including a measure of the extent to which product markets are dominated by a few sellers as an explanatory variable. The two manufacturing samples were combined and a variable indicating the four-firm concentration ratio in the worker's three-digit industry group[19] along with a union-member-concentration ratio interaction variable were added to the regression specification.

The results of several alternative specifications of the wage regression are summarized in Table 8. In addition to the controls, regression 1 includes only the employer size and union status variables. Regression 2,

which adds the concentration variables, indicates that all three factors—
employer size, unionism, and market structure—are important factors in
the wage determination process in manufacturing. Of particular interest
is the result that the estimated coefficients on the employer size variables
decline quite modestly—by only about 15 percent—with the inclusion of
an explicit measure for product market structure. For the largest size
group the estimated wage premium declines from 16 to 14 percent moving
from regression 1 to 2.

Regression 3 indicates the consequences of measuring employer size
at the worker level as opposed to relying on an industry measure that is
imputed to individual workers on the basis of their industry affiliation.
The size dummies are replaced with the natural logarithm of the average
value of shipments in the worker's three-digit industry.[20] Although the
coefficient of the new size variable is positive and significant, there is a
modest decline in the overall explanatory power of the equation (R^2 falls
from .577 to .566). More importantly, the new size variable alters the
magnitude of the estimated union and concentration impacts. Union membership, which now is the only structural variable measured at the worker
level, increases in estimated impact, while concentration and percent
union, which like the new size variable are measured at the industry level,
decline in estimated impact. Regression 4 returns the sample to blue-collar
workers. The notable consequences are moderate increases in the coefficients on the union membership and (in absolute terms) the union-con-
centration interaction variables.

Stratified Employer Size Estimates

Specialization of work tasks associated with large employers may lead
to greater investments in firm-specific human capital. If so, and if firms
use wage premiums to reduce turnover and thereby protect their investments,[21] this would show up in a regression that controls imperfectly for
firm-specific human capital as an estimated size premium. As a *very* rough
way of examining this issue the sample is stratified according to three
employer size categories (1–99, 100–999, and 1000 +) and wage regressions are estimated for each sample. These results are summarized in
Table 9.

The estimates indicate important structural differences in the wage determination process. Consistent with earlier evidence, the estimated relative wage premium associated with union membership is greater in small
firms (19 percent in the under-100 sample versus only 3 percent in the
1000-and-over sample). Conversely, the estimated impact of percent
union more than doubles moving from the first to second size category,
but then declines slightly with the final size category. The race coefficients

Table 9. Regression Estimates of the Determinants of Log Hourly
Earnings: Sample Stratified by Employer Size
(absolute values of t-statistics are in parentheses)

Explanatory Variable	Employer Size Under 100	Employer Size 100–999	Employer Size 1000 and Over
RACE	−.050	−.004	−.039
	(3.11)	(.18)	(2.92)
SEX	−.234	−.249	−.233
	(20.30)	(17.55)	(23.36)
EDUCATION	.040	−.002	−.007
	(3.54)	(.13)	(.47)
(EDUCATION/10)^2	.018	.146	.184
	(.43)	(2.48)	(3.79)
JOB TENURE	.012	.015	.016
	(3.80)	(3.98)	(5.74)
(JOB TENURE/10)^2	−.026	−.046	−.046
	(4.28)	(7.14)	(10.53)
OTHER EXPERIENCE	.018	.006	.009
	(7.29)	(1.60)	(3.06)
(OTHER EXPERIENCE/10)^2	−.024	−.017	−.021
	(8.58)	(3.52)	(5.69)
(EDUCATION × JOB TENURE)/100	.023	.058	.071
	(1.03)	(2.39)	(4.13)
(EDUCATION × OTHER EXPERIENCE)/100	−.064	.021	−.002
	(4.37)	(.92)	(.11)
UNION MEMBER	.176	.056	.031
	(11.35)	(3.96)	(3.11)
PERCENT UNION	.152	.324	.275
	(2.70)	(5.15)	(8.86)
PART-TIME	−.082	−.048	−.084
	(7.54)	(2.87)	(6.25)
Sample Size	7693	3619	7239
R^2	.439	.507	.530

Note: Data and variables are described in Table 1. Also included as explanatory variables are marital status (3), SMSA (2), region (3), occupation (8), and industry (8) dummies.

Table 10. Regression Estimates of the Determinants of Log Hourly Earnings: Sample Stratified by Union Status and Employer Size
(absolute values of t-statistics in parentheses)

Explanatory Variable	Employer Size Under 100		Employer Size 100–999		Employer Size 1000 +	
	Union	Nonunion	Union	Nonunion	Union	Nonunion
RACE	−.083 (1.94)	−.038 (2.23)	−.037 (5.55)	.004 (.18)	−.031 (1.64)	−.036 (2.02)
SEX	−.280 (7.39)	−.230 (19.01)	−.261 (10.10)	−.265 (15.87)	−.189 (11.79)	−.243 (19.34)
EDUCATION	.070 (2.05)	.036 (2.99)	−.052 (1.70)	−.004 (.20)	−.031 (1.42)	.013 (.69)
$(\text{EDUCATION}/10)^2$	−.082 (.67)	.032 (.71)	.238 (2.28)	.173 (2.42)	.211 (2.78)	.124 (1.87)
JOB TENURE	.014 (1.69)	.010 (2.99)	.008 (1.14)	.016 (3.54)	.002 (.53)	.022 (5.99)
$(\text{JOB TENURE}/10)^2$	−.038 (2.29)	−.026 (3.92)	−.042 (3.54)	−.051 (6.64)	−.023 (3.47)	−.052 (9.40)

OTHER EXPERIENCE	.031 (3.31)	.017 (6.62)	−.012 (1.41)	.009 (1.95)	.007 (1.30)	.008 (2.19)
(OTHER EXPERIENCE/10)^2	−.032 (2.87)	−.023 (7.99)	.004 (.35)	−.019 (3.43)	−.021 (3.23)	−.021 (4.47)
(EDUCATION × JOB TENURE)/100	.024 (.34)	.041 (1.66)	.078 (1.82)	.074 (2.46)	.090 (3.34)	.057 (2.47)
(EDUCATION × OTHER EXPERIENCE)/100	−.147 (2.70)	−.059 (3.87)	.102 (2.13)	.007 (.25)	−.001 (.00)	.007 (.34)
PERCENT UNION	.588 (4.14)	.092 (1.51)	.363 (3.53)	.257 (3.32)	.293 (6.99)	.209 (4.69)
PART-TIME	.047 (1.11)	−.094 (8.29)	.064 (1.77)	−.058 (3.06)	.023 (.98)	−.109 (6.64)
Sample Size	782	6911	963	2656	2520	4719
R^2	.485	.408	.451	.532	.364	.583
SEE	.349	.381	.311	.333	.291	.340

Note: Data and variables are described in table 1. Also included as explanatory variables are marital status (3), SMSA (2), region (3), occupation (8), and industry (8) dummies.

273

indicate that blacks have smaller discounts in large firms, perhaps attributable to government EEO activities since employers with 100 or more
employees are required to file an annual information report with the Equal
Employment Opportunity Commission.

Regarding the argument that size premiums represent an offset against
turnover costs, the variable that is probably the best proxy for firm-specific human capital—the tensure function (tenure, tenure squared, and
education × tenure)—monotonically increases in estimated impact with
size. At sample means the marginal return to tenure increases from 1.2
percent in small firms (1–99) to 1.8 percent in large (1000 +) firms. At the
means and taking account of the interaction terms, the marginal return
to schooling (another potential proxy for firm-specific human capital) increases moderately moving from small to large firms. Before attempting
to draw any tentative conclusions, however, a final effort is made to bring
unionism back into the analysis in a more direct way.

Employer Size and Unionism (Again)

To pursue further the issue of possible cost offsets associated with size
premiums and to take a final look at the interaction between size and
unionism the sample was stratified by both size and union status. The
wage equation estimates are summarized in Table 10. (Separate union and
size stratifications with the sample restricted to manufacturing are summarized in the Appendix.) Focusing on the returns to schooling and tenure
at overall sample means, among union workers the marginal return to
both schooling and job tenure decreases moderately with firm size, while
among nonunion workers the return to schooling increases moderately
and to tenure almost doubles going from small to large firms. Union–
nonunion differences in the marginal returns to schooling and tenure are
respectively modest and nonexistent in small firms (in firms with 1–99
workers the marginal returns to schooling and tenure are respectively 3.3
and 1.2 percent for union workers and 4.0 to 1.2 percent for nonunion
workers) but quite substantial in large firms (in firms with 1000 or more
workers the marginal returns to schooling and tenure are respectively 3.0
and 1.0 for union workers and 5.0 and 2.2 for nonunion workers).

Since the regression specification allows for the possibility of substantial nonlinearities in the estimated relation between wages and schooling/
tenure, there is always the possibility that focusing on marginal returns
at the means may provide an incomplete picture. As an alternative, one
can compare the wage increases associated with an arbitrary change in
the schooling–tenure–other experience vector. For example, the wage
gain associated with going from 10 years schooling, 1 year job tenure,

and 1 year other experience to 14 years schooling, 15 years job tenure, and 10 years other experience is roughly 40 percent for both union and nonunion workers in small firms. In contrast, in large firms the same change implies roughly a 30 percent wage increase for union workers but a 55 percent increase for nonunion workers. Both this result and the above comparison of marginal returns thus suggest that the big differences between union–nonunion schooling and tenure profiles that are commonly observed are found in large but not in small firms.

Regarding the related issue of monitoring costs, several pieces of evidence provide at least indirect support for the hypothesis of increased monitoring costs with size. First there is the relatively strong showing of the plant-level size measures discussed earlier—monitoring difficulties should be more closely related to the actual work situation. Second, another aspect of the wage structure that is interesting to consider in the monitoring context is the dispersion of wages. A very crude indication of wage dispersion is provided by the standard errors of the estimate that are presented in the last line of Table 10. At each size level, dispersion is less in the union sector. Moreover, within sectors dispersion tends to decrease with size. Finally, monitoring difficulties may cause firms to adopt production technologies characterized by more rigid working conditions and greater firm-specific human capital. Oi (1983), for instance, contends that in an attempt to reduce monitoring costs large employers incur greater recruiting and training costs and adopt production technologies characterized by rigid schedules and fixed factor proportions which limit the opportunities for discretionary behavior thereby tending to lower monitoring requirements. Thus earlier discussions of the role of working conditions and premiums to protect investment in firm-specific human capital can also be given a monitoring costs interpretation if one takes a broader view of what underlying forces contribute to heterogeneity across firms.

III. CONCLUSIONS

Numerous studies have found that large employers pay higher wages. This study confirms that result. In a major departure from past analyses, however, the data that are analyzed cover the entire work force and provide worker-specific information on employer size. The results offer not only a better understanding of the true independent role played by employer size in the wage determination process, but also provide better estimates of the wage impacts of more traditional factors such as unionism. The study finds that, other things equal, wages are 13 percent higher when firm size exceeds 1000 and 8 percent higher when it is in the 500–999 range than when it is less than 25.

Regarding the interaction of employer size and union membership in the wage determination process, the study yields three major results. First, the estimated union–nonunion relative wage differential is much greater in small firms. Second, including a worker-specific measure of employer size in the wage equation decreases the estimated wage impact of union membership, but only moderately. Finally, the big differences between union and nonunion schooling and tenure profiles that are commonly observed are found among workers in large firms but not among workers in small firms.

Although the study does not provide a definitive answer to the question of what exactly might be responsible for the observed size–wage relation, it does provide evidence that helps to discriminate at least somewhat among the likely candidates. The results indicate that the estimated size effect is a generalized phenomenon found in nearly all sectors of the economy and that it is large even after explicitly controlling for market structure. It thus appears that the size premium is not primarily attributable to a sharing of rents by employers operating in concentrated product markets. On the other hand, findings that plant size is important independent of firm size and that schooling and job tenure—variables which serve as a proxy for firm-specific skills—have successively larger estimated coefficients with increases in employer size are not inconsistent with arguments that premiums are related to working conditions and that they serve as an offset against other components of the employer's cost function. In the end, however, the issue of what factors are actually responsible for the strong observed positive association between employer size and wages remains very much an open question.

ACKNOWLEDGMENT

I would like to thank Charles Brown, H. Gregg Lewis, William Reece, and Jack Triplett for helpful comments and suggestions. Points of view or opinions stated in this document do not necessarily represent the official position or policy of the Department of Labor.

NOTES

1. In any given month, the CPS sample is composed of a rotating group of addresses. A particular address is in the same 4 consecutive months, out 8, and then in 4 more months. Only rotation groups 4 and 8 are asked the earnings questions. However, individuals in

rotation groups 3 and 7 are asked the earnings questions in the next month's survey. For these individuals, responses to the earnings questions in the June survey are added to their data record. This matching process roughly doubles the number of participants in the May supplement for whom earnings data are available. A description of the CPS, including a detailed account of the basic survey questionnaire and the sampling and interviewing procedures, is contained in U.S. Bureau of the Census (1978).

2. In a recent study of the relationship between the two concepts, Miller (1978) finds that "there is a quite pervasive and strong relationship between size of firm and size of plant within each industry" (p. 867). Experiments conducted using the plant-level size variables are described in Section III.

3. For private sector workers percent union figures are taken from Freeman and Medoff (1979), Table 2, column 3. For government workers the source is "Selected Earnings and Demographic Characteristics of Union Members, 1970," BLS Report 417, 1972.

4. The proportionate wage impact of a dummy variable in a log-linear regression is computed from its estimated coefficient by taking the antilog and subtracting 1.

5. It is probable that the personal characteristics variables do not fully capture all worker-specific differences in productive ability. To the extent that these unmeasured abilities are correlated with employer size, the wage regression will incorrectly attribute a relative wage impact to employer size. The same is true of the estimated wage impact of union membership (Mellow, 1981).

6. If the standard synthetic measure of potential labor force experience, age − years schooling − 6, and its square are the only experience variables, the estimated wage premium associated with the largest employer-size category is 30 percent; the estimated impacts associated with the other size variables increase proportionately.

7. See, for instance, Masters (1969) and Ashenfelter and Johnson (1972). The figures in Table 1 indicate substantial increases in the proportion of workers who are union members with increases in employer size.

8. As noted by Professor Lewis in his Conference remarks, this estimate of the union–nonunion relative wage premium is notably lower than estimates typically obtained using May CPS data. As a result of the Conference discussion, I conducted the following experiment to explore the implications of excluding from the analysis nonrespondents to the employer size questions. A total of 3987 observations met all sample inclusion requirements except response to the employer size question. These observations were assigned a dummy and added to the sample. Reestimating the Table 2, regression 4 specification, the estimated coefficient on the employer size nonresponse dummy is .060. The coefficients on the other employer size variable change only slightly; for instance, the coefficient on EXLG is now .123. The coefficient on UNION MEMBER increases by 1 percentage point to .085, while that on PERCENT UNION increases slightly to .265.

9. Here, arguments run in both directions. Rosen (1969), for instance, contends the impact should be greater because large employers will be in industries where percent unionized (and hence union power) is high. However, included in our wage equation is an explicit measure of percent union. [If percent union is excluded from the regression 7 specification the coefficients on EXLG, UNION MEMBER, and UNION MEMBER X EXLG are: .137 (17.02), .105 (10.56), and − .028 (2.14).] Alternatively, if organizing and servicing costs are higher per worker in small employers, those small employers who are in fact organized will have presented the best opportunities for wage gains. Thus, although unionism will be much less pervasive among small employers it will be found in those presenting the most attractive possibilities for wage gains. This latter proposition is related to arguments emphasizing the simultaneous relation between unionism and wages. See Ashenfelter and Johnson (1972), Johnson (1975), and Duncan and Leigh (1980) for further discussion.

10. For a discussion of the relation between the percent of workers organized in a product

market and the wages received by union and nonunion workers, see Rosen (1969) and Freeman and Medoff (1981). Lewis (1980) stresses the importance of including both union status *and* union coverage variables in estimating the relative wage impact of unionism in wage regressions using data on individual workers.

11.   In interpreting the estimated impact of percent union, a possible complicating factor (examined in the next section) is incomplete control for other industry characteristics such as product market concentration. In addition, the percent union measure is a nationwide average. Some sectors (e.g., construction), however, operate in more restricted product markets. In such instances the nationwide measure may be somewhat inefficient at indicating actual conditions. Also, see Appendix Table A1, which presents union-stratified results with the sample limited to manufacturing.

12.   In an analysis based on establishment data that measure the dollar cost of fringes, Freeman (1981) finds that unionism has a greater proportional impact on total compensation than on wages.

13.   A compensating payment for adverse working conditions is also consistent with Brown and Medoff's (1978) finding of a positive union productivity effect.

14.   In addition to altering specification of the explanatory vector, Duncan and Stafford use detailed information on work breaks and training activities to construct adjusted wage variables.

15.   One could speculate that sample composition might account for part of the difference. Duncan and Stafford analyze blue-collar workers in manufacturing, while our sample is economywide. If the sample is limited to blue-collar workers in manufacturing, the coefficients on UNION MEMBER and PERCENT UNION in a specification identical to regression 5 of Table 2 are .093 (8.06) and .298 (9.35). If the plant-level size measures are then added to the equation, the estimated coefficients decline to .070 (6.07) and .248 (7.85), respectively.

16.   See Rees (1961) or Levinson (1967) for an extensive discussion of the interaction between unionism and market structure in the determination of wages.

17.   For durable goods manufacturing, the intermediate size variables are all insignificant, intermittently so for the other industry groups. Additionally, the 500–999 cells are typically quite small. Consequently, although the discussion formally pertains to the comparison between the largest size group and the excluded group, it is in fact frequently similar to what would be found in a direct estimation of the differential wage effect between large and small firms, with 1000 employees serving as the delimiting size criteria.

18.   This conslusion is also supported by the insensitivity of estimated size impacts to the inclusion of industry dummies in the earlier Table 2 regressions.

19.   Constructed from information in U.S. Bureau of the Census (1972), Table 5. Reported four-digit SIC concentration ratios were weighted by the value of industry shipments to obtain three-digit measures. Three-digit industry is the most detailed breakdown available with CPS data.

20.   Constructed from information contained in U.S. Bureau of the Census (1972), Table 5. This variable is included by Freeman and Medoff (1981) in wage regressions using CPS data with similar results.

21.   For a general discussion of the economic gains to the employer from wage premiums that serve to offset the higher wage costs, see Oi (1962) and Reynolds (1978), pp. 187–8. Regarding the impact of size wage premiums on turnover, our conclusion implicitly assumes that increases in firm-specific skills and advertising economies associated with size result in a given wage premium providing a greater cost offset there than in small firms. Alternatively, if personnel costs are an increasing function of average monthly turnover and its variance small firms may have a greater incentive to offer wage premiums because it would otherwise be necessary to "overstaff" the personnel office.

APPENDIX:
ADDITIONAL ESTIMATES WITH SAMPLE RESTRICTED TO MANUFACTURING

Table A1. Regression Estimates of the Determinants of Log Hourly Earnings in Manufacturing: Union and Nonunion Samples (absolute values of t-statistics are in parentheses)

	Means			
Explanatory Variable	*Union Sample*	*Nonunion Sample*	*Union Sample*	*Nonunion Sample*
Employer Size:				
SMALL (25–99)	.08	.15	−.157 (3.45)	.001 (.00)
MED (100–499)	.13	.16	−.156 (3.63)	.043 (1.91)
LG (500–999)	.05	.06	−.155 (3.15)	.095 (3.24)
XLG (1000+)	.71	.51	−.030 (.75)	.140 (6.81)
RACE	.11	.09	−.087 (3.66)	−.043 (2.10)
SEX	.22	.36	−.230 (12.04)	−.276 (18.89)
EDUCATION	11.23	12.39	.0003 (.00)	.008 (.47)
(EDUCATION/10^2)	1.32	1.61	.178 (1.99)	.104 (1.71)
JOB TENURE	10.76	7.37	.017 (3.68)	.013 (3.59)
(JOB TENURE/10)^2	2.10	1.32	−.026 (3.29)	−.037 (6.40)
OTHER EXPERIENCE	11.45	11.34	.003 (.58)	.0004 (.09)
(OTHER EXPERIENCE/10)^2	2.37	2.51	−.004 (.54)	−.006 (1.43)
(EDUCATION × JOB TENURE)/100	1.18	.92	−.037 (1.12)	.081 (3.37)
(EDUCATION × OTHER EXPERIENCE)/100	1.18	1.30	−.014 (.37)	.038 (1.60)
PERCENT UNION	.44	.34	.341 (5.91)	.121 (2.80)

(*continued*)

279

	Means			
Explanatory Variable	Union Sample	Nonunion Sample	Union Sample	Nonunion Sample
CON RATIO	.40	.34	.017 (.38)	.190 (2.60)
PART-TIME	.03	.06	.009 (.21)	−.065 (2.60)
Sample Size			1480	2865
R^2			.440	.627

Note: Data and variables are described in table 1. Also included as explanatory variables are marital status (3), SMSA (2), region (3), and occupation (8) dummies.

Table A2. Regression Estimates of the Determinants of Log Hourly Earnings In Manufacturing: Sample Stratified by Employer Size (absolute values of t-statistics are in parentheses)

Explanatory Variable	Employer Size Under 100	Employer 100–999	Employer Size 1000 and Over
RACE	−.114 (3.19)	−.083 (2.31)	−.042 (2.12)
SEX	−.317 (11.57)	−.268 (11.52)	−.248 (15.94)
EDUCATION	.005 (.17)	−.004 (.15)	−.042 (2.00)
$(EDUCATION/10)^2$	.144 (1.40)	.168 (1.76)	.269 (3.73)
JOB TENURE	.008 (1.15)	.015 (2.55)	.010 (2.58)
$(JOB\ TENURE/10)^2$	−.032 (2.42)	−.044 (4.61)	−.033 (5.91)
OTHER EXPERIENCE	.008 (1.20)	−.003 (.56)	−.003 (.57)
$(OTHER\ EXPERIENCE/10)^2$	−.010 (1.33)	−.0005 (.05)	−.007 (1.18)
(EDUCATION × JOB TENURE)/100	.099 (1.82)	.060 (1.65)	.081 (3.27)
(EDUCATION × OTHER EXPERIENCE)/100	−.020 (.49)	.059 (1.55)	.052 (1.70)

(continued)

280

Table A2. (*Continued*)

Explanatory Variable	Employer Size Under 100	Employer 100–999	Employer Size 1000 and Over
UNION MEMBER	.148	.110	.105
	(2.55)	(2.30)	(3.61)
PERCENT UNION	−.100	.264	.213
	(.84)	(3.07)	(5.12)
CON RATIO	.219	−.065	.175
	(1.79)	(.63)	(3.30)
CON RATIO × UNION MEMBER	.014	−.211	−.163
	(.08)	(1.53)	(2.65)
ln (average value of shipments)	−.002	.012	.023
	(.09)	(.84)	(3.40)
PART-TIME	−.059	−.044	−.023
	(1.76)	(.99)	(.60)
Sample Size	928	905	2512
R²	.503	.610	.535

Note: Data and variables are described in table 1. Also included as explanatory variable are marital status (3), SMSA (2), region (3), and occupation (8) dummies.

REFERENCES

Ashenfelter, Orley, and George E. Johnson (1972), "Unionism, Relative Wages and Labor Quality in U.S. Manufacturing Industries." *International Economic Review* 13(October):488–508.

Bloch, Farrell E., and Mark S. Kuskin (1978), "Wage Determination in the Union and Nonunion Sectors." *Industrial and Labor Relations Review* 31(January):183–192.

Brown, Charles, and James L. Medoff (1978), "Trade Unions in the Production Process." *Journal of Political Economy* 86(June):355–378.

Duncan, Greg J., and Frank P. Stafford (1980), "Do Union Members Receive Compensating Wage Differentials?" *American Economic Review* 70(June):355–371.

Duncan, Gregory M., and Duane E. Leigh (1980), "Wage Determination in the Union and Nonunion Sectors: A Sample Selectivity Approach." *Industrial and Labor Relations Review* 34(October):24–34.

Freeman, Richard B. (1981), "The Effect of Unionism on Fringe Benefits." *Industrial and Labor Relations Review* 34(July):489–509.

Freeman, Richard B., and James L. Medoff (1979), "New Estimates of Private Sector Unionism in the United States." *Industrial and Labor Relations Review* 32(January): 143–174.

——— (forthcoming), "The Impact of the Percent Organized on Union and Nonunion Wages." *Review of Economics and Statistics*, 63(November):561–572.

Haworth, Charles T., and Carol Jean Reuther (1980), "Industrial Concentration and Interindustry Wage Determination." *Review of Economics and Statistics* 60(February):85–95.

Johnson, George E. (1975), "Economic Analysis of Trade Unionism." *American Economic Review* 65(May):23–28.

Lester, Richard (1967), "Pay Differentials by Size of Establishment." *Industrial Relations* (October):57–67.

Levinson, Harold M. (1967), "Unionism, Concentration and Wage Changes: Toward A Unified Theory." *Industrial and Labor Relations Review* 20(January):198–205.

Lewis, H. Gregg (1963), *Unionism and Relative Wages in the United States*. Chicago: University of Chicago Press.

——— (1980), "Interpreting Unionism Coefficients in Wage Equations." Duke University, mimeograph.

Masters, Stanley. (1969), "Wages and Plant Size: An Interindustry Analysis." *Review of Economics and Statistics* 51(August):341–345.

Mellow, Wesley (1981), "Unionism and Wages: A Longitudinal Analysis." *Review of Economics and Statistics* 63(February):43–52.

Miller, Edward M. (1978), "Size of Firm and Size of Plant." *Southern Economic Journal* 44(April):861–872.

Oi, Walter (1962), "Labor as a Quasi-Fixed Factor." *Journal of Political Economy* 70(December):538–555.

——— (1983), "The Fixed Employment Costs of Specialized Labor." In Jack E. Triplett (ed.), *The Measurement of Labor Cost*. Conference on Research in Income and Wealth, Studies in Income and Wealth, Vol. 48. Chicago: University of Chicago Press for the National Bureau of Economic Research.

Parsley, C. J. (1980), "Labor Union Effects on Wage Gains: A Survey of Recent Literature." *Journal of Economic Literature* 43(March):1–32.

Pugel, Thomas A. (1980), "Profitability, Concentration and the Interindustry Variation in Wages." *Review of Economics and Statistics* 62(May):248–253.

Rees, Albert (1961), "Union Wage Gains and Enterprise Monopoly." In *Essays on Industrial Relations Research-Problems and Prospects*. Detroit: Wayne State University Press.

Rees, Albert, and George P. Schultz (1970), *Workers and Wages in Urban Labor Markets*. Chicago: The University of Chicago Press.

Reynolds, Lloyd G. (1978), *Labor Economics and Labor Relations*, 7th ed. Englewood Cliffs, N.J.: Prentice-Hall.

Rosen, Sherwin (1970), "Unionism and the Occupational Wage Structure in the United States." *International Economic Review* 11(June):269–286.

——— (1971), "Trade Union Power, Threat Effects and the Extent of Organization." *Review of Economic Studies* (August):185–196.

Stigler, George J. (1962), "Information in the Labor Market." *Journal of Political Economy* Supplement(October):94–105.

U.S. Bureau of the Census (1973), *1972 Census of Manufactures, Special Report Series*. Washington, D.C.: U.S. Government Printing Office.

——— (1978), "The Current Population Survey." Technical Analysis Paper No. 40.

Weiss, Leonard W. (1966), "Concentration and Labor Earnings." *American Economic Review* 56(March):96–117.

DISCUSSION

H. Gregg Lewis

I. COMMENTS ON MINCER'S PAPER

For some time I have been collecting and reviewing post-1963 papers that contain estimates of union–nonunion relative wage differentials in the United States. The number of these papers is large, certainly well over 100 and perhaps as many as 200 by the end of this year. The bulk of the estimates come from wage *level* equations fitted by ordinary least squares (OLS) to individualworker (micro) data at a given date or period on wages, union status, and other variables. The chief sources of these data are the 1967 Survey of Economic Opportunity (SEO), the May Current Population Surveys (CPS), the National Longitudinal Surveys (NLS), the Panel Study of Income Dynamics (PSID), and other Michigan surveys.

Among wage equations fitted to data with broad coverage of wage and salary workers few of these micro, OLS, level estimates (in natural logarithmic units) are below .10 and few above .25 with a central tendency near the middle of this range. I suspect that when I have completed my attempt to reconcile differences among these estimates, their dispersion

New Approaches to Labor Unions.
Research in Labor Economics, Supplement 2, pages 283–290.
Copyright © 1983 by JAI Press Inc.
All rights of reproduction in any form reserved.
ISBN: 0-89232-265-9

will be considerably smaller than these numbers may suggest. There is also a strong suggestion in these studies that the union–nonunion differential is higher for workers with characteristics associated with low wages than for their opposites.

The selection process determining the union status of individual workers surely is not a random one. Furthermore there can be no doubt that *all* of the OLS fitted wage equations have left out wage-determining variables. Thus there are good grounds for suspecting that these OLS level estimates are not free of bias. My priors are that typically the bias is upward and I have a hunch that generally the higher the estimate, the greater its upward bias. Let a union through collective bargaining with an employer fix a wage for a given worker quality and quality of working conditions than otherwise would be obtained. The higher wage provides the employer both the opportunity (more job applicants) and the incentive (higher labor cost) to select higher-quality workers.

The subject has not suffered from being neglected by econometricians. We now have a substantial number of papers purporting to deal with the problem of selectivity bias in the OLS level estimates. I divide them into two broad categories of which the first I call "simultaneous equations" papers which cover two headings in Freeman and Medoff's Table 3, namely "Simultaneous Equations Bias" and "Sample Selection Bias." Because Freeman and Medoff discuss most of these papers, I will be brief. The resulting estimates range from outlandishly low (negative) to outlandishly high, are more dispersed than the estimates they were designed to correct, and appear to be sensitive to equation specification. These papers have not shaken me from my judgment that the OLS level estimates are upward-biased, despite the contrary suggestion in some of them. Nor do I believe that the OLS level estimates are so seriously upward biased that in truth the union–nonunion differential is negative, though that is suggested in some other of these papers. Instead, I have come to the conclusion that we know too little about union status selection to model the "simultaneous equations" reliably.

The second set of papers attempting to correct for the biases in OLS level estimates exploits the panel (before-and-after) feature of the NLS, PSID, and May CPS. Freeman and Medoff have stated well the virtues of panel data and I won't repeat their argument here. However, neither they nor Mincer have summarized the results of the panel studies, so I will take a few minutes to do so.

PSID Studies

1. Duncan (1977)
    1970–71 to 1973–74, male household heads.
    Level estimate (1970–71): .21.
    Panel estimate (1973–74 minus 1970–71): .11.

2. Duncan (1979)

   1972, 1977, male household heads, 23–38 years of age in 1972.
   Level estimate not reported but probably >.2.
   Panel estimate: .13–.14.

3. Kenny (1978)

   1970–74, male household heads.
   Level estimate not reported.
   Panel estimate .08.

4. Raisian (1981)

   1967–77, male household heads.
   Level estimate: .20–.21 from other papers by him.
   Panel estimate: .05–.06.

5. Moore and Raisian (1981)

   1967–77, male household heads.
   Level estimate: .20.
   Panel estimate: .07.

NLS Studies

6. Brown (1980)

   1966–71, 1973, young men.
   Level estimate: .13.
   Panel estimate: .08.

7. Chamberlain (1978)

   1969–71, young men.
   Level estimate (1971): .19.
   Panel estimate: .11–.12.

8. Chamberlain (1981)

   1969–1971, young men.
   Level estimate: .19.
   Panel estimate: .11.

CPS Studies

9. Mellow (1981)

   1974–75, 1977–78, wage and salary workers.
   Level estimate: .19 for 1977, .18 for 1978.
   Panel estimate: .08 for 1974–75, .06–.08 for 1977–78.

All of these estimates of the union–nonunion wage differential are in log-natural units.[1]

Although level estimates comparable to the panel estimates are not reported in all nine of these papers, I think that it is safe to say that all nine agree that the panel estimates are substantially below corresponding level estimates and suggest that the economywide mean union–nonunion relative wage differential is in the range .05–.15. This is very comforting for me. My judgment that the level estimates are upward-biased is supported. (More than that, these findings indicate that my 1963 estimate of .10–.15 for the overall mean differential in 1958 is not as far out of the ballpark as some critics would have it.)

I turn to Mincer's panel estimates of the union–nonunion wage differential presented in Sections II and III of his paper. For me the key feature in his estimates is his classification of workers by their interfirm mobility status (as well as by union status) and among movers by quit vs. layoff. Consider first his findings from the PSID reported in Tables 1, 3, 5, and A4. For purposes of comparison, I first note that the *level* estimates of the union–nonunion differential implied by his Tables 1 and 5 are:

All ages: .17
<30: .22
≥30: .15.

What are the corresponding panel estimates? That depends on how one interprets Tables 3, 5, and A4. First suppose that union status *change* is accurately reported in the PSID and that Mincer had fitted wage equations with only the three right-hand unionism variables:

$$\Delta U^*M, \quad \Delta U^*S, \quad \text{and } U^*M,$$

where M and S are dummies for movers and stayers, respectively; $\Delta U = 1$ for joiners (U_{01}); $\Delta U = -1$ for leavers; $\Delta U = 0$ otherwise; and $U = 1$ for the U_{00} and U_{11} groups (workers who did not report a change in union status). Then the coefficient of ΔU^*S estimates the union–nonunion differential for stayers, the coefficient of ΔU^*M minus that for U^*M is the corresponding estimate for movers. From Table 3, I have calculated that these estimates are:

	All Ages	<30	≥30
Movers	.01	.00	.01
Stayers	.02	.04	.01
Both	.02	.03	.01

the corresponding figures implied by Table 5 are close to these. These estimates do not ignore any of the data.

In contrast, Mincer's estimates are based only on the coefficients for U_{01} (joiners) and U_{00} (nonunion workers who did not change union status) for *movers*, ignoring the stayers and the union leavers. His estimates of the union–nonunion differential are:

	All Ages	<30	≥30
Table 5	.097	.102	.137
Table 3	.047	.059	.033

There are good grounds, I think, for suspecting that union status change suffers seriously from reporting error among stayers in the PSID. Contrary to what I would expect if there were no reporting errors, there were $2\frac{1}{2}$ times as many union status changers who were stayers than status changers who were movers. Furthermore, the coefficients for stayers in Tables 3 and 5 are consistent with the view that U_{01} and U_{10} are seriously misreported.

But why ignore union leavers (U_{10}) among the PSID movers? There are two good reasons for doing so. First, the year 1 coefficients in Table 5 do not suggest that these workers were unionized in year 1. Second, of 12 estimates of the union–nonunion differential calculated for mover-leavers only one was positive and barely so at that. (Furthermore, the estimates are not appreciably better when the mover-leavers are classified by quit vs. layoff or by industry change.)

Thus I do not quarrel with Mincer's ignoring the stayers and the mover-leavers in the PSID data. But why compare U_{01} only with U_{00} among movers? There are also the U_{11}, the unionized workers who did not change status. I have combined U_{00} and U_{11} and then subtracted their average wage growth from that for U_{01}:

	All Ages	<30	≥30
Table 5	.087	.099	.119
Table 3	.044	.061	.020

These all-ages estimates are close to the panel estimates in the Duncan (1977), Kenny, Raisian, and Moore, and Raisian studies.

I turn now to consider briefly Mincer's estimates from the NLS data based on the collective bargaining coverage (CB) definition of union status. The level estimates calculated from Table 4 are:

	Young	Old
1969	.21	.05
1971	.22	.08

The corresponding panel estimates from Tables 2 and 4 that ignore none of the unionism coefficients are:

	Young	Old
Table 2	.08	.03
Table 4	.07	.03

Mincer's panel estimates which are based only on the coefficients for U_{01} and U_{00} among movers are:

	Young	Old
Table 2	.07	.155
Table 4	.07	.12

where the figures for the older men have little statistical reliability. There is clearly less strong a case for ignoring the stayers and the mover-leavers in the NLS data for young men than in the PSID data. The unreliability of Mincer's estimates for the older men stems in part from the small sample (12 or 13 persons) who were mover-joiners.

Thus, except possibly for the NLS older men, Mincer's paper supports the findings of earlier panel studies: Estimates of the union–nonunion wage differential from micro, OLS, level wage equations contain a substantial upward bias. However, I am not yet convinced that the before-and-after estimates from panel data are not biased downward. Basically the panel studies estimate the differential by comparing the wage growth of workers who changed union status with that of workers who did not. That the fraction of the relatively few status changers who report status change without reporting employer change is large, especially in the PSID, suggests serious misreporting of status change and likely downward bias in panel estimates. Mincer's paper gives some support to this view and suggests ignoring the stayers, which I am reluctant to do in general.

But even if the stayers are ignored, there remain important possibilities not only of reporting error, but also of selectivity bias. Movers are likely to be a highly select group and among them the mover-status changers. To what groups in the population do the Mincer estimates of union–nonunion wage differentials pertain? For example, do his panel estimates for young white male wage and salary workers in the NLS panel pertain to the population from which the NLS sample was drawn or to a portion of this population for which the differential is well below average?

II. COMMENTS ON MELLOW'S PAPER

This paper started out as BLS Working Paper 116, April 1981, which Mellow sent to me soon after it was issued. We have had a continuing and not yet finished correspondence since then. He has given me much time as well as hundreds of pages of computer printouts much of which does not appear in his paper. The present version of the paper, of course, has much in common with that of April, though all of the statistical tables are different at least in terms of the numbers they contain.

I have sent comments on the paper to Mellow and for the most part I do not repeat them. Instead I will report what I have learned from our interchange including information from both versions of the paper, his letters to me, and the computer printouts.

1. Obviously I have learned that there are substantial employer-size and plant-size differentials: the larger the plant or firm, the higher the relative wage. This is not a new finding, but it is the first real evidence that I know of coming from micro data. But why should there be such a differential? I doubt that it has anything to do with monopoly. Is it a compensatory differential for higher labor quality? For inferior working conditions?

2. Introducing employer or plant size or both as right-hand variables in the wage equation lowers the estimated union–nonunion differential (from wage equations with a substantial set of right-hand variables) by about 2 percentage points. This is the first evidence I have seen on this question. (I do not regard 2 points as negligible.)

3. The estimated union–nonunion differential declines with employer size from about .15 to .20 for firms with <100 employees to below .05 for firms with 1000 or more employees. In a sense this finding, though new, is not surprising. Unions tend to raise *and flatten* most profiles. This finding is interesting in another context. Most studies from which estimates of union–nonunion differentials by industry may be derived show a considerably below average differential in manufacturing. Most of this difference disappears when employer size is held constant.

4. Introducing percent unionized by industry as a control variable lowers the estimated mean union–nonunion differential by about 2 points. This confirms a finding made in only a few other studies.

5. Most studies that provide separate estimates of the union–nonunion differential by color show that for blacks higher than that for whites. Not so in Mellow's study; the difference is reversed, though not strongly. Why so?

6. The overall mean union–nonunion differential that I have calculated from Mellow's equations range from .075 to .097. These are *not* panel estimates, but cross-section estimates. They are the lowest cross-

section estimates from micro data with broad worker coverage that I have seen. From Mellow's 1981 panel study I calculated cross-section estimates for 1977 of .19 and for 1978 of .18. Why are his 1979 estimates so low? Part of the explanation is the expanded set of right-hand variables in the 1979 wage equations—employer size, percent unionized, job tenure, and a full quadratic in schooling, tenure, and other experience. Across equation comparisons indicate that absent these additional variables, the estimated differential would have been about .13–.14 in 1979, still substantially below typical estimates from the May CPS in earlier years of 1970s. Could it have been nonresponse? Mellow's 1979 coverage was wage and salary workers who reported answers to new questions on tenure, employer, and plant size. Were there an appreciable number of workers who did not answer these new questions? Were they somewhat high union–nonunion differential workers?[2]

6. These last questions lead to a general question. Coverage statements explicitly or implicitly state that nonrespondents to questions whose answers are required in fitting wage equations are excluded. What are the characteristics of the nonrespondents? What biases are suggested by the answer to the preceding question?

7. Desire for measurement accuracy may get you into trouble. One of the real problems facing students of wages is that of getting least moderately accurate data on the wage itself. It is easy to argue, for example, with the May CPS data that the wage per hour reported by those paid by the hour is probably more accurate a measure of the wage for these workers than is obtained by asking them for their usual weekly earnings and usual weekly hours and dividing the first by the second. (Indeed, what does "usual" in this context mean?) It then seems like a small step to restrict the sample to those paid by the hour who reported their hourly wage. But it isn't. Evidence: When Mellow did this, quite unintentionally to be sure, the estimated union–nonunion differential rose from .075 (usual hourly earnings) to .174, which is not exactly a small difference.

NOTES

1. All of the studies outlined, except the following three, are listed in Mincer's references.

Chamberlain, Gary (1981), "Multivariate Regression Models for Panel Data." Mimeograph, April.
Duncan, Greg J. (1977), in *Five Thousand American Families,* Vol. VI.
Moore, William J., and John Raisian (1981), "Unionism and Wage Rates in the Public and Private Sectors: A Comparative Time-Series Analysis." Mimeograph, October.

2. Both of these questions have affirmative answers. Exclusion of nonrespondents lowered Mellow's estimates of the union-nonunion differential by perhaps as much as .01.

PART IV

ARE NEW APPROACHES TO

LABOR UNIONS NEEDED?

THE IMPACT OF COLLECTIVE BARGAINING:

CAN THE NEW FACTS BE EXPLAINED BY MONOPOLY UNIONISM?

R. B. Freeman and J. L. Medoff

ABSTRACT

In this paper we focus our attention on the question of whether union–nonunion differences in nonwage outcomes can be explained in terms of standard price-theoretic responses to union wage effects, as opposed to the real effect of unionism on economic behavior.

We reach three basic conclusions. First, unions and collective bargaining have real economic effects on diverse nonwage variables which cannot be explained either in terms of price-theoretic responses to union wage effects or be attributed to the poor quality of econometric "experiments." Second, we find that while sensitivity analyses of single-equation results and longitudinal experiments provide valuable checks on cross-sectional findings,

New Approaches to Labor Unions.
Research in Labor Economics, Supplement 2, pages 293–332.
Copyright © 1983 by JAI Press Inc.
All rights of reproduction in any form reserved.
ISBN: 0-89232-265-9

multiple-equations approaches produce results which are too sensitive to small changes in models or samples to help resolve the questions of concern. Finally, on the basis of these findings we conclude that the search for an understanding of what unions do requires more than the standard price-theoretic "monopoly" model of unionism. New (and/or old) perspectives based on institutional or industrial relations realities, contractarian or property rights theories, or other potential sources of creative views are also needed.

The recent outpouring of empirical studies on the impact of collective bargaining on the economy has provided us with a large body of new evidence regarding differences between union and nonunion workers and union and nonunion enterprises along many dimensions other than rates of pay.

Can the observed union–nonunion differences in nonwage outcomes be explained primarily in terms of preunion characteristics of firms or individuals? Can the observed differences be explained as a response to the effect of unions on wages? Or does the new evidence suggest that unions have an important impact on economic performance through routes ignored in the standard monopoly model of the institution?

The need for and value of new theories of trade unionism depend on the answers to these questions.

In our initial review of recent literature[1] we focused largely on the question of whether union–nonunion differences obtained in cross-section studies were illusions, which primarily reflected the poor quality of our econometric "experiments." In this paper we wish to focus on the question of whether union–nonunion differences in nonwage outcomes can, in fact, be explained in terms of standard price-theoretic responses to real wage effects, as opposed to the real effect of unionism on economic behavior.

The paper is divided into four sections. Section I summarizes the recent empirical findings about union–nonunion differences in nonwage outcomes on which the interpretative debate focuses. The second section examines the results of econometric probes designed to assess whether the effects set out in Section I are best interpreted as illusory due to innate differences between union–nonunion workers or firms, as real for price-theoretic reasons, or as real for reasons that go beyond standard price theory. The final section lays out our conclusions regarding the implications of the evidence for the standard price-theoretic or monopoly model of unionism as opposed to other perspectives, both old and new.

We reach three basic conclusions:

(1) Unions and collective bargaining have real economic effects on diverse nonwage variables which cannot be explained either in terms of

price-theoretic responses to union wage effects or as illusions, attributable to the poor quality of our econometric "experiments."

(2)   Some econometric techniques for probing union–nonunion differences provide useful insights into the real effects of unions while others do not. In particular, we find that sensitivity analyses of single-equation results and longitudinal experiments provide valuable checks on cross-sectional findings while multiple-equations approaches produce results which are much too sensitive to small changes in models or samples to help resolve the questions of concern.

(3)   On the basis of these findings we conclude that the search for an understanding of what unions do requires more than the standard price-theoretic "monopoly" model of unionism. New (and/or old) perspectives based on institutional or industrial relations realities, contractarian or property rights theories, or other potential sources of creative views are also needed.

I.   THE EVIDENCE IN QUESTION

It is important at the outset to lay out the union–nonunion differences in economic variables on which modern work has focused. Accordingly, this section briefly summarizes the central findings of recent research, including for purposes of comparison and ensuing analysis results on wages as well as nonwage outcomes. As a guide to the discussion, Table 1 gives the central findings of these studies categorized by the following substantive issues: the level and structure of compensation; internal and external mobility; work rules, (management) flexibility, and (employee) satisfaction; and inputs, productivity, and profits. The reader will notice that our set of issues is not exhaustive. We have, in particular, neglected such important topics as the internal operation of unions, strikes, and the survival of the organization itself, in part because these topics do not lend themselves to the union–nonunion comparisons which form the bulk of research on the topics in the table. In addition, we concentrate exclusively on the private sector. While, as noted, we have no pretense that our set of issues is all-encompassing and while our listing of relevant references is undoubtedly incomplete, we believe that the table provides a reasonably accurate picture of the empirical results in question.

A.   The Level and Structure of Compensation

The first and probably still the most widely studied issue is the differential between union and nonunion wages. The early literature on this differential was summarized in Lewis's influential 1963 book, *Unionism and Relative Wages in the United States*. Since the publication of Lewis's book, a number of new sources of individual-level data (such as the May

Table 1. Recent Evidence on Union/Nonunion Differences Based on Cross-Sectional Data

Variable (Price Theoretic Control)	Finding	Partial Listing of Relevant References
Level and Structure of Compensation		
Wage Rates	All else (measurable) the same, union/nonunion hourly wage differential is between 10% and 20%.	Ashenfelter (1976), Freeman & Medoff (1981a), Lewis (1980), Mellow (1981a), Oaxaca (1975), Welch (1980).
Cyclical Responsiveness of Wage Rates	Union wages are less responsive to cyclical variation in market conditions than are nonunion wages.	Ashenfelter (1976), Hamermesh (1972), Johnson (1981), Lewis (1963), Medoff (1979), Medoff and Mitchel (1980a, 1980b), Fay (in process), Parson (1968), Raisian (1979).
Determinants of Compensation Differential	Other things equal, the union compensation advantage is higher the greater the percentage of a market's workers who are organized. The effects of market concentration on wage differentials is unclear. The differentials appear to be very large in some regulated markets. They appear to decline as firm size increases.	Dalton & Ford (1977), Donsimoni (1978), Ehrenberg (1979), Freeman & Medoff (1981a), Hayden (1977), Hendricks (1975), Kahn (1978), Kochan (1980), Lee (1978), Mellow (1981b), Weiss (1966).
Fringes (Wages or total compensation held fixed)	All else the same, union/nonunion hourly fringe differential is between 20% and 30%. The fringe share of compensation is higher at a given level of compensation.	Duncan (1976), Freeman (1981), Goldstein & Pauly (1976), Leigh (1979), Solnick (1978), Viscusi (1980).
Wage Dispersion	Wage inequality is much lower among union members than among comparable nonmembers and total wage dispersion appears to be lowered by unionism.	Freeman (1980c, forthcoming), Hyclak (1979–1980), Plotnick (1981).
Wage Structure	Wage differentials between workers who are different in terms of race, age, service, skill level, and education appear to be lower under collective bargaining.	Ashenfelter (1976), Bloch & Kuskin (1978), Johnson & Youmans (1971), Kiefer & Smith (1977), Leigh (1978), Pfeffer & Ross (1980), Schoeplein (1977), Shapiro (1978).

Table 1. (Continued)

Variable (Price Theoretic Control)	Finding	Partial Listing of Relevant References
Internal & External Mobility		
Promotions (Wages and "labor quality" held fixed)	Seniority independent of productivity is rewarded substantially more in promotion decisions among union members than among otherwise comparable nonunion employees.	Halasz (1980), Medoff & Abraham (1980b, 1981b), Yanker (1980).
Quits (Wages and "labor quality" held fixed)	The quit rate is much lower for unionized workers than for similar workers who are nonunion.	Blau & Kahn (1981), Block (1978a), Farber (OLS Results 1979), Freeman (1976, 1980a, 1980b), Kahn (1977), Leigh (1979).
Temporary layoffs (Wages and "labor quality" held fixed)	There is much more cyclical labor adjustment through temporary layoffs in unionized manufacturing firms than in otherwise comparable firms that are nonunion.	Blau & Kahn (1981), Medoff (1979).
Terminations (Wages and "labor quality" held fixed)	Terminations are more likely to be on a last-in-first-out basis among union employees, *ceteris paribus*.	Blau & Kahn (1981), Medoff & Abraham (1981a, 1981b).
Work Rules, Flexibility and Satisfaction		
Rules (Wages held fixed)	There are important differences in the prevalence and nature of various rules in union and nonunion settings, such as those stipulating the role of company service and the way grievances are to be handled. Union work places appear to be run more by rules, with more rigidity in the scheduling of hours and less worker flexibility.	Freeman (1980a), Kochan & Bloch (1977), Kochan & Helfman (1977), Medoff & Abraham (1981b).
Management Practices	Management in unionized cement firms appears to be more professional (less paternalistic or authoritarian), more	Clark (1980a).

(continued)

297

Table 1.   (Continued)

Variable (Price Theoretic Control)	Finding	Partial Listing of Relevant References
	standards oriented, and more in touch with work performance than management in similar nonunion firms.	
Management Flexibility (Factor prices held fixed)	Management in unionized manufacturing firms appears less able to substitute nonproduction worker hours for production worker hours but seems no less able to substitute capital for production labor than similarly situated nonunion management.	Freeman & Medoff (forthcoming b).
Satisfaction with Jobs Overall (Wages held fixed)	The stated level of overall job satisfaction is lower, but the wage gain required to induce a job change is higher for union members than for otherwise comparable employees who are not members.	Borjas (1979), Freeman (1976, 1978a), Kochan & Helfman (1979), Mandelbaum (1980).
Evaluation of Rules and Conditions (Wages held fixed, where appropriate)	Unionized workers state that they are more satisfied with their wages and fringes, less satisfied with their supervision, and less satisfied with their working conditions than nonunion workers. The extent to which stated job security grows with tenure is substantially greater under unionism. While the probability of viewing promotions as fair declines with service among nonunion employees, it increases among union members.	Duncan & Stafford (1980), Freeman & Medoff (1982), Kochan & Helfman (1979), Viscusi (1980).
Inputs, Productivity, and Profits		
Pre-firm Quality of Work Force	Other things equal, workers in unionized firms tend to have more "human capital".	Allen (1979), Brown & Medoff (1978), Farber (1979), Frantz (1976), Kahn (1979), Kalachek & Raines (1980).

Table 1.   (Continued)

Variable (Price Theoretic Control)	Finding	Partial Listing of Relevant References
Capital Intensity (Wages held fixed)	Unionized firms in manufacturing, construction, and underground bituminous coal appear to have higher capital–labor ratios than similar nonunion enterprises.	Allen (1979), Brown & Medoff (1978), Clark (1980b), Connerton, Freeman & Medoff (1979), Frantz (1976).
Productivity (Capital intensity and "labor quality" held fixed)	In manufacturing and construction and in the underground bituminous coal industry in nonturbulent times, unionized enterprises appear to have greater productivity than those that are nonunion, all else equal. In underground coal, productivity appeared to be lower under unionism in the turbulent years around 1975.	Allen (1979), Brown & Medoff (1978), Connerton, Freeman & Medoff (1979), Frantz (1976).
Input, Productivity, Profits (continued)		
Profitability (Industry, type of business held fixed)	The rate of profit per unit of capital appears to be lower under unionism.	Brown & Medoff (1978), Clark (forthcoming), Frantz (1976), Freeman & Medoff (forthcoming, b), Hayden.

Current Population Survey—CPS) which permit estimation of the wages effect have become available. With microdata of this kind, it is possible to compare the wages of union and nonunion workers with similar demographic characteristics who are also in the same detailed industry and/ or occupation. As Johnson (1975) has reviewed some of this work, our summary will be brief. The post-Lewis micro data estimates (derived with ordinary least squares—OLS) have generally found wage differentials noticeably above the 10–15 percent range given in Lewis's book. However, the analyses that have looked within more detailed cells, especially those with industry as a dimension, have tended to yield estimated differentials near the top end of the 10–15 percent range. This makes very good sense given that the studies summarized by Lewis normally examined a very narrowly defined group of workers. Another form of data which has been used in recent studies pertains to individual establishments. These data (from surveys such as the Employer Expenditures for Employee Compensation Survey—EEC) permit the estimation of wage effects for production or nonproduction workers at firms of the same size within the same three-digit Standard Industrial Classification (SIC) industry. Estimates using these data are quantitatively closer to those of Lewis, yielding union–nonunion differences of 10 percent or so. All told, with rare exception, recent studies confirm the existence of a sizable union–nonunion wage differential.

Another important aspect of the union wage effect which has been examined is the difference between union and nonunion wage adjustments to varying economic conditions. The recent work on the cyclical variation in wage rates has confirmed the earlier finding of Lewis that the union–nonunion wage differential has tended to be greater during economic downturns, which suggests that the reduction in (the growth of) real wage rates in response to a reduction in product demand is smaller under trade unions. Interestingly, the work of Johnson (1981) and Mitchell (1981a) and an analysis of Current Wage Developments establishment-level data suggest that the union wage effect grew substantially during the 1970s to a point where it is roughly comparable to its level in the 1930s.

One key question to ask about the union–nonunion wage differentials is, "How do they vary across settings?" Recent empirical work on this subject has been based on the notion that union wage gains will be high where the elasticity of demand for labor, and hence the cost of increased relative wages in terms of lost members, is low. The evidence that, at least in the manufacturing and construction sectors of our economy, union wages but not nonunion wages grow with the fraction organized in the relevant product market is consistent with this claim; this is because a high percentage organized is likely to be associated with a low demand elasticity for union products and thus a low demand elasticity for union members. Other work has concentrated on the effect of market regulation on the union wage effect. Ehrenberg (1979) presents evidence consistent with the claim that union wages are raised by the regulation of public utilities. Hayden (1977) argues that the sizable impact of unionism on trucker wages (40 percent or so) is attributable both to ICC regulation of the sector and to the National Master Freight Agreement, which created industrywide bargaining.

A significant piece of the new work on union effects has been concerned with the composition and distribution of compensation. With regard to fringe benefits, recent analyses have demonstrated that the "union fringe effect" is bigger, in percentage terms, than the "union wage effect." Data from the 1968, 1970, and 1972 EEC indicate, for example, that holding constant the characteristics in employees' establishments, blue-collar workers covered by collective bargaining received fringe benefits that were about 28 to 36 percent higher than those of blue-collar workers who were not covered (compared to a union wage advantage of 8 to 15 percent). For workers receiving the same total compensation per hour, the fringe share of labor cost was markedly higher in the union setting (Freeman, 1981). Looking at separate fringes, the largest union–nonunion percentage differentials on a per hour basis are for pensions, life, accident and health insurance, and vacation pay.

Since their inception, unions in our country have been concerned with wage inequality as well as the level of wage rates. The practice which most exemplifies unions' efforts on this front is the long-standing policy of pushing for "standard rates," that is, uniform rates for comparable workers across establishments and for given occupational classes within establishments. Estimates presented in Freeman (1980c) show that, for blue-collar workers, wage inequality is substantially lower among union members than among similar nonmembers. Consistent with this, estimates of separate wage equations for union and nonunion workers have found that virtually all standard wage-determining variables are associated with smaller earnings differentials under unionism. Moreover, union wage policies appear to contribute to the equalization of wages by decreasing the differential between covered blue-collar workers and noncovered white-collar workers. If we add the decrease in inequality due to wage standardization and the decrease due to reduction in the white-collar–blue-collar differential to the increase due to the greater wages of blue-collar union workers, we find that the net effect of unionism is to reduce total wage inequality. Evidence on inequality of earnings across standard metropolitan statistical areas (SMSAs) and states and over time also shows a negative relationship between unionism and dispersion in pay. In short, it appears that the structure of wages in the United States has been compressed by the wage policies of organized labor. Finally in related work, several studies show union wage impacts to be larger for blue-collar as opposed to white-collar workers, for younger as opposed to older employees, and for the less as opposed to the more educated; some studies indicate a greater wage effect for blacks than for whites, but others do not.

B. Internal and External Mobility

The new work on unionism has, as noted earlier, turned attention to outcomes other than the wage level. One of the most important set of issues receiving this attention involves the impact of unionism on the internal and external mobility of employees. To evaluate the effects of unionism on firms' employment policies (the awarding of promotions, the ordering of layoffs, etc.) it is necessary to have knowledge of what is actually happening inside both union and nonunion firms. Survey evidence collected by and discussed in Medoff and Abraham (1980b, 1981a, 1981b) and recent case studies have provided relevant information concerning the role of seniority independent of performance in firms' promotion and termination decisions. With respect to promotions, the survey data reveal that whereas 68 percent of private-sector unionized employees outside of agriculture and construction work in settings where senior employees are favored substantially when promotion decisions are made only 40 percent of the nonunion work force is employed in such settings. When the analysis is restricted to hourly employees, the estimates of concern are 68 percent for union members and 53 percent for the nonunion labor force. Regressions with the survey data which include controls for firm size, industrial sector, and geographic region yield differences similar to those just given. Moreover, case studies of a number of U.S. firms tell the same story: company service counts more in promotion decisions in union settings.

Another important mobility issue relates to the effect of unionism on the turnover behavior of workers. Recent evidence using newly available information on the job changes of thousands of individuals and on industry-level turnover rates shows that with wages and diverse other factors held constant, unionized workers have substantially lower quit rates than nonunion workers who are comparable in other respects. The reduction in quits and the accompanying increase in tenure appear to be as substantial for blacks as for whites and greater for older than for younger workers.

With less ability to reduce (the growth of) real wage rates and with lower quit rates, unionized firms can be expected to make greater use of other adjustment mechanisms, such as average hour reductions and layoffs. Both establishment-level and individual-level data sets demonstrate that, holding fixed wages, worker characteristics, and industry conditions, temporary layoffs and recalls are a more important form of labor adjustment in unionized manufacturing firms than in otherwise comparable firms that are nonunion. Moreover, the use of temporary layoffs relative to the use of average hours reductions appears to be greater under unionism. Hence, it seems that the layoff/recall syndrome which has received much recent attention is, for the most part, a unionized manufacturing (in particular, durables) phenomenon.

With respect to the order of layoffs, evidence from the seniority survey just cited reveals that among those who had witnessed workforce reductions rules protecting senior workers against being permanently laid off before their junior coworkers are more prevalent and stronger under trade unions. For hourly employees, 95 percent of the responses pertaining to groups covered by collective bargaining indicated that seniority in and of itself receives substantial weight in termination decisions, compared to 70 perecent of the responses pertaining to noncovered groups. As for "strength," 68 percent of the survey responses pertaining to unionized hourly employees stated that a senior worker would *never* be involuntarily terminated before a junior worker, whereas only 28 percent of the responses pertaining to nonunion hourly employees stated that this is so. These surveys could not be explained in terms of company characteristics and are consistent with the findings of Blau and Kahn (1981) who used individual-level data.

C. Work Rules, Flexibility, and Satisfaction

Other personnel practices and procedures also appear to be affected by the presence of unionism. In Clark's (1980a, 1980b) study of six cement firms which were recently unionized, management practices appear to have changed significantly with the coming of a union, in directions which can be labeled "productivity-oriented." These observations gain credence from the fact that they are similar to those of Sumner Slichter, James Healy, and E. Robert Livernash, who conducted a myriad of case studies concerning the relationship between unionism and management behavior for their classic 1960 opus, *The Impact of Collective Bargaining on Management*. It should be noted that, with evidence of the type which has been collected, it is difficult to infer whether managers were moved from non–cost-minimizing behavior to cost-minimizing behavior or whether the type of behavior which is cost-minimizing is different in union and in nonunion environments. Nevertheless, it is apparent from this work that management responds to the shock and sustained pressure of unionism in ways which cannot be fully understood with a standard price-theoretic model.

It would seem reasonable, given what is believed about the objective function of the typical union, to find less management flexibility in unionized establishments than in otherwise comparable establishments that are nonunion. Consistent with this view, evidence drawn primarily from the *1972 Census of Manufactures* and the EEC show that within U.S. manufacturing the ease of substitution for productive labor, particularly substitution of nonproduction for production labor, is lower under trade unionism. However, it should be mentioned that the limited evidence does *not* indicate that unionism is associated with a lower elasticity of substitution between labor and capital and thus with whatever technological change is embodied in new capital.

Several recent studies examining the impact of unionism on the stated job satisfaction of workers have found union workers expressing less satisfaction, or in some instances no more satisfaction, with their jobs than similar nonunion workers, when compensation is held fixed, and even when compensation is *not* held constant. At the same time, however, union members are also more likely to state that they ae "unwilling to change jobs under any circumstance" or "would never consider moving to a new job" than are their "more satisfied" nonunion counterparts, even when the wage is fixed. One interpretation of these results is that the collective voice of unionism provides workers with a channel for expressing their preference to management and that this increases their willingness to complain about undesirable conditions.

Evidence has also been accumulated concerning workers' stated satisfaction with particular aspects of their jobs. Some of the findings are: (1) union members are much more likely to state that they are happy with their wages and fringes than are otherwise comparable nonunion employees; (2) there appears to be a strong tendency for unionized workers to state they are less happy with their supervisors and have worse relations with them; (3) there is a tendency for unionized workers to report their physical work conditions are less desirable then those reported by unionized workers; (4) the extent to which stated job security grows with tenure is substantially greater under unionism; and (5) while the probability of viewing promotions as fair is negatively related to seniority in nonunion settings, it is positively related to seniority under unionism.

D. Inputs, Productivity, and Profits

When unions raise wages or otherwise alter labor costs, enterprises can be expected to change factor inputs and modes of organization in such ways as to raise the marginal revenue product of labor up to the point where it equals the new marginal cost of labor. Two of the most important ways in which firms could potentially do this are to hire "higher-quality" workers and to increase their capital/labor ratios. Evidence has been offered showing that blue-collar union workers do in fact have somewhat more "human capital" than similar nonunion workers. With May CPS data for 1973–1975, blue-collar union members are found to be three to four years older than otherwise comparable nonunion blue-collar workers, and to have slightly more education. Separate wage equations for males and females, which differentiate workers by schooling, age, and region, lead to the conclusion that unionized production labor has about 6 percent more "human capital" within two-digit manufacturing industries (Brown and Medoff, 1978). It should be noted, however, that an index of labor quality based on weights from wage regressions is at best only a crude approximation to an index based on "true" productivity weights, as is implied by evidence that a substantial fraction of seniority–earnings differential cannot be explained by seniority–productivity differentials (Medoff, 1977; Medoff and Abraham, 1980a, 1981a). Moreover, it should be recognized that indices of the sort being discussed ignore potentially very important, but not measured, worker characteristics.

With respect to capital/labor ratios, evidence from the 1972 Census of Manufactures suggests that, as expected, capital/labor ratios are higher in unionized settings within two-digit manufacturing industries. What is perhaps more surprising is that the substantially higher capital/labor ratio under trade unions cannot be fully explained by the union wage effect (nor by the union effect on total compensation). Thus, even one of the major price-theoretic response variables seems to be affected by unionism in ways that possibly go beyond the standard compensation-level path.

A number of studies conducted during the past few years have sought to isolate "as well as is possible with existing data" the effect of trade unionism on the productivity of otherwise comparable workers utilizing the same amount of capital. The Brown and Medoff (1978) study, based on 1972 state-by-industry data for U.S. manufacturing, found that unionized enterprises had higher productivity than otherwise comparable nonunion establishments within the same two-digit SIC industries. The magnitude of the effect varied from 27 percent (when they allowed the regression to determine the elasticity of output with respect to capital) to 7 percent (when they imposed an estimate of the output–capital elasticity which was viewed as an upper bound to the true value). Studies of particular manufacturing industries—wooden household furniture and cement—have also found a positive productivity differential. Allen reports a sizable positive differential in construction, using a value output measure. His result is supported by the findings of Mandelstamm (1965), who avoided the potential problems of measuring output in dollar terms by having union and nonunion contractors cost out an identical project.

That unionism can be associated with lower as well as higher productivity has been documented for the U.S. underground bituminous coal sector, where unionized mines were estimated to be about 28 percent more productive than comparable nonunion mines in 1965, but more than 30 percent less productive a decade later. One potential explanation for the observed change in union–nonunion productivity differentials is that the "quality" of industrial relations in that sector appeared to change over time.

Note that in all of these studies the relationship between unionism and productivity is estimated with the price-theoretic responses to higher wages held fixed. Thus, the higher productivity is *not* due to employers substituting higher-quality labor or capital for the more expensive uncovered workers, at least to the extent that can be discerned with the existing measures of those variables. As a result, some effort has been devoted to determining the nonstandard routes which may underlie the apparent union impact on productivity. One relevant finding is that roughly one fourth of the union–nonunion productivity differential in the manufacturing sector can be explained by the union–nonunion differential in quit rates. Other evidence suggests that a significant piece of the union productivity effect can be explained by the union–nonunion differential in the quality of management practices.

The association of unionism and profitability has been examined only recently, in part because, like labor quality and capital, profits are an extremely difficult variable to measure. While there is undoubtedly considerable variation across data sets, the available evidence suggests that in general unionism is associated with a lower return to capital. In some cases, the gross profit margin (profit as a percent of value added) is not noticeably different in union than nonunion sectors, but the capital/labor ratio is higher under trade unions, producing a lower return to capital. In other cases, the gross profit margin as well as the return to capital appears lower. That unionism does not always reduce profitability, however, is also apparent: Hayden found profits as well as wages in trucking rising after the Teamsters negotiated the first National Master Freight Agreement in 1964. All told, on the basis of existing and ongoing studies, it does appear that productivity under unionism is not sufficiently greater than productivity in nonunion settings to offset the higher compensation plus the higher capital intensity, which would be necessary if profits per unit of capital were to be left unaffected.

II. ECONOMETRIC PROBES INTO THE REALITY OF THE NONWAGE EFFECTS OF UNIONS

As noted in Table 1, most studies of the union impact on factors other than the wage level try to control for the wage effect and potential price-theoretic responses to higher union wages, and have found that the bulk of the union–nonunion differences under discussion cannot be explained in terms of measurable price-theoretic variables. For instance, the substantial union–nonunion differential in quit probabilities exists even when individuals' wages and fringes are held constant. Or to choose another example, the union–nonunion productivity differentials discussed above were estimated with models which controlled for labor quality and capital intensity.

Analysts in the industrial relations tradition interpret the existence of significant union effects above and beyond measured price-theoretic routes as real—reflecting the nature of the economy's basic institutions. These individuals believe that the key task for research on trade unions involves gaining a better understanding of the origins, operations, and interactions of the institutions, since the non–price-theoretic actions of firms and unions matter greatly in determining economic performance.

Devotees of the standard price-theoretic model perceive the union–nonunion differences in nonwage variables quite differently: they see these results as illusory, due in part perhaps to inability to control adequately for preunion characteristics of workers or firms and/or to a failure to capture the relevant price-theoretic routes due to the poor quality of the empirical experiment conducted. This point of view leads to the search for observed or unobserved differences which existed between individuals or firms before they were unionized or for important price-theoretic stimuli or responses which had not been captured by the models or with the data of concern and which could be causing the estimated union–nonunion differences. Since these alternative views, and a third view that even union wages effects are illusory, have been discussed in our earlier work,[2] we concentrate here only on the econometric efforts to evaluate the hypotheses.

At the onset, it is important to recognize that the econometric problems of concern occur because the observed union–nonunion differences do not come from the "ideal" experiment needed to estimate the effects of unions on economic outcomes. This experiment would involve unionizing a randomly chosen nonunion individual or firm, while holding all else of relevance in the world fixed, and observing the resultant changes. Unfortunately, all of the statistical "experiments" conducted depart from the ideal, at least to some extent, for two reasons. First, all the relevant factors cannot be held perfectly fixed when we compare unionized individuals or firms to nonunion individuals or firms or even to themselves when they were nonunion. Second, it is unlikely that individuals or firms with similar measured characteristics became unionized on a random basis.

The absence of a series of ideal experiments sets the stage for the econometric efforts at probing the reality of the observed union–nonunion differences in nonwage variables, on which we focus next.

A.   Potential Econometric Explanations and Assessments of Their Validity

The real reason you have obtained those union–nonunion differences is that you have omitted (mismeasured, not observed) a key variable which is correlated with unionization, and that variable is . . .

But you have the wrong causality. It is not that unionism causes . . .; it is that . . . causes unionism.

It seems obvious that your results are due to selectivity; there is an unobserved factor out there which affects whether or not workers are unionized and the market outcome of concern.

—Frequently heard assertions at seminars throughout the U.S.

There are three key econometric problems than can arise in doing empirical work on the impact of unionism (or any factor) on economic outcomes: omitted, mismeasured, or unobserved variable bias; simultaneous equations bias; and sample selection bias. Each of these potential reasons why estimated union–nonunion differences might be spurious arises because of the aforementioned lack of an ideal experiment. These potential problems have been appealed to in attempts to explain the observed union–nonunion differentials depicted in Table 1. Those whose priors come from the price-theoretic monopoly view have used the three potential forms of bias to argue that the observed differentials in Table 1 are illusions.

There are various methods for dealing with each of the potential bias problems which arise in analyses of cross-sectional data. Heuristically, these methods can be divided into three broad categories: (1) Approaches which probe the cross-sectional results through various forms of "sensitivity" analysis designed to see how results might be "driven" by the poor quality of the experiment. In this category we include such techniques as: expanding the list of controls; using the omitted-variable-bias formula; imposing coefficients on mismeasured variables; and using the variance–covariance matrix of coefficients to examine the sensitivity of results to alleged experimental problems. Given outside information on, for example, the relationship between the omitted variable and included variables or on the degree of measurement error in the variables of concern or on the likely magnitude of selected coefficients, estimates can be made of the likely impact of omitted, mismeasured, or unobserved variables. By making particularly strong assumptions or picking particularly large (or small) values of the relevant correlation coefficients, one can "stack the deck" against the estimated union effect and thus get a good notion of its strength. (2) Techniques which seek to treat the alleged experimental problem through complex systems of equations in which very strong assumptions are used to identify the "true" union impact. Such techniques can be used to deal with unobserved mismeasured variables but are most commonly used to treat the simultaneous equations and sample selection problems. The methodology is to postulate a "true" model which enables one to deal with the alleged experimental problem and to solve the resultant equations to obtain the coefficient of concern. (3) Approaches which seek to obtain new and better-quality data designed specifically to deal with particular experimental problems, especially measurement error and omitted variables. Perhaps the most common way of bringing new data to bear on union effects is to examine longitudinal (before/after) rather than cross-sectional data. Longitudinal information provides what is perhaps the most direct way of dealing with the essential cross-sectional data problem—that we are comparing *different* people or firms rather than conducting the ideal experiment described earlier. If one obtains longitudinal data in which omitted, mismeasured, or unobserved variables are constant over time, one can obtain estimates of union effects purged of biases due to these problems. Similarly, by enabling us to compare outcome variables before and after unionization, such data provide the proper recursive structure for dealing with both the "union causes" versus "causes unionism" question and the problem of cross-sectional selectivity bias.

It is important to recognize, however, that longitudinal studies are themselves subject to potential experimental problems not unlike those with cross-sectional data. One potential difficulty is that when persons change jobs, other relevant variables are also likely to change, such as occupation or industry or tasks at work, which may be omitted, mismeasured, or unobserved in the analysis. Another potential problem is that classical measurement error bias may become more severe because the systematic parts of variables are differenced away. Third, since only a limited number of persons are likely to change union status in a given period of time, longitudinal studies may be prone to a sample selection problem not unlike that in cross-sectional studies. Longitudinal calculations reveal the effects of changing union status on the position of workers (firms) who change: If those persons (firms) differ in some fundamental way from other workers, the results may not generalize to the entire population. Whether the selectivity of union and nonunion changers is an important phenomenon and, if so, in what way it affects results are unclear a priori.[3]

Recognizing the problems of longitudinal analyses does not of course vitiate the fact that before/after data provide a distinct and real set of potential experiments which can go a long way toward dealing with the potential difficulties with cross-sectional work discussed above. By following the same individual (firm) over time as he/she/it changes status from nonunion to union or vice versa, one is able to control in a more natural way for all missing or unobserved variables which do not change over time. The longitudinal data are an invaluable complementary form of information to the more widely used cross-sectional data.

B.   Results of Econometric Probes

Much recent work on unionism has used the econometric techniques alluded to earlier to probe the union–nonunion differentials summarized in Table 1. What have been the results of these efforts to obtain better estimates of the "true" union effect on economic outcomes? To what extent are the Table 1 differences "moved" by sensitivity probes which use new data or information to evaluate the effect of omitted, mismeasured, or unobserved variables in a specified study? How sensitive are the empirical results to probes which rely on extensive cross-sectional modeling in which unionization is taken as endogenous, for reasons of either simultaneity or selectivity? What are the results of panel or longitudinal studies designed to deal with the potential "experimental" problems with cross-sectional analyses? In short, what does the evidence say about possible ways of answering, and about possible answer to, the frequently heard seminar assertions regarding the potential problems with the cross-sectional investigations of the impact of collective bargaining?

Our review of the relevant econometric studies yields three conclusions. First, the econometric probes do not invalidate the findings summarized in Table 1 by attributing all or the vast bulk of observed differences to the inadequacies of the experimental comparisons. Studies which probe the sensitivity of cross-sectional findings to omitted, mismeasured, or unobserved variables show that while these experimental problems appear to bias union coefficients somewhat, they are far from the sole explanation of the ordinary least squares (OLS) regression results. Studies which use longitudinal data to deal with the problems of unobserved factors, simultaneity, or sample selectivity tend to yield lower estimates of union effects than do OLS studies using cross-sectional information, but they also fail to eliminate the bulk of estimated impacts. Studies which seek additional data regarding the potential causality of union effects through surveys of firms also tend to find real union impacts on behavior.

Second, union–nonunion differences in the nonwage outcomes of concern appear to be no more affected, and in some instances to be less affected, by the absence of the perfect experimental data than are the union–nonunion differences in wages. Moreover, the relevant analyses suggest that both sets of differences are real. Furthermore, the studies examined imply that probes of the wage differential can be expected to shed much light on the likely outcome of probes of other differentials.

Third, studies which use systems of equations with cross-sectional data to "correct for" potential simultaneous equations and sample selection bias provide very little insight into whether the Table 1 union–nonunion differences are real or illusory. The models employed rely on "restrictions" or "exclusions" which are far from convincing. More importantly, the results show great instability in the face of seemingly small changes in the model or the sample analyzed. In some cases the systems yield union effects much below those obtained with OLS; in others they yield effects much above those from OLS; and in yet others the systems of equations give about the same results as does OLS. In a surprisingly large number of cases, the systems yield results so implausible on a priori grounds as to be dismissed out of hand. While this instability and implausibility do not demonstrate that the OLS union–nonunion differences are unbiased, it does indicate that the system of equations methodology does not offer a reliable and useful way of improving on these estimates.

We consider next the evidence regarding these conclusions. We review first the results of efforts to probe cross-sectional findings with sensitivity analysis, better data designed to deal with omitted variables, and systems techniques. Then we review the growing body of evidence which uses longitudinal experiments to check on the cross-sectional findings.

C.   Probing the Cross-Sectional Evidence

Table 2 summarizes some recent efforts to assess the validity of cross-sectional findings using one or more of the methods discussed in the preceding section. For each study the table shows the type of bias being focused on, the econometric technique employed, the variable analyzed, the data used, the key empirical results, and the appropriate references. While our listing is undoubtedly incomplete, we believe it is broadly representative of the pattern of results in extant work. Because of the initial concentration of quantitative analyses on wages, the table is top-heavy with the results of econometric probes into the union wage effect.

The first and undoubtedly the most widely used technique for dealing with data inadequacies is to test the sensitivity of results to the inclusion of detailed industry or occupation controls in the data set under study. Addition of such controls in some sense leads to finer experiments by focusing on union effects within more detailed groupings. Alternatively, to the extent that missing or mismeasured variables differ across the relevant sectors, inclusion of a large number of variables can be justified by pointing out that they help control for those variables. Even when one might argue that exclusion of detailed controls is theoretically "correct," it is useful to know whether these variables "matter." In many studies attempts are made to obtain information on the posited missing variables at an industry level and to add those variables in place of the dummy controls. This provides a means of evaluating what industry dummies in fact stand for, but offers a weaker test of the extent to which results stand up to addition of numerous covariance controls.

In most cases in which additional controls are added to analyses, either by augmentation of data sets with industry-level variables or by inclusion of numerous industry or occupation dummy variables, the greater refinement of the comparison set reduces the estimated impact of unionism. But this occurs only up to the point of, say, "one" or "two-digit" industry or occupation controls. Additional controls appear to have only a modest effect on the estimates. Consider, for example, the effect of adding industry controls to the equations estimating the effect of unionism on the usual hourly pay of private, male wage and salary workers using 1976 May CPS data. With a standard log-linear hourly earnings functional form which includes race, years of education, age minus years of education

Table 2. Evidence of Econometric Probes Into Union/Nonunion Differences Using Cross-Sectional Data[a]

Issue and Technique	Variable, Data Set, Sample	Result	Reference
Omitted, Mismeasured, or Unobserved Variable Bias			
Enter additional dummy variable(s), or other variables to obtain finer comparisons	*Wages: quits; layoffs; dispersion; productivity; etc.* Diverse Diverse	Addition of various dummies for 2- and where possible 3-digit Census or SIC industry or for occupation can reduce but not eliminate estimated union/ nonunion differential; similar results from adding average characteristics using industry figures and from adding variables capturing work place characteristics.	Diverse studies.
Set coefficient on mismeasured variable at predetermined level	*Productivity* Census of Manufactures; CPS All workers in manufacturing industries	Union coefficient is reduced substantially by forcing estimated coefficient of capital/labor variable to equal an upper bound of capital's share of value added in Census of Manufactures data set, but still implies that unionized establishments are moderately more productive (by a lower bound of 7%).	Brown & Medoff (1978).
Use omitted variable formula to discern likely bias	*Quits* CPS; PSID; NLS Older Men; NLS Younger Men; All Workers	Correcting for omitted fringe benefits variable and mismeasured alternate earnings variable can most likely reduce large union coefficient by no more than $\frac{1}{4}$.	Freeman (1980b).
	Productivity Cement company data Production workers	Capturing true labor quality is unlikely to greatly reduce the union productivity effect in cement.	Clark (1980a, 1980b).

Collect new data	*Productivity* Cement company data; Underground bituminous coal mine data Production workers	Physical output data for cement plants and coal mines obtained to deal with problems of distinguishing output variation from price variation indicate that the fact that the earlier union productivity studies used a value measure cannot explain the estimated positive union effect; in addition, these data point to the importance of the quality of labor-management relations as a mediating factor in the union-productivity relationship.	Clark (1980a, 1980b), Connerton, Freeman & Medoff (1978).
	Role of Seniority per se Surveys of companies All workers	Union/nonunion differences in the relationships between seniority and both terminations and promotions cannot be explained in terms of an unobserved union/nonunion differential in the relationship between seniority and contribution to firm.	Medoff & Abraham (1980b, 1981a).
Construct unobserved variable model	*Fringes* EEC Production workers	Magnitude of union coefficient is sensitive to precise model for unobserved establishment characteristics, but qualitative conclusion that unions are associated with higher fringe benefits is not.	Freeman (1981).
Simultaneous Equations Bias			
Replace a union variable with a predicted union variable	*Wages* E&E; Census All workers	Union/nonunion wage differential declines for 49 manufacturing industries from 37% with OLS to 27% in a 2-SLS model.	Pencavel (1970)

(continued)

313

Table 2. (Continued)

Issue and Technique	Variable, Data Set, Sample	Result	Reference
	Wages E&E; Census All workers	Union/nonunion wage differential declines for 2-digit SIC manufacturing industries from 46% OLS to 19% or 4% in 2-SLS models and to −9% in a 3-SLS model.	Ashenfelter Johnson (1972).
	Wages; quits E&E; Census Production workers	Both wage and quit differentials grow substantially (in absolute value) with data for 3-digit SIC manufacturing industries, when 2-SLS replaces OLS; the wage differential rises from 50 to 80%.	Kahn (1977).
	Wages SEO All workers	Wage differential reduced from 11% to 6% by fitting a system of equations in which the estimated union coefficient is unbiased by assumption.[b]	Schmidt & Strauss (1976); Olsen (1978); Schmidt (1978).
	Wages; quits NLS Young Men All workers	Wage differential rises with selectivity correction from 32% to 51%; differential in quit probability switches from significant negative (−.487) to near significant positive (.878).	Farber (1979).
	Wages NLS Young Men All workers	With selectivity adjustment, union differential rises from 22/38% to 28/105% for young and middle-aged black employees and from 25/13% to 37/46% for young and middle-aged white employees.	Leigh (1980b).

314

	Data	Results	Citation
	Wages CPS detailed occupational data Hospital workers	Results vary with data set and model, with estimated differentials moving, in many cases quite substantially, in both directions (presented in Table 4).	Cain et al, (1980); McLaughlin, (1980); Podgursky, (1980).
	Wages PSID: Michigan Time Use Survey All workers	Differential increases from 19% to 24% with union made endogenous on work conditions.	Duncan & Stafford (1980).
	Dispersion Aggregate Industry All workers	Union impact of reducing dispersion is not significantly affected by simultaneity adjustment.	Hirsch.
Sample Selection Bias Add an inverse Mills ratio term to outcome equation or estimate a system which explicitly recognizes correlation between selection and outcome equation.	*Wages* NLS Older Men All workers	Coefficients in separate union and nonunion equations are only moderately affected by addition of inverse Mills ratio; estimated union/nonunion differential rises moderately.	Duncan & Leigh (1980).
	Wages SEO Operatives	Sizeable wage differential declines slightly (from 18% to 16%) with selectivity correction.	Lee (1978).
	Wages PSID All workers	Estimated union wage differential rises significantly to 40% from its OLS value of 13% in one calculation and modestly in another (from 6% to 9%).	Neumann (1977).
	Wages CPS detailed occupation data Hospital workers	Results vary with data set and model with estimated differentials moving, in many cases quite substantially, in both directions to large positive or large (in absolute value) negative (see Table 5 for specific results).	Cain et al, (1980), McLaughlin (1980), Podgursky (1980).

(continued)

315

Table 2. (Continued)

Issue and Technique	Variable, Data Set, Sample	Result	Reference
	Wages CPS detailed occupation data Health care employees	Sizeable increases in wage differential for nurses aides (to 89%); moderate increases for health aides and technical workers; decline to −6% for nurses.	Feldman, Lee, and Hoffbeck (1980).
	Wages Survey of Hospital Directors of Nursing	Union coefficient in wage equation goes from insignificant positive (OLS) to insignificant negative (2-SLS).	Sloan & Elnicki (1979).
	Turnover Hospital survey data set Health care workers	Percentage reduction in turnover associated with unionism is large (50%) even when 2-SLS is used to correct for selectivity.	Becker (1978).

Notes:

[a] The following abbreviations are used throughout this table and the remainder of the paper for data sources: CPS represents the Current Population Survey, E&E represents *Employment and Earnings*, EEC represents the Expenditure for Employee Compensation survey, NLS represents the National Longitudinal Survey, PSID represents the Panel Study of Income Dynamics survey, and SEO represents the Survey of Economic Opportunity, and for statistical techniques: OLS represents ordinary least squares, 2-SLS represents two-stage least squares, and 3-SLS represents three-stage least squares.

[b] This result is reported in the Schmidt response to Olsen's piece, which pointed out a flaw in the original Schmidt & Strauss model.

minus 6 and its square, three region dummies, and a blue-collar dummy variable, the effect of adding industry controls on the estimated coefficient of the union membership dummy (member = 1) is shown in the accompanying tabulation.

Industry Controls	Estimated Union Member Coefficient in May 1976 CPS (Standard Error)
None	.29
	(.01)
One-Digit census (20)	.21
	(.01)
Two-Digit census (45)	.19
	(.01)
Three-Digit census (200)	.18
	(.01)

As is common in such sensitivity probes, the reductions (in absolute value) in union coefficients approach zero very quickly as the number of industry dummies grows, and the estimated union–nonunion differences of concern does not vanish.

Addition of other variables designed to reflect union–nonunion comparisons by holding fixed workplace conditions likely to cause compensating differentials yields similar results: union–nonunion wage differentials diminish but do not disappear. The most sizable reduction, obtained by Duncan and Stafford (1980), showed that addition of variables relating to the nature and intensity of work to a ln (wage) equation reduced a union coefficient estimate of .29 to .19. Other studies by Brown (1980) and Leigh (1981), however, show no such relation between union–nonunion differentials and characteristics of workplaces.

There have been a limited number of studies which have sought to evaluate the effect of measurement error or omitted variables on estimated union–nonunion differentials. In their study of productivity, Brown and Medoff (1978) probed the extent to which the coefficient on unionism could be explained by classical measurement error in the capital/labor ratio by exploiting the fact that with the Cobb–Douglas production function, under profit maximization, the coefficient of this ratio should equal capital's share of value added. Because unionization and capital/labor ratio are positively correlated, they found that mismeasurement of the capital intensity variable may have substantially biased upward the estimated impact of unionism on productivity. However, even when the coefficient of the capital/labor variable was forced to equal an upper-bound estimate of capital's share, there remained a nonnegligible positive union productivity effect. In a study of quits, Freeman (1980a,b) used the omitted-variable-bias formula to assess the sensitivity of the apparent union effect on quits to the omission of fringe benefits from the analysis and to measurement error in alternative wages. The formula was applied using information from other data sets in conjunction with strong assumptions designed to yield lower-bound estimates of the union effect. The lower-bound estimates showed a significant and large effect about half as large as the initial OLS impact. In another study dealing with omitted variables, Clark (1980a,b) examined the likely effect of omitted labor quality on the union–nonunion productivity differential. Using a formula describing how labor quality enters the production process, and exogenous information on possible quality changes during the period since his sample of cement plants had gone from nonunion to union, he concluded that only a small piece of the differential he had originally estimated could be explained by this uncaptured workforce dimension.

There have been some recent efforts to generate new data sets to deal with omitted or mismeasured variable problems. To determine whether union effects on productivity, measured by value added, might be due to union effects on the price rather than the output component of value added, Connerton, Freeman, and Medoff gathered data on tons of coal, while Clark gathered data on tons of cement. The coal study found sizable positive union productivity effects when industrial relations in the sector appeared to be good but negative effects in a period of seemingly poor industrial relations. The cement study found positive union effects on physical output per worker in that industry. To determine whether union–nonunion differentials in the extent to which seniority reduces the probability of termination and increases the chance of promotion could be explained by an unobserved union–nonunion differential in the relationships between company service and current contribution, Medoff and Abraham (1981b) asked companies to compare the termination and promotion probabilities of senior and junior employees whose performance was equal. Based on more than 500 responses, it was concluded that the greater importance attached to seniority per se under unionism could not be explained in terms of an uncaptured differential in the way performance and seniority were related.

Finally, recently developed "unobservables" models (see Chamberlain, 1977) were used by Freeman (1981) to assess the possibility that part of the estimated union impact on fringes was due to an omitted firm characteristic. The analysis showed that the extent to which the OLS differential could be attributed to unobserved firm differences depended greatly on the way the model was constructed. When it was assumed that there was no within-firm spillover from blue-collar unionization to white-collar fringes, the original fringe differential was reduced substantially by the firm-effects correction. Hence, any conclusion concerning the impact of unobserved firm effects on the union–nonunion fringe differential depends crucially on one's a priori logic concerning the "true" unobservable model to be used.

D. Simultaneous Equations

Several analysts have sought to explore the causality of observed union effects using simultaneous equations models in which unionism is endogenous, i.e., determined by the equations of the system. In the outcome equation(s) the actual union variable is replaced by a predicted variable. Identification of the system is obtained either by exclusion of one (or more) variables from the outcome equation, but not from the unionism equation, or on the basis of different functional forms for the two equations.

The first analyses using the simultaneous equations technique focused on industry aggregates. Both Ashenfelter and Johnson (1972) and Pencavel (1970) showed that, depending on the particular model employed, a large positive OLS union–nonunion wage differential in U.S. manufacturing was substantially reduced; Ashenfelter and Johnson estimated a differential of 46 percent with a single equation (OLS) model, a differential of 19 percent with one two-stage model, a differential of 4 percent with another two-stage model, and a differential of −8 percent with a three-stage model. The more recent work on manufacturing by Kahn (1977), who used three-digit SIC data, whereas the previous researchers used two-digit data, but followed the same general procedure, generated quite different results: substantial *increases* (in absolute value) in both the union wage and quit effects upon correcting for the endogeneity of unionism. Kahn's estimated wage differential rose from 50 to 80 percent when he changed his technique from OLS to two-stage least squares, and his estimated quit effect also rose noticeably. In a later study, Kahn (1979) attempted to control for union-induced increases in labor quality. Using this three-digit SIC manufacturing data, he found a wage differential of about 50 percent with a two-stage model versus 25 percent with an OLS model. Hence, seemingly small changes in the models employed and in the degree of data aggregation have yielded very different results with systems designed to correct for potential simultaneous equations bias in analyses of aggregate cross-sectional data.

A widely divergent pattern of results has also been obtained when roughly similar simultaneous equations models have been estimated with similar bodies of individual-level data. Schmidt (1978), relying on functional form for identification, reported a decline in the effect of unionism from 10 percent to 4 percent with SEO data (his two-equation model was not, however, needed to obtain unbiased estimates, since it assumed away the correlation that gives rise to the bias problem). On the other hand, Duncan and Stafford (1980) showed an increase in the estimated coefficient of unionism when unionism was made endogenous in their model which focused on work conditions, as did Leigh (1980a). Applying a simultaneous equations model with both a wage and a quit equation to the young men NLS data, Farber (1979) obtained an increase in the union wage effect while at the same time switching the sign on the standard quit effect from negative to positive, the opposite of Kahn's quit result. Farber found his results somewhat puzzling. Overall, in the regressions cited in Table 2 (including those from Cain et al. presented in detail in Table 3), there is an alarming amount and pattern of instability when actual unionism is replaced by predicted unionism; in somewhat more than half the cases, the estimated union coefficient rises, counter to expectation, often to rather large values, while in many cases in which the coefficient declines it becomes negative.

While most authors have not discussed the sensitivity of their findings to minor changes in specification, the statements of those who have indicate that the instability discussed above is not a purely cross-researcher phenomenon, since a given individual working with a given data set appears likely to find that slight changes in specification lead to large changes in results. For example, Duncan and Stafford (1980, p. 367) wrote that "the estimated union coefficient [is] sensitive to the exogenous variables omitted from the [wage] equation." Similarly, Mitchell (1980, p. 204) stated: "In general simultaneous-equation estimates require assumptions concerning which variables are exogenous and which serve to identify particular equations. Experiments by this author suggest that changing assumptions can produce wide variations in results ranging from negative union wage effects to ridiculously large positive effects."

Perhaps the most far-reaching work on the stability of models which replace a union variable by a predicted value, in the context of a model in which unionism is taken as endogenous, has been done at the University of Wisconsin by Cain et al. (1980), McLaughlin (1980), and Podgursky (1980). Their findings for the wage differential, summarized in Table 3, show that the same simultaneous equation model, estimated with data for comparable employee groups, yields results which swing back and forth over a highly implausible range (from −84 percent to 95 percent).[4] The Podgursky results, which show the union–nonunion wage differential swinging from a positive 10 percent with OLS to a most certainly absurd negative 72 percent using a two-stage least squares procedure, are particularly striking as they relate to one of the groups most frequently studied in the literature.

We conclude that the highly sensitive results obtained with both aggregate industry and industry-level data sets when unionism is "predicted" raise serious questions about the usefulness of the simultaneous equation methodology for analyses of what unions really do. The technique appears to be trying to squeeze out of the data more than the data contain; it does not, in our view, provide a reliable way of addressing the illusion/reality question.

E. Sample Selection

The recently popular technique for dealing with potential sample selection bias—adding an inverse Mills ratio term to outcome regressions, which corrects for the potential bias under certain assumptions (see Heckman, 1976)—has been used in a number of analyses of the union–nonunion wage differential. In the first such piece, Lee (1978), using exclusion of variables as well as functional form for identification, reduced slightly the OLS wage differential for operatives (from 17 to 16 percent) with data from the SEO. Leigh (1980b), fitting models very similar to those used by Lee, analyzed NLS data for both older and younger men. He found that wage differentials were increased, rather than decreased, by the selectivity adjustment in both samples. In several cases they were increased by extremely large amounts; in three or six sets he presented, the selectivity-adjusted percentages were at least three times as large as the OLS estimates. Another very substantial increase in estimated wage differentials was obtained by Neumann (1977); with PSID data for 1974 his adjusted estimate was 40 percent while his OLS estimate was 13 percent. However, when Neumann used average data for 1968–1974, the difference was much smaller: 9 percent versus 6 percent. Overall, the results from adding sample selectivity "correction" terms to wage regressions appear to be as unstable and divergent as those obtained with simultaneous equations "corrections." Studies that differ only slightly in specification, data, or group covered show wide differences in the impact of the "corrections" on OLS results.[5]

Work focusing on the wage differential in a given sector, hospitals, tends to confirm this judgment. Becker (1978) and Sloan and Elnicki (1979) found that selectivity adjustments reduced estimated union coefficients, whereas the results in Table 3 from Cain et al. (1980) and McLaughlin (1980) for various groups in this sector show as many increases as decreases in the union coefficient upon addition of the inverse Mills ratio to regressions using the same survey data and model. In yet another study, Feldman et al. (1980) obtained increases in the union wage effect for several occupations in the health sector but obtained decreases in the union wage effect for nurses when they corrected for selectivity.

Podgursky's (1980) work with the CPS files provides yet additional evidence which calls into question the usefulness of the inverse Mills ratio

Table 3. Results of "Wisconsin" Regressions With CPS Data in Which Unionism is Treated as a Predicted Endogenous Variable or in Which There is a Sample Selection Term

Group	OLS Union Effect	Union Effect With Predicted Unionism	Union Effect With Inverse Mills Ratio
Cain, et al. (1980)[b] Hospital employees	Percentage Wage Differential[a] (level of significance)		
privated nonprofessional workers	6 (.10)	64 (.06)	31 (.05)
private, registered nurses	−15 (>.10)	16 (>.10)	−6 (>.10)
government, nonprofessional workers	−3 (.07)	95 (.06)	16 (>.10)
private, technicians	−20 (.10)	31 (>.10)	4 (>.10)
government, registered nurses	3 (>.10)	−24 (>.10)	1 (>.10)
private, licensed practical nurses	16 (>.10)	13 (>.10)	28 (>.10)
government, technicians	−10 (>.10)	−84 (>.10)	−72 (>.10)
government, licensed practical nurses	20 (>.10)	55 (.07)	21 (>.10)
McLaughlin (1980)[c] Hospital employees	Percentage Wage Differential[a] (t-statistic)		
private nonprofessional workers	6 (1.74)	36 (1.69)	22 (1.30)
private, registered nurses	3 (.66)	16 (.46)	6 (.22)
government, nonprofessional workers	4 (1.41)	5 (.07)	−22 (.51)
government, registered nurses	0 (.00)	−57 (1.37)	−27 (.77)
Podgursky (1980)[d] Private sector Production workers	10 (3.0)	−72 (4.3)	−63 (4.0)

Notes:

[a] These differentials give the estimated percentage amount by which the wages of union members exceed those of otherwise comparable nonunion employees. Although the data were transformed where necessary to yield differentials, the original t-statistic or level of significance (depending on what the author presented) is given.

322

technique for analyses of union–nonunion differentials. In his work on private sector production workers, an initial positive OLS differential of 10 percent (significant at the .01 level) becomes a highly dubious negative 63 percent (again significant at the .01 level) when an inverse Mills ratio term is added to a wage equation.

What is one to make of the aberrant results obtained with the simultaneous equations (predicted unionism) technique and with the inverse Mills ratio technique for examining whether observed union–nonunion differences are real or illusory? We believe that the empirical results just presented strongly suggest that there is little to be learned from using either of the two techniques for analyzing the impact of unionism. Unfortunately, there seems to be no obvious "best" way to identify the systems of concern, and the results obtained seem to be highly sensitive to the one chosen, as well as to the data and sample with which it is used. While the problems addressed by the techniques may be real, the econometric solutions offered can do little to solve them with extant cross-sectional data. Econometric manipulations of these data do not appear to be a good substitute for better data, for experiments more suitable to answering the problems of concern, or for genuine institutional or theoretical knowledge about the interactions between union, employers, and workers.

F. Longitudinal Data

The results of some recent studies of union effects that exploit the before/after nature of longitudinal data sets to obtain estimates of the effect of unionism on the same person or firm are summarized in Table 4. These studies, which ask, "How does the charcteristic of a worker

---

[b] The data set used to derive these estimates is a pooled file of 1973–1976 May CPS microdata. The dependent variable for each occupational group in the particular government/nongovernment sector was the real hourly wage rates of individual hospital workers. Regressors in the OLS Union Effect model included a zero-one union status dummy variable as well as a vector of personal characteristics, region of country, size of SMSA, year, and sub-occupation group. In the Union-Effect-With-Predicted-Unionism model, predicted union status (provided by a probit computation) replaced the zero-one union status variable. In the Union-Effect-With-Inverse-Mills-Ratio model, the hazard ratio was added as a regressor to the OLS Union Effect model. Interactions of the union status dummy variable with variables for race, year, and full-time/part-time status were included in each model. The significance level refers to the combined effect of the set of union and union-interaction variables.

[c] The data set used and the variables included in the models are essentially the same as in note b above, except that part-time workers were excluded. The only important difference in the specification is that interactions terms were not included as additional regressors in the McLaughlin regressions. In fact, the McLaughlin results are virtually identical to the Cain, et al. specifications without the interaction terms.

[d] The data set used was the March, 1971 CPS. The dependent variable in these regressions is the log of annual earnings of full-time, full-year, nonfarm, private sector production workers. In addition to a zero-one union status dummy variable and a percent-of-industry unionized variable, regressors included a vector of personal characteristics, region of country, size of SMSA, industry, and industrial concentration.

Table 4. Evidence of Econometric Probes into Union/Nonunion
Differences Using Longitudinal Data

Variable, Data Set, Sample	Result	Reference
Wages NLS Young Men All workers	Changes in wages from going union to nonunion (UN) as opposed to remaining union (UU) and of going nonunion to union (NU) as opposed to remaining nonunion (NN) are about six-tenths as large as the comparable cross-sectional differentials.	Chamberlain (1980).
Wages May CPS All workers	Wage Differential of about 8% in longitudinal analysis compared to 19% in cross-sectional analysis.	Mellow (1979).
Wages; Work Conditions PSID; Michigan Time Use Survey All workers	Change in wages; UN 7%; NU 55%; UU 33%; NN 40%; Estimated UN change in "choice of work" is positive while NU change is negative. Estimated UN changes in "freedom to increase work hours" is near zero while NU change is negative and substantially so in absolute value.	Duncan & Stafford (1980).
Wages; Work Conditions NLS Young Men All workers	Change in wages; UN 45%; NU 118%; UU 71%; NN 81%. Estimated UN change in "progress at work" is positive while NU change is negative. Estimated UN change in "job pace" is positive while NU change is zero.	Leigh (1980a).
Permanent Separations; Fringes; Wages PSID NLS Young and Old Men All workers	Men who join unions have sizeable reduction in quits; reduction related to union wage gains; joiners also obtain less training than nonunion workers; union wage effect of 20% among young reduced in half; results for old men less clear.	Mincer (1981).
Quits PSID	Quits differential in longitudinal study is roughly the same as in comparable cross-section investigations.	Freeman (1978b).
Tenure; Dispersion NLS Young Men Blue-collar Workers	Tenure and dispersion differentials in longitudinal study are quite consistent with those from comparable cross-sectional analyses.	Freeman (1982).
Productivity Cement company data Production workers	NU change is approximately equal to the comparable cross-sectional differential.	Clark (1980a, 1980b).

(firm) change when he/she (it) goes from union to nonunion status or vice versa?'' yield estimates of union wage and nonwage effects which, while frequently smaller (in absolute value) than those obtained in comparable cross-sectional analyses, are always quite consistent with the cross-sectional findings. In contrast to the attempts to deal with the problem of causality and selectivity with systems of equations, in no case does a longitudinal analysis result "blow up." Finally, but perhaps more importantly for the present discussion, the nonwage union–nonunion differentials seem to be inexplicable in terms of unobserved (or observed) fixed price-theoretic or monopoly effects.

As was the case with cross-sectional studies, there are still more longitudinal analyses of wage rates than of other outcomes of concern. The magnitude of the difference between longitudinal and cross-sectional estimates of union wage effects varies somewhat by study. Chamberlain found that the effect of unionism estimated with the longitudinal data in the young men NLS was about six-tenths as large as the effect estimated with cross-sectional data. Mincer found the longitudinal effect roughly two-thirds as large as the cross-sectional effect. Mellow's analysis of the May–May matched CPS tapes, by contrast, obtained a longitudinal effect that was about 40 percent of that estimated in CPS cross-sectional regressions. One possible explanation of the greater difference between the CPS results and other results is that in the CPS, unlike the other surveys, workers do not typically respond for themselves, raising the possibility of greater measurement error in the union variable using the CPS than using the other surveys. As noted earlier, classical measurement error can be expected to become a more serious problem in longitudinal than in cross-sectional data. Finally, with respect to wages, Duncan and Stafford, and Leigh, have presented figures on the change in wages for workers who switch union status and those who remain union or nonunion. These figures, given in Table 4, provide several interesting comparisons which illuminate the nature of the longitudinal experiment. From them one can compare the wage changes of workers who were nonunion in the first period and become union members in the second period to the wage changes of workers who were nonunion in both periods or to the changes of those who began as members but left their unions or to the changes of workers who were unionized in both periods. A similar set of comparisons can also be made for workers who began as union members but left their union. Each comparison provides an answer to a different question concerning the impact of unionism on wage rates. For present purposes, it suffices to note that in all relevant comparisons, the results in Table 4 show a substantial union wage impact of a magnitude somewhat smaller than, but consistent with, the Table 1 findings.

Turning to the other outcome variables a longitudinal analysis of quit behavior with Panel Survey Income Dynamics data produced estimated coefficients on the union variable roughly equal to those obtained in cross-sectional analyses. This finding is consistent with longitudinal analyses of quits, permanent separations, and tenure on NLS data for men (Freeman, 1981b).

Longitudinal studies have also roughly replicated the cross-sectional differentials for fringes, dispersion, and productivity. In the case of fringes, Mincer (1981), using NLS data for working men, found estimates of union–nonunion differentials whose magnitudes differ only modestly from comparable cross-sectional estimates. With respect to dispersion, Freeman (in process), analyzing young male blue-collar workers, observed that among those who moved from union to nonunion employment there was a substantial increase in wage dispersion, while among those who moved in the opposite direction there was a significant decrease, with both changes in dispersion only modestly smaller (in absolute value) than the cross-sectional dispersion differential. Finally, with regard to productivity, Clark (1980a) found only a modest diminution in his estimated effect of unionism on productivity in the cement industry when he went to a before/after data file.[6]

Overall, the longitudinal analyses suggest that much of the cross-sectional union–nonunion differentials presented in Table 1 are "real" and cannot be explained in terms of price-theoretic or monopoly effects. Since, as noted earlier, it is likely that there are some potential problems with analyses which estimate union impacts by focusing on marginal as opposed to average workers, we endorse neither the longitudinal nor the cross-sectional results as *the* answer. However, the fact that they regularly point in the same direction—there is much more to unions than their monopoly power—is reassuring.

III. CONCLUSIONS

This paper has reviewed a significant body of evidence regarding the impact of trade unionism on economic performance and sought to evaluate antithetical views regarding whether estimated differences in nonwage outcomes between union and nonunion workers and firms are real effects which can be fully understood in terms of monopoly unionism. The review has yielded conclusions on both the substantive questions at hand and the methodologies which have been used to address their validity.

With respect to the reality of the differences in nonwage variables, the preponderance of evidence indicates that union effects estimated with cross-sectional data are real. This statement is based on econometric probes into the cross-sectional findings and analyses of longitudinal data sets. While both types of investigations have shown that cross-sectional union effects tend to be somewhat overstated, no effect has been explained away as due solely to the poor quality of the relevant econometric experiment. Moreover, since the effects of unions on nonwage outcomes come from models which generally hold fixed the level of wages and variables affected by wages, the evidence supports the view that unions do much more than simply raise wages through their monopoly power.

Thus, our examination of the existing evidence indicates that the new facts about the impact of collective bargaining cannot be fully explained by monopoly unionism. For this reason, we have offered elsewhere our "collective voice/institutional response" view of trade unions.[7] While we feel that this view is of value for understanding the institution, it is our belief that other views which go beyond monopoly unionism can also play major roles in explaining what unions do.

With respect to methods for evaluating the quality of standard cross-sectional experiments, some techniques appear more useful than others. In particular, we have found that sensitivity analyses of single-equation results and longitudinal experiments provide valuable checks on cross-sectional findings while multiple-equations approaches produce results which are much too unstable to help resolve the questions of concern.

Our conclusions seem to have three messages for future research on trade unionism. First, the operating assumption that trade unions have important and real nonwage effects which cannot be explained in price-theoretic terms in strongly supported by the extant evidence. Second, the search for a valid answer to the question of what unions do should involve more than just manipulating existing data with sophisticated techniques; it should have at its heart the collection of new evidence concerning the functions and operations of trade unions and their interactions with firms and employees. Third, the illusion/reality question should be asked not only of empirical results on the impact of collective bargaining, but also of the efforts to probe these findings. In sum, monopoly unionism appears unable to explain much of the impact of collective bargaining, even with the assistance of econometric model builders.

ACKNOWLEDGMENT

This paper is a revised version of an earlier study; see Freeman and Medoff (1981b).

NOTES

1. See Freeman and Medoff (1981b).
2. See Freeman and Medoff (1981b).
3. Several arguments can be advanced regarding the possible problems involved in inferring union effects for the population from what happens to a sample of changers. To see the first, consider wages. To the extent that voluntary job changing is viewed as an in-

vestment in mobility, there is likely to be a tendency for both union and nonunion job changers to experience the same wage gains, as both would change only if they could earn the appropriate return. This would bias comparisons of the differences in the wage growth of union-to-nonunion and nonunion-to-union changers toward zero. One would most likely get better estimates by looking solely at changers who left their firm involuntarily for reasons unrelated to their individual actions (e.g., those whose firms went out of business). Another point is that observed wage changes of union-status changers depend on where the changers were in the relevant wage distribution. If union or nonunion changers came disproportionately from either end of the distribution of concern, the estimated wage changes would not reflect those that would result from a person selected at random.

4. Specifically, counting the number of cases in Tables 2 and 3 in which actual unionism was replaced by predicted unionism shows 8 instances in which union coefficients declined from OLS levels, 4 to negative values, and 12 in which the coefficient rose compared to OLS values, 5 of which reached levels in excess of .40 ln point.

5. Specifically, counting the number of cases in Tables 2 and 3 in which a selectivity correction term was introduced shows 10 instances in which union coefficients declined from OLS levels, 6 to negative values, and 11 in which the coefficients rose compared to OLS values, 2 of which reached levels in excess of .40 ln point.

6. Brown and Medoff (1978) gathered data by two-digit industry for 1929 and 1953 to use with data on unionization in these two years found in Lewis (1963, pp. 289–90) in an effort to capture productivity before and after unionization. They regressed the change in ln (value added/labor) on the change in ln (capital/labor) and the change in fraction unionized. With only 20 observations they could not estimate the union productivity effect with any precision. The estimated coefficient on the change in fraction-unionized variable ranged from negative to positive depending on the data used and the assumptions made.

7. See Freeman and Medoff (1979 and forthcoming, b).

REFERENCES

Allen, Steven G. (1979), "Unionized Construction Workers Are More Productive." Mimeograph.

Ashenfelter, Orley (1976), "Union Relative Wage Effects: New Evidence and a Survey of Their Implications for Wage Inflation." Mimeograph.

Ashenfelter, Orley, and George E. Johnson (1972), "Unionism, Relative Wages, and Labor Quality in U.S. Manufacturing Industries." *International Economic Review* 13(October):488–507.

Becker, Brian (1978), "Hospital Unionism and Employment Stability." *Industry Relations* 12(February):96–101.

Blau, Francine D., and Lawrence M. Kahn (1981), "The Exit-Voice Tradeoff in the Labor Market: Some Additional Evidence." Mimeograph.

Bloch, Farrell E., and Mark S. Kuskin (1978), "Wage Determination in the Union and Nonunion Sectors." *Industrial and Labor Relations Review* 31(January):183–192.

Block, Richard N. (1978), "The Impact of Seniority Provisions on the Manufacturing Quit Rate." *Industrial and Labor Relations Review* 31(June):355–378.

Borjas, G. J. (1979), "Job Satisfaction, Wages, and Unions." *Journal of Human Resources* 14(Winter):21–40.

Brown, Charles (1980), "Equalizing Differences in the Labor Market." *Quarterly Journal of Economics* 94(February):113–134.

Brown, Charles, and James Medoff (1978), "Trade Unions in the Production Process." *Journal of Political Economy* 86(June):355–378.

Cain, Glen G., Brian E. Becker, Catherine G. McLaughlin, and Albert E. Schwank (1980), "The Effect of Unions on Wages in Hospitals." Mimeograph.

Chamberlain, Gary (1977), "Are Brothers as Good as Twins?" In Paul Taubman (ed.), *Kinometrics: The Determinants of Socio-Economic Success Within and Between Families.* Amsterdam: North-Holland, pp. 287–298.

――― (1981), "Multivariate Regression Models for Panel Data." Mimeograph.

Clark, Kim B. (1980a), "The Impace of Unionization on Productivity: A Case Study." *Industrial and Labor Relations Review* 33(July):451–469.

――― (1980b), "Unionization and Productivity: Micro-Econometric Evidence." *Quarterly Journal of Economics* 95(December):613–639.

――― (1983), "The Impact of Unionization on Firm Performance: Profits, Growth and Productivity." Harvard Business School Working Paper, HBS 83-990.

Connerton, M., R. B. Freeman, and J. L. Medoff (1979), "Productivity and Industrial Relations: The Case of Bituminous Coal." Mimeograph.

Dalton, James A., and E. J. Ford, Jr. (1977), "Concentration and Labor Earnings in Manufacturing and Utilities." *Industrial and Labor Relations Review* 31(October):45–60.

Doeringer, P. B., and M. J. Piore (1971), *Internal Labor Markets and Manpower Analysis.* Lexington, Mass.: Heath.

Donsimoni, Marie-Paule Joseph (1978), "An Analysis of Trade Union Power: Structure and Conduct of the American Labor Movement." Ph.D. Thesis, Harvard University.

Duncan, Greg J. (1976), "Earnings Functions and Nonpecuniary Benefits." *Journal of Human Resources* 11(Fall):462–483.

Duncan, Greg J., and Duane E. Leigh (1980), "Wage Determination in the Union and Nonunion Sectors: A Sample Selectivity Approach." *Industrial and Labor Relations Review* 34(October):24–34.

Duncan, Greg J., and Frank P. Stafford (1980), "Do Union Members Receive Compensating Wage Differentials?" *American Economic Review* 70(June):355–371.

Ehrenberg, Ronald (1979), *The Regulatory Process and Labor Earnings.* New York: Academic Press.

Farber, Henry S. (1980), "Unionism, Labor Turnover, and Wages of Young Men." In Ronald G. Ehrenberg (ed.), *Research in Labor Economics*, Vol. 3, Greenwich, Conn.: JAI Press Inc., pp. 33–53.

Feldman, Roger, Lung-Fei Lee, and Richard Hoffbeck (1980), "Hospital Employees' Wages and Labor Union Organization." Mimeograph.

Frantz, John (1976), "The Impacet of Trade Unions on Productivity in the Wood Household Furniture Industry." Senior Honors Thesis, Harvard College.

Freeman, Richard B. (1976), "Individual Mobility and Union Voice in the Labor Market." *American Economic Review* 66(May):361–368.

――― (1978a), "Job Satisfaction as an Economic Variable." *American Economic Review* 68(May):135–141.

――― (1978b), "A Fixed Effect Logit Model of the Impact of Unionism on Quits." Mimeograph.

――― (1980a), "The Effect of Unionism on Worker Attachment to Firms." *Journal of Labor Research* 1(Spring):29–61.

――― (1980b), "The Exit-Voice Tradeoff in the Labor Market, Unionism, Job Tenure, Quits, and Separations." *Quarterly Journal of Economics* 94(June):643–673.

――― (1980c), "Unionism and the Dispersion of Wages." *Industrial and Labor Relations Review* 34(October):3–23.

――― (1981), "The Effect of Trade Unionism on Fringe Benefits." *Industrial and Labor Relations Review* 34(July):489–509.

――― (1983), "The Longitudinal Estimates of the Nonwage Impacts of Unionism." In process.

Freeman, R. B., and James L. Medoff (1979), "The Two Faces of Unionism." *The Public Interest* 57(Fall):69–93.

——— (1981a), "The Percent Organized Wage Relationship for Union and Nonunion Workers." *Review of Economics and Statistics* 63(November):561–572.

——— (1981b), "The Impact of Collective Bargaining: Illusion or Reality." In J. Steiber, R. B. McKersie and D. Q. Mills (eds.), *U.S. Industrial Relations 1950–1980: A Critical Assessment*. Madison, Wisc.: Industrial Relations Research Association, pp. 47–97.

——— (forthcoming, a), "Substitution Between Production Labor and Other Factors in Unionized and Nonunionized Manufacturing." *Review of Economics and Statistics*.

——— (forthcoming, b), *What Do Unions Do?*

Goldstein, Gerald, and Mark Pauly (1976), "Group Health Insurance as a Local Public Good." In R. Rosett (ed.), *The Role of Health Insurance in the Health Services Sector*. New York: National Bureau of Economic Research, pp. 73–110.

Halasz, Peter (1980), "What Lies Behind the Slope of the Age-Earnings Profile?" Senior Honors Thesis, Harvard College.

Hamermesh, Daniel (1972), "Market Power and Wage Inflation." *Southern Economic Journal* 39(October):204–212.

Hayden, James F. (1977), "Collective Bargaining and Cartelization: An Analysis of Teamster Power in the Regulated Trucking Industry." Senior Honors Thesis, Harvard College.

Heckman, James D. (1976), "The Common Structure of Statistical Models of Truncation, Sample Selection, and Limited Dependent Variables and a Simple Estimator for Such Models." *Annals of Economics and Social Measurement* 5:475–492.

Hendricks, Wallace (1973), "Labor Market Structure and Union Wage Level." *Economic Inquiry* 13(September):401–416.

——— (1976), "Conglomerate Mergers and Collective Bargaining." *Industrial Relations* 15(February):75–87.

Hirsch, Barry (1982), "The Interindustry Structure of Unionism, Earnings, and Earnings Dispersion." *Industrial and Labor Relations Review*. 36(7).

Hyclak, Thomas (1979), "The Effect of Unions on Earnings Inequality in Local Labor Markets." *Industrial and Labor Relations Review* 33(October):77–84.

——— (1980), "Unions and Income Inequality: Some Cross-State Evidence." *Industrial Relations* 19(Spring):212–215.

Johnson, George E. (1973), "Economic Analysis of Trade Unionism." *American Economic Review* 65(May):23–28.

——— (1981), "Changes Over Time in the Union/Nonunion Wage Differential in the United States." Mimeograph.

Johnson, George E., and Kenneth Youmans (1971), "Union Relative Wage Effects by Age and Education." *Industrial and Labor Relations Review* 24(January):171–179.

Kahn, Lawrence M. (1977), "Union Impact: A Reduced Form Approach." *The Review of Economics and Statistics* 59(November):503–507.

——— (1978), "The Effect of Unions on the Earnings of Nonunion Workers." *Industrial and Labor Relations Review* 31(January):205–216.

——— (1979), "Unionism and Relative Wages: Direct and Indirect Effects." *Industrial and Labor Relations Review* 32(July):520–532.

Kalachek, Edward, and Frederic Raines (1980), "Trade Unions and Hiring Standards." *Journal of Labor Research* 1(Spring):63–75.

Kiefer, Nicholas, and Sharon Smith (1977), "Union Impact and Wage Discrimination by Region." *Journal of Human Resources* 12(Fall):521–534.

Kochan, Thomas A. (1980), *Collective Bargaining and Industrial Relations*. Homewood, Ill.: Richard D. Irwin, Inc.

Kochan, Thomas A., and Richard N. Block (1977), "An Interindustry Analysis of Bargaining Outcomes: Preliminary Evidence from Two-Digit Industries." *Quarterly Journal of Economics* 91(August):431–452.

Kochan, Thomas A., and David E. Helfman (1981), "The Effects of Collective Bargaining on Economic and Behavioral Job Outcomes." In Ronald G. Ehrenberg (ed.), *Research in Labor Economics*, Vol. 4. Greenwich, Conn.: JAI Press, Inc.

Lee, Lung-Fei (1978), "Unionism and Wage Rates: A Simultaneous Equations Model with Qualitative and Limited Dependent Variables." *International Economic Review* 19(June):415–433.

Leibenstein, Harvey (1966), "Allocative Efficiency vs. 'X-Efficiency.'" *American Economic Review* 56(June):392–415.

Leigh, Duane E. (1978), "Racial Discrimination and Labor Unions: Evidence from the NLS Sample of Middle-Aged Men." *Journal of Human Resources* 13k(Fall):568–577.

―――― (1979), "Unions and Nonwage Racial Discrimination." *Industrial and Labor Relations Review* 32(July):439–450.

―――― (1980a), "Do Union Members Receive Compensating Wage Differentials?" Mimeograph.

―――― (1980b), "Racial Differentials in Union Relative Wage Effects: A Simultaneous Equations Approach." *Journal of Labor Research* 1(Spring):95–114.

Lewis, H. Gregg (1963), *Unionism and Relative Wages in the United States*. Chicago: University of Chicago Press.

―――― (1980), "Interpreting Unionism Coefficients in Wage Equations." Mimeograph.

Mandelbaum, David (1980), "Responses to Job Satisfaction Questions as Insights into Why Men Change Employers." Senior Honors Thesis, Harvard College.

Mandelstamm, Allen B. (1965), "The Effects of Unions on Efficiency in the Residential Construction Industry: A Case Study." *Industrial and Labor Relations Review* 18(July):503–521.

McLaughlin, Catherine G. (1980), "The Impact of Unions on Hospital Wages." Ph.D. Thesis, University of Wisconsin—Madison.

Medoff, James L. (1977), "The Earnings Function: A Glimpse Inside the Black Box." Mimeograph.

―――― (1979), "Layoffs and Alternatives Under Trade Unionism in U.S. Manufacturing." *American Economic Review* 69(June):380–395.

Medoff, James L., and Katharine G. Abraham (1980a), "Experience, Performance, and Earnings." *Quarterly Journal of Economics* 95(December):703–736.

―――― (1980b), "Years of Service and Probability of Promotion." Mimeograph.

―――― (1981a), "Involuntary Terminations Under Explicit and Implicit Employment Contracts." Mimeograph.

―――― (1981b), "The Role of Seniority at U.S. Work Places: A Report on Some New Evidence." Mimeograph.

―――― (1981c), "Are Those Paid More Really More Productive?: The Case of Experience." *Journal of Human Resources* (Spring):186–216.

Medoff, James L., and Jon A. Fay (1983), "Cyclical Labor Adjustment in U.S. Manufacturing."

Mellow, Wesley (1981a), "Unionism and Wages: A Longitudinal Analysis." *Review of Economics and Statistics* 63(February):43–52.

―――― (1981b), "Employer Size and Wages." Mimeograph.

Mincer, Jacob (1980), "The Economics of Wage Floors." Mimeograph.

―――― (19), "Union Effects: Wages, Turnover & Job Training." NBER Working Paper No. 808. Cambridge, Mass.: National Bureau of Economic Research.

Mitchell, Daniel J. B. (1980a), "Some Empirical Observations of Relevance to the Analysis of Union Wage Determination." *Journal of Labor Research* 1(Fall):193–215.

―――― (1980b), *Unions, Wages, and Inflation*. Washington, D.C.: The Brookings Institution.

Moore, William J., and John Raisian (1980), "Cyclical Sensitivity of Union/Nonunion Relative Wage Effects." *Journal of Labor Research* 1(Spring):115–132.

Neumann, George (1977), "Union Wage Differentials and the Decision to Join Unions."
    Mimeograph.

Oaxaca, Ronald L. (1973), "Estimation of Union/Nonunion Wage Differentials Within Oc-
    cupational/Regional Subgroups." *Journal of Human Resources* 10(Fall):529–536.

Olsen, Randall J. (1978), "Comment on 'The Effect of Unions on Earnings and Earnings
    on Unions: A Mixed Logit Approach.'" *International Economic Review*
    19(February):259–261.

Pencavel, John (1970), *An Analysis of the Quit Rate in American Manufacturing Industry*.
    Princeton, N.J.: Princeton University, Industrial Relations Section.

Pfeffer, Jeffrey, and Jerry Ross (1980), "Union–Nonunion Effects on Wage and Status
    Attainment." *Industrial Relations* 19(Spring):140–151.

Pierson, Gail (1968), "The Effect of Union Strengths on the U.S. 'Phillips Curve.'" *Amer-
    ican Economic Review* 58(June):456–467.

Plotnick, Robert (1980), "Trends in Male Earnings Inequality." Mimeograph, November.

Podgursky, Michael John (1980), "Trade Unions and Income Inequality." Ph.D. Thesis,
    University of Wisconsin—Madison.

Raisian, John (1979), "Cyclic Patterns in Weeks and Wages." *Economic Inquiry*
    17(October):475–495.

Rice, Robert G. (1968), "Skill, Earnings and the Growth of Wage Supplements." *American
    Economic Review* 56(May):583–593.

Schmidt, Peter (1978), "Estimation of a Simultaneous Equations Model with Jointly De-
    pendent Continuous and Qualitative Variables: The Union-Earnings Question Revis-
    ited." *International Economic Review* 19(June):453–465.

Schmidt, Peter, and Robert P. Strauss (1976), "The Effect of Unions on Earnings and Earn-
    ings on Unions: A Mixed Logit Approach." *International Economic Review*
    17(February):204–212.

Schoeplein, Robert N. (1977), "Secular Changes in the Skill Differential in Manufacturing,
    1952–1973." *Industrial and Labor Relations Review* 30(April):314–324.

Shapiro, David (1978), "Relative Wage Effects of Unions in the Public and Private Sectors."
    Industrial and Labor Relations Review 31(January):193–204.

Simon, Herbert (1955), "A Behavioral Model of Rational Choice." *Quarterly Journal of
    Economics* 69(February):99–118.

Slichter, Sumner, James Healy, and E. Robert Livernash (1960), *The Impact of Collective
    Bargaining on Management*. Washington, D.C.: The Brookings Institution.

Sloan, Frank, and Richard A. Elnicki (1979), "Determinants of Professional Nurses'
    Wages." In Richard M. Scheffer (ed.), *Research in Health Economics*, Vol. 1. Green-
    wich, Conn.: JAI Press Inc., pp. 217–254.

Solnick, L. M. (1978), "Unionism and Fringe Benefit Expenditures." *Industrial Relations*
    17(February):102–107.

Viscusi, W. Kip (1978), "Wealth Effects and Earnings Premiums for Job Hazards." *Review
    of Economics and Statistics* 60(August):408–416.

———— (1980), "Union, Labor Market Structure, and the Welfare Implications of the Quality
    of Work." *Journal of Labor Research* 1(Spring):175–192.

Weiss, Leonard (1966), "Concentration and Labor Earnings." *American Economic Review*
    56(March):96–117.

Welch, Stephen W. (1980), "Union–Nonunion Construction Wage Differentials." *Industrial
    Relations* 19(Spring):152–162.

Williamson, O. E., M. L. Wachter, and J. E. Harris (1975), "Understanding the Employment
    Relation: The Analysis of Idiosyncratic Exchange." *The Bell Journal of Economics*
    6(Spring):250–278.

Yanker, Robert H. (1980), "Productivity Versus Seniority: What is the Determining Factor
    in Regard to Wages and Promotion?" Senior Honors Thesis, Harvard College.

SAMPLE SELECTIVITY AS A PROXY
VARIABLE PROBLEM:
ON THE USE AND MISUSE OF GAUSSIAN
SELECTIVITY CORRECTIONS

Gregory M. Duncan

I. INTRODUCTION

As might be gleaned from the title, this paper builds on Heckman's (1978) insight that sample selectivity can be viewed as an omitted-variables problem. Here I show that if the errors are not Gaussian,[1] then using the Gaussian selectivity correction formulas proposed by Heckman leads to a problem akin to the errors-in-variables problem, or, more precisely, to the proxy variable problem. In particular, I use this intrepretation to explain seeming anomalies noted recently by many in the literature. These anomalies include the following: (1) the coefficient estimate on the selectivity correction variable is generally statistically insignificant (Dun-

New Approaches to Labor Unions.
Research in Labor Economics, Supplement 2, pages 333–345.
Copyright © 1983 by JAI Press Inc.
All rights of reproduction in any form reserved.
ISBN: 0-89232-265-9

can, 1980; Westin and Gillen, 1978; Freeman and Medoff, 1981); and (2) the same coefficients estimated in studies using different data sets vary a good deal while at the same time the estimated standard errors of these coefficients would suggest a good deal of stability (Freeman and Medoff, 1981).

The paper is divided into three parts. First, the sample selectivity problem and the effects of ignoring it are reviewed. Second, two common procedures for correcting the sample selectivity problem when the errors are Gaussian are discussed. Third, I discuss the consequences of using the Gaussian correction when the errors are not Gaussian. I conclude with a discussion of whether it is better to omit the selectivity correction as suggested by Freeman and Medoff (1981) or to use a Gaussian correction in the presence of non-Gaussian errors, thus accepting a proxy variable bias. I argue, based on the work of Goldberger (1980) and of Aigner (1974), that it will be generally better to go with a poor proxy for the selectivity variable rather than to drop the variable entirely.

II. THE SELECTIVITY BIAS PROBLEM

The basic selectivity bias model is sufficiently well known to most labor economists and econometricians that it will be considered only briefly. Consider a population and random drawings from that population. For each drawing (observation) three or more dependent variables could be observed, say, the union preference measure U_t, something akin to the utility of being in a union, the union wage rate W_t^u, and the nonunion wage rate W_t^n. If all were observed, then the relationship between these and personal characteristics of the individual might be represented by a system of linear equations:

$$W_t^u = X_t^T \beta_u + \epsilon_t^u \tag{1}$$

$$W_t^n = X_t^T \beta_n + \epsilon_t^n \tag{2}$$

$$U_t = Z_t^T \gamma + \delta_t. \tag{3}$$

The vectors of explanatory variables X_t and Z_t are exogenous and may or may not be mutually exclusive.[2] It is reasonable to expect that the effect of similar unobserved variables in each equation would render the errors correlated across equations. So a reasonable model for the errors is that they have zero means with constant variances and covariances. Suppose that W_t^u represents the union wage that would be obtained by a person drawn at random from the population if he or she belonged to a union, *whether or not he or she actually belonged to a union*. Inference in such an ideal situation is easy; one runs ordinary least squares (OLS) on Eq. (1) and proceeds as usual. Unfortunately, this ideal experiment is rarely performed. That is, we do not observe union wages for those who do not belong to unions (but we do observe the nonunion wage). Let us say that if $U_t \geq 0$, a person belongs to a union, whereas if $U_t < 0$, a person does not belong to a union. The experiment actually performed is then the following:

$$W_t^u = X_t^T \beta + \epsilon_t^u \quad \text{if} \quad U_t \geq 0 \tag{1'}$$

$$W_t^n = X_t^T \beta_n + \epsilon_t^n \quad \text{if} \quad U_t < 0. \tag{2'}$$

That is, a person is drawn at random from the population, and if $U_t \geq 0$, we observe the union wage and union status; otherwise we observed the nonunion wage and union status.[3]

What will OLS results applied to equation (1) above tell us if the experiment performed is that represented by equations (1') and (2') above?[4] To see we note that

$$E(W_t) = X_t^T \beta + E(\epsilon_t \mid u_t \geq 0), \tag{4}$$

while $V(W_t) = V(\epsilon_t : u_t \geq 0)$. Johnson and Kotz (1972) show that

$$E(\epsilon_t : u_t \geq 0) = E(\epsilon_t \mid \delta_t \geq - Z_t^T \gamma)$$

$$= \frac{\sigma_{\delta\epsilon}}{\sigma_\delta^2} E(\delta_t \mid \delta_t \geq -Z_t^T \gamma),$$

while

$$V(\epsilon_t \mid u_t \geq 0) = \sigma_\epsilon^2 - \sigma_{\delta\epsilon}(\sigma_\delta^{-2} - \sigma_\delta^{-2} V(\delta_t \mid \delta_t \geq -Z_t^T)\sigma_\delta^{-2})\sigma_{\delta\epsilon}$$

$$= \sigma_\epsilon^2 - \frac{\sigma_{\delta\epsilon}^2}{\sigma_\delta^4} (\sigma_\delta^2 - V(\delta_t \mid \delta_t \geq -Z_t^T \gamma))$$

Let us concentrate on the relationship between Eqs. (1) and (1'). Based on these formulas, Heckman (1978) points out that applying OLS to (1) will suffer from two sources of misspecification: (1) an omitted variable bias and (2) heteroskedasticity. The omitted-variable interpretation arises from treating $E(\delta_t \mid \delta_t \geq -Z_t^T \gamma)$ as a relevant explanatory variable with coefficient $\sigma_{\delta\epsilon}/\sigma_\delta^2$. If this variable is orthogonal to the explanatory variables in (1), then OLS will still yield unbiased estimates of β. Note, however, that the errors might still be heteroskedastic so that the usual regression tests would be invalid. However, if $\sigma_{\delta\epsilon}$ is zero, then OLS will yield good estimates of β and valid test statistics. Rather than simply saying that if neither of the two conditions obtains, one faces an omitted-variable bias, let us examine what such OLS estimates could tell us.

OLS performed on (1) when (1') obtains yields the coefficients of the best linear approximation to $E(W_t \mid X_t \text{ and } U_t \geq 0)$. This can be easily seen by examining Kendall and Stuart (1979) or White (1981).[5] If one is

interested in questions such as what is the effect of personal characteristics on the wage *of a union member,* then the OLS estimates of the
regression

$$W_t^u = X_t^T \alpha + V_t \tag{1''}$$

can be used to answer that question. Note that α in (1'') is not the β_u in
(1); it will differ by the degree of the omitted-variable bias. Moreover,
the error term V_t has a different distribution than does that of ϵ_t. In particular (see again White, 1981), the V_t will be heteroskedastic so that even
if $\hat{\alpha}_{OLS}$ is a good estimator, tests based on $\hat{\alpha}_{OLS}$ and the usual regression
formulas for standard errors will be incorrect (White, 1981). This is be-
cause when there is heteroskedasticity the usual formula for the variance–
covariance matrix of the coefficient estimator is incorrect. The correct
formula is given in Eicker (1967), Hinkley (1977), White (1980), and in
multivariate situations by Duncan (1981b). In this case it would be

$$V(\hat{\alpha}_{OLS}) = \frac{(X^T X)^{-1} \sum_{i=1}^{N} \hat{V}_i^2 X_i X_i^T (X^T X)^{-1}}{N},$$

where $\hat{V}_i = W_i - X_i^T \hat{\alpha}_{OLS}$ and X_i^T is the row vector corresponding to the
ith observation on the independent variables.

In conclusion, in answer to the question of when to employ and how
to interpret regression results: First, if there is no selectivity or if the
errors in the status equation are independent of or uncorrelated with the
errors in the regression equation [e.g., equation (1) above], then subject
to the usual qualifications the OLS estimates may be used to answer
questions about the parent population relationships between the dependent variable and the independent variables. All tests will be valid using
the usual statistics.

Second, if there is selectivity but the selectivity variable is orthogonal
to the other explanatory variables, then OLS estimates may be used to
draw inferences about the parent population relationships in Eqs. (1) and
(2), but the usual tests may be invalid due to possible heteroskedasticity.
However, use of a heteroskedastic robust estimate of the variance–covariance matrix of the OLS coefficients, in place of the usual estimate,
will allow accurate testing in the usual fashion. One simply replaces, in
a test statistic, the usual estimates by the heteroskedastic robust ones and
then proceeds as usual.

Finally, if there is a selectivity bias, a regression of the dependent
variable on the independent variables will not allow any direct inference
on the relationship between these variables in the parent population. Instead, such estimates will explain the relationship between these variables
in an unrepresentative sample, one that takes selectivity as given.

Although the regression estimates may be precise, it is the case that they are precise estimates of the wrong things. For we are generally interested in the coefficients of the best linear predictor of W_t given X_t; but what we obtain are estimates of the coefficients of the best linear predictor of W_t given X_t and the selection rule. The two are different. Estimates of the latter cannot be used to make inferences about the former.

As an example consider only Eqs. (1) and (3) above. Let $w_t = W_t^u$ if $U_t \geq 0$ but let it be unobserved otherwise. Assume that $Z_t^T = (X_t^T, Z_t^{1T})$ so that X and Z have common elements. Moreover, assume that $E(\epsilon_t^u|\delta_t)$ is linear in δ_t, $V(\epsilon_t^u|\delta_t)$ is independent of δ_t, and δ_t is uniformly distributed over some interval. That is, we are discussing a rigorously formulated linear probability model. It is easy to show that under these conditions $E(\epsilon_t^u|U_t \geq 0) = \mu + X_t^T\beta_1 + Z_t^{1T}\gamma_1$, where the interpretation of the parameters is unimportant. Now $V(\epsilon_t^u|U_t \geq 0)$ will be quadratic in X_t^T and Z_t^{1T}. If one performs ordinary least squares on

$$W_t = X_t^T\beta_u + E(\epsilon_t^u|U_t \geq 0) + \epsilon_t^*$$

$$= \mu + X_t^T(\beta_u + \beta_1) + Z_t^{1T}\gamma_1 + \epsilon_t^*,$$

one does not obtain estimates of β_u but of $(\beta_u + \beta_1)$. The standard errors are wrong, though easily corrected, due to heteroskedasticity induced by the dependence of $V(\epsilon_t^u|U_t \geq 0)$ on quadratic terms. One may find that $\beta_u + \beta_1$ is estimated quite precisely—but that does not change the fact that estimates of β_u are not being obtained. If estimates of β_u are desired, one must obtain estimates of β_1 as well; speaking loosely, this uses up degrees of freedom and one would expect less precise estimates will be obtained if β_u, β_1, and γ_1 are all estimated than when $(\beta_1 + \beta_u)$ and γ_1 are estimated. Thus it is easy to believe that ordinary least squares estimates of $(\beta_u + \beta_1)$ are more precise than selectivity corrected estimates of β_u. But, reiterating, least squares yields estimates of $(\beta_1 + \beta_u)$, not β_u, and it is β_u we are generally interested in.

III. SELECTIVITY BIAS CORRECTIONS

Given that one does not wish to employ OLS for the reasons mentioned above, one must correct for the selectivity. Current approaches include maximum-likelihood, instrumental variables, weighted nonlinear least squares, or selectivity adjusted ordinary least squares. The maximum-likelihood and instrumental variable techniques are not given much play in current practice.[6] Nonlinear least squares is somewhat more popular, but most popular is selectivity adjusted ordinary least squares which was developed by Heckman (1974) and used by many (see Freeman and Medoff in this volume for a survey of applications to union issues).

The selectivity adjustment technique, in current practice, depends upon an assumption that the errors in the status equation are Gaussian. (Most papers assume more, but all that is required is that the error in the status equation be Gaussian.) In the case of Gaussian δ_t we have

$$E(\delta_t \mid \delta_t \geq -Z_t\gamma) = \sigma_\delta \frac{f(-Z_t\gamma/\sigma_\delta)}{1 - F(-Z_t\gamma/\sigma_\delta)}$$

$$= \sigma_\delta\gamma\left(\frac{-Z_t\gamma}{\sigma_\delta}\right)$$

and

$$V(\delta_t \mid \delta_t \geq -Z_t\gamma) = (-Z_t\gamma)\lambda\left(\frac{-Z_t\gamma}{\sigma_\delta}\right) + \sigma_\delta^2,$$

where $f(\cdot)$ is the standard Gaussian density, $F(\cdot)$ is the standard Gaussian distribution, and $\lambda(\cdot)$ is the inverse Mills ratio. Consequently, if $\lambda(\cdot)$ were known for each observation, one has the heteroskedastic regression model

$$W_t^u = X_t\beta_u + \phi\lambda_t + \eta_t, \tag{5}$$

where

$$\lambda_t = \lambda\left(\frac{-Z_t\gamma}{\sigma_\delta}\right);$$

$$\phi = \frac{\sigma_{\epsilon\delta}}{\sigma_\delta} \quad E(\eta_t) = 0; \text{ and}$$

$$V(\eta_t) = \sigma_\delta^2 - \lambda_t Z_t\gamma.$$

The common form for the variances is known, so if λ_t, γ, and σ_δ^2 are known, then weighted least squares could be employed to estimate (β, ϕ). Since γ/σ_δ and σ_δ are unknown, it is common practice to estimate them. The procedure is as follows: First, a probit estimation procedure, usually maximum-likelihood, is carried out to yield consistent estimates of γ/σ_δ. One then estimates λ_t by $\hat{\lambda}_t = \lambda(-Z_t\hat{\gamma}/\hat{\sigma}_\delta)$. (Note that one typically cannot estimate γ and σ_δ separately.) Second, ordinary least squares is applied to the equation

$$W_t = X_t\beta + \phi\hat{\lambda}_t + \eta_t^* \tag{6}$$

and initial consistent estimates of β and ϕ are obtained. One cannot stop here because the errors η_t^* are heteroskedastic. Note also that they differ from η_t in Eq. (1') above by a term $\phi(\lambda_t - \hat{\lambda}_t)$ which results from the fact that λ_t had to be estimated. Third, the estimated residuals

$$\hat{\eta}_t = w_t - X_t\hat{\beta} + \hat{\phi}\hat{\lambda}_t$$

are formed and σ_δ^2 is estimated by

$$\hat{\sigma}_\delta^2 = \sum_{i=1}^{N} \frac{(\hat{\eta}_t^2 + \hat{\lambda}_t Z_t \hat{\gamma})^2}{N}.$$

Fourth, the variances $V(\eta_t)$ are estimated using

$$\hat{V}(\eta_t) = \hat{\sigma}_\delta^2 - \hat{\lambda}_t Z_t \hat{\gamma}.$$

Finally, weighted least squares is done on

$$W_t = X_t \beta + \phi \hat{\lambda}_t + \eta_t^*$$

using as weights the $\hat{V}(\eta_t)$.

This is common practice but it is wrong. The key reason, as pointed out by Heckman (1978), Lee and Trost (1980), and others, is that in estimating the variance of η_t^* one only accounts for the heteroskedasticity induced by selectivity. Unaccounted for are the heteroskedasticity and the serial dependence induced by using an estimate, $\hat{\lambda}_t$, rather than λ_t itself. Consequently the correct estimate variance–covariance matrix of the estimates of β and ϕ is not the one printed by the computer, and so the usual tests will not yield correct inferences.

Correct formulas can be obtained from the aforementioned works by Heckman and the others. However, my own preference now is to apply nonlinear weighted least squares in the fifth step above. That is, instead of doing weighted least squares on

$$W_t = X_t \beta + \phi \hat{\lambda}_t + \eta_t^*$$

using $\hat{V}(\eta_t)$ as weights, I do nonlinear least squares on

$$W_t = X_t \beta + \phi \lambda(-Z_t \theta) + \eta_t$$

using $\hat{V}(\eta_t)$ as weights. Note that I have replaced γ/σ_δ by θ to indicate that separate estimates of γ and σ_δ typically cannot be obtained at this stage (they can, of course, with a more complete estimation procedure such as maximum-likelihood, or a system of nonlinear least squares estimation procedure). Following this procedure, one uses the asymptotic standard errors and other statistics, as printed by the computer, in the usual fashion. One need not write special variance-correction packages to account for the use of an estimate of λ_t, because a separate estimate is not used.

As near as I can tell few, if any, of the papers mentioned in the recent survey by Freeman and Medoff (1981) used the correct variance–covariance formulas; consequently, it is likely that the estimated standard errors are incorrect. This could explain why the estimated standard errors in the studies cited by Freeman and Medoff are at odds with the intersample variation of coefficients between studies. This suspicion is easily handled by finding out what the various authors actually did and if the wrong formulas were used when correcting them. But I do not think this is the problem; I have looked at my own work, work I have done with Duane Leigh, and other work, and only once, in a context unrelated to economics, much less labor economics, did using the correct formulas make much difference. This is not to say that the correct formulas should not be used; they should, as argued below. It does say that the explanation for the divergence between estimated measures of stability, the estimated standard errors, and actual variability as measured by intersample variation in estimated coefficients is likely to lie elsewhere. In the next section I suggest that the explanation lies, in fact, in the assumption that the errors δ_t in the status equation are Gaussian. This means that the above procedures may be acceptable only when the errors δ_t are Gaussian or when there is some transformation of the errors δ_t that will achieve Gaussianity.

IV. ABNORMAL SELECTION ERRORS AS ERRORS IN VARIABLES

The title of this section[7] is lifted from a paper of Goldberger (1980), who together with myself (Duncan, 1980, 1981a), Poirier (1978), Olsen (1981), Crawford (1979), Hausman and Wise (1977), and others have suggested that the Gaussian assumption may not be inconsequential in selectivity models the way it is in straight regression models. Goldberger finds, based on Monte Carlo results, that misspecifying the error distribution slightly leads to extreme biases in selectivity-corrected regressions. However, he concludes that using a Gaussian correction factor is better than using none at all. My own work on maximum-likelihood estimators leads to the same conclusions for the special cases of censored and truncated regression models (see Duncan, 1980).

One consequence of using a Gaussian selectivity correction for non-Gaussian errors is a bias, but one possibly less severe than that faced when the selectivity issue is ignored. A second consequence of misspecifying the error distribution is that the associated correction for heteroskedasticity will also be incomplete so that even if the direction of bias is known, selectivity-corrected statistics of the types discussed in the previous section will be unusable since the standard errors are calculated incorrectly. For example, if an estimate is biased toward zero (as we suggest below these might be), then an estimate found by a t-test to be significantly larger, or smaller, than zero rightly leads one to conservatively reject the hypothesis that the coefficient is really zero, *provided* that the variance estimate used in the t-statistic is correctly calculated.

To see this we return to Eq. (4) and note that

$$W_t = X_t\beta + \phi E(\delta_t \mid \delta_t \geq -Z_t\gamma) + \eta_t.$$

For simplicity assume that γ/σ_δ is known so that λ_t is known as well. Then if we use the Gaussian selectivity correction factor λ_t in place of $E(\delta_t: \delta_t \geq -Z_t\gamma)$, it is like using a variable measured in error. Consider the identity

$$\lambda_t = E(\delta_t \mid \delta_t \geq -Z_t\gamma) + (\lambda_t - E(\delta_t \mid \delta_t \geq -Z_t\gamma))$$

and treat $S_t = \lambda_t - E(\delta_t \mid \delta_t \geq -Z_t\gamma)$ as though it were a random error (of course it really is not, but this is only a technical detail which is inconsequential for the intuitive understanding of what is going on). Let us therefore write

$$\lambda_t = E_t + S_t.$$

Now S_t need not have mean zero, so we may continually overestimate or underestimate E_t; hence let us write

$$\lambda_t = E_t + S + S_t^*,$$

where S is the mean of S_t, and S_t^* has zero mean. Thus the effect of misspecifying the error distribution of δ_t is similar to that of applying OLS to a heteroskedastic errors-in-variables or proxy variable model. An additional problem is that the constant will be biased by $\phi\delta$. Using the reasoning of the above sections, it is clear that the heteroskedastic robust covariance estimator will be a consistent estimator of variance of the limiting distribution of the OLS estimator applied to the equation

$$W_t = X_t\beta + \phi\lambda_t.$$

Immediately, we see a likely explanation for the phenomenon noted in the introduction. We have statistical insignificance because the estimate of ϕ is biased downward, as is generally the case with errors-in-variables models. Also the standard errors are calculated incorrectly (though the direction of bias also could be downward). Hence, the usual standard errors will not accurately reflect the true stability of the estimates, so it is not surprising to find small (incorrectly) estimated standard errors in the presence of a great deal of intersample instability. Of course, the fact that one uses a estimate $\hat{\lambda}_t$ for λ_t will further disturb matters, but I think only to a second order. Nonetheless, its effect is obvious: It will exacerbate the inaccurate calculation of the standard errors as well as contribute to the errors-in-variables problem.

V. RECOMMENDATIONS FOR PRACTICAL APPLICATION

The practitioner is now faced with three options. First, ignore the selectivity problem. Second, employ a Gaussian correction. Third, apply some sort of robust non-Gaussian correction. Practically, the typical researcher faces only the first two. Using the framework above the choice is tantamount to that of omitting or including a proxy. The difference is the heteroskedasticity caused by selectivity.

There is an extensive literature on the question of whether to include or omit a proxy variable. Let us recall the results of Aigner (1974). Aigner shows that in the standard linear model with homoskedastic errors using even a poor proxy will usually be better in terms of mean square error than omitting such a proxy.[8] Aigner's basic result is that omitting the variable will dominate if the relative error is large *and* the sample size is small, *and* the correlation between the variable measured in error with the other variables in the regression is small. The latter case is the one mentioned above where the selectivity term is orthogonal to the other variables—in that case there is no bias, just an efficiency loss. The second case is not important here since the data sets we are discussing are large. Finally, as shown in Duncan (1981a), the rank correlation between the true selectivity term and the Gaussian selectivity term is 1, so it is doubtful that a great deal of the variation in the Gaussian selectivity term can be attributed to the error in approximation (which we are treating as an error in variable).

This argument must be qualified in our context by the fact that these results were developed for the homoskedastic case and ours is heteroskedastic. I do not think this will change the above argument. Nevertheless, it is useful to recount the findings of Goldberger (1980) on exactly the point of whether it is better to neglect the selectivity correction or include it. Goldberger finds that the bias is less when a misspecified selectivity variable is included than when it is not. He does not investigate mean squared error.

Based on the foregoing, my recommendation is to go with the Gaussian correction, but use a heteroskedastic robust estimate of the covariance matrix of the estimates (see Appendix).

Readers who follow this advice are likely to discover that their estimates are still not as precise as ordinary least squares estimates. All that the use of heteroskedastic robust covariance estimators will do is insure that one has the right measure of precision. They cannot make imprecise estimates precise. This imprecision is to be expected and should not be taken as support for omitting the correction. Recall that the experiment actually performed in many of these studies is the selection conditioned one (see Section II). The linear regression that those who abjure the selectivity correction would have us use tells us about a linear relationship between the independent and dependent variables in the experiment that was actually performed. To the extent that OLS is a technique designed for just such a purpose, it is not surprising that precise stable estimates are obtained. However, we are usually interested in using data from the selectivity-conditioned experiment to make inferences about an experiment that was never performed, the experiment made implicit in Eqs. (1) and (2). Since we make the data do more work, it is reasonable to assume that the results will be less efficient. Alternatively, in extending the data from inferences about the selected population to inferences about the parent population, we necessarily bring along fewer a priori restrictions— consequently efficiency and precision suffer.

Finally, a good deal of work is currently in progress on exactly what to do about non-Gaussian errors. Poirier (1978) suggests the use of a Box–Cox transform to obtain normality. Olsen (1981) suggests the use of a more flexible distribution. I have suggested two robust estimators. In the first (Duncan, 1980), I jointly estimate the underlying density function, the coefficients, and a measure of scale. In the second (Duncan, 1981a), I use order statistics and instrumental variables to obtain consistent and asymptotic estimates. None of these latter techniques has been applied often enough for an assessment of their suitability for mass use. I mention them as evidence that help is on the way.

APPENDIX

In this appendix I show how I would do a Gaussian selectivity correction for the model in the text. Begin by employing the four step procedure described in the text. Next, perform weighted nonlinear least squares as suggested in the text, but obtain the matrix of gradients for each observation. For simplicity, write

$$\frac{W_t^u}{\sqrt{\hat{V}_t}} = \frac{g(X_t, \beta, \theta, \phi)}{\sqrt{\hat{V}_t}} + \eta_t^u.$$

Obtain $g_t^* = (\partial g/\partial \beta, \partial g/\partial \theta, \partial g/\partial \phi)$ for each t; these can usually be obtained from a nonlinear least squares program. Let

$$\hat{\eta}_t^* = \frac{W_t^u - g(X_t, \hat{\beta}, \hat{\theta}, \hat{\phi})}{\sqrt{\hat{V}_t}} , \qquad t = 1, \ldots, N,$$

be the normalized residual returned by the computer. Estimate the variance of $(\hat{\beta}, \hat{\theta}, \hat{\phi})$ by

$$\hat{V}^* = N \left(\sum_{t=1}^{N} g_t^* g_t^{*T} \right)^{-1} \sum_{i=1}^{N} (\eta_i^*)^2 g_i^* g_i^{*T} \left(\sum_{t=1}^{N} g_t^* g_t^{*T} \right)^{-1}.$$

According to Fox et al. (1980), this will be a heteroskedastic robust estimate of the variance–covariance matrix of $(\hat{\beta}, \hat{\theta}, \hat{\phi})$.

ACKNOWLEDGMENTS

This paper owes its inception to Joseph Reid and Walter Oi, who encouraged me to elaborate upon an informal remark I made during the New Approaches to Labor Unions Conference, held at Virginia Polytechnic Institute, Blacksburg, Va., October 1981. My colleague, Duane Leigh, gave invaluable insight and advice. I am the source of any errors found herein.

NOTES

1. I use the term *Gaussian* in place of the more usual *normal*. Gaussian errors are normally distributed.
2. For simplicity, $U_t = Z_t^T\gamma + \delta_t$ is the reduced form and does not contain a wage rate or wage differential.
3. We shall call Eq. (3) above the union status equation.
4. It might be noted that a common practice of pooling union and nonunion wage equations and using a union dummy variable is equivalent to asserting that, except for the intercept terms, the coefficients in each Eq. (1) and (2) above are equal. In addition to the problems mentioned below, this has the effect of imposing an erroneous constraint, another source of bias. We will not discuss this special case further.
5. Poirier and Melino (1978) show that generally the coefficients of a variate in truncated regression models do not correspond to the change in the conditional expectation for a change in the variate.
6. See, however, Hausman and Wise (1977).
7. Much of this section is taken from Duncan (1981b).
8. Before Aigner's paper, McCallum (1972) and Wickers (1972) had demonstrated that the bias of OLS estimates using the proxy variable is lower than that of OLS excluding the proxy.

REFERENCES

Aigner, D. J. (1974), "MSE Dominance of Least Squares with Errors-of-Observations." *Journal of Econometrics* 2(December):365–372.

Crawford, D. L. (1979), *Estimating Models of Earnings from Truncated Samples*. Unpublished Ph.D. dissertation, Department of Economics, University of Wisconsin.

Duncan, G. M. (1980), "A Relatively Distribution Robust Censored Regression Estimator." Washington State University, Working Paper.

——— (1981a), "An Instrumental Variable Correction for Non-Gaussian Selectivity Models." Washington State University, Working Paper.

——— (1981b), "Estimation in Heteroscedastic Systems." *International Economic Review* (forthcoming).

Duncan, G. M., and D. E. Leigh (1980), "Wage Determination in the Union and Nonunion Sectors: A Sample Selectivity Approach." *Industrial and Labor Relations Review* 34(October):24–34.

Eicker, F. (1967), "Limit Theorems for Regressions with Dependent and Unequal Errors." In *Fifth Berkeley Symposium in Probability and Mathematical Statistics,* Vol. I. Berkeley: University of California Press.

Fox, T., D. Hinkley, and K. Larntz (1980), "Jackknifing in Nonlinear Situations." *Technometrics* 22(1):28–33.

Freeman, R., and J. Medoff (1981), *The Impact of Collective Bargaining: Illusion or Reality.* Mimeograph, March.

Goldberger, A. (1980), "Abnormal Selection Bias." University of Wisconsin, SSRI Working Paper.

Hausman, J., and D. Wise (1977), "Social Experimentation, Truncated Distributions, and Efficient Estimation." *Econometrica* 45:919–938.

Heckman, J. (1976), "A Common Structure for Truncation Sample Selection, Limited Dependent Variables, and a Simple Estimator for Such Models." *Annals of Economic and Social Measurement* 5:475–492.

—— (1978), "Sample Selectivity as a Specification Error." *Econometrica* 47:153–161.

Hinkley, D. (1977), "Jackknifing in Unbalanced Situations." *Technometrics* 19:285–292.

Hurd, M. (1979), "Estimation in Truncated Samples when There is Heteroscedasticity." *Journal of Econometrics* 11:247–258.

Johnson, D., and S. Kotz (1972), *Distributions in Statistics: Continuous Multivariate Distribution.* New York: John Wiley and Sons.

Kendall, M., and A. Stuart (1979), *The Advanced Theory of Statistics,* Vol. II, (Fourth Ed.). New York: Hafner Press, Chap. 28.

Lee, L. F., and R. P. Trost (1978), "Estimation of Some Limited Dependent Variable Models with Application to Housing Demand." *Journal of Econometrics* 8:357–382.

McCallum, B. T. (1972), "Relative Asymptotic Bias from Errors of Observation and Measurement." *Econometrica* 40(July):757–758.

Olsen, R. J. (1979), "Tests for the Presence of Selectivity Bias and Their Relation to Specifications of Fundamental Form and Error Distributions." Yale University, Department of Economics Working Paper.

Poirier, D. J. (1978), "The Use of the Box-Cox Transformation in Limited Dependent Variable Models." *Journal of the American Statistical Association* 73:284–287.

Poirier, D., and A. Melino (1978), "A Note on the Interpretation of Regression Coefficients within a Class of Truncated Distributions." *Econometrica* 46:1207–1210.

Westin, R., and D. Gillen (1978), "Parking Location and Transit Demand: A Case Study of Endogenous Attributes in Dissaggregated Mode Choice Models." *Journal of Econometrics* 8:75–101.

White, H. (1980), "A Heteroscedastic Consistent Covariance Matrix Estimator and A Direct Test for Heteroscendasticity." *Econometrica* 48:817–838.

—— (1981), "Using Least Squares to Approximate Unknown Regression Functions." *International Economic Review* 21:149–170.

Wickers, M. R. (1972), "A Note on the Use of Proxy Variables." *Econometrica* 40:759–762.

CONCLUDING COMMENTS

John Burton and Gordon Tullock

I. SOME GROUNDS FOR UNEASE

In his Preface, Reid expresses "unease" about the present state of labor union economics. It seems to us that one possible result of reading the reports of the conference would be to increase this feeling of unease. There is still much confusion about what labor unions are in terms of their fundamental economic characteristics. Efforts to analyze their economic effects necessarily suffer.

If we look historically through the explanations of what labor unions are or do, we find that there is no current way of selecting among them. The very traditional view held by many honest union members that labor unions exist to raise the wages of all labor is thought to be absurd by most economists. There is one thing to be said in its favor, which is that apparently at least a small amount of effort is put in politically by labor unions in essentially charitable efforts to help nommembers. This is, however, a very minor aspect of union activity and is totally dominated by various political activities, the net result of which is to injure nonmembers.

New Approaches to Labor Unions.
Research in Labor Economics, Supplement 2, pages 347–353.
Copyright © 1983 by JAI Press Inc.
All rights of reproduction in any form reserved.
ISBN: 0-89232-265-9

The second obvious easy explanation of union behavior is that they are attempting to maximize the well-being of their members. Such an approach continues to inspire some theoretical work in the modern debate on the economic analysis of unionism (e.g., Oswald, 1982a,b). Actually, this approach may be divided into two categories, depending on whether you are talking about the present membership or some kind of time continuum in which future members are also to be benefited. The results of these two subsections would of course be different, but as far as we can see union behavior does not aim at maximizing either of these variables. The fundamental defect of the approach, in either variant, is that it implicitly assumes that the union always acts as the fair and perfect agent of the union members. Faith and Reid's paper in this volume should do much to dispel this notion. As they argue, there are solid economic reasons for assuming that the union is likely to be an imperfect agent—and not necessarily even an agent of the members.

Another possible explanation is that the union in fact exists for the benefit of its current management, who are the controllers, although not the owners, of the organization. This approach also may be subdivided into three categories. The first is one in which the union leaders find some way of converting or indeed perverting the operation of the union to their personal financial advantage. Lentz (1982) has done some work on this. In the extreme, this analysis leads to Gregg Lewis's (1956) analysis of the "boss-dominated" monopoly union. This is a case in which the members of the union essentially gain nothing out of their membership (except that they are not beaten up by the organizers) and the entire profit goes to the organizers. However, not even in the most Mafia-controlled unions would this model appear to be completely accurate. The second variant assumes that the union executive is unable to reap pecuniary advantage in the manner suggested above but is able to use its managerial discretion to maximize leadership utility along nonpecuniary avenues, such as the size of the union organization and their personal security of tenure. This is the so-called political model of the union, advanced initially by Ross (1944). Although Ross himself rejected an economic analysis of such a trade union model, his analysis may be seen as a forerunner of Baumol's (1959) model of the managerial enterprise. In the Baumol model the managers of the corporation maximize their utility by maximizing the size of their empire (specifically, the revenue of the enterprise), subject to the attainment of a "satisfactory" level of returns for stockholders. In the political model of the union, the managers of the union maximize the size of their empire (specifically, the total membership of the union), subject to the constraint of providing a "satisfactory" level of benefits to the rank and file. Perhaps not surprisingly, given this theoretical similarity, the Ross model of the union suffers from the same basic analytical defect as the Baumol model of the corporation. Neither model specifies clearly what determines the satisficing level of returns to stockholders and union members respectively (Burton, 1982). If this constraint is not sharply defined—and it is not in either model—then we cannot determine whether the arena for managerial discretion is large and significant or small and thus trivial for analysis.

The third variant of this general approach also holds that the union is indeed a business run by its management but that it is one of those businesses which are engaged in the competitive business of forming a monopoly. In other words, the union attempts to form a monopoly of labor to deal with the management in its particular industry, but the management of the union faces competition in its organization of the monopoly. For example, another group of people who break away from the union might compete with it. Another example: The union has to offer to younger people who are thinking of a lifetime career a satisfactory prospect or they won't enter the unionized industry and eventually the union will die out. The seeds of this approach once again may be seen as laying in Lewis's (1956) treatment and Lazear's paper here is a development of it. Personally, we find such an approach quite attractive; not least because it allows of the possibility of tieing in the economic analysis of trade unions to the more general study of rent-seeking institutions and activities.[1] One important question-mark hanging over such an approach, however, concerns the assumed environment and avenue of union rent-seeking. In both the Gregg Lewis and Lazear models of the rent seeking union, the assumed context of union operation is that of private sector pecuniary markets, and the assumed avenue of rent seeking is the standard monopoloid practice of establishing and enforcing a supracompetitive price for unionized labor services. Neither the assumed environment of action or the strategy of rent seeking analyzed are inclusive of all possibilities and may indeed be less important in the real world than these other possibilities. As regards the environment, the public sector is becoming an increasingly important arena for trade unionism in both America and Britain. Here, furthermore, unions would seem to be seeking rent not only by market closure but by obtaining the support of the state in transferring wealth to union members and leaders from taxpayers. Moreover, even in the private sector, rent seeking by trade unions (and professional associations) may sometimes, or even often, rest more upon regulatory capture by the state than the direct enforcement of a supracompetitive price for labor services by the union itself. Minimum wage laws, the legal privileges conferred on independent trade unions by the Wagner Act, and the Davis–Bacon Act are perhaps to be seen as instances of this little-analyzed avenue of union rent seeking in the private sector.

To conclude at this juncture: no one model of the trade union is without defects; in some cases, these defects are clearly mortal.

II. MAXIMUM "UNEASE": THE FREEMAN-MEDOFF ANALYSIS OF UNIONISM

Our unease about the credibility of the foundations of some approaches to theorizing about unions reaches maximum intensity regarding Freeman and Medoff's (FM hereafter) analysis of unionism.

There can be no dispute that FM and their colleagues—collectively embodying the so-called Harvard school approach to unionism—have done much in recent years to provide us with a large body of new empirical studies on unionism. What worries us—and what worried many participants at the conference—is partly the lack of theory underpinning their empirical research. Charges of "measurement without theory" and "blackbox economics" have not gone unvoiced or unheard.

However, it is not fair or true to say that FM are entirely without some theoretical formulation behind their empirical studies. The basic FM "model" of unionism may be briefly recapitulated as follows.

Unionism has two "faces" (Freeman and Medoff, 1979). One is its monopoly face, long analyzed by economists. Trade unions are a labor cartel that raises (relative) wages above the competitive level. FM do not deny this aspect of unionism but suggest that the monopoly model alone is unable to explain the total impact of unionism on firms and the economy. Trade unions also have a "collective voice/institutional response" face and impact. Trade unions are an (effective) means of channeling median employee preferences to employers. The "institutional response," they assert, is that X-inefficiency is squeezed out of managers. Overall organizational efficiency, labor productivity in particular, and thus the general functioning of the economy are improved. A balanced view of unionism requires that we take both faces into account. In other writings, they assert that the productivity-enhancing effect of unionism roughly offsets its wage-raising impact; indeed they claim that in many settings the former is more important than the latter. Thus the impact of unionism on the economy is, on net, benign.

There are obvious problems with this set of propositions. It is not impossible, incidentally, to think of reasons why trade unions may improve labor productivity (see the paper by Faith and Reid, in this volume). This is not the problem with FM's analysis. *The* problem is that if unions act to improve productivity more than they add to wages—as FM assert is often the case—we might expect business enterprises to be glad, if not overjoyed, to have unions organizing their workers. It is very commonly the other way about.

FM answer this charge by the point that the enterprise is concerned with profits, and not productivity per se (Freeman and Medoff, 1982). In empirical studies, it has often been found that the presence of unionism lowers the rate of return on capital for the enterprise. Thus business opposition to unionism is explained by FM.

But is it, really? Consider Figure 1.[2] Here the curve MP^n represents the firm's demand for labor when laborers are nonunionized. The (real) wage rate, set by competitive market forces, is W_c. The firm hires N_c workers. Now, assume a union enters the scene and successfully organizes (all) employees. With this strike-threat power established, they manage to jack up the wage to (say) W_u. But we must not forget the other face of unionism. They also increase (marginal) productivity; and "usually" (FM allege) by the same amount as the percentage increase in wages. Reflecting this assumption, we exhibit the marginal productivity schedule of unionized labor as MP^u.

Consider now the two triangles abc and def, which represent the producer's surplus in the pre- and postunion situations. They are exactly the

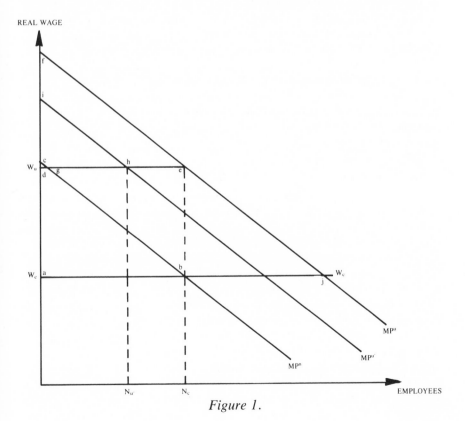

Figure 1.

same in size. Moreover, the ratio of the wage rate to the marginal productivity of labor is exactly the same in the two situations. As basic theory of the firm informs us, the disturbance of this ratio (or some other factor price/factor marginal productivity ratio) is necessary to cause a profit-maximizing firm to alter its purchasing of labor inputs. The profit-maximizing firm would in fact be indifferent as between the two situations as portrayed in Figure 1. There has been no decline in returns to the firm.

For there to be a reduction in producer surplus in the postunion situation as compared to the preunion one, there are two possibilities. One would be that MP^u is in the same position as MP^n; unionism raises the marginal productivity schedule not at all, and the producer's surplus declines from triangle abc to dgc. The other possibility is that unionism raises productivity, as FM allege, but by less than they raise wages. In this case, the postunion situation is shown by some curve in between the positions MP^n and MP^u, such as $MP^{u'}$. In this case, the producer's surplus of the profit-maximizing firm declines from abc to dhi and the firm reduces employment from Nc to Nu'.

The heart of the puzzle surrounding FM's work is that if unions do the things they say they do to productivity, profits are not reduced by unionism and may even be raised. Conversely, if unions do the things they say they do to enterprise profits, then this implies that unionism does less to raise productivity than they assert. Thus our unease about the consistency of their "model" of the impacts of unionism.

Moreover, if enterprise owners are concerned with maintaining and increasing their profits, as FM clearly assume they are, why did they not squeeze the X-inefficiency out of the managers *before* the arrival of a union upon the scene? This, after all, would have jacked up the producer's surplus from the area of abc to that of triangle ajf.

There are clearly some loose ends in the FM story about unionism.

III. SOME MORE POSITIVE REFLECTIONS

We have sought to expose some grounds for our dissatisfaction with some of the contemporary work on the economics of unionism, and with FM's work in particular. However, we would not wish to leave this matter on such a negative note. There are, in fact, some positive and hopeful signs about the current debate about the economic analysis of unionism, as witnessed by the contents of this volume.

The most important advance is that the old and played out game of finding a new answer to the old question "What do unions maximize?" is increasingly less in evidence. Economists are increasingly addressing the more important question of the nature of the trade union, defined in terms of its fundamental economic characteristics as an institution. In approaching these matters, economists are more and more drawing upon elements of both the property rights and public choice paradigms. This is a promising development.

Second, there is increasing attention to the operation of trade unions in the political market, whereas previously the implicit assumption of much economic research has been that unions operate in the labor (and perhaps goods) market, and that arena alone. (Here, Kurth's paper in this volume is indicative of the more general development). This development leads on directly to the possibility of locating the study of unionism within the more general framework of the economic analysis of rent-seeking.

In full perspective, then, it seems to us that there is something valuable in the new approaches to labor unions debate. In this sense the conference was a success; there should be more. We are confronted with a very difficult problem, and stimulating research on it is the only thing we can do. The papers presented here certainly did not solve the basic problems, but they increase the information base upon which further progress can, we hope, be made. Mao Tse-tung's slogan, "We have made but the first step of a 10,000 Li march" perhaps fits the conference, but we have to start somewhere. Retrospectively, we may seem to have made many steps, rather than one.

NOTES

1. On the latter, see Buchanan et al. (1980).

2. The ensuing treatment has benefited from discussions with Joe Reid and John Pettengill on these matters.

REFERENCES

Baumol, W. J. (1959), *Business Behavior, Value and Growth*. New York: Harcourt, Brace and World.

Buchanan, J. M., R. D. Tollison, and G. Tullock, eds. (1980), *Toward a Theory of the Rent-Seeking Society*. College Station, Tex.: Texas A & M University Press.

Burton, J. (1982), "The Economic Analysis of the Trade Union as a Political Institution." In J. J. Rosa (ed.), *The Economics of Trade Unions*. Paris: Bonnel Editions.

Freeman, R. B., and J. L. Medoff (1979), "The Two Faces of Unionism." *The Public Interest* 57(Fall):69–93.

———— (1982), "Comment." *Policy Review* No. 16(Spring):3–6.

Lentz, B. (1982), "The Determinants of Union Staff Salaries: A New Meaning to Business Unionism?" In J. J. Rosa (ed.), *The Economics of Trade Unions*. Paris: Bonnel Editions.

Lewis, H. G. (1959), "Competitive and Monopoly Unionism." In P. D. Bradley (ed.), *The Public Stake in Union Power*. Charlottesville: University of Virginia Press, pp. 181–208.

Rosa, J. J., ed. (1982), *The Economics of Trade Unions*. Paris: Bonnel Editions.

Ross, A. M. (1948), *Trade Union Wage Policy*. Berkeley: University of California Press.

Oswald, A. J. (1982a), "The Microeconomic Theory of the Trade Union." *Economic Journal*, forthcoming.

———— (1982b), "Trade Unions, Wages and Unemployment: What Can Simple Models Tell Us?" *Oxford Economic Papers*, forthcoming.